Introduction to
THE DIGITAL
COMPUTER

Introduction to

THE DIGITAL
COMPUTER

John O'Malley
UNIVERSITY OF FLORIDA

HOLT, RINEHART and WINSTON, Inc.

NEW YORK   SAN FRANCISCO
CHICAGO   ATLANTA   DALLAS
MONTREAL   TORONTO
LONDON   SYDNEY

This book is dedicated to my parents,
CECILE and MART O'MALLEY

Preface

This textbook presents basic topics in combinational switching circuits and digital computers at a level suitable for scientifically minded students with good high school backgrounds. It is primarily a *hardware* book having little programming material.

This textbook, unlike a reference book, has extensive developments of a limited number of topics as opposed to limited developments of a large number of topics. Also, it has many examples, particularly in the first half of the book, where one or more examples follow almost every introduced topic. This format encourages self-study as does that of the problems at the ends of the chapters.

The problems provide almost instant feedback to students on their understanding of fundamental concepts. For each topic there is at least one corresponding problem with answers, carefully checked for accuracy, followed by very similar problems without answers. By working the problems with answers, students can determine their need to go back to the text for further study before attempting the problems without answers. The problems are short, requiring little manipulation, and they test the students' understanding of basic concepts instead of innate cleverness.

A student can readily understand the material in this book without being an electrical engineering or a mathematics major. The only prerequisites are a good high school course in physics and some scientific aptitude. Students in my classes who have majored in fields as divorced from electrical engineering as geography and political science have done well with this material.

Most students will be pleased with the non-esoteric practical approach of this book. For example, the introduction of switching algebra is purely pragmatic—few theorems and minimum formalisms—but with an adequate foundation for most purposes. After studying this material a student will be able to apply it perhaps even better than a person who has had (and perhaps "been had" by) a formalistic, rigorous, abstract presentation.

Although this is a hardware book, it has an introduction to assembly language programming in Chapter 10. The following chapter contains hardware material dependent upon this assembly language programming. But an instructor can, if he prefers, skip these two chapters and still provide his students with an adequate first treatment of digital computers.

The material in this book suffices for a single semester course or, if supplemented, for a two-quarter sequence, the first quarter of which is on combinational switching circuits and the second quarter on digital computers. In either case, the material on combinational switching circuits is an adequate foundation for a subsequent course on sequential switching circuits.

By limiting the number of topics, I have undoubtedly omitted some that many professors believe are very important. But with the book written so that most of the material can be readily understood from self-study, instructors should be able to devote much class time to the development and explanation of those pet topics not contained in this book.

Also, with limited coverage, this book usually presents only one way of doing things. For example, it has only one minimization technique—the Karnaugh map—and only one method for most arithmetic operations. This limitation is reasonable and even necessary for an introductory course from which students should receive an overall picture of the hardware features of digital computers and have much of the mystery removed.

From my experiences with this book, I suspect that few books are written without the help and even the sacrifices of many persons. This is certainly a fact with this textbook and deserves acknowledgment and an expression of appreciation. First, as regards sacrifices, I thank my students for not complaining (at least to me) when they, on occasion, suffered through worse than usual discussions—never lectures—when I took some time from class preparation in order to work on this book. Also, I thank my wife, Lois Anne, and my children, Martin, Elaine, John,

Timothy, Margaret, Cecilia, and Mathew, for being patient and understanding during the many hours this book took me from them.

As regards help, I thank Dr. Wayne Chen, chairman of the Department of Electrical Engineering of the University of Florida, for creating an environment conducive to book writing. By encouraging writing and providing material aids, he has given faculty members ample opportunities to satisfy their writing urges. I also thank Dr. W. W. Peterson (University of Hawaii) for allowing me to use some material in Chapter 11 based on his work. I thank Carolyn Lyons for her excellent typing. And, finally, I thank the students in my classes who delighted in correcting errors in the text and problems.

March 1972   JOHN O'MALLEY

Contents

Introduction to
THE DIGITAL COMPUTER

1

Number
Systems

In this chapter we study the decimal number system, the binary number system, and to a lesser degree the octal and the hexadecimal number systems. It may seem unnecessary to consider the decimal number system since it is so familiar. However, attention can be focused on the structure and features of the decimal number system without regard for arithmetic operations since these are so well known. Knowledge gained from the study of the decimal number system is an aid in the study of the other number systems.

The popularity of the decimal system probably results from humans having ten fingers. If God had endowed us with, say, eight fingers instead, then perhaps the octal number system would be the most popular. Thus, in a sense the extensive use of the decimal system is a matter of chance and not because it is better suited for calculations than other number systems.

Only one number system—the binary system—is well suited, at present, for direct implementation in a digital computer and many other digital applications. In an electronic digital computer application each different digit of a number system is represented by a different physical quantity—for example, different voltages, currents, states of conduction, and so on. Thus direct implementation of, say, the decimal system requires components having ten different physical quantities. Other considerations require these components to be small, light, cheap, and fast. Components satisfying these latter requirements seldom possess the necessary ten distinct quantities. In fact, many of these components have just *two* distinct quantities, and for this reason electronic digital systems are inherently binary systems.

To appreciate better the need for the binary system, we will now consider a few of the typical electrical components of electrical digital systems. A popular storage device—the flip-flop—is used extensively because its output voltages can be changed very rapidly. Inherently, flip-flops produce just two voltage levels and consequently are binary devices. Another component—the relay—also has just two states: a relay is either open or closed. Electronic components such as transistors are, for minimum errors, often operated in just two conditions, saturation and cutoff, and thus are binary devices, at least when operated in this manner.

From the foregoing it is evident that the binary number system is best for many of the components of present-day digital systems. Unfortunately, the binary number system requires a large number of digits —in general, more than three times that of the decimal system.

This large number of digits can be avoided for hand calculations by use of an octal or hexadecimal shorthand. The octal system reduces the number of digits by a factor of approximately 3 and the hexadecimal system reduces it by a factor of approximately 4. The use of either of these systems for a shorthand is convenient for it is very easy to convert a binary number into either an octal or a hexadecimal number.

1.1   DECIMAL NUMBER SYSTEM

The *decimal number system* has *ten* different symbols: 0, 1, 2, 3, 4, 5, 6, 7, 8, and 9. The number of symbols is the *base* or *radix*. Note that the symbol for the base is a combination of the first two symbols; there is no single symbol for ten.

This being a *positional number system,* the value of a number depends not only on the symbols used but also on the symbol positions. For example, 6325 and 3625 contain the same symbols but have entirely different values.

The adjacent positioning of the symbols is a contraction. As an illustration, 6325 is a contraction of $6 \times 10^3 + 3 \times 10^2 + 2 \times 10^1 + 5 \times 10^0$. The number raised to the various powers is, of course, the base.

A *radix point* or, in this case, decimal point, designates the separation of the negative powers of the base from the nonnegative powers. Consider 321.406 which is a contraction of $3 \times 10_2 + 2 \times 10_1 + 1 \times 10^0 + 4 \times 10^{-1} + 0 \times 10^{-2} + 6 \times 10^{-3}$. The decimal point is between digits 1 and 4—the multipliers of 10^0 and 10^{-1}, respectively. Thus the digit to the left of the decimal point is the multiplier of the zero power of the base and the digit to the right is the multiplier of the minus one power of the base.

In this example and in general, the nonnegative powers equal in value the number of digits between the digit of interest and the radix point. Each negative power is the negative of the number of digits that the digit of interest is to the right of the radix point.

This extended number representation applies not only to the decimal number system but also to all number systems we will consider. In general, a number of a positional number system with radix r and digits a_i is representable as

$$a_n r^n + \ldots + a_1 r^1 + a_0 r^0 + a_{-1} r^{-1} + a_{-2} r^{-2} + \ldots$$

wherein

$$0 \leq a_i \leq r - 1$$

In using this representation in our following considerations of the binary, octal, and hexadecimal number systems, we will, for convenience, express each radix and radix power in decimal.

1.2 BINARY NUMBER SYSTEM

The base or radix of the *binary number system* is two. Thus this system has just two distinct digits: 0 and 1, which are often referred to as *bits*. The base, which is 10, has an equivalent value of two in the decimal system. An example of a binary number is 1011.101, which is a contraction of $1 \times 2^3 + 0 \times 2^2 + 1 \times 2^1 + 1 \times 2^0 + 1 \times 2^{-1} + 0 \times 2^{-2} + 1 \times 2^{-3}$.

A binary number cannot be recognized as such by inspection. Unless otherwise specified, it could be a decimal number, or an octal number, or a number of any system having the symbols 0 and 1. When the base of a number is not obvious, it is indicated by a subscript, for example, 1011.101_2.

The correspondence between twelve decimal numbers and equivalent binary numbers is presented in Table 1.1. The decimal equivalences of the binary numbers can be verified by assigning weights of 1, 2, 4, and 8 to 1's in, respectively, the first, second, third, and fourth columns from the right.

Table 1.1   Decimal-Binary Equivalence

Decimal	Binary	Decimal	Binary
0	0	6	110
1	1	7	111
2	10	8	1000
3	11	9	1001
4	100	10	1010
5	101	11	1011

Addition and Subtraction

Addition in binary is quite simple as is evidenced by the addition Table 1.2, which is a convenient and conventional way of indicating that $0 + 0 = 0$, $0 + 1 = 1 + 0 = 1$, and $1 + 1 = 10$. From these few relations any number of binary numbers can be added.

Table 1.2   Binary Addition

		Augend		
	+	0	1	
Addend	0	0	1	Sum
	1	1	10	

One difficulty in adding binary numbers is the large number of carries that often occur. Some examples of addition follow, each of which has several carries:

```
                                      1  11  1
      1 1 1        1 1 1 1 1         ₁110.11
      1101         11101.101          11.1
    +1011        + 1110.11         +1110.011
    ------        ----------        ----------
    11000         101100.011        11000.101
```

In the third example a carry extends over two places. This extension is not unusual in the addition of more than two binary numbers, but it is rare in the addition of decimal numbers.

Binary subtraction is more difficult than addition but no more so than decimal subtraction is more difficult than decimal addition. As in decimal subtraction we subtract the smaller magnitude number from the larger magnitude number and adjust the sign of the difference accordingly. That is, the number with the smaller magnitude is the subtrahend and the number with the larger magnitude is the minuend. The smaller number is easily recognized; it has fewer digits to the left of the binary point. If both numbers have the same number of integer digits, the smaller number is the one having the first zero from the left that is matched with a one in the same position in the other number.

The principal difficulty in binary subtraction occurs when a one in the subtrahend is below a zero in the minuend, as is illustrated in the second position from the right for the following two numbers:

$$11001 \quad \text{minuend}$$
$$-10011 \quad \text{subtrahend}$$

There are two popular methods for handling this situation, and they follow directly from similar methods for decimal subtraction.

The first method: In the case of a one in the subtrahend and a zero in the corresponding position in the minuend, borrow a one from the left of the zero in the minuend. In this borrow, change the first one on the left to a zero and all in-between zeros to ones.

Example 1.1   Subtract 10011 from 11001.

Solution   With the above method the approach is

$$
\begin{array}{c}
11001 \\
-10011 \\
\hline
\end{array}
\quad \rightarrow \quad
\begin{array}{c}
101^10\ 1 \quad \text{borrow} \\
-100\ 1\ 1 \\
\hline
001\ 1\ 0 \quad \text{difference}
\end{array}
$$

Note that the second and third bits of the minuend change in the generation of the borrow for the fourth digit. The result should be checked by adding the difference to the subtrahend.

$$
\begin{array}{c}
110 \\
+10011 \\
\hline
11001
\end{array}
$$

The sum is the minuend as it always is if no error is made.   ∎*

This first method is the conventional borrow method that is completely analogous to the borrow method of decimal subtraction. The other method requires addition.

The second method: In the case of a one in the subtrahend and a zero in the corresponding position in the minuend, change this zero to 10 and add one to the number to the left of the one in the subtrahend.

This method is easily justified since it is equivalent to adding the same number to both minuend and subtrahend, which, of course, does

---

* The symbol ∎ indicates the end of a solution.

not change the difference. For the problem of Example 1.1 this method requires 100 and then 1000 to be added to both minuend and subtrahend.

Example 1.2   Subtract 10011 from 11001 using the second method.

Solution

$$
\begin{array}{r}
11001 \\
-10011 \\
\hline
0
\end{array}
\quad\rightarrow\quad
\begin{array}{r}
110^101 \\
-101\ 11 \\
\hline
10
\end{array}
\quad\rightarrow\quad
\begin{array}{r}
11^10^101 \\
-11\ 1\ 11 \\
\hline
1\ 10
\end{array}
$$

Of course, the result is the same as with the first method.   ■

These methods apply if the binary numbers are integers, fractions, or mixed numbers.

Multiplication and Division

Multiplication in binary is presented in Table 1.3. The essence of Table 1.3 is that zero times a digit is zero and one times a digit is that digit. The rule for positioning the radix point in the product is exactly the same as that in the decimal number system.

Table 1.3   Binary Multiplication

		Multiplicand		
		0	1	
Multiplier	0	0	0	Product
	1	0	1	

Example 1.3   Multiply 101.1 by 110.1

Solution

$$
\begin{array}{r}
1\ 0\ 1.1 \\
\times\ 1\ 1\ 0.1 \\
\hline
1\ 0\ 1\ 1 \\
0\ 0\ 0\ 0 \\
1\ 0\ 1\ 1 \\
1\ 0\ 1\ 1 \\
\hline
1\ 0\ 0\ 0\ 1\ 1.1\ 1
\end{array}
$$

multiplicand
multiplier

product   ■

From Example 1.3 we see that, in general, for a one in the multiplier we write the multiplicand and shift left one position before writing again. For a zero in the multiplier we just shift left.

Division in binary is much simpler than in decimal. Either the divisor divides exactly once or it does not divide. For division we mark off, starting from the left in the dividend, a number of digits equal to the number of digits in the divisor. If the number marked off is larger (noted by the position of the zeros from the left), then the divisor divides into this number exactly once. If the number marked off is smaller, then another digit is included and the divisor always divides into this number exactly once. Subtraction follows and the procedure continues as in decimal division. The position of the radix point of the quotient is determined exactly as in decimal division.

The process of binary division is perhaps best illustrated by an example. Example 1.4 is taken from the multiplication Example 1.3: the multiplier is divided into the product. Thus the quotient should be the multiplicand.

Example 1.4   Divide 100011.11 by 110.1

Solution

```
                              1 0 1.1      quotient
divisor    1 1 0.1 | 1 0 0 0 1 1.1 1      dividend
                     1 1 0 1
                     ─────────
                       1 0 0 1 1
                       1 1 0 1
                       ─────────
                         1 1 0 1
                         1 1 0 1
                         ─────────
                         0 0 0 0
```

Binary and Decimal Conversion

To convert a binary number into its decimal equivalent, we express the binary number in expanded form as powers of the base 10, which is decimal two. For example, 11011.101_2 is in decimal: $1 \times 2^4 + 1 \times 2^3 + 1 \times 2^1 + 1 \times 2^0 + 1 \times 2^{-1} + 1 \times 2^{-3} = 16 + 8 + 2 + 1 + \frac{1}{2} + \frac{1}{8} = 27.625$.

Although some convenient algorithms exist for rapid conversion, it is not essential to know them unless one does a considerable amount of conversion.

In the conversion of a decimal number to its binary equivalent we consider the integer part of the decimal number separate from the fraction part and apply a *different* rule to each part. Of course the decimal integer part converts into a binary integer and the decimal fraction into a binary fraction. The conversion is done entirely in decimal arithmetic.

The rule for converting a decimal integer to a binary integer is

Divide the decimal number by the base two. Place the remainder to one side and then divide the base two into the integer part of the quotient. Place the remainder from this second division to one side and then divide the base two into the integer part of the second quotient, and so on. Repeat this procedure until a quotient is zero. The binary equivalent is the number obtained by arranging the remainders in *reverse order*.

This procedure is best understood from an example.

Example 1.5   Convert the decimal number 123 into its binary equivalent.

Solution

$$
\begin{array}{r|l}
 & \text{remainders} \\
2\,|\,123 & \\
\hline
\quad 61 & 1 \\
2\,|\,61 & \\
\hline
\quad 30 & 1 \\
2\,|\,30 & \\
\hline
\quad 15 & 0 \\
2\,|\,15 & \\
\hline
\quad 7 & 1 \\
2\,|\,7 & \\
\hline
\quad 3 & 1 \\
2\,|\,3 & \\
\hline
\quad 1 & 1 \\
2\,|\,1 & \\
\hline
\quad 0 & 1 \\
\end{array}
$$

The remainders arranged in reverse order provide the answer 1111011, which is the binary equivalent of decimal 123. It is not necessary to arrange the division process as was done in this example. Instead, each step can immediately follow the prior one.

$$
\begin{array}{r|l}
 & \text{remainders} \\
2\,|\,123 & \\
\hline
2\ |\,61 & 1 \\
2\ |\,30 & 1 \\
2\ |\,15 & 0 \\
2\ |\,7 & 1 \\
2\ |\,3 & 1 \\
2\ |\,1 & 1 \\
\hline
0 & 1 \\
\end{array}
$$

The justification for this rule is that in converting a decimal number into its binary equivalent, we are simply trying to determine the a_n's of

$$\ldots + a_3 \times 2^3 + a_2 \times 2^2 + a_1 \times 2^1 + a_0 \times 2^0$$

wherein each a_n is zero or one. The first division by two results in

$$\ldots + a_3 \times 2^2 + a_2 \times 2^1 + a_1 + \underbrace{a_0/2}_{} \quad \text{remainder}$$

$$\underbrace{\ldots + a_3 \times 2^2 + a_2 \times 2^1 + a_1}_{\text{integer}}$$

Obviously, the part of the quotient including a_1 and to the left is an integer and a_0 is the remainder. Thus the remainder from the first division is a_0. Similarly, the remainder from the second division is a_1, and so on. The remainders from the repeated divisions yield the a_n's and these a_n's are in order commencing with the least significant.

The rule for converting the fractional part of a decimal number into an equivalent binary fraction is

> Multiply the fractional part of the decimal number by two. Place the integer part to one side and multiply the resulting fractional part by two. Again put the integer part of the product to one side and multiply the resulting fractional part by two, and so on. Repeat this procedure until the fractional part of the product is zero or until the number of digits is that desired. The integer parts of the products form the binary fraction with the integers arranged *in the order* in which they were obtained.

Example 1.6   Convert decimal 0.6875 to binary.

Solution

	integer
$2 \times 0.6875 = 1.375$	1
$2 \times 0.375 = 0.75$	0
$2 \times 0.75 = 1.5$	1
$2 \times 0.5 = 1.0$	1

Thus 0.6875 in decimal is 0.1011 in binary.   ■

This procedure is easy to justify. The decimal fraction is converted into binary by a determination of the a_n's in

$$a_{-1} \times 2^{-1} + a_{-2} \times 2^{-2} + a_{-3} \times 2^{-3} + \cdots$$

in which each of the a_n's is either zero or one. If this expression is multiplied by two the product is

$$a_{-1} + \underbrace{a_{-2} \times 2^{-1} + a_{-3} \times 2^{-2} + \ldots}_{\text{fraction}}$$

The portion of the product to the right of a_{-1} is less than one and thus is a fraction; a_{-1} is the integer portion of the product. If the product has an integer part of one, then a_{-1} is one. If the integer part is zero, then a_{-1} is zero.

For a_{-2} only the fractional part of the first product is considered:

$$a_{-2} \times 2^{-1} + a_{-3} \times 2^{-2} + \ldots$$

This, when multiplied by two, is

$$a_{-2} + \underbrace{a_{-3} \times 2^{-1} + \ldots}_{\text{fraction}}$$

Again, the portion of the product to the right of a_{-2} is a fraction and a_{-2} is the integer part of the second product. Repetition of this process provides the rest of the binary digits.

It is of interest that a terminating fraction in decimal may not be terminating in binary (for example, $0.1_{10} \rightarrow 0.0001100110011 \ldots _2$), but a terminating fraction in binary is always terminating in decimal.

1.3   OCTAL NUMBER SYSTEM

Since the base or radix of the *octal number system* is eight, this system has eight symbols: 0, 1, 2, 3, 4, 5, 6, and 7. The correspondences among the decimal, binary, and octal number systems for the first twenty nonnegative integers are shown in Table 1.4.

Table 1.4   Decimal-Binary-Octal Equivalence

Decimal	Binary	Octal	Decimal	Binary	Octal
0	0	0	10	1010	12
1	1	1	11	1011	13
2	10	2	12	1100	14
3	11	3	13	1101	15
4	100	4	14	1110	16
5	101	5	15	1111	17
6	110	6	16	10000	20
7	111	7	17	10001	21
8	1000	10	18	10010	22
9	1001	11	19	10011	23

The first eight integers of the octal and decimal systems are the same. For the next eight integers the octal integers appear to be two greater than the corresponding decimal integers. This observation is important in the addition and subtraction of octal numbers.

Addition and Subtraction

For our purposes we need never add more than two octal numbers at one time. Consequently, the following discussion is limited to that consideration. In adding two octal digits, most of us will want to think in terms of decimal addition. With this viewpoint the rule is

> If the sum of two octal digits is seven or less, the result is the same as in decimal, but if the sum (in terms of decimal addition) is more than seven, then the octal sum is *two greater* than would be the result in decimal addition.

The following examples, which are all in octal, illustrate this rule.

$$
\begin{array}{r}
2 \\
+3 \\
\hline
5
\end{array}
\qquad
\begin{array}{r}
2 \\
+7 \\
\hline
11
\end{array}
\qquad
\begin{array}{r}
4 \\
+6 \\
\hline
12
\end{array}
\qquad
\begin{array}{r}
24 \\
+37 \\
\hline
63
\end{array}
\qquad
\begin{array}{r}
3072 \\
+5763 \\
\hline
11055
\end{array}
$$

Octal subtraction can also be considered from a decimal viewpoint. The rule is

> In the subtraction of one octal digit from a larger digit the result is the same as in decimal. If the digit in the subtrahend is larger, then (with the borrow approach) borrow from the next nonzero digit to the left in the minuend. That is, decrease this digit by one and make sevens of any in-between zeros. The difference is *two less* than the result in decimal.

The following are some examples.

$$
\begin{array}{r}
7 \\
-3 \\
\hline
4
\end{array}
\qquad
\begin{array}{r}
37 \\
-21 \\
\hline
16
\end{array}
\qquad
\begin{array}{r}
406 \\
-207 \\
\hline
\end{array}
\rightarrow
\begin{array}{r}
37^16 \\
-20\ 7 \\
\hline
17\ 7
\end{array}
\qquad
\begin{array}{r}
40672 \\
-3725 \\
\hline
\end{array}
\rightarrow
\begin{array}{r}
4066^12 \\
-372\ 5 \\
\hline
4\ 5
\end{array}
\rightarrow
\begin{array}{r}
37^166^12 \\
-3\ 72\ 5 \\
\hline
34\ 74\ 5
\end{array}
$$

Instead of the borrow approach one can use the addition approach as presented in the binary discussion. Following is an example.

$$
\begin{array}{r}
40672 \\
-3725 \\
\hline
\end{array}
\rightarrow
\begin{array}{r}
4067^12 \\
-373\ 5 \\
\hline
4\ 5
\end{array}
\rightarrow
\begin{array}{r}
40^167^12 \\
-4\ 73\ 5 \\
\hline
74\ 5
\end{array}
\rightarrow
\begin{array}{r}
4^10^167^12 \\
-1\ 4\ 73\ 5 \\
\hline
3\ 4\ 74\ 5
\end{array}
$$

In these examples, several steps with many repeated numbers are shown to aid understanding. In actual practice one simply pencils in the changes or makes the changes mentally.

In subsequent chapters we will use octal numbers only for shorthand representations of binary numbers or as an aid in converting from decimal to binary. For these purposes we will never multiply or divide octal numbers and thus we will not need to know the octal multiplication table.

Octal and Decimal Conversion

The rule for converting an octal number to an equivalent decimal number is the same as for binary except that powers of eight are used instead of powers of two. For example, 314.72 in octal is $3 \times 8^2 +$ $1 \times 8^1 + 4 \times 8^0 + 7 \times 8^{-1} + 2 \times 8^{-2} = 192 + 8 + 4 + \frac{7}{8} + \frac{2}{64} =$ 204.90625 in decimal.

Decimal numbers convert to octal numbers with the same procedure as explained with binary numbers except that eight is used instead of two. Also the justification for the conversion rules is similar to those for binary, the only difference being that the powers are of eight instead of two. It should be noted that a terminating decimal fraction may not have a terminating octal fraction equivalent.

Example 1.7   Convert the decimal number 379.375 into an equivalent octal number.

Solution   For the integer part

$$
\begin{array}{rl}
 & \text{remainder} \\
8\overline{)379} & \\
\overline{47} & 3 \\
8\overline{)47} & \\
\overline{5} & 7 \\
8\overline{)5} & \\
\overline{0} & 5
\end{array}
$$

and thus 573 octal is equivalent to 379 decimal. Now for the fraction part

$$8 \times 0.375 = 3.0$$

The complete result is that 573.3 octal is equivalent to 379.375 decimal.   ■

Octal and Binary Conversion

In octal-to-binary conversion each octal digit is replaced by its three-digit binary equivalent. Of course, in each binary number any leading zeros in the integer or trailing zeros in the fraction can be ignored.

Example 1.8   Convert 376.4502 octal into its binary equivalent.

Solution

3	7	6	.	4	5	0	2
↓	↓	↓	↓	↓	↓	↓	↓
011	111	110	.	100	101	000	010

or 376.4502 octal is 11111110.10010100001 in binary.   ■

The conversion from binary to octal is just the reverse of the above. That is, the binary digits are grouped by threes from the right and from the left of the binary point and then each group is replaced by its octal equivalent. In the binary fraction part, zeros are added, if necessary, to complete the rightmost group.

Example 1.9 Determine the octal equivalent of the binary number

$$11101110.01111$$

Solution We group the bits by threes as follows:

$$011 \quad 101 \quad 110. \quad 011 \quad 110$$

The leading zero for the integer part is not necessary, but the trailing zero for the fraction is essential for completing the last group. After this grouping, we replace each group with its octal equivalent:

011	101	110	.	011	110
↓	↓	↓		↓	↓
3	5	6	.	3	6

The equivalent octal number is 356.36. If the trailing zero is not added the result is 356.33, which is incorrect. ∎

The justification for this conversion rule—really for both rules—is that the grouping of the binary numbers into groups of three, in effect, forms numbers times powers of eight. This is perhaps best understood from a specific example. Again consider 011 101 110.011 110, which can be considered a contraction for $11 \times 2^6 + 101 \times 2^3 + 110 \times 2^0 + 011 \times 2^{-3} + 110 \times 2^{-6}$. If this is converted to octal, term by term, the result is

$$3 \times 8^2 + 5 \times 8^1 + 6 \times 8^0 + 3 \times 8^{-1} + 6 \times 8^{-2} = 356.36$$

Obviously, the grouping by three results in the powers of the binary base directly converting into powers of the octal base, and for this reason the conversion is so convenient.

The conversion rules and these examples illustrate why octal numbers are a convenient shorthand for representing binary numbers. The equivalent octal numbers have only approximately one-third as many digits, and the conversion from binary to octal, and vice versa, is easy and fast.

This shorthand has another justification. In some computers the basic binary numbers on which the computer operates have parts that are multiples of three bits. That is, each part of these numbers is either three bits, six bits, nine bits, and so on. Consequently, conversion of these numbers to octal contains an exact conversion for each part. As will be seen, this is a very convenient feature.

The conversion between decimal and binary numbers is usually most conveniently done through octal. If a decimal number is to be converted to binary, less work is required in converting the number to octal and then the octal number to binary than in converting the decimal number directly to binary. Also, in converting a binary number to a decimal number, it is easier to convert the binary number to octal and then the octal number to decimal than it is to convert the binary number directly into decimal.

1.4   HEXADECIMAL NUMBER SYSTEM

In some computers the parts of binary numbers considered as units are multiples of four bits each instead of three bits. Consequently, an octal shorthand is not suitable. In this case the *hexadecimal system* is used because in the conversion from binary to hexadecimal the binary digits are grouped by fours.

Since the base of the hexadecimal system is sixteen, this system has sixteen different symbols. The conventional symbols are the ten decimal digits and the first six letters of the alphabet.

Table 1.5 gives the correspondences for the first twenty nonnegative integers of the decimal, binary, and hexadecimal systems.

Table 1.5   Decimal-Binary-Hexadecimal Equivalence

Decimal	Binary	Hexadecimal	Decimal	Binary	Hexadecimal
0	0	0	10	1010	A
1	1	1	11	1011	B
2	10	2	12	1100	C
3	11	3	13	1101	D
4	100	4	14	1110	E
5	101	5	15	1111	F
6	110	6	16	10000	10
7	111	7	17	10001	11
8	1000	8	18	10010	12
9	1001	9	19	10011	13

In the conversion of a hexadecimal number to decimal, each hexadecimal digit is expressed in terms of its decimal equivalent and then multiplied by the appropriate power of sixteen, which power should be apparent from prior discussions.

Example 1.10   Convert CA6.2C to decimal.

Solution $CA6.2C \rightarrow 12 \times 16^2 + 10 \times 16^1 + 6 \times 16^0 + 2 \times 16^{-1}$
$+12 \times 16^{-2} = 3072 + 160 + 6 + 0.125 + 0.046875$
$= 3238.171875$ ∎

The conversion of a decimal number to hexadecimal form should be obvious from the discussions of decimal-to-binary and decimal-to-octal conversions.

Example 1.11   Convert 3476.1875 to hexadecimal.

Solution   The integer part must be considered separately.

$$
\begin{array}{r}
\text{remainder} \\
16\overline{)3476} \\
218 \quad\quad 4 \\
16\overline{)218} \\
13 \quad\quad 9 \\
16\overline{)13} \\
0 \quad\quad 13 \to D
\end{array}
$$

Now consider the fraction part.

$$16 \times 0.1875 = 3.0$$

The result is D94.3 hexadecimal, which is equivalent to 3476.1875 decimal. ■

The conversion from binary to hexadecimal, and vice versa, is similar to that for octal except that the bits are grouped into groups of four bits each instead of three. Justification for this conversion follows from that given for the octal-binary conversion.

Example 1.12   Convert 11011011.1111101101 binary into hexadecimal.

Solution   We group the bits into groups of four to the right and left of the binary point and then insert the hexadecimal equivalent for each group.

$$
\begin{array}{cccc}
1101 & 1011.1111 & 1011 & 0100 \\
\downarrow & \downarrow \quad \downarrow \quad \downarrow & \downarrow & \downarrow \\
D & B \quad . \quad F & B & 4
\end{array}
$$

The desired hexadecimal number is DB.FB4. ■

The conversion from hexadecimal to binary is the reverse procedure.

Example 1.13   Convert FEB6.AC4 hexadecimal into binary.

Solution

$$
\begin{array}{ccccccc}
F & E & B & 6 \quad . \quad A & C & 4 \\
\downarrow & \downarrow & \downarrow & \downarrow \quad \downarrow \quad \downarrow & \downarrow & \downarrow \\
1111 & 1110 & 1011 & 0110.1010 & 1100 & 0100
\end{array}
$$

The binary equivalent is 1111111010110110.1010110001. ■

We will not consider the addition and subtraction of hexadecimal numbers since in subsequent chapters we will use octal, exclusively, for a binary shorthand.

PROBLEMS ▪▪▪▪▪▪▪▪▪▪▪▪▪▪▪▪▪▪▪▪▪▪▪▪▪▪▪▪▪▪▪▪▪▪▪▪▪

1.1 Perform the indicated operations on the following binary numbers:

(a) 1101 + 110

(b)   111.011
          1111.11
      +111001.1

(c) 10011 − 110

(d) 1001.1101 − 11100.001

(e)   111.01
          1111.1
          1011.11
      +1101.111

(f) 11001.01 − 111.1

Answers   (a) 10011;   (b) 1010000.101;   (c) 1101;
          (d) −10010.0101   (e) 110000.011;   (f) 10001.11

1.2 Repeat Problem 1.1 for

(a) 1101.1 + 111.101

(b)   111.01
          1011.11
      +11110.01

(c) 11011 − 101

(d) 1001.01 − 10110.101

(e)   111.101
          1110.11
          11111.01
      +101110.011

(f) 1100.01 − 111.1

1.3 Repeat Problem 1.1 for

(a) 10111.001 + 111.00111

(b)   1111.11
          11101.11
      +111110.111

(c) 1110001 − 1111

(d) 111.0001 − 10000.01

(e)   11.01
          111.111
          1111.1111
      +11111.11111

(f) 1.1 − 0.0001

1.4 Perform the indicated binary multiplications and divisions.

(a) 101 × 1101

(b) 11011 × 1100.1

(c) 111011.01 × 1111.001

(d) 10100 ÷ 100

(e) 100011.11 ÷ 101.1

(f) 101010001.1 ÷ 11011

Answers   (a) 1000001;   (b) 101010001.1;
          (c) 1110000000.00101;   (d) 101;   (e) 110.1;
          (f) 1100.1

1.5 Repeat Problem 1.4 for

(a) 1101 × 110011

(b) 11010.1 × 1101.01

(c) 1011101.011 × 10110.101

(d) 1001000 ÷ 110

(e) 10000000.01 ÷ 1101.1

(f) 110101001.11101 ÷ 110011.101

1.6 Repeat Problem 1.4 for

(a) 110 × 1111

(b) 1111.1 × 1111.1

(c) 100111.101 × 11110111.1
(d) 110001 ÷ 111
(e) 101010001.1 ÷ 1100.1
(f) 1110000000.00101 ÷ 1111.001

1.7 Convert the following binary numbers to decimal:
(a) 100111   (b) 10101.101   (c) 10001001.001
Answers   (a) 39;   (b) 21.625;   (c) 137.125

1.8 Repeat Problem 1.7 for
(a) 1100111   (b) 1100.111   (c) 1100110101.0111

1.9 Repeat Problem 1.7 for
(a) 1111111   (b) 11111.1111   (c) 11111111.11111111

1.10 Convert the following decimal numbers to binary:
(a) 146   (c) 14.6
(b) 1928.875   (d) 19⅔
Answers   (a) 10010010;   (b) 11110001000.111;
                  (c) 1110.100110011001 . . .;   (d) 10011.001110 . . .

1.11 Repeat Problem 1.10 for
(a) 1689   (b) 1430.625   (c) 178.3

1.12 Repeat Problem 1.10 for
(a) 762   (c) 999.99
(b) 0.01   (d) 10.1

1.13 Perform the indicated operations on the following octal numbers:
(a) 324 + 564   (f)   46.23
(b) 710.145 + 217.633   327.12
(c) 352 − 163   +4652.327
(d) 1236.47 − 765.2377   (g) 473.63 − 754.321
(e) 40002.3 − 675.77
Answers   (a) 1110;   (b) 1130;   (c) 167;   (d) 251.2301;
                  (e) 37104.31;   (f) 5247.677;   (g) −260.471

1.14 Repeat Problem 1.13 for
(a) 472 + 326   (e)   47.653
(b) 410.23 + 367.55   327.734
(c) 456 − 324   +467.772
(d) 4723.636 − 724.647   (f) 5346.72 − 600321.1

1.15 Repeat Problem 1.13 for
(a) 673 + 444   (e)   77.7
(b) 101.11 + 111.1   777.77
(c) 401 − 372   +7777.777
(d) 2436.203 − 777.77   (f) 600000.2001 − 5732.4377

1.16 Convert the following octal numbers to decimal:
(a) 110011   (b) 1234.54   (c) 7006.302
Answers   (a) 36873;   (b) 668.6875;   (c) 3590.37890625

1.17 Repeat Problem 1.16 for
(a) 30076   (b) 6403.2   (c) 400602.244

1.18 Repeat Problem 1.16 for
(a) 7777   (b) 77.77   (c) 1010.101

1.19 Convert the following decimal numbers to octal:
(a) 3094   (c) 250.3
(b) 2906.5625   (d) $37\frac{1}{9}$

Answers   (a) 6026;   (b) 5532.44;   (c) 372.23146 . . . ;
          (d) 45.0707 . . .

1.20 Repeat Problem 1.19 for
(a) 1000   (c) 2345.46875
(b) 100   (d) $46\frac{3}{13}$

1.21 Repeat Problem 1.19 for
(a) 1296   (c) 777.7
(b) 10,000   (d) $5\frac{1}{7}$

1.22 Convert the following binary numbers to octal:
(a) 101101   (c) 1000111101.01
(b) 110010111011.01011011

Answers   (a) 55;   (b) 6273.266;   (c) 1075.2

1.23 Repeat Problem 1.22 for
(a) 1101011   (c) 110111.0111
(b) 10111111011.0110111

1.24 Repeat Problem 1.22 for
(a) 10111   (c) 1111111.11111
(b) 1101101111.1101111111

1.25 Convert the following octal numbers to binary:
(a) 76002   (b) 773406.245

Answers   (a) 111110000000010;
          (b) 111111011100000110.010100101

1.26 Repeat Problem 1.25 for
(a) 23077   (b) 432.7066

1.27 Repeat Problem 1.25 for
(a) 770362   (b) 413072.635

1.28 Convert the following hexadecimal numbers to decimal:
(a) 4A6   (b) ABD.C8

Answers   (a) 1190;   (b) 2749.78125

1.29 Repeat Problem 1.28 for
(a) CAB   (b) FE6.8C4

1.30 Repeat Problem 1.28 for
(a) BEAD   (b) F79.B3C

1.31 Convert the following binary numbers to hexadecimal:
(**a**) 110111001   (**b**) 110001101.10011

Answers (**a**) 1B9;   (**b**) 18D.98

1.32 Repeat Problem 1.31 for
(**a**) 1001110101   (**b**) 1100111001.1000101

1.33 Repeat Problem 1.31 for
(**a**) 1111111111   (**b**) 1111111.1111111

1.34 Convert the following hexadecimal numbers to binary:
(**a**) CD3F   (**b**) 8F2A.5EF

Answers (**a**) 1100110100111111;
         (**b**) 1000111100101010.010111101111

1.35 Repeat Problem 1.34 for
(**a**) ACD8   (**b**) 3FD2.ACD

1.36 Repeat Problem 1.34 for
(**a**) BEEF   (**b**) 4BC2.6EF

1.37 Convert the following decimal numbers to hexadecimal:
(**a**) 329.5   (**b**) 7495.34   (**c**) $17\frac{1}{7}$

Answers (**a**) 149.8; (**b**) 1D47.570A3D . . .
         (**c**) 11.249249 . . .

1.38 Repeat Problem 1.37 for
(**a**) 492.25   (**b**) 9294.85   (**c**) $72\frac{13}{21}$

1.39 Repeat Problem 1.37 for
(**a**) 1000   (**b**) 3228.96   (**c**) $4\frac{7}{8}$

1.40 Write the first 25 numbers in the following number systems. Use decimal digits and then letters of the alphabet.
(**a**) base 18   (**b**) base 25   (**c**) base 13

Answers (**a**) 0, . . . , 9, A, . . . , H, 10, 11, . . . , 16;
         (**b**) 0, . . . , 9, A, . . . , O;
         (**c**) 0, . . . , 9, A, B, C, 10, . . . , 1A, 1B

1.41 Repeat Problem 1.40 for the first 30 numbers in the number systems of
(**a**) base 17   (**b**) base 31   (**c**) base 11

1.42 Repeat Problem 1.40 for the number systems of
(**a**) base 14   (**b**) base 19   (**c**) base 12

1.43 Make the following indicated conversions directly without using the decimal number system. For symbols use decimal digits and then letters of the alphabet, if needed.
(**a**) 21.012_3 to base 9   (**c**) 3214.3212_5 to base 25
(**b**) 543.32_6 to base 36

1.44 Repeat Problem 1.43 for
    (a) 231.21_4 to base 16   **(c)** $F.9E6_{16}$ to base 4
    (b) $AM9.4F_{25}$ to base 5

1.45 Convert 316.25_{10} to an equivalent number in the following number systems. Use decimal digits and then letters of the alphabet, if necessary.
    (a) base 5   **(b)** base 13   **(c)** base 25

    Answers   **(a)** 2231.1111 . . . ;   **(b)** 1B4.3333 . . . ;
                   (c) CG.6666 . . .

1.46 Repeat Problem 1.45 for decimal number 726.625 to an equivalent number in a number system of
    (a) base 3   **(b)** base 27   **(c)** base 17

1.47 Repeat Problem 1.45 for decimal number 1429.78 to an equivalent number in a number system of
    (a) base 6   **(b)** base 12   **(c)** base 19

2

Switching
Algebra

In this chapter an algebra is presented that is essential for the design of circuits used in digital computers and other digital applications. These circuits are called *switching circuits*—they act similar to switches—and the algebra used in their design is preferably termed *switching algebra*, although it is sometimes referred to as Boolean algebra. This algebra provides a systematic method for designing these circuits. Our study of this algebra will be purely pragmatic; we will discuss very little that is not essential for circuit design.

There are two types of switching circuits: *combinational* and *sequential*. Combinational switching circuits produce outputs that are functions only of the *present* inputs, and sequential circuits produce outputs that are dependent not only on the present inputs but also on *past* inputs; that is, these circuits have memories.

This chapter is limited to the design of combinational circuits. Other chapters, however, have circuits that contain such elements as flip-flops having this memory feature.

2.1   BASIC OPERATIONS

In switching algebra the variables can have only one of two values: 0 and 1. There are no negative numbers, no fractions, and just the two values of 0 and 1. The variables are usually denoted by letters. And, as in ordinary algebra, a variable may be a function if it is expressed in terms of other variables (an expression). Of course, the value of the function depends on the values of these other variables.

AND

The product operation in switching algebra is called AND. It is designated by dots as in $A \cdot B \cdot C$ or more simply by adjacently placed variables: ABC. The AND operations on the two values 0 and 1 are

$$0 \cdot 0 = 0, \quad 0 \cdot 1 = 0, \quad 1 \cdot 0 = 0, \quad \text{and} \quad 1 \cdot 1 = 1$$

Another way of explaining this operation is to say that 1 AND anything equals that anything and 0 AND anything equals 0. For example, $1 \cdot (ABC) = ABC$ but $0 \cdot (ABC) = 0$, regardless of the value of ABC. The AND operation obeys the commutative law, that is, $AB = BA$. Also, it obeys the associative law: $A(BC) = (AB)C$.

Note particularly that $X \cdot X \cdot X \ldots = X$, as can easily be proved by substituting in, one at a time, the two values (0 and 1) that the variable X can have.

The AND operation, as well as the others we will discuss, are perhaps best understood from a *truth table,* which is simply a listing of all possible values of the variables with the corresponding values resulting from the operation (or operations). In this table the values of the variables are usually listed, for convenience, such that if considered to be binary numbers, they occur in increasing value.

For AND and the two variables A and B the truth table is

A	B	$A \cdot B$
0	0	0
0	1	0
1	0	0
1	1	1

As should be apparent from this table and the explanation of the AND operation, a truth table for the AND of more than two variables has, in the right column, all 0's except for the last entry, which is 1, regardless of the number of variables.

OR

Addition in switching algebra is called OR. A plus sign ($+$) is usually used to designate it. This operation obeys the commutative and associative laws, that is, $A + B = B + A$ and $A + (B + C) = (A + B) + C$. The OR operation on the values of 0 and 1 are

$$0 + 0 = 0, \qquad 0 + 1 = 1, \qquad 1 + 0 = 1, \qquad \text{and} \qquad 1 + 1 = 1$$

In other words, 1 OR anything equals 1 and 0 OR anything equals that anything. For example, $1 + AB(C + D) = 1$ and $0 + AB(C + D) = AB(C + D)$. Note that $X + X + X + , \ldots , = X$.

The truth table for OR and the two variables A and B is

A	B	$A + B$
0	0	0
0	1	1
1	0	1
1	1	1

A truth table for the OR of more than two variables has 1's in the right column except for the first entry which is 0.

AND and OR obey a distributive law, that is, $A(B + C) = AB + AC$.

NOT

There is a third basic operation: NOT. If a quantity is NOT 1, then it must be 0 since there are only two values, 0 and 1. And, if a quantity is NOT 0, then it must be 1. This NOT operation is often denoted by an overline as in $\overline{A}$. However, the prime, as in A', is also popular. We will use the overline exclusively. From the above, obviously $\overline{0} = 1$ and $\overline{1} = 0$.

The truth table for NOT and the variable A is

A	$\overline{A}$
0	1
1	0

When the NOT operation is applied to an expression such as the NOT of $A\overline{B} + C$, $\overline{A\overline{B} + C}$, this latter expression is called the *complement* of the first expression. In other words, the first expression has been complemented, or the complement of it has been taken.

These operations can perhaps be better understood from some examples.

Example 2.1 Evaluate the following expressions for $A = 1$, $B = 0$, $C = 1$, and $D = 1$: (a) $A\overline{B} + C$; (b) $(\overline{A} + B)(C + \overline{B}D)$; and (c) $A\overline{B}(C + D\overline{E})$.

Solution   (a) $A\bar{B} + C = 1 \cdot \bar{0} + 1 = 1$ since 1 OR anything is 1; (b) with $\bar{A} + B = 0 + 0 = 0$, $(\bar{A} + B)(C + \bar{B}D) = 0$ regardless of the value of $(C + \bar{B}D)$; (c) because $A\bar{B} = 1 \cdot 1 = 1$ and $C = 1$, we have $1 \cdot (1 + D\bar{E}) = 1$ and there is no need to evaluate $D\bar{E}$.   ■

2.2   EXPRESSIONS

Sum-of-Products (SOP) Expressions

An expression such as $A\bar{B} + CD + AC$, comprising several product terms summed together, is called a *sum-of-products* expression or just a *sum of products*. We will often use the acronym *SOP* for these expressions.

Care should be taken in identifying SOP expressions. As an illustration, the expression $(A + B)\bar{C} + \bar{B}D$ is not an SOP but can be converted to one by multiplying out the first two factors. The result is $A\bar{C} + B\bar{C} + \bar{B}D$, which is a sum of products.

Product-of-Sums (POS) Expressions

The expression $(A + \bar{B})(C + D)(\bar{A} + C)$ of multiplie a factors of sums is called a *product-of-sums* expression or simply just d product of sums. We will often use the acronym *POS*. In a POS each factor contains only sums of single variables; there cannot be any product terms as, for example, in the first factor of $(A + \bar{B}C)(A + D)$. However, with theorems we will study we can convert such an expression to a POS: $(A + \bar{B})(A + C)(A + D)$.

Equivalent Expressions

Two expressions are *equivalent* if for every set of values of the variables the two expressions have the *same* value. For example, the expressions $A\bar{B} + B$ and $A + B$ are equivalent.

This equivalence can be shown by means of a truth table.

A	B	$A\bar{B} + B$	$A + B$
0	0	0	0
0	1	1	1
1	0	1	1
1	1	1	1

Since the two expressions have the same value for each combination of variable values, they are equivalent, or $A\bar{B} + B = A + B$.

Note that for two variables a truth table has four rows; for three variables, eight rows; and, in general, *for n variables, a truth table has* 2^n *rows*.

Example 2.2   Determine if the expressions $AB + \bar{B}C$ and $AB + \bar{A}C$ are equivalent.

Solution   Equivalency can be determined from a truth table. If in forming this table we have a row for which the expressions have different values, we need go no further; the expressions are not equivalent. Otherwise, we must complete the table.

A	B	C	$AB + \bar{B}C$	$AB + \bar{A}C$
0	0	0	0	0
0	0	1	1	1
0	1	0	0	0
0	1	1	0	1
1	0	0		
1	0	1		
1	1	0		
1	1	1		

Because the fourth row has different values for the expressions, the two expressions are not equivalent, and it is not necessary to complete the table.   ∎

Complement Expressions

Two expressions are *complements* of one another if for every set of variable values, the two expressions have *different* values. Thus in a truth table, complement expressions have *no* agreement of values in any row.

Example 2.3   Determine if the expression $AB + \bar{C}$ is the complement of $(\bar{A} + \bar{B})C$ or, in other words, if $\overline{AB + \bar{C}} = (\bar{A} + \bar{B})C$.

Solution   We will form a truth table and see if the expressions values differ in every row.

A	B	C	$AB + \bar{C}$	$(\bar{A} + \bar{B})C$
0	0	0	1	0
0	0	1	0	1
0	1	0	1	0
0	1	1	0	1
1	0	0	1	0
1	0	1	0	1
1	1	0	1	0
1	1	1	1	0

Since the two expressions differ for every set of values, they are complements of one another. If in forming the table, we have a row for which the two expression values are the same, we would, of course, terminate our work without completing the table, since the expressions could not possibly be complements of one another, regardless of the remaining values. ■

There are rules for determining the complement of an expression, but before studying these rules we need to define *literal*. A literal is the occurrence of a variable or its complement. For example, the expression $\bar{A}B + AC + B\bar{C}$ contains only three variables but has six literals. Each of the three terms has two literals.

The following rules for forming the complement of an expression apply to expressions having no terms such as $\overline{AB}$ or factors such as $(\overline{A+B})$. That is, the expressions have no complement of more than one variable. If they do, then these rules should be applied first to these variables and then to the whole expression. Or, the variables in these terms or factors can be replaced by a single variable and then these rules applied. At the end of the work a substitution can be made back to the original variables.

Rules for complementing an expression:

1. Change each AND to OR and each OR to AND; then
2. Complement each literal and each 1 and 0.

From these rules

$$\overline{A + B + C + \ldots} = \bar{A} \cdot \bar{B} \cdot \bar{C} \cdot , \ldots , \text{ and}$$
$$\overline{A \cdot B \cdot C \cdot \ldots} = \bar{A} + \bar{B} + \bar{C} + \ldots$$

Example 2.4   What is the complement of $A\bar{B} + C$?

Solution   Applying the rules, we obtain

$$A \quad \cdot \quad \bar{B} \quad + C$$
$$\downarrow \qquad \downarrow$$
$$\text{step 1} \qquad (A + \bar{B}) \quad \cdot \quad C$$
$$\downarrow \qquad \downarrow \qquad \downarrow$$
$$\text{step 2} \qquad (\bar{A} + B) \quad \cdot \quad \bar{C}$$

and thus $\overline{A\bar{B} + C} = (\bar{A} + B)\bar{C}$. ■

Example 2.5   Determine the complement of $\overline{A\bar{B}} + C(D + \bar{E}F)$.

Solution   Here it may be advisable to assign $G = A\bar{B}$ temporarily; then

$$\bar{G} + C \quad \cdot \quad (D + \bar{E} \quad \cdot \quad F)$$
$$\downarrow \qquad \downarrow \qquad \downarrow \qquad \downarrow$$
$$\text{step 1} \qquad \bar{G} \quad \cdot \quad [C + D \quad \cdot \quad (\bar{E} + F)]$$
$$\downarrow \qquad \downarrow \qquad \downarrow \qquad \downarrow \qquad \downarrow$$
$$\text{step 2} \qquad G \quad \cdot \quad [\bar{C} + \bar{A} \quad \cdot \quad (E + \bar{F})]$$

and with the substitution back for G, the result is $A\bar{B}[\bar{C} + \bar{D}(E + \bar{F})]$. ■

From working a few examples, a person quickly acquires the facility to combine these several steps into one step for most expressions.

The proof for these rules, although fairly straightforward, will not be presented here but they can be found in the literature. These rules for complementing are called *De Morgan's theorem* or theorems.

Dual Expressions

Since in the next section we will make some use of expressions called *dual expressions,* they will be defined here. The dual of an expression is obtained in exactly the same way as the complement, with one exception: the literals are *not* complemented.

In general, there is *no* special relation between dual expressions. That is, from the value of one expression, the value of the dual expression cannot be ascertained. However, the dual of the dual of an expression is equivalent to the original expression. This will be called taking the double dual, and is very useful for converting an SOP to a POS.

In the next section duals are used in the discussion of some switching algebra theorems. It is a fact that the dual of a theorem is also a valid theorem.

Example 2.6   Convert $X\overline{Y} + \overline{X}\overline{Z}$ into an equivalent POS expression by taking the double dual.

Solution   The dual of $X\overline{Y} + \overline{X}\overline{Z}$ is $(X + \overline{Y})(\overline{X} + \overline{Z})$. This must be multiplied out in order for the second dual, when it is taken, to be a POS.

$$(X + \overline{Y})(\overline{X} + \overline{Z}) = X\overline{Z} + \overline{X}\overline{Y} + \overline{Y}\overline{Z}$$

The dual of this last expression is $(X + \overline{Z})(\overline{X} + \overline{Y})(\overline{Y} + \overline{Z})$ and it is the equivalent of $X\overline{Y} + \overline{X}\overline{Z}$. The reader should verify this last statement using a truth table or by multiplying out the POS and simplifying the resulting SOP with theorems presented in the next section. In fact, if simplification theorems are used, the POS can be simplified to $(X + \overline{Z})(\overline{X} + \overline{Y})$. ∎

An alternative to taking the dual twice is complementing twice. But this procedure involves more work because of the added complementing of the literals.

2.3   THEOREMS

Of the many switching algebra theorems, this section contains only the few that are most important in our study and that we have not already considered.

In these theorems we will use only single variables, but the theorems are also valid if the variables are replaced by expressions. For example De Morgan's theorem, already discussed, might be represented by $\overline{X + Y + Z} = \overline{X}\overline{Y}\overline{Z}$. But, a problem may have $\overline{A\overline{B} + \overline{C} + \overline{D}E}$. Obviously this theorem is applicable if X is replaced by $A\overline{B}$, Y by $\overline{C}$, and Z by $\overline{D}E$, or $\overline{A\overline{B} + \overline{C} + \overline{D}E} = \overline{A\overline{B}} \cdot \overline{\overline{C}} \cdot \overline{\overline{D}E} = (\overline{A} + B) \cdot C \cdot (D + \overline{E})$.

One of the most important theorems is $XZ + \overline{X}YZ = XZ + YZ$. This theorem states that if an expression has two terms, one of which is contained in the other except for the complementing of one variable, that variable can be deleted in the larger term. In the theorem example the term XZ is contained in the larger term $\overline{X}YZ$ except for the complementing of X (that is, the complementing of X is different in the two terms). The variable X can, therefore, be deleted from the larger term. From the dual of this theorem it is apparent that the same simplification applies to factors: $(X + Z)(\overline{X} + Y + Z) = (X + Z)(Y + Z)$. An important special case of this theorem, applied to terms, is $X + \overline{X}Y = X + Y$.

The following proof for this theorem, which proof is by means of a truth table, is only for the factor part of the theorem. The table perhaps will be made more complete than necessary to ensure that the use of a truth table is fully understood. Actually, only the first column and the last two columns are essential.

XYZ	$X + Z$	$\overline{X} + Y + Z$	$Y + Z$	$(X + Z)(\overline{X} + Y + Z)$	$(X + Z)(Y + Z)$
000	0	1	0	$0 \cdot 1 = 0$	$0 \cdot 0 = 0$
001	1	1	1	$1 \cdot 1 = 1$	$1 \cdot 1 = 1$
010	0	1	1	$0 \cdot 1 = 0$	$0 \cdot 1 = 0$
011	1	1	1	$1 \cdot 1 = 1$	$1 \cdot 1 = 1$
100	1	0	0	$1 \cdot 0 = 0$	$1 \cdot 0 = 0$
101	1	1	1	$1 \cdot 1 = 1$	$1 \cdot 1 = 1$
110	1	1	1	$1 \cdot 1 = 1$	$1 \cdot 1 = 1$
111	1	1	1	$1 \cdot 1 = 1$	$1 \cdot 1 = 1$

Since the two factor expressions have the same value for all possible combinations of values of variables, they are equivalent.

Example 2.7 Simplify $A\overline{B}CD + ABDE + A\overline{C}DE$.

Solution The expression can be written $AD[\overline{B}C + (B + \overline{C})E]$. Since $\overline{\overline{B}C} = B + \overline{C}$, the $(B + \overline{C})$ factor can be deleted. The simplified expression is $A\overline{B}CD + ADE$. ∎

Example 2.8 Simplify $(A + \overline{B} + C + D)(A + B + C + D + E)$.

Solution   The variable B is complemented in one factor but not in the other. Thus it can be eliminated in the larger factor, which, except for $\bar{B}$, includes the smaller factor. The simplified expression is $(A + \bar{B} + C + D)$ $(A + C + D + E)$. ∎

Another important theorem is $X + XY = X$ and its dual $X(X + Y) = X$. These theorems are almost self-evident. The first one perhaps can be proved easiest by factoring out the X on the left side. Then this side becomes $X(1 + Y) = X \cdot 1 = X$. In the second theorem, multiplying through by X produces $X \cdot X + XY$. But, $X \cdot X = X$, and so this left side becomes $X + XY$, which has just been shown to equal X.

These theorems may be better appreciated when expressed in words. The first theorem states that if a smaller term appears in a larger term, then the larger term is redundant (can be made zero). The second theorem says the same thing about factors, but here the larger redundant factor is replaced by 1 instead of 0.

Example 2.9   Simplify $(A + B + C + D)(A + B + C + D + E)$.

Solution   Since the factor $(A + B + C + D)$ appears in the larger factor, the larger factor can be replaced by 1 without affecting the value of the expression for any set of values of variables. That is

$$(A + B + C + D)(A + B + C + D + E) = A + B + C + D. \quad ∎$$

A very important theorem that is the basis for an important simplification method—the Karnaugh map—as well as other simplification methods, is $XYZ + X\bar{Y}Z + XY\bar{Z} + X\bar{Y}\bar{Z} = X$ and the dual

$$(X + Y + Z)(X + \bar{Y} + Z)(X + Y + \bar{Z})(X + \bar{Y} + \bar{Z}) = X$$

These theorems are difficult to put into words, but in them some variables must occur in all possible combinations such as YZ, $\bar{Y}Z$, $Y\bar{Z}$, and $\bar{Y}\bar{Z}$, which means that *the number of terms or factors must be a power of two*. Also, some literals must remain the same in all these terms or factors. If this is the case, then the SOP or POS can be simplified to a single term or factor comprising the literals that do not change. Also, *the number of variables that are eliminated is* n, this n being that of 2^n, the total number of terms or of factors.

Example 2.10   Simplify $ABCD + A\bar{B}CD + AB\bar{C}D + ABC\bar{D} + A\bar{B}\bar{C}D + A\bar{B}C\bar{D} + AB\bar{C}\bar{D} + A\bar{B}\bar{C}\bar{D}$.

Solution   The variables B, C, and D occur in all possible combinations, while the only other literal, A, is constant throughout the eight terms (note that eight is a power of two). Thus these terms can be simplified to the single term A. ∎

Example 2.11   Simplify $(A + B)(A + \bar{B})$.

Solution   The variable B occurs in all possible combinations, and since the other literal, A, is the same in both factors, the POS reduces to A.   ∎

Many other theorems can be used in the simplification of switching algebra expressions, but for most purposes these theorems are more difficult to use than the simplification method of the Karnaugh map, which is presented later in this chapter. Thus, since the theorems presented above will suffice for our purposes, we will not consider any others.

2.4   EXPANDED EXPRESSIONS

We must study both expanded sum-of-products expressions and expanded product-of-sums expressions since they are the bases for some systematic simplification procedures. Also they are used to obtain switching functions from truth tables.

Expanded Sum-of-Products (ESOP) Expressions

An *expanded sum of products* is a sum of products in which every term contains all variables, either complemented or uncomplemented. These terms are called *minterms,* and the expressions are often referred to by the acronym *ESOP*.

Any term missing a variable can be expanded by multiplying it by the variable plus its complement. This multiplication does not affect the value of the expression for any set of values of variables since the variable plus its complement equals 1. Often, duplicate minterms result as a consequence of this expansion. Of course, there is no reason for having two like terms, and thus a duplicate minterm should be deleted.

Example 2.12   Convert the SOP $A\bar{B} + BC$ into an *ESOP*.

Solution   It can be presumed from the specified expression that there are only three variables: A, B, and C. Thus each minterm must contain these three variables. C can be included in the first term by multiplying this term by $C + \bar{C}$, and A in the second term by multiplying it by $A + \bar{A}$: $A\bar{B}(C + \bar{C}) + (A + \bar{A})BC = A\bar{B}C + A\bar{B}\bar{C} + ABC + \bar{A}BC$.   ∎

A very important feature of an expanded sum of products is that *each minterm is 1 for only one set of values of variables.* For example, in the expression $A\bar{B}C + A\bar{B}\bar{C} + ABC + \bar{A}BC$, the first term is 1 only for $A = 1$, $B = 0$, $C = 1$; the second term is 1 only for $A = 1$, $B = 0$, and $C = 0$; the third term for $A = 1$, $B = 1$, and $C = 1$; and the fourth term for $A = 0$, $B = 1$, and $C = 1$. There are eight different combinations of values of three variables, and for four of these this expression is 1 and for the other four it is 0.

We will now consider the different functions or expressions that can be formed from a specified number of variables. With two variables we can form 2^2 different ESOP terms (AB, $\overline{A}B$, $A\overline{B}$, and $\overline{A}\overline{B}$). In an expression each term can be present or absent; that is, there are two possibilities for each term. Hence the number of different functions of two variables is $2^{2^2} = 16$. Three variables can form $2^3 = 8$ different possible minterms. Again in any one function each minterm has just two possibilities—it can be present or absent. Thus there are $2^{2^3} = 2^8 = 256$ different functions of three variables. In general, there are 2^{2^n} different functions of n variables.

Because writing all the terms for an ESOP function is burdensome, a shorthand is sometimes used in which the letter P with a subscript designates each minterm. The subscript for each minterm is determined by assigning a 0 to a variable if it is complemented and a 1 if not. Then the resulting 0's and 1's are interpreted as a binary number the decimal equivalent of which is used for the subscript. For three variables A, B, and C, the shorthand is

$$\begin{array}{ll}
\overline{A}\,\overline{B}\,\overline{C} - P_0 & A\,\overline{B}\,\overline{C} - P_4 \\
\overline{A}\,\overline{B}C - P_1 & A\,\overline{B}C - P_5 \\
\overline{A}\,B\overline{C} - P_2 & A\,B\overline{C} - P_6 \\
\overline{A}\,BC - P_3 & A\,BC - P_7
\end{array}$$

This shorthand is often convenient. For example, suppose that the complement of a function F of three variables A, B, and C is desired, where $F = P_0 + P_3 + P_7$. The complement $\overline{F}$ must contain the P terms not present in F; that is, $\overline{F} = P_1 + P_2 + P_4 + P_5 + P_6$. This fact should be apparent since the values that make the missing P terms 1 make F a 0, and vice versa. Another way of understanding this result is from a truth table.

A	B	C	F		$\overline{F}$	
0	0	0	1	(P_0)	0	
0	0	1	0		1	(P_1)
0	1	0	0		1	(P_2)
0	1	1	1	(P_3)	0	
1	0	0	0		1	(P_4)
1	0	1	0		1	(P_5)
1	1	0	0		1	(P_6)
1	1	1	1	(P_7)	0	

Expanded Product-of-Sums (EPOS) Expressions

In an *expanded product-of-sums* expression or function, each factor contains all variables. These factors are called *maxterms*, and the expressions are often referred to by the acronym *EPOS*.

A POS can be converted to an EPOS by use of the theorem $(A + B)(A + \bar{B}) = A$, in reverse. Duplicate factors can originate from this process and, of course, the duplicates should be deleted. It should be fairly apparent that *each maxterm is 0 for only one set of values*. This is a very important feature of EPOS expressions.

Example 2.13   Convert $(A + \bar{B})(B + C)$ into an EPOS and determine the variable values for which each factor is 0.

Solution   C must be included in the first factor. This can be done as follows: $A + \bar{B} = (A + \bar{B} + C)(A + \bar{B} + \bar{C})$. The missing variable A can be included in the second factor in a similar fashion: $B + C = (A + B + C)(\bar{A} + B + C)$. Thus $(A + \bar{B})(B + C) = (A + \bar{B} + C)(A + \bar{B} + \bar{C})(A + B + C)(\bar{A} + B + C)$. The first factor in the EPOS is 0 only for $A = 0$, $B = 1$, and $C = 0$; the second factor for $A = 0$, $B = 1$, and $C = 1$; the third factor 0 only for $A = 0$, $B = 0$, and $C = 0$; and the fourth factor only for $A = 1$, $B = 0$, and $C = 0$.   ∎

Functions can be formed by including or excluding these factors. With a little thought it is evident that the same formula for the number of expressions that was developed in the ESOP discussion applies as well to EPOS.

A shorthand is useful for maxterms. In the shorthand each maxterm is represented by an S having a subscript that is determined by substituting 0 for each uncomplemented variable and 1 for each complemented variable. This subscript determination is just the opposite of that for the P's. For three variables A, B, and C

$$
\begin{array}{ll}
A + B + C - S_0 & \bar{A} + B + C - S_4 \\
A + B + \bar{C} - S_1 & \bar{A} + B + \bar{C} - S_5 \\
A + \bar{B} + C - S_2 & \bar{A} + \bar{B} + C - S_6 \\
A + \bar{B} + \bar{C} - S_3 & \bar{A} + \bar{B} + \bar{C} - S_7
\end{array}
$$

De Morgan's theorem can easily be used with this shorthand by noting $\bar{P}_n = S_n$. Hence, if $F = P_1 + P_2 + P_7$, then $\bar{F} = \bar{P}_1\bar{P}_2\bar{P}_7 = S_1S_2S_7$. Also, assuming three variables, $\bar{F} = P_0 + P_3 + P_4 + P_5 + P_6$, as has been discussed. If this latter function is complemented, the result is $F = S_0S_3S_4S_5S_6$.

Thus, if we have one expression for F in expanded form, we can quickly obtain another expanded expression for F and two for $\bar{F}$. If the original expanded expression for F is in terms of P, then the equivalent expression in terms of S is obtained by using the subscripts not present in the P expression. The expressions for $\bar{F}$ contain the P terms and S factors not present in the expressions for F.

Example 2.14 Given F as a function of four variables, A, B, C, and D, and $F = P_0 + P_4 + P_7 + P_9 + P_{13} + P_{14} + P_{15}$, obtain F as an EPOS and $\bar{F}$ both as an EPOS and an ESOP.

Solution The subscripts missing in the ESOP are 1, 2, 3, 5, 6, 8, 10, 11, and 12. Hence

$$F = S_1 S_2 S_3 S_5 S_6 S_8 S_{10} S_{11} S_{12}$$

From the subscripts for F, obviously

$$\bar{F} = S_0 S_4 S_7 S_9 S_{13} S_{14} S_{15} = P_1 + P_2 + P_3 + P_5 + P_6 + P_8 + P_{10} + P_{11} + P_{12}$$

It will be left as an independent exercise for the reader to convert the P terms and S factors into terms and factors of the variables A, B, C, and D. ■

We now have sufficient knowledge to obtain a function in EPOS and also ESOP forms from a specification of input and output values. The *input* values are the values of variables and the *output* values are the corresponding values of the function.

Example 2.15 A function is desired of three variables A, B, and C. The function is to be 1 only if two and only two of these variables are 1.

Solution The first step in obtaining the function is the formation of a truth table from the specification of the inputs and corresponding outputs.

A	B	C	F
0	0	0	0
0	0	1	0
0	1	0	0
0	1	1	1
1	0	0	0
1	0	1	1
1	1	0	1
1	1	1	0

The 1's and 0's are placed under F in agreement with the specification of the problem.

We have two choices for F: (1) Obtain F as an ESOP from the 1's in the F column; or (2) obtain F as an EPOS from the 0's in the F column. For approach (1) we recognize that each P term produces a 1 value for a certain combination of variable values. And since the F column has three 1's, the ESOP expression for F has three P terms. The first P term is 1 if $A = 0$, $B = 1$, and $C = 1$. Obviously, this P term is $\bar{A}BC$ or P_3. The second P term, which is 1 if $A = 1$, $B = 0$, and $C = 1$, is $A\bar{B}C$ or P_5. Of course, it is no accident that the subscript for the P term is the decimal equivalent of the binary number corresponding to the variable 0's and 1's. Thus the third P term can be quickly found to be P_6 or $A B \bar{C}$. The result is $F = P_3 + P_5 + P_6 = \bar{A} B C + A \bar{B} C + A B \bar{C}$.

For an EPOS each maxterm produces a zero for a certain combination of values of the variables. Since F is 0 for five different combinations of variable values, the EPOS has five factors. The first factor is 0 if $A = 0$, $B = 0$, and $C = 0$ and is obviously $(A + B + C)$ or S_0. Similarly, and from the binary number interpretation, the other factors are S_1, S_2, S_4, and S_7. Thus

$$F = S_0 S_1 S_2 S_4 S_7$$
$$= (A + B + C)(A + B + \bar{C})(A + \bar{B} + C)(\bar{A} + B + C)(\bar{A} + \bar{B} + \bar{C}) \quad \blacksquare$$

To find the ESOP in general, consider the rows for which F is 1. The number of minterms equals the number of these rows. If in one of these rows a 0 is underneath a variable, then that variable is complemented in the corresponding term. For a 1 it is not complemented.

For an EPOS in general, we consider the rows for which F is 0. The number of maxterms equals the number of these rows. If for one of these rows a 1 is underneath a variable, then that variable is complemented, but otherwise not. This rule is just the opposite of that for the P terms.

2.5 MINIMUM EXPRESSIONS

Switching functions in either EPOS or ESOP forms are seldom desirable for realization with hardware (relays, resistors, diodes, transistors, and so on). Often the expression desired is the one for which the hardware requirements for implementation are least expensive. Of course other considerations may be important, such as size, weight, shock resistance, radiation resistance, and reliability. Also, for integrated circuits, in which many components are purchased as a single package, the considerations for optimum design may be different than if the components are available only individually. Thus there are many considerations in an optimum design, and we cannot hope in this introduction to treat them thoroughly. Yet we should consider some aspects of optimization.

To this end we will select the one design that is often of most interest—the one requiring fewest components. Also, as will be shown, the functions of interest are often SOP's or POS's. Consequently, the POS that results in minimum hardware is called *minimum product of sums* (*MPOS*) and the SOP for minimum hardware is called *minimum sum of products* (*MSOP*). As usual, we will often use the acronyms.

In many cases these minimum expressions are not unique; there may be several of them.

In the next chapter the hardware requirements are shown to be directly related to the number of literals in an expression. Accordingly, MPOS's can be defined as the POS expressions (there may be more than one) or functions having the fewest literals of any POS satisfying the specified problem. Similarly, the MSOP expressions or functions are those SOP expressions or functions that satisfy the problem and have fewest literals. Since an MSOP expression may have a different number of literals than an MPOS, we must often determine both an MPOS and an MSOP and realize (with circuits) the one having fewer literals.

In another section of this chapter we will study the Karnaugh map which will permit graphical determinations of MPOS's and MSOP's, but since we have not yet studied any systematic minimization techniques, we will have to try to obtain minimum functions by the use of theorems.

Example 2.16   Find an MSOP expression for the function F specified in the following truth table.

A	B	C	F
0	0	0	0
0	0	1	1
0	1	0	0
0	1	1	1
1	0	0	0
1	0	1	0
1	1	0	1
1	1	1	1

Solution   From the 1 entries of F, it is evident that $F = \overline{A}\,\overline{B}C + \overline{A}BC + AB\overline{C} + ABC$. Since this is an ESOP, it perhaps can be minimized. The first two terms combine: $\overline{A}\,\overline{B}C + \overline{A}BC = \overline{A}C(\overline{B} + B) = \overline{A}C$. And, the last two terms also combine: $AB\overline{C} + ABC = AB(C + \overline{C}) = AB$. Thus $F = \overline{A}C + AB$. This appears to be an MSOP function but perhaps is not. With a systematic procedure, such as the Karnaugh map, the functions obtained are minimum, unless, of course, an error is made.   ■

2.6   DON'T CARES

Often, certain combinations of variable values are not of interest. Perhaps in the hardware realization of the switching function, the physical quantities corresponding to these values never occur, or even if they do occur the resulting output may have no effect because of the action of other hardware. Whatever the reason, it is a fact that certain variable value combinations are often not of concern and yet they have rows in the truth table. These combinations, which are called *don't cares*, have entries under F of Φ: a one superimposed on a zero. For each don't-care output, we select a 1 or 0, depending upon which gives us a minimum expression.

Example 2.17   A function of two variables A and B is to be 1 if A is 0 and B is 1. The function is unspecified if A is 1 and B is 0. For other values of the variables, the function is 0. Determine an MPOS.

Solution   The problem specification put in the form of a truth table is

A	B	F
0	0	0
0	1	1
1	0	Φ
1	1	0

For a determination of an MPOS we make the don't-care output 1 and find a POS. Then, we make the don't care 0 and determine another POS. Finally, we compare the two POS expressions and use the one having fewer literals. With the don't care having a value of 1, there are two 0 entries, and from them $F = (\bar{A} + \bar{B})(A + B)$. With the don't care having a value of 0, $F = (\bar{A} + \bar{B})$ $(A + B)(\bar{A} + B)$, which, after multiplying out and simplifying, becomes $F = \bar{A}B$. Obviously, this second result is the MPOS. Incidentally, it is also the MSOP, but do not infer from this result that the same don't-care assignments give both an MPOS and an MSOP. Often, different don't-care assignments are necessary. ∎

From Example 2.17 it is evident that one don't care doubles the amount of work in determining an MPOS or MSOP since both values for the don't care must be considered. For two don't cares the amount of work is quadrupled since there are four different combinations of don't cares that must be considered: (0,0), (0,1), (1,0), and (1,1). With three don't cares there are eight different combinations of values. It is easy to see that the amount of work in the truth table-theorem approach increases greatly with the number of don't cares. Fortunately, the Karnaugh map approach permits the consideration of don't cares with little additional work.

2.7   LOGIC DIAGRAMS

In the realization of a switching algebra function, the variable values are represented by physical quantities, often voltages. For example, $+1$ V could be an algebraic 0 and $+3$ V a 1. Also, circuits of diodes, resistors, transistors, and other electrical components produce the operations of AND, OR, and NOT. At this point of our study, it is of no importance exactly what circuits perform these operations, but yet some representations for these operations are desirable.

Because various implementations are possible, it is customary to use diagrams with certain operation symbols that have been standardized but, unfortunately, not universally accepted. For AND, OR, and NOT these symbols are illustrated in Figure 2.1. Occasionally, small circles are used for NOT. The circuits for performing these operations are called *gates*.

AND   OR   NOT

Figure 2.1   Logic symbols.

Example 2.18   Show $F = A\bar{B} + \bar{C}(\bar{A} + BD)$ in logic diagram form. The inputs are A, B, C, and D.

Solution   The block diagram solution of Figure 2.2 should be apparent. Intermediate expressions are shown as an aid in understanding, but they are not usually necessary. ◾

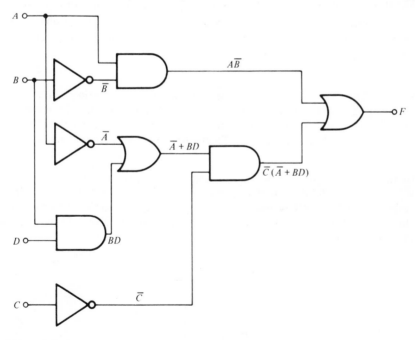

Figure 2.2   Example 2.18.

An important concept of realizations is that of *levels*. The number of levels of a realization equals the *maximum* number of components that any part of the input must pass through in order to reach the output. Of course, the part of the input of interest in determining levels is that part passing through the most gates.

In Example 2.18 some of the input must pass through four gates; for example, D passes through an AND gate, an OR gate, an AND gate, and finally an OR gate. Although some of the input does not have to pass through this number of gates, no part of the input passes through more gates. Thus this is a four-level circuit.

One reason the number of levels is important is because of the time delay of a signal in passing through a component corresponding to a level. Although the delays in some components are extremely short—maybe of the order of a few nanoseconds—these delays are often significant. Thus the circuit with fewest delays, and thus fewest levels, is often preferred.

If complements of the variables are available, and they often are, an MSOP or an MPOS can *always* be realized in two levels since an MSOP expression is basically AND followed by OR and an MPOS expression is OR followed by AND. If complements are *not* available, three levels may be necessary.

Unfortunately, realizations with fewest components are often obtained with greater than two levels. As a result, the requirements for maximum speed and for a most economical realization may be opposed, necessitating a compromise.

Example 2.19   Obtain a logic diagram realization for a function of three variables (A, B, and C) that is to be 1 when only one of the variables is 1 or when none of the variables is 1. Complements of the variables are available. The realization is to be in two levels.

Solution   The steps for determining a logic diagram realization are (a) forming a truth table; (b) determining an EPOS and an ESOP from the truth table; (c) minimizing these expressions and selecting the expression having fewer literals; and (d) implementing this expression in the form of a logic diagram. The truth table for this problem is

A	B	C	F
0	0	0	1
0	0	1	1
0	1	0	1
0	1	1	0
1	0	0	1
1	0	1	0
1	1	0	0
1	1	1	0

The ESOP is, from the truth table, $\bar{A}\bar{B}\bar{C} + \bar{A}\bar{B}C + \bar{A}B\bar{C} + A\bar{B}\bar{C}$. The first two terms combine to $\bar{A}\bar{B}$, the first and third terms to $\bar{A}\bar{C}$ (any term can be used any number of times in minimizing since $X = X + X + , \ldots , + X$), and the first and fourth terms to $\bar{B}\bar{C}$. Thus $F = \bar{A}\bar{B} + \bar{A}\bar{C} + \bar{B}\bar{C}$. This happens to be an MSOP expression, as can be verified later when Karnaugh maps are studied.

From the truth table, the EPOS function is

$$F = (A + \bar{B} + \bar{C})(\bar{A} + B + \bar{C})(\bar{A} + \bar{B} + C)(\bar{A} + \bar{B} + \bar{C})$$

The first and fourth factors simplify to $(\bar{B} + \bar{C})$, the second and fourth factors to $(\bar{A} + \bar{C})$ (a factor can be used any number of times since $X = X \cdot X \cdot , \ldots , \cdot X$), and the third and fourth factors to $(\bar{A} + \bar{B})$. Thus

$$F = (\bar{B} + \bar{C})(\bar{A} + \bar{C})(\bar{A} + \bar{B})$$

This is an MPOS, and again this fact is not evident at present but can easily be shown from a Karnaugh map. Since the two expressions have the same number of literals, both of them will be realized. The realizations are shown in Figure 2.3. ∎

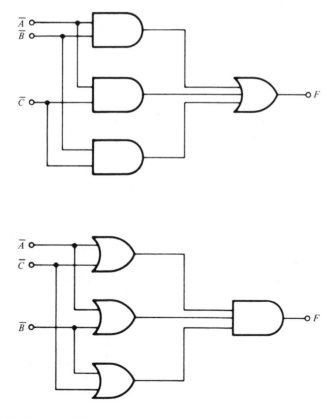

Figure 2.3 Example 2.19.

2.8   NAND AND NOR

Two switching algebra operations will now be introduced that are extremely important—at least as important as AND, OR, and NOT. These are NAND and NOR.

NAND

NAND is equivalent to AND followed by NOT, and in logic diagrams is designated by (for three inputs) the symbol illustrated in Figure 2.4(a). Since, for example, $\overline{X \cdot Y, \ldots, Z} = \overline{X} + \overline{Y} +, \ldots, \overline{Z}$, NAND can also be considered as OR preceded by NOT, or symbolically, for three inputs, as is illustrated in Figure 2.4(b). A NAND gate, for logic diagram considerations, can have any number of inputs, but for practical realizations is limited. This matter is discussed in the next chapter.

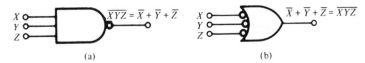

(a)   (b)

Figure 2.4   NAND symbols.

The NAND operation, which is sometimes designated by a stroke (/), does *not* obey the associative law; that is, $(A/B)/C \neq A/(B/C)$. The left side when reduced to AND, OR, and NOT is $(A/B)/C = \overline{\overline{AB}/C} = \overline{\overline{AB}C} = AB + \overline{C}$. But the right side is $A/(B/C) = A/\overline{BC} = \overline{A \cdot \overline{BC}} = \overline{A} + BC$. Since $AB + \overline{C} \neq \overline{A} + BC$, NAND does not obey the associative law. This is an academic matter for present purposes and will cause no problem.

Any switching algebra function can be realized with only NAND gates; no other gates are necessary. We will show the sufficiency of NAND by producing the operations of AND, OR, and NOT from the NAND operation. Actually, this is more than sufficient for it is a fact that NOT and *either* AND or OR, two of these operations, are all that are necessary for generating any switching function. The proof of this fact will not be presented here.

A two-input NAND gate can produce NOT if the same signal is applied to both inputs, as is shown in Figure 2.5(a). In actual construction, the gate has only one input, as will be shown in the next chapter.

Since NAND is AND followed by NOT, a NAND gate followed by NOT produces AND—the two NOT's cancel. See Figure 2.5(b).

NAND is also OR preceded by NOT. Thus, if NOT gates are placed

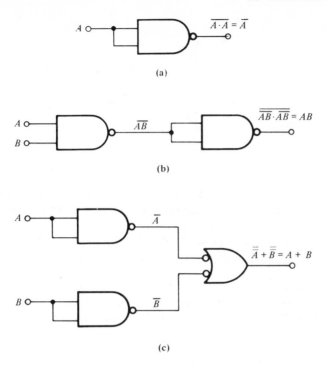

Figure 2.5 NOT, AND, and OR from NAND.

at the inputs of a NAND gate, the two NOT's cancel leaving OR. See Figure 2.5(c).

This proof of the sufficiency of NAND is intended to be for academic purposes only. As a rule, circuits are not implemented with NAND gates in this fashion for they are often uneconomical. However, NAND gates are frequently used exclusively. We will now consider how to use them for two-level circuits.

If complements of the variables are available, *any* function can be realized with a two-level NAND circuit having several NAND gates at the first level that provide inputs to a single NAND gate at the second level. *For this realization, the variables applied at the input level of NAND gates are those appearing in the MSOP, with each input NAND gate corresponding to a different term.*

The variables are selected in this manner because a two-level NAND circuit is basically an AND-OR circuit, which is the type of circuit needed for implementing an SOP. The NAND operation in the first level can be considered as AND followed by NOT, and that in the second level as OR preceded by NOT. The two NOT's cancel, leaving AND followed by OR, as is illustrated in Figure 2.6. Of course, NAND symbols need not be drawn in this manner for two-level NAND realizations.

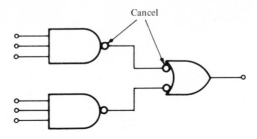

Figure 2.6 AND-OR from two-level NAND's.

NAND realizations of more than two levels may be more economical, but a consideration of such circuits is beyond the scope of this book.

Example 2.20   Realize $F = (X + Y)(\overline{X} + \overline{Y})$ with a two-level NAND diagram. Complements of the variables are available.

Solution   Convert this POS to an SOP, and preferably to an MSOP, for a determination of the variables to apply to the NAND gates in the first level. The MSOP is obviously $X\overline{Y} + \overline{X}Y$. Thus the realization is as shown in Figure 2.7.   ■

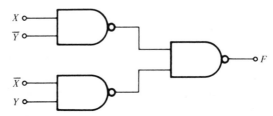

Figure 2.7 Example 2.20.

The truth table for NAND is extremely simple considering the power of this operation. Regardless of the number of variables, all function values are 1 except for one entry: all of the variables equal to 1. For three variables the truth table is

A	B	C	$\overline{ABC}$
0	0	0	1
0	0	1	1
0	1	0	1
0	1	1	1
1	0	0	1
1	0	1	1
1	1	0	1
1	1	1	0

NOR

The NOR operation is equivalent to OR followed by NOT or to AND preceded by NOT. In symbolic representation, NOR is (for four variables) shown in Figure 2.8.

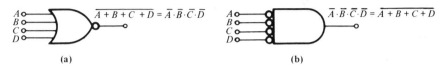

(a)   (b)

Figure 2.8 NOR symbols.

NOR, which is sometimes designated by an arrow ($\downarrow$), does *not* obey the associative law: $(A \downarrow B) \downarrow C \neq A \downarrow (B \downarrow C)$. The proof of this will be left as an exercise for the reader.

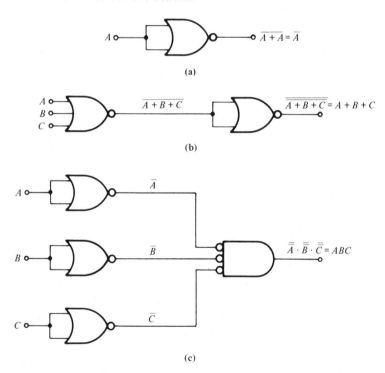

Figure 2.9 NOT, OR, and AND from NOR.

Like NAND, the NOR operation alone is sufficient for realization of any switching algebra function. A NOT gate can be produced from a two-input NOR gate with the same signal applied to both inputs [Figure 2.9(a)]. Of course, in practice a single-input circuit is used, as will be shown in the next chapter. OR is the result if a NOR gate is followed by a NOT gate: the two NOT's cancel, leaving OR. See Figure 2.9(b). Finally, an AND gate is formed if a NOR gate is preceded by NOT gates. See Figure 2.9(c).

As a practical matter, this use of NOR gates is usually uneconomical. As with NAND, any function can be realized with a two-level NOR circuit having several NOR gates at the first level that provide inputs to a single NOR gate at the second level. *For two-level realizations, the variables used should be those appearing in the MPOS, with each first-level NOR gate corresponding to a different factor.*

The justification for this realization is apparent if the first-level NOR gates are considered as OR followed by NOT and the second-level NOR gate as AND preceded by NOT. The two NOT's of the two levels cancel leaving the OR-AND combination which is needed for realizing an MPOS in two levels (Figure 2.10).

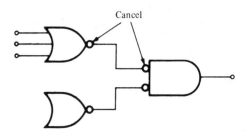

Figure 2.10 OR-AND from two-level NOR's.

Example 2.21 Show a two-level block diagram realization of NOR gates for $F = ABC + \bar{A}\bar{B}$. Complements are available.

Solution Convert the function to POS form and, of course, preferably MPOS form, for the desired realization. This conversion can be accomplished in several ways. By the double dual method it is

$$ABC + \bar{A}\bar{B} \xrightarrow{\text{dual}} (A + B + C)(\bar{A} + \bar{B}) = \bar{A}B + \bar{A}C + A\bar{B} + \bar{B}C$$

This intermediate result should be minimized to ensure that when the dual of it is taken, the result is an MPOS. Minimizing this expression is difficult from the few theorems we have studied, but with a systematic method, the result can be easily obtained as $\bar{A}B + A\bar{B} + \bar{B}C$. From the dual of this, the result is

$$F = (\bar{A} + B)(A + \bar{B})(\bar{B} + C)$$

Because of the three factors, three NOR gates are needed for the first level, as is shown in the realization of Figure 2.11. ∎

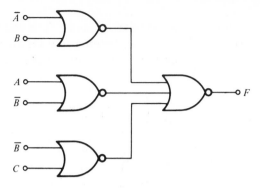

Figure 2.11 Example 2.21.

NOR realizations of more than two levels are often more economical, but the study of the design of these circuits is beyond the scope of this book.

The truth table for NOR is as singular as that for NAND. For NOR, all of the function values are 0 except the one for which all input variables are 0. That is (for three variables)

A	B	C	$\overline{A + B + C} = \overline{A}\overline{B}\overline{C}$
0	0	0	1
0	0	1	0
0	1	0	0
0	1	1	0
1	0	0	0
1	0	1	0
1	1	0	0
1	1	1	0

2.9   KARNAUGH MAPS AND MINIMIZATION

The *Karnaugh map* is a very convenient graphical method for obtaining an MPOS and an MSOP. It is quick to use and nearly foolproof for functions of up to five variables. Some persons have facility with maps of six variables and even seven. However, for those persons that use Karnaugh maps only occasionally, facility with maps of five variables and less is probably all that can be expected. The presentation here will be directed to the development of skills with the three-, four-, and five-variable maps.

Three-Variable Karnaugh Maps

A Karnaugh map contains squares, one for each row of a corresponding truth table. In fact, a Karnaugh map can be considered to be a special representation of a truth table. Each square corresponds to a different row, and 1's or 0's are entered into the squares depending upon the function values for the corresponding rows. For example, the truth table

A	B	C	F
0	0	0	0
0	0	1	1
0	1	0	0
0	1	1	0
1	0	0	1
1	0	1	0
1	1	0	0
1	1	1	1

and the Karnaugh map shown in Figure 2.12(a) contain the same information.

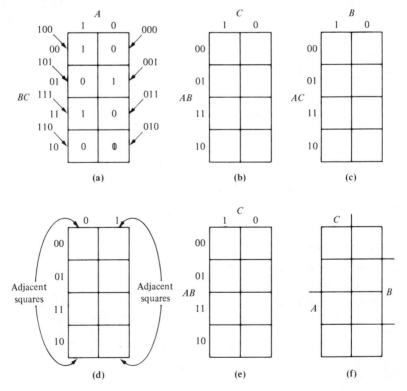

Figure 2.12   Three-variable Karnaugh maps.

The squares corresponding to the various rows are shown. In fact, they are shown twice: the numbers heading the rows and columns indicate the rows as well as the numbers 000, 001, and so on, with arrows extended from them. These latter numbers are shown here only to ensure a complete understanding of the correspondence between the squares and the rows of a truth table. They will not be included in any other Karnaugh maps.

The ordering of the rows of the map should be noted: 00, 01, 11, and 10. The numbering of the last two rows is *inverted* from the natural ordering. There is a good reason for this inverted ordering. With it, the P terms corresponding to adjacent squares are the same except for one complement. That is, if one square corresponds to the P term ABC, then an adjacent square corresponds to $\overline{A}BC$. In fact, we will define adjacent squares to be those having corresponding P terms that differ in only one complement. With this definition, the top row is adjacent to the bottom row even though they are not truly physically adjacent.

In this map it makes *no* difference how the variables are assigned before the function values are inserted. The variable C could head the columns and AB the rows, as shown in Figure 2.12(b), or AC the rows and B the columns, as in Figure 2.12(c). Also, the 1 column can be on the right instead of the left. The only real restriction of the map is that squares corresponding to adjacent P terms be physically adjacent, and this includes the folding of the map so that the top edge meets the bottom edge to make the top row adjacent to the bottom row. See Figure 2.12(d).

The map is preferably drawn without designating the row and column headings with 0's and 1's. Instead, the variables are placed where they appear uncomplemented for the P terms. In other words, they are placed where the 1's would be. As an illustration, Figures 2.12(e) and (f) are different forms of the same map, but the second map is easier to write and also to use.

Now that we have discussed the construction of the three-variable Karnaugh map, we can consider how to use the map to obtain an MSOP. For an MSOP, the squares containing 1's are of concern. Two adjacent squares with 1's combine to give a single product term having *one* less than the number of variables of a P term. Thus, for a three-variable map, the terms of two adjacent 1-squares combine into a single term of two variables.

In Figure 2.13(a) two adjacent 1-squares are shown combined or grouped by a loop drawn around them. This grouping causes the elimination of one variable which is the one that changes from one square to the other; that is, it is complemented in one square and not in the other. This grouping accomplishes the following:

$$\overline{A}BC + ABC = BC(\overline{A} + A) = BC$$

Four adjacent squares *in the form of a rectangle* can be grouped to yield a product term having *two* less variables than the number of variables corresponding to each square. For a three-variable map, the four squares grouped in a rectangle combine to give a term having a single variable. The two variables that drop out are the ones that change over the group.

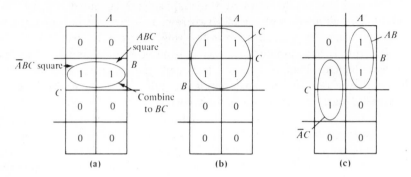

Figure 2.13 Karnaugh map groupings.

An example is shown in Figure 2.13(b), in which the two variables A and B drop out of the resulting term. This elimination is evident from the four P terms of the four squares: $A\bar{B}C$, ABC, $\bar{A}\bar{B}C$, and $\bar{A}BC$, for which $F = A\bar{B}C + ABC + \bar{A}\bar{B}C + \bar{A}BC$. We can easily reduce this function to $F = C$ by grouping terms; perhaps the reader should do this for an exercise. However, a theorem is directly applicable. This theorem, which has been presented, applies to a number of terms (or factors) that are some power of two (2, 4, 8, 16, 32, and so on) and in which some variables are in all possible combinations of forms as regards complements, (such as AB, $\bar{A}B$, $A\bar{B}$, and $\bar{A}\bar{B}$), and in which the other variables in each term are the same. These terms combine such that the variables that change drop out, leaving only a single term of the variables that are constant. In a Karnaugh map, the 1-squares must be in a rectangular group to satisfy these conditions and the number of squares per group must be a *power of two*. In this example, the variables A and B go through all possible combinations and thus drop out, leaving only C.

As mentioned, the pattern of 1's must be rectangular in order to be grouped. The Karnaugh map of Figure 2.13(c) has four 1-squares, but since these squares are not in a single rectangle, no two variables go through all possible combinations. The MSOP is obtained from this map by forming two groups.

Several rules must be followed in forming groups in a Karnaugh map. For an MSOP each 1-square must be in at least one group since all P terms must be considered. And the groups, which must contain 2, 4, 8, 16, and so on 1-squares, should be as large as possible, because

the larger the group the fewer the number of variables in the corresponding term. Specifically, for two squares in a group, the term has one
less variable. For four squares, the term has two less variables. For
eight squares, the term has three less variables, and so on. Finally,
no more groups should be formed than are necessary to include all
the 1-squares since the fewer the number of groups, the fewer the number
of terms.

Example 2.22   Determine an MSOP for the function specified in the map of
Figure 2.14(a).

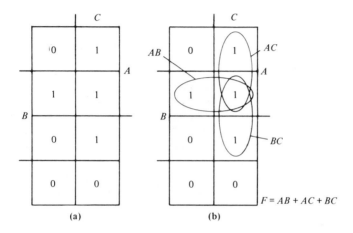

Figure 2.14   Example 2.22.

Solution   Although the number of 1-squares is a power of two (4), the 1-squares
are not in the form of a rectangle such that each 1-square is adjacent
two other 1-squares. Thus they cannot be combined into a single group. In fact,
three groups must be used as shown in Figure 2.14(b), and $F = AB + AC + BC$.

■

The ABC square is used three times in the above solution. There
is nothing wrong with this since $ABC = ABC + ABC + ABC$. In addition to the fact that each 1-square can be used as many times as desired,
each 1-square must be used at least once if only to form a group comprising just itself. Of course, the groups should be as large as possible and
should be a minimum in number.

Don't cares are inserted on the maps as ϕ. From inspection, it is
usually apparent whether the don't cares should be assigned as 1's or
0's. Of course, the don't-care assignments are independent; that is, some
don't cares can be assigned as 1's and others as 0's.

Example 2.23   Determine an MSOP corresponding to the map of Figure 2.15(a).

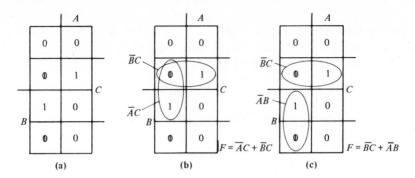

(a)   (b)   (c)

Figure 2.15   Example 2.23.

Solution   If both don't cares are made 0's, the two 1-squares will be spaced which condition is obviously undesirable. If the don't care of square $\bar{A}\bar{B}C$ is made a 1, there will be two groups, each having two squares. The other don't care may be considered a 0 or a 1; it makes no difference even though different expressions result. In the map of Figure 2.15(b), it is considered a 0 and in the map of Figure 2.15(c), a 1. Both $F = \bar{A}C + \bar{B}C$ and $F = \bar{B}C + \bar{A}B$ are acceptable MSOP's, although they are not equivalent. However, they do have the same values for the non-don't-care cases. This example illustrates that there may be several MSOP functions.   ∎

Karnaugh maps are equally applicable for determining MPOS expressions. An MPOS can be determined in several ways, one of which is to obtain an MSOP from the map for $\bar{F}$ and then complement this function to obtain the desired function F as an MPOS.

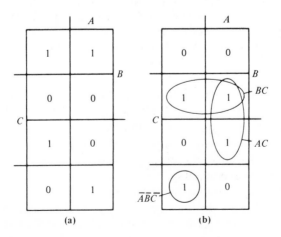

(a)   (b)

Figure 2.16   Example 2.24.

Example 2.24 Obtain an MPOS corresponding to the map of the function F shown in Figure 2.16(a).

Solution The complement approach will be used. A map of $\bar{F}$ is formed by replacing the 0's by 1's and the 1's by 0's on the F map. Then an MSOP is found for $\bar{F}$, and this function complemented. See Figure 2.16(b).

$$\bar{F} = \bar{A}\bar{B}\bar{C} + BC + AC$$

and

$$F = (A + B + C)(\bar{B} + \bar{C})(A + \bar{C})$$

is the MPOS.　• ∎

After acquiring some facility with maps, a person can determine an MPOS without making a map of $\bar{F}$. Instead, he can work with the 0's of the F map and mentally complement the literals and form sums. This is done in the following example. Also, the use of don't cares in MPOS situations is illustrated.

Example 2.25 Find an MPOS, given the map of F illustrated in Figure 2.17(a).

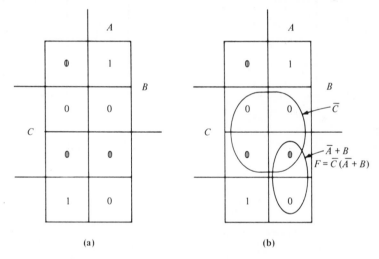

(a)   (b)

Figure 2.17 Example 2.25.

Solution The three don't cares have eight possible different combinations of 0's and 1's. However, little complexity is introduced by these don't cares, and the solution of Figure 2.17(b), $F = \bar{C}(\bar{A} + B)$, is fairly obvious. ∎

Several features of three-variable maps have yet to be mentioned. One of these is that it is entirely possible to have several MPOS's or several MSOP's even if there are no don't cares. Also, in forming a map, we often omit the 0 entries; they are "understood." This omission saves a little work and makes the map less cluttered.

Four-Variable Karnaugh Maps

A four-variable Karnaugh map comprises two three-variable maps. The map has, of course, sixteen squares, and they are arranged in a square as shown in Figure 2.18(a). In this map the top row is adjacent the bottom row and the left side is adjacent the right side. Note the inverted ordering in the rows and columns. Incidentally, the adjacencies are easily determined, if forgotten. One merely has to check the P terms corresponding to two squares to see if they differ in only one complement.

A preferred form of this map does not have the numbered rows and columns but has just the variables instead, as illustrated in Figure 2.18(b).

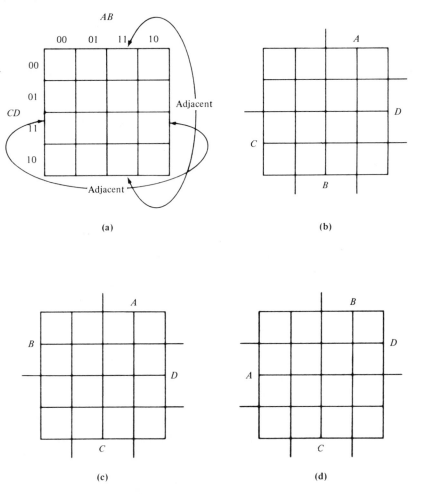

Figure 2.18   Four-variable Karnaugh maps.

Four-variable Karnaugh maps can have several arrangements. The only requirement is preservation of adjacencies. In Figures 2.18(c) and (d) are illustrated two differently arranged maps, and there are others.

A four-variable map is used in exactly the same manner as a three-variable map. Of course, there are more adjacencies to consider. Especially it should be noted that the four corners form a four-group.

Example 2.26 Following is a truth table specifying a function. Determine an MPOS and an MSOP and show implementations with AND-OR, NAND, and NOR. Complements of the variables are available.

A	B	C	D	F
0	0	0	0	1
0	0	0	1	0
0	0	1	0	Φ
0	0	1	1	0
0	1	0	0	Φ
0	1	0	1	1
0	1	1	0	0
0	1	1	1	1
1	0	0	0	1
1	0	0	1	0
1	0	1	0	0
1	0	1	1	0
1	1	0	0	0
1	1	0	1	1
1	1	1	0	1
1	1	1	1	Φ

Solution The first step in the solution is the construction of a four-variable map as is done in Figure 2.19(a). The don't-care assignment for an MSOP is apparent: the don't care in the $ABCD$ square should be considered a 1 and all the others 0's. The grouping is then as shown in Figure 2.19(b), and

$$F = ABC + BD + \overline{B}\overline{C}\overline{D}$$

For the MPOS expression, we are *not* restricted to the choice of don't cares made in determining the MSOP. If a different choice is made, the MSOP and the MPOS are not equivalent, but they have the same values for all non-don't-care inputs. In this case, however, the MSOP and an MPOS (it is not unique) have the same don't-care assignments. One grouping for an MPOS, $F = (B + \overline{C})$ $(B + \overline{D})(\overline{B} + C + D)(A + \overline{C} + D)$, is shown in Figure 2.19(c).

Because the MSOP has fewer literals, it will be used in the AND-OR realization. See Figure 2.19(d). The MSOP expression should be used for the two-level NAND realization which is shown in Figure 2.19(e) and, of course, the MPOS is used for a two-level NOR realization shown in Figure 2.19(f). ∎

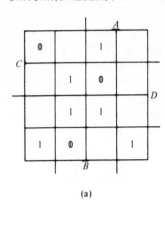

(a)

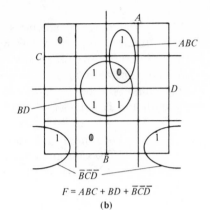

$$F = ABC + BD + \overline{B}\overline{C}\overline{D}$$

(b)

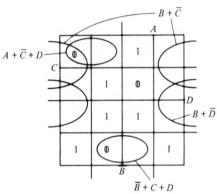

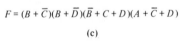

$$F = (B + \overline{C})(B + \overline{D})(\overline{B} + C + D)(A + \overline{C} + D)$$

(c)

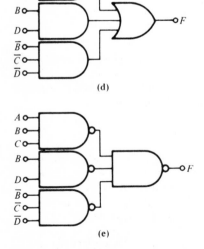

(d)

(e)

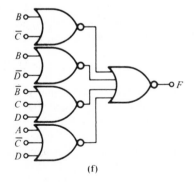

(f)

Figure 2.19 Example 2.26.

In combining squares, it is advisable, in general, to first consider the squares that combine in the smallest groups, and then the squares that combine in the next to smallest groups, and so on. In fact, errors may result otherwise. For example, consider the map of Figure 2.20. In determining an MSOP, it is tempting to form a group of four squares. But if this is done, the resulting SOP will not be minimum, as the reader can demonstrate for himself.

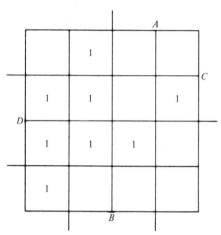

Figure 2.20 Karnaugh map with an apparent four-square group.

Five-Variable Karnaugh Maps

We will consider two versions of the five-variable map: the *layer* map and the *waffle-iron map*. In each of these, the map is essentially two four-variable maps.

A suitable five-variable layer map is shown in Figure 2.21(a), but a preferred form is in Figure 2.21(b).

The five-variable map has all the adjacencies of the four-variable map and, in addition, the adjacencies obtained by placing one map over the other to form two layers. That is, the map also has *up and down adjacencies*. Some adjacent squares are shown in the map of Figure 2.21(c).

Example 2.27 Given the five-variable map of Figure 2.22(a), determine an MPOS and an MSOP.

Solution For the MSOP, the solution is fairly obvious: $F = \bar{A}\bar{B} + A\bar{C}DE + ABC\bar{D}$ as shown in Figure 2.22(b). The grouping for the MPOS is more difficult, but after some thought is seen to be as shown in Figure 2-22(c), and

$$F = (A + \bar{B})(\bar{A} + B + \bar{C})(\bar{A} + C + D)(\bar{B} + \bar{C} + \bar{D})(\bar{A} + \bar{D} + E)$$

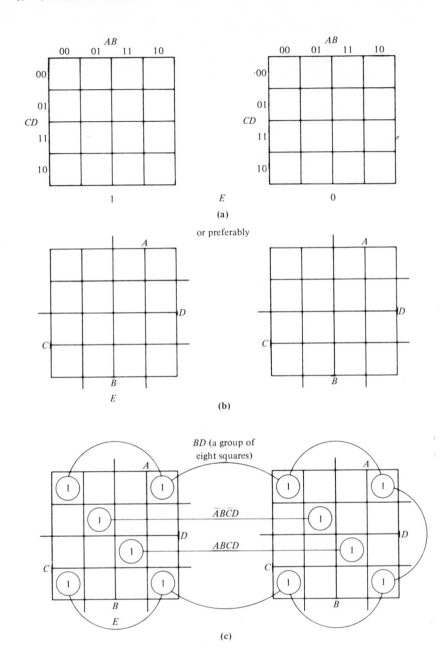

Figure 2.21   Five-variable layer Karnaugh maps.

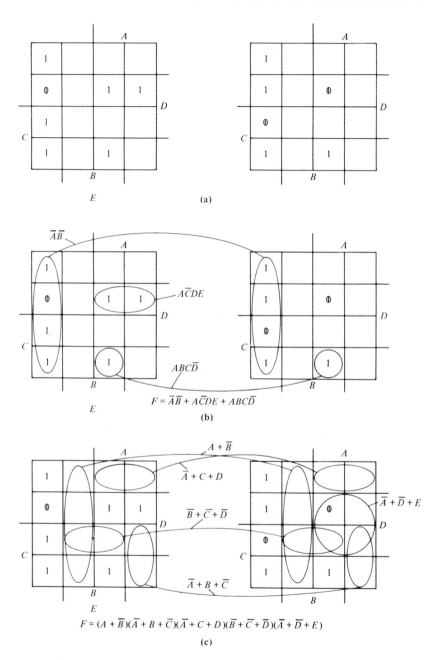

Figure 2.22 Example 2.27.

It should be noted that there are other equivalent expressions for the MPOS; it is not unique. ▪

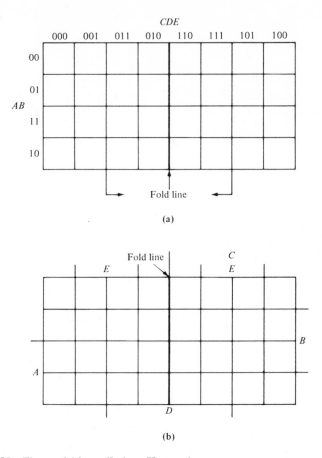

Figure 2.23   Five-variable waffle-iron Karnaugh maps.

The waffle-iron, five-variable map is illustrated in Figures 2.23(a) and (b). This map has a top and bottom adjacency that can be seen by folding one map over the other about the fold line.

Example 2.28   Given the map of Figure 2.24(a), obtain an MPOS and an MSOP.

Solution   The grouping of the 1-squares for the MSOP is apparent and is shown in Figure 2.24(b). Thus $F = B\bar{E} + A\bar{B}C + \bar{A}\bar{B}DE$. The grouping for the MPOS of Figure 2.24(c) is less apparent. With this grouping, $F = (\bar{B} + \bar{E})(\bar{A} + B + C)(A + B + E)(A + D + \bar{E})$. This MPOS and MSOP are equivalent since they have the same don't-care assignments. ▪

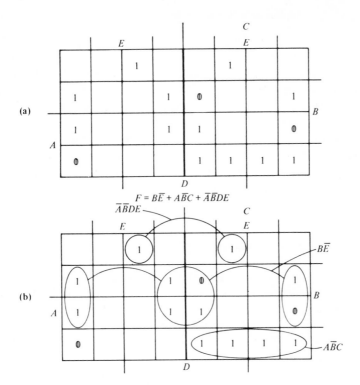

$$F = B\overline{E} + A\overline{B}C + \overline{A}\overline{B}DE$$

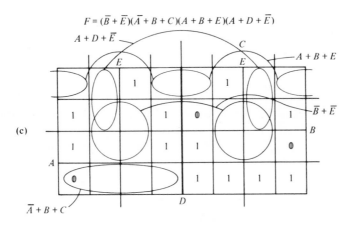

$$F = (\overline{B} + \overline{E})(\overline{A} + B + C)(A + B + E)(A + D + \overline{E})$$

Figure 2.24 Example 2.28.

Six-Variable Karnaugh Maps

A six-variable Karnaugh map comprises two five-variable maps. Again, the map has a layer version and waffle-iron version. The layer version is illustrated in Figure 2.25(a). In it four maps are placed on top of one another, at least mentally, for a determination of the adjacencies. The waffle-iron version has two fold lines, as shown in Figure 2.25(b).

No examples will be presented for the six-variable maps because these maps are not required for the work that follows. Also, if one has this many (or more) variables perhaps he should consider another method, such as the McCluskey-Quine method, which is described in the literature.

2.10   EXCLUSIVE OR

Additional switching algebra operations could be presented, but most of these are not germane to the present study. However, there is one of vital importance to other studies that we will use occasionally: $EXCLUSIVE\ OR$, which has the symbol $\oplus$. For two variables, the EXCLUSIVE OR truth table is

A	B	$A \oplus B$
0	0	0
0	1	1
1	0	1
1	1	0

This operation differs from OR (sometime referred to as INCLUSIVE OR) in the last row. For this table, $A \oplus B = A\overline{B} + \overline{A}B$. In comparison, $A + B = AB + A\overline{B} + \overline{A}B$.

In general, the EXCLUSIVE OR of an odd number of 1's is one and for an even number of 1's is zero.

$$0 \oplus 1 \oplus 1 \oplus 0 \oplus 1 = 1$$
but
$$1 \oplus 1 \oplus 0 \oplus 1 \oplus 1 = 0$$

With this knowledge and a little thought, we should realize that rather complicated expressions EXCLUSIVE OR'd together can be greatly simplified with Karnaugh maps. We can represent each expression on a different Karnaugh map and then superimpose the maps. From these, we form a single map having 1's in squares for which the superimposed maps have an odd number of 1's.

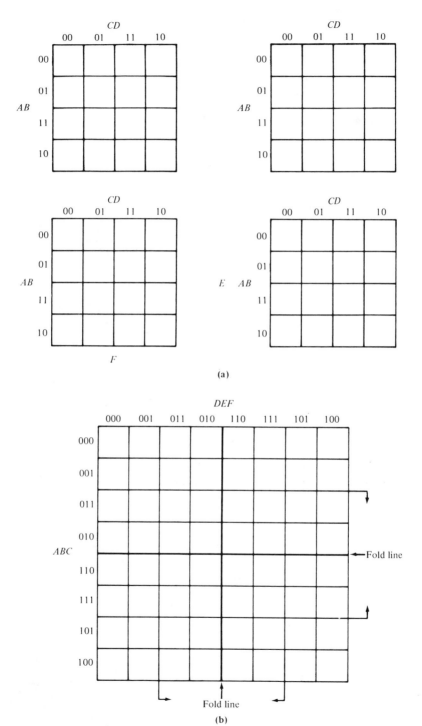

Figure 2.25 Six-variable Karnaugh maps.

Example 2.29   Convert $F = (A\bar{B} + C) \oplus (\bar{A}\bar{B} + BC) \oplus (A\bar{C} + \bar{A}\bar{B})$ to an MSOP.

Solution   Each expression is placed in map form as illustrated in Figure 2.26(a).

A superimposing of the maps produces a single map having 1's in squares in which the superimposing produces an odd number of 1's. See Figure 2.26(b). The SOP from the resultant map is $F = AB\bar{C} + \bar{B}C$. This use of the maps is much easier than trying to manipulate the variables individually.   ∎

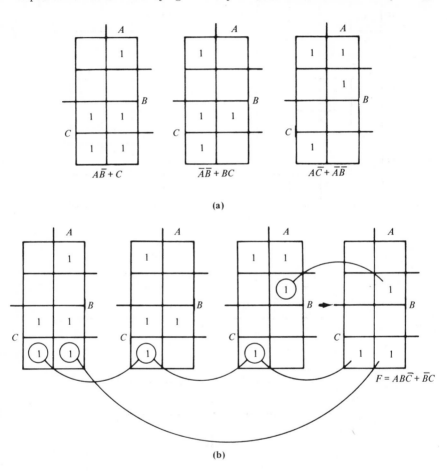

(a)

(b)

Figure 2.26   Example 2.29.

2.11   POSITIVE AND NEGATIVE LOGIC

The topic of *positive* and *negative logic* perhaps should be delayed until the next chapter because it relates to hardware implementation as contrasted to the study of switching algebra, which is the principal subject of this chapter. However, it is also related to many of the topics discussed in this chapter, such as the logic diagrams, and even to the algebraic operations. Thus positive and negative logic will be discussed here.

Voltage levels in digital computers and other switching circuit applications often represent the 0's and 1's which are, at the same time, switching algebra values and also binary numbers. Of course, two voltages are used. If the more positive voltage (both voltages can be negative, both positive, or one positive and one negative, with respect to ground) represents the 1 and the more negative voltage the 0, then, by definition, positive logic is used. If the more negative voltage represents the 1, then negative logic is used.

The type logic has a direct bearing on the operation that an implemented gate performs. For example, consider a two-input gate constructed to operate according to the following voltage truth table in which the plus sign indicates the more positive voltage and the minus sign the more negative voltage. The third column comprises the outputs for the inputs indicated in the first two columns.

A	B	F
−	−	−
−	+	−
+	−	−
+	+	+

If positive logic is used, $+ \rightarrow 1$ and $- \rightarrow 0$, then the corresponding algebraic truth table is

A	B	F
0	0	0
0	1	0
1	0	0
1	1	1

The operation is AND. However, if negative logic is used, $- \rightarrow 1$ and $- \rightarrow 0,$ the algebraic truth table is

A	B	F
1	1	1
1	0	1
0	1	1
0	0	0

and the operation is OR. Thus this component can be either an AND gate or an OR gate, depending on the logic used. That is, no determination can be made from the circuit alone as to whether it is an AND gate or an OR gate. However, gates are usually assigned names corresponding to the operations performed with positive logic.

The above illustrates that an AND gate for positive logic is an OR gate for negative logic. It will be left to the reader to establish that an OR gate for positive logic is an AND gate for negative logic.

Consider a two-input gate that produces the following voltage truth table.

A	B	F
−	−	+
−	+	+
+	−	+
+	+	−

For a positive logic assignment, the corresponding switching algebra truth table is

A	B	F
0	0	1
0	1	1
1	0	1
1	1	0

which is a truth table for NAND. If negative logic is used, the algebraic truth table is

A	B	F
1	1	0
1	0	0
0	1	0
0	0	1

which is a truth table for NOR. It is true, in general, not just for two inputs, that a NAND gate for positive logic is a NOR gate for negative logic. Also, a NOR gate for positive logic is a NAND gate for negative logic.

The reader can demonstrate to himself that a NOT gate is a NOT gate, regardless of the logic.

In summary

Positive Logic		Negative Logic
AND	↔	OR
OR	↔	AND
NAND	↔	NOR
NOR	↔	NAND
NOT	↔	NOT

When negative logic is used, it is often designated on the logic diagram. This designation is desirable because in the same switching circuit, positive logic may be used in one part of the circuit and negative logic in another. This is mixed logic. One way of indicating negative logic is by small circles that overlap the gate symbol lines, as is illustrated in Figure 2.27. These circles should not be confused with the small non-overlapping circles sometimes used for NOT gates.

Figure 2.27 Negative logic designations.

The consequences of mixed logic are readily determinable from a consideration of negative logic as the equivalent of the use of a NOT gate. Perhaps this fact is obvious, but it will be verified by examples. Consider a two-input gate that is an AND gate for positive logic. The voltage and switching algebra truth tables are

A	B	F
−	−	−
−	+	−
+	−	−
+	+	+

A	B	F
0	0	0
0	1	0
1	0	0
1	1	1

Suppose negative logic is employed at the output and only the output. The corresponding switching algebra truth table is

A	B	F
0	0	1
0	1	1
1	0	1
1	1	0

which is, of course, the truth table for a NAND gate. Thus the change of the output logic from positive to negative logic is the equivalent of the insertion of a NOT gate. This is generally true and is not limited to this one example.

Example 2.30   Given a NAND gate for positive logic, but with negative logic applied at the input [see Figure 2.28(a)], what is the logic function performed?

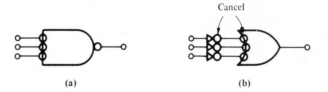

(a)   (b)

Figure 2.28   Example 2.30.

Solution   The change of logic at the input is equivalent to the use of NOT gates at the input and the application of positive logic. And since NAND is equivalent to NOT followed by OR, the result is just OR [Figure 2.28(b)].   ■

Example 2.31   In the logic diagram of Figure 2.29(a) the gates are indicated for positive logic. What is F in terms of the applied variables?

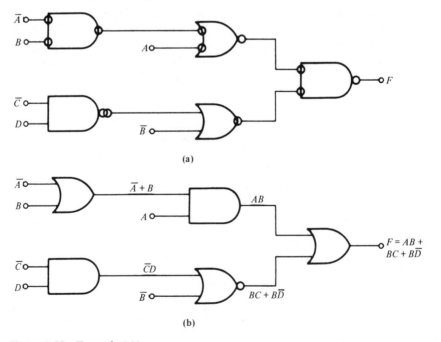

(a)

(b)

Figure 2.29   Example 2.31.

Solution   If negative logic is considered the equivalent of the insertion of NOT
gates, this diagram can be modified to an all-positive logic diagram
by inserting NOT gates mentally. Then the AND gate with $\bar{A},B$ inputs, which
has negative logic inputs and outputs, obviously becomes an OR gate. The following NOR gate with negative logic at both inputs produces AND since NOR is
equivalent to NOT followed by AND, and the two NOT's effectively cancel at
the inputs, leaving AND. The right-most gate, the NAND gate with negative
logic inputs, is equivalent to an OR gate: NAND is equivalent to NOT followed
by OR and the NOT's cancel at the inputs. The NAND gate with $\bar{C},D$ inputs
has a negative logic output, and the result is obviously an AND gate. The following OR gate with a negative logic output acts like a NOR gate. The result is the
equivalent all-positive logic diagram of Figure 2.29(b) from which clearly
$F = AB + BC + B\bar{D}$.   ∎

2.12   COMPLETE EXAMPLES

At this point of the discussion all of us should be able
to synthesize some switching systems. Of course, the systems will be in
logic diagram form since the circuits for implementing the logic operations have not yet been studied; they are presented in the next chapter.
But being able to synthesize a system in logic diagram form is an accomplishment since an engineer may not do any design of the circuit
implementation, but instead purchase the gates he needs. In these times
of integrated circuits, few electrical engineers design the circuits. Rather,
most purchase the circuit components they need. With this viewpoint,
the synthesis procedure for many and perhaps most applications can be
considered to be the producing of a logic diagram from the problem
specifications, followed by the purchase and interconnection of the components indicated on the diagram.

Example 2.32   A half adder is needed. It is to be constructed of NOR gates.
Complements of the variables are available.

Solution   A half adder, which adds two binary digits, has two inputs, one for
each digit, and two outputs, one for the sum bit and one for the carry
bit. We will call the two input digits A and B, the sum output bit S, and the
carry C [see Figure 2.30(a)]. From our study of binary arithmetic we can easily
formulate a truth table.

A	B	S	C
0	0	0	0
0	1	1	0
1	0	1	0
1	1	0	1

From the truth table, $S = A \oplus B = (\bar{A} + \bar{B})(A + B)$, which is the MPOS
needed for the NOR realization, and $C = AB$. Preferably, both operations should
use common gates, as much as possible, for minimum gate requirements. Since
procedures for producing an optimum design for a multi-output circuit are beyond

the scope of this book, we will use just trial and error. After a little study we can obtain the logic diagram of Figure 2.30(b).

This half adder was so simple to design that a Karnaugh map was not needed to determine the MPOS for the S bit. However, in general, the minimization step is necessary. Also, it should be noted that the 1's and 0's of direct concern in a half adder are binary numbers. But, in the synthesis procedure the 1's and 0's are treated as switching algebra values once the truth table has been obtained. ∎

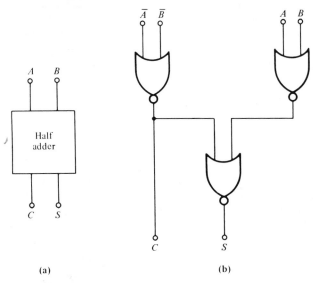

(a)   (b)

Figure 2.30 Example 2.32.

Example 2.33   Design a half subtractor using only NAND gates. Complements of the variables are available.

Solution   A half subtractor circuit subtracts one binary digit from another, say $X - Y$. Two outputs must be provided, one for the difference bit D and one for the borrow bit B. See Figure 2.31(a). A 1 is generated on the difference bit line when 0 is subtracted from 1 and on both output bit lines when 1 is subtracted from 0. The following truth table for a half subtractor should be apparent from the presentation of binary numbers in Chapter 1.

X	Y	D	B
0	0	0	0
0	1	1	1
1	0	1	0
1	1	0	0

From the truth table, $D = X \oplus Y = \overline{X}Y + X\overline{Y}$, which is the MSOP needed for the NAND realization, and $B = \overline{X}Y$. Again, for an optimum design, the same circuits, as much as possible, should be used to provide both outputs. By trial and error we obtain the diagram of Figure 2.31(b). ∎

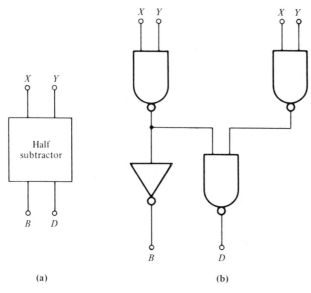

Figure 2.31   Example 2.33.

The realizations of this section are in terms of logic diagrams. In the next chapter circuits will be studied that are used in the construction of the gates.

PROBLEMS ▬▬▬▬▬▬▬▬▬▬▬▬▬▬▬▬▬

2.1   Evaluate the following expressions for $A = 0$, $B = 1$, $C = 0$, and $D = 1$.
(a) $A\bar{B}(1 + C)$
(b) $\bar{C}(\bar{A} + B)(\overline{AB} + C)$
(c) $[A(\bar{B} + C) + D(C + B)](A\bar{C} + D)$

Answers   (a) 0;   (b) 1;   (c) 1

2.2   Evaluate the expressions of Problem 2.1 for $A = 1$, $B = 1$, $C = 0$, and $D = 0$.

2.3   Show a truth table for $F = A\bar{B}(AB + \bar{B})$.

Answers	A	B	F
	0	0	0
	0	1	0
	1	0	1
	1	1	0

2.4   Show a truth table for $F = A\bar{B}(C + \bar{D}) + ACD$.

2.5   Determine if the expressions $AB + AC$ and $(A + \bar{C})(A + C)(B + C)$ are equivalent.

Answer   They are equivalent.

2.6   Determine if the expressions $\bar{B}CD + \bar{A}BC + AB\bar{C}$ and $AB\bar{C} + A\bar{B}CD + \bar{A}BC\bar{D} + \bar{A}CD$ are equivalent.

2.7   Determine if the expression $A\bar{B}C + \bar{A}(C\bar{D} + B)$ is the complement of $(\bar{A} + B + \bar{C})(A + \bar{C} + D)(A + \bar{B})$.

Answer   It is.

2.8   Determine if the expression $AB + (\bar{C} + D)(\bar{A} + \bar{B})$ is the complement of $\bar{A}C\bar{D} + \bar{B}C\bar{D}$.

2.9   Determine the complements of the following expressions:
(a) $A\bar{B} + C(\bar{D} + E)$
(b) $A\bar{B} + \bar{C}\bar{D}(E + \bar{F}G)$
(c) $A\bar{B}(C + \bar{D}E) + \bar{A}\bar{B}C + \bar{B}(C + D)$

Answers   (a) $(\bar{A} + B)(\bar{C} + D\bar{E})$;   (b) $(\bar{A} + B)[CD + \bar{E}(F + \bar{G})]$;
(c) $[\bar{A} + B + \bar{C}(D + \bar{E})](A + B + \bar{C})(B + \bar{C}\bar{D})$

2.10   Determine the complements of the following expressions:
(a) $(A + \bar{C})(D + \bar{E}F) + A\bar{B}$
(b) $\overline{\bar{A}\bar{B}(C + D\bar{E})} + A\bar{B}(C + D)$
(c) $A\bar{C}D(E + \bar{F}G) + HI\bar{J}(K + L\bar{M})$

2.11   Convert $AB + \bar{B}C$ to an equivalent POS by taking the double dual.

Answer $(A + \bar{B})(B + C)$

2.12   Convert $A\bar{B}C + ABD + B\bar{C}D$ to an equivalent POS by taking the double dual.

2.13   Simplify the following expressions:
(a) $A\bar{B}C + (\bar{A} + B)C\bar{D}$
(b) $A\bar{C}(B + D) + \bar{B}\bar{D} + C$
(c) $(A\bar{B} + C + D)(\bar{A} + B + C + D + E)$
(d) $(A\bar{B} + C\bar{D} + E + F)(\bar{A} + B + E + F)(\bar{C} + D + E + F)$

Answers   (a) $A\bar{B}C + C\bar{D}$;   (b) $A + C + \bar{B}\bar{D}$;
(c) $C + D + A\bar{B}E$;   (d) $E + F$

2.14   Simplify the following expressions:
(a) $A + \bar{C}D + CDE + \bar{A}B$
(b) $AC\bar{D} + A\bar{B}\bar{C} + A\bar{B}D$
(c) $(A + C + D)(A + C + \bar{D} + E)$
(d) $(A + \bar{C} + B)(A + \bar{C} + D)(\bar{B} + \bar{D})C$

2.15   Simplify the following expressions:
(a) $ABC + A\bar{B}C + (\overline{\bar{A} + \bar{B} + \bar{C}})(\bar{A} + B + \bar{C})$
(b) $(A + B + C)(A + \bar{B}\bar{C})(A + \bar{B} + C)(A + B + \bar{C})$

Answers   (a) AC;   (b) A

2.16 Simplify the following expressions:
(a) $ABCD + AB\overline{C}D + \overline{A}BCD + \overline{A}B\overline{C}D$
(b) $(A + \overline{B})(\overline{B} + C)(\overline{B} + \overline{C})$

2.17 Convert each of the following expressions to an ESOP:
(a) $\overline{A}\overline{B} + \overline{B}C$ (c) $(A + B)(\overline{A} + \overline{B})$
(b) $A + \overline{B}C$ (d) $(A + B)(\overline{B} + \overline{C})$

Answers   (a) $\overline{A}\overline{B}C + \overline{A}B\overline{C} + A\overline{B}C$;   (b) $A\overline{B}C + AB\overline{C} + A\overline{B}\overline{C} + ABC + \overline{A}\overline{B}C$;   (c) $A\overline{B} + \overline{A}B$;   (d) $A\overline{B}C + A\overline{B}\overline{C} + AB\overline{C} + \overline{A}B\overline{C}$

2.18 Convert each of the following expressions to an ESOP:
(a) $A\overline{B} + C$ (c) $(A + \overline{B}C)(A + \overline{B}D)$
(b) $A\overline{B} + \overline{C}D$ (d) $(A + \overline{B})(C + D)$

2.19 Convert each of the expressions of Problem 2.17 to an EPOS.

Answers   (a) $(A + \overline{B} + C)(A + \overline{B} + \overline{C})(\overline{A} + B + C)(\overline{A} + \overline{B} + C)(\overline{A} + \overline{B} + \overline{C})$
(b) $(A + B + C)(A + \overline{B} + C)(A + \overline{B} + \overline{C})$
(c) $(A + B)(\overline{A} + \overline{B})$
(d) $(A + B + C)(A + B + \overline{C})(A + \overline{B} + \overline{C})(\overline{A} + \overline{B} + \overline{C})$

2.20 Convert each of the expressions of Problem 2.18 to an EPOS.

2.21 Given $F = P_0 + P_3 + P_5$ as a function of three variables. Determine F as a product of S factors and $\overline{F}$ as a sum of P terms and also as a product of S factors.

Answers $F = S_1S_2S_4S_6S_7$; $\overline{F} = P_1 + P_2 + P_4 + P_6 + P_7$
         $= S_0S_3S_5$

2.22 Given $F = P_1 + P_4 + P_{11} + P_{12}$ as a function of four variables. Determine F as a product of S factors and $\overline{F}$ as a sum of P terms and also as a product of S factors.

2.23 A function F of four variables A, B, C, and D is to be one if and only if two of the four variables are one. Express the function as an EPOS and also as an ESOP.

Answers $F = AB\overline{C}\overline{D} + A\overline{B}C\overline{D} + A\overline{B}\overline{C}D + \overline{A}BC\overline{D} + \overline{A}B\overline{C}D + \overline{A}\overline{B}CD$;
$F = (A + B + C + D)(A + B + C + \overline{D})$
$(A + B + \overline{C} + D)(A + \overline{B} + C + D)$
$(A + \overline{B} + \overline{C} + \overline{D})(\overline{A} + B + C + D)$
$(\overline{A} + B + \overline{C} + \overline{D})(\overline{A} + \overline{B} + C + \overline{D})$
$(\overline{A} + \overline{B} + \overline{C} + D)(\overline{A} + \overline{B} + \overline{C} + \overline{D})$

2.24 A function F of four variables A, B, C, and D is to be one if and only if one or three of the four variables are one. Express the function as an EPOS and also as an ESOP.

2.25 Show $F = A\bar{B}\bar{C}(D + \bar{E}H) + AE\bar{H}$ in logic diagram form. Use AND, OR, and NOT gates. The inputs are A, B, C, D, E, and H.

Answer   See Figure 2.32.

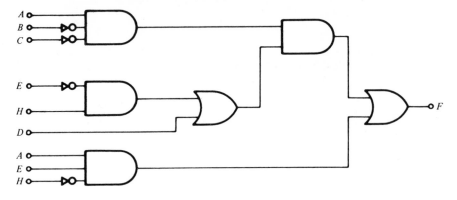

Figure 2.32 Problem 2.25.

2.26 Show $F = (A + \bar{B}C)(\bar{C}D + H) + \bar{A}E(B + \bar{C})$ in logic diagram form. Use AND, OR, and NOT gates. The inputs are A, B, C, D, E, and H.

2.27 A function of three variables A, B, and C is to be one if and only if two or all three variables are one. Complements of the variables are available. Use AND and OR gates. Show two two-level realizations in logic diagram form.

2.28 Realize the function of Problem 2.27 with a two-level NAND diagram and then with a two-level NOR diagram.

Answer   See Figures 2.33(a) and (b).

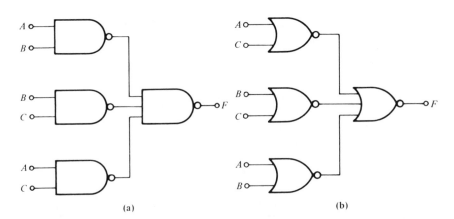

(a)   (b)

Figure 2.33 Problem 2.28.

2.29 A function of four variables A, B, C, and D is to be one if and only if three or all four variables are one. Complements of the variables are available. Use AND and OR gates. Show two two-level realizations in logic diagram form.

2.30 Realize the function of Problem 2.29 with a two-level NAND diagram and then with a two-level NOR diagram.

2.31 Determine an MSOP and an MPOS for each of the functions entered on maps in Figures 2.34(a), (b), and (c).

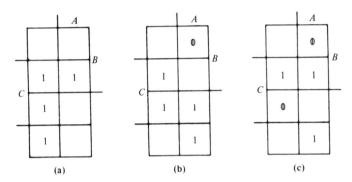

(a)   **(b)**   **(c)**

Figure 2.34 Problem 2.31.

Answers   **(a)** $BC + \overline{A}\overline{B}$; $(\overline{B} + C)(\overline{A} + B)$;   **(b)** $\overline{A}C + A\overline{B}$;
$(\overline{A} + \overline{B})(A + C)$;   **(c)** $BC + A\overline{C}$; $(B + \overline{C})(A + C)$

2.32 Determine an MSOP and an MPOS for each of the functions entered on maps in Figures 2.35(a), (b), and (c).

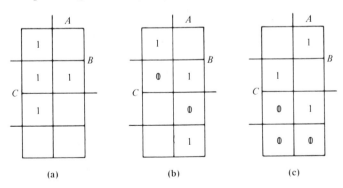

(a)   **(b)**   **(c)**

Figure 2.35 Problem 2.32.

2.33 Determine an MSOP and an MPOS for each of the functions entered on maps in Figures 2.36(a), (b), and (c).

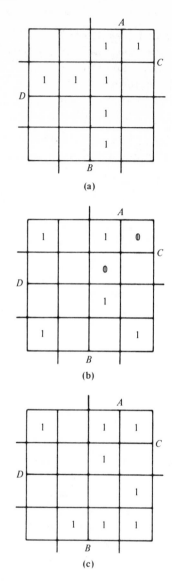

Figure 2.36   Problem 2.33.

Answers   (a) $AB + \bar{A}CD + AC\bar{D}$; $(\bar{A} + B + \bar{D})(A + D)$
$(A + C)(B + C)$

(b) $ABD + AC\bar{D} + \bar{B}\bar{D}$; $(B + \bar{D})(A + \bar{B})$
$(\bar{B} + C + D)$

(c) $ABC + A\bar{B}\bar{C} + BC\bar{D} + \bar{B}C\bar{D}$; $(B + \bar{C} + \bar{D})$
$(\bar{B} + C + \bar{D})(A + B + C)(A + \bar{B} + \bar{C})$

2.34   Determine an MSOP and an MPOS for each of the functions entered on maps in Figures 2.37(a), (b), and (c).

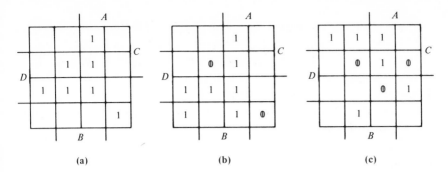

Figure 2.37   Problem 2.34.

2.35   Determine an MSOP and an MPOS for both functions entered on maps in Figures 2.38(a) and (b).

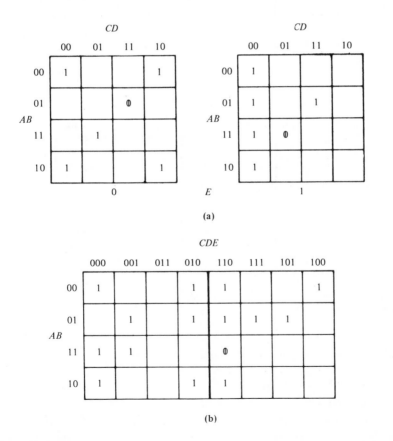

(a)

(b)

Figure 2.38   Problem 2.35.

Answers   (a) $\overline{A}BCD + AB\overline{C}D + \overline{B}\overline{D}\overline{E} + \overline{C}\overline{D}E; (A + C + \overline{D})$
$(\overline{C} + D + \overline{E})(\overline{A} + \overline{B} + \overline{C})(\overline{B} + D + E)(B + \overline{D})$
(b) $\overline{A}BCE + A\overline{C}\overline{D}\overline{E} + B\overline{C}\overline{D}E + \overline{A}D\overline{E} + \overline{B}D\overline{E} + \overline{A}\overline{B}\overline{E};$
$(A + \overline{B} + D + E)(\overline{A} + \overline{C} + D)(\overline{A} + \overline{B} + \overline{D})$
$(C + \overline{D} + \overline{E})(B + \overline{E})$

2.36   Determine an MSOP and an MPOS for both functions entered on maps in Figures 2.39(a) and (b).

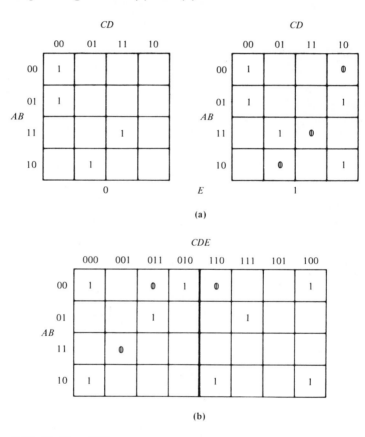

(a)

(b)

Figure 2.39   Problem 2.36.

2.37   Convert each of the following to an MSOP:
(a) $(A + B) \oplus (\overline{A} + C) \oplus (B + \overline{C})$
(b) $A\overline{B}(C + D) \oplus \overline{B}\overline{C} \oplus \overline{A}B\overline{C}$
(c) $(A\overline{B} + C\overline{D}) \oplus (E\overline{F} + G)$

Answers   (a) $\overline{A}C + \overline{A}B + BC$;   (b) $\overline{A}\overline{B} + AB\overline{C} + A\overline{C}\overline{D}$;
(c) $\overline{A}C\overline{G}\overline{E} + \overline{A}C\overline{G}F + \overline{A}D\overline{G}\overline{E} + \overline{A}D\overline{G}F + B\overline{C}\overline{G}\overline{E} +$
$B\overline{C}\overline{G}F + BD\overline{G}\overline{E} + BD\overline{G}F$

2.38   Convert each of the following to an MSOP:

(a) $(\overline{A} + B)(A + C) \oplus (AB\overline{C} + \overline{A}C) \oplus A\overline{B}$

(b) $(A + B\overline{C})(\overline{A} + \overline{B}) \oplus (\overline{A}C + AB) \oplus (A\overline{C} + \overline{B}C) \oplus$
   $(\overline{A} + B)(A + \overline{C})$

(c) $(A\overline{B} + C)(\overline{B} + \overline{C}) \oplus (E\overline{F} + G)H$

2.39   Determine F in the logic diagram of Figure 2.40.

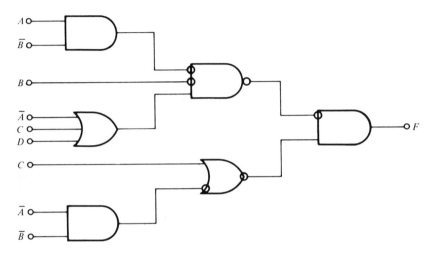

Figure 2.40   Problem 2.39.

Answer $F = \overline{A}\overline{B}\overline{C}$

2.40   Determine F in the logic diagram of Figure 2.41.

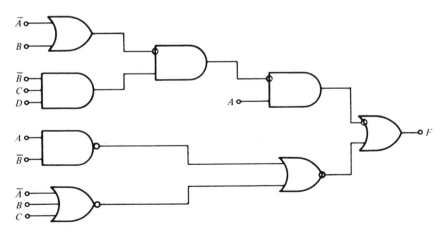

Figure 2.41   Problem 2.40.

3

Logic
Circuits

At this point of our study we should be able to construct a logic diagram for performing any desired operation that is *combinational* in nature, that is, for which the output at any time depends only on the input at that time. Of course, this implementation is in the form of logic blocks—no circuit details are shown. Still the logic diagram can be the step immediately preceding actual construction of the circuit, since circuits for performing the various logic operations are often purchased as a unit and not constructed in detail. Thus an engineer can construct an operable digital circuit and yet be fairly ignorant of many of the details of the circuit.

Some engineers must, of course, have sufficient knowledge to construct the circuits. These are the relatively few engineers who design the circuits that are purchased by others. But a detailed knowledge of digital circuits is not needed by most engineers using digital circuits. Also, digital circuit design is such a swiftly changing field that knowledge gained at any one time is considerably obsolete in a few years. Consequently it is certainly at least questionable whether it is worth gaining this knowledge, taking the time and effort to obtain it, unless a person is specializing in digital circuit design and can thus keep abreast of this field by continued study. However, an engineer using digital circuits should have a sufficient knowledge of details of these circuits so that he can select the type of circuit best suited for the job at hand. He should know some of the limitations of these circuits and enough to do further study of these circuits if that is necessary.

In view of this situation, digital circuits are presented in this chapter sufficiently to meet many of the needs of the circuit user but not nearly to the extent needed by the digital circuit designer.

Not all digital circuits will be considered. There are too many for an introductory book or for any book that is not limited to digital circuits. However, the circuits presented here are those that are the most popular at the present time in the United States. Relay circuits, diode circuits, and transistor circuits are presented in that order.

3.1 RELAY LOGIC

Although relays have slow operating speeds compared to electronic devices, such as diodes and transistors, they are suitable for many digital circuit applications, particularly those that, in addition to not requiring high speeds, have high power devices to be controlled or in which noise is a problem. Railroad systems for controlling the movement of trains and dial telephone systems have relays as a major switching component as do many other switching systems. One of the earliest computers had relays, exclusively, for switching elements. Relays are also used in the peripheral equipment (for example, card readers) of digital computers.

The study of relay circuits is therefore practical from an implementation viewpoint. Also, this study serves as an introduction to the slightly more difficult studies of diode and transistor digital circuits.

Physical Features of Relays

Relays comprise a coil and two (or more) contact springs, as shown in Figure 3.1(a). One of the springs is mounted on an iron armature (not shown) that moves into the coil when current flows in the coil. This movement causes the springs to either touch or separate, depending upon the type of contact. A pair of springs forms a contact.

There are three types of contacts and they are distinguished by the relay coil energization required to make the springs touch. These three are the *normally open* (*N/O*), the *normally closed* (*N/C*), and *transfer contacts*.

An N/O contact has springs that are separated when there is no current in the relay coil but which touch when current flows. Since the nonenergized state is considered to be the normal state and is that shown in circuit diagrams, an N/O contact is illustrated with separated springs, as in Figure 3.1(a). The spring without the arrow is the spring that moves (in some relays both springs move) and touches the other spring when the coil is energized.

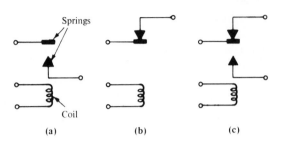

Figure 3.1   Relays.

An N/C contact has springs that touch when the coil is not energized and that separate when current flows in the coil. Its circuit symbol is shown in Figure 3.1(b).

A relay with transfer contacts has three springs per contact pair, each of which comprises a normally open contact and a normally closed contact sharing a common operating spring, as shown in Figure 3.1(c).

A relay may have many springs associated with it. In fact, some relays are constructed of nothing but transfer contacts piled one on top of the other and all operated by the same armature. For our purposes we will consider each different relay to have as many springs as are needed for the circuit. Again, for emphasis, there may be many springs but only one relay.

A relay circuit has an input circuit and an output circuit that are electrically isolated from one another. The coils are in the input circuit and the contacts in the output circuit, as shown in Figure 3.2. For our present purposes we can consider the output circuit to be a single output line and some contacts that can connect this line to ground. Thus the output circuit has just two possible conditions of operation: the output line is connected to ground or it is not connected to ground. In the latter case there is an open circuit.

One of these physical conditions can be assigned to correspond to the logical 1 and the other to the logical 0. Usually the assignment is that ground on the *output* line produces a logical 1 for the function corresponding to the condition of that line. Another way of saying the same thing is that a conduction path through contacts is usually considered to be a logical 1 and an open circuit a 0.

In the *input* circuit each relay coil has just two conditions of operation: energized or not energized. Usually the condition of energization corresponds to the logical 1 and the condition of deenergization to the logical 0. Also, as shown in Figure 3.2, there is often a dc voltage source in the input circuit connected to a terminal of each coil. Then, if ground is applied at an input terminal, a coil is energized, and the state of the coil becomes 1. Thus, for both the input terminals and the output line, the presence of ground is indicative of a logical 1.

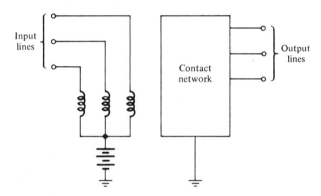

Figure 3.2 Relay circuit.

Each input terminal has a switching variable associated with it, as is shown for a single terminal and a variable A in Figure 3.3. If terminal A is a 1 or, in other words, is physically grounded, the coil is energized. Since this energization also corresponds to a 1, the variable can also be associated with the coil.

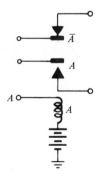

Figure 3.3 Relay with variable assignments.

The variables are also associated with the contacts, and this association is determinable from what has already been discussed. That is, when a coil is energized a conducting path exists through its N/O contacts, which path corresponds to a 1. And since there should be agreement between the variables in both the input and output circuits, it is necessary that an N/O contact correspond to the variable assigned to the coil so that both have the same values at the same times. That is, if A is assigned to the coil, then A *must be assigned to the N/O contacts* for that relay. Similarly, an N/C contact must be assigned or associated with the complement of the variable assigned to the coil, for when the coil is energized, and thus associated with a 1, the N/C contacts are open, which condition corresponds to a 0. Consequently, if A is associated with a coil, then $\overline{A}$ *is associated with the N/C contacts.* This discussion is summarized, graphically, in Figure 3.3.

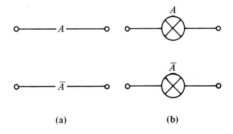

(a)   **(b)**

Figure 3.4 Symbols for contacts.

In a diagram of a relay circuit the details of the relays are seldom shown since they are so well known and the diagram can be simplified considerably by the omission of the details. The coils are usually not shown and some designation such as that in Figure 3.4(a) or (b) is used for the contacts.

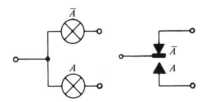

Figure 3.5 Transfer contact assignment.

In general, a relay design should employ as many transfer contacts as possible since these contacts require fewer springs. For a transfer-contact realization the design must be such that the contacts corresponding to the variables and their complements are in sets with each set having a common terminal, as shown in Figure 3.5. Obviously, with .this arrangement there is a saving of one spring per set as compared to a realization with two individual contacts: an N/O contact and an N/C contact.

Parallel and Series Connections

If a pair of contacts is placed in parallel as in Figure 3.6(a), a conduction path occurs if either contact A OR contact B is closed. And since conduction corresponds to a 1, *a parallel connection of contacts produces OR.*

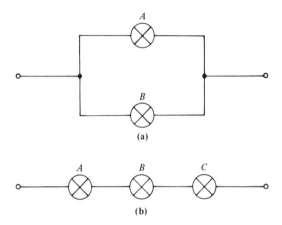

Figure 3.6 Parallel-connected and series-connected contacts.

If contacts are placed in series as in Figure 3.6(b), conduction occurs only if contacts A AND B AND C are closed. Thus the operation *AND is obtained by placing contacts in series.*

Example 3.1   Show a relay circuit for producing $F = A(\bar{B} + C\bar{D})$.

Solution   Four relays are needed since there are four variables. From the knowledge that series connections produce AND, parallel connections OR, and N/C contacts NOT, the realizations of Figures 3.7(a) and (b) are fairly apparent.   ■

In the design of relay circuits there is *no* concern for levels, since in almost any application for which relays are suited, switching speed must not be a major concern. If it were, faster components than relays would be used. With levels of no concern, the most desirable expression for relay implementation is usually that having fewest literals since it requires fewest contacts. Of course, the design should include transfer contacts where possible, but unfortunately there is no systematic procedure for optimizing their use. Thus, in implementing a switching function, we will try to arrange the variables such that the number of literals is a minimum and then in the construction use transfer contacts expediently.

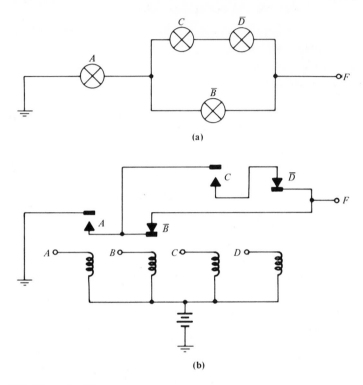

(a)

(b)

Figure 3.7   Example 3.1.

The implemented expressions or functions are *seldom* put in a POS or an SOP. However, an MPOS or an MSOP will often be a convenient point of departure for obtaining the desirable form.

Example 3.2   A 115 V lamp is controlled by three switches A, B, and C. The lamp is to light when any two of the switches are closed. It makes no difference if the lamp is on or off when all three switches are closed. The relays require 24 V for the coils. Design the relay circuit.

Solution   The first step in the realization is the formation of a Karnaugh map from the specifications. The entries for the map are obvious from the specifications, and the completed map is shown in Figure 3.8(a). From this map

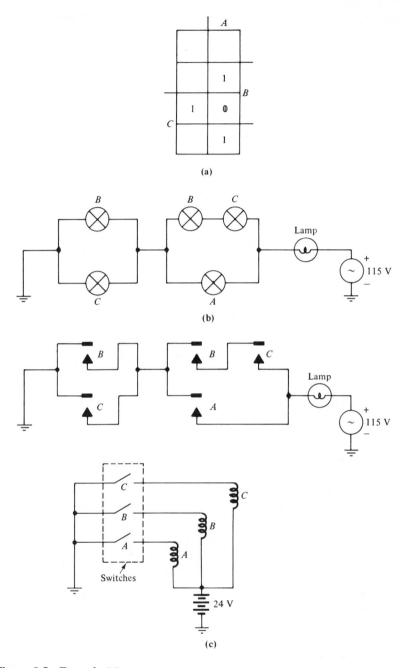

Figure 3.8 Example 3.2.

obviously $F = AB + BC + AC = (B + C)(A + C)(A + B)$. These expressions can be rearranged to minimize the number of literals: $F = A(B + C) + BC = (B + C)(A + BC)$. With the same number of literals in both expressions, and no opportunity to use transfer contacts with either (there are no complements of variables), it is purely arbitrary which expression is realized. The second one is shown in Figures 3.8(b) and (c).

In Figure 3.8(c) relays B and C each have two pairs of contacts and, although not shown, the operating springs are, for any one relay, connected to the same armature. Thus, although the two pairs of contacts for, say, B are spaced and not shown directly over coil B, they are operated by the same armature. ■

From this point on, the contacts and the coils will seldom be shown since they are not needed for an understanding of how the relays are connected; the connections should be obvious once the symbol diagram is obtained. The inclusion of the coils and the contacts clutters the diagrams and hinders rather than aids comprehension.

Bridges

Contacts arranged in *bridge form* often provide more economical circuits than parallel-series connected contacts. Unfortunately, no systematic procedure exists for obtaining a bridge circuit directly from a switching function expression. However, it is very easy to find either a POS or an SOP from a bridge. Each factor of a POS corresponds to a set of contacts that if open prevent conduction and thus produce a 0. For an SOP each term corresponds to a set of contacts that if closed produce conduction and thus a 1.

Example 3.3   Determine a POS and an SOP for the bridge of Figure 3.9(a).

Solution   To determine a POS we draw lines (all possible lines) through contacts such that the lines pass completely across the bridge, as shown in Figure 3.9(b). The contacts on each line, if open, prevent conduction and thus correspond to a factor. Hence

$$F = (\overline{A} + D)(\overline{A} + C + E)(B + C + D)(B + E)$$

For the SOP we need only determine all conduction paths through the bridge, for the contacts along each path correspond to a term. There is a conduction path through $\overline{A}$ and B, another one through $\overline{A}$ and C and E, and also one through D and C and B, and, finally, one through D and E. Thus

$$F = \overline{A}B + \overline{A}CE + BCD + DE.$$ ■

As mentioned, it is quite another matter to obtain a bridge from an expression.

Example 3.4   Design a relay circuit for realizing $F = CDE + \overline{C}\overline{D}\overline{E}$. Use nine springs.

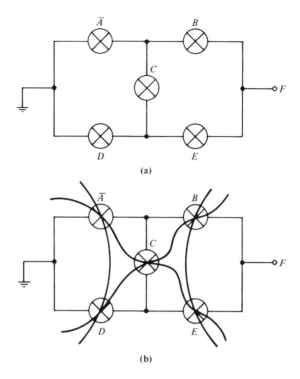

Figure 3.9 Example 3.3.

Solution   A straightforward approach results in the realization of Figure 3.10(a).
This is a ten-spring realization if transfer contacts are used for con-
tacts C, $\bar{C}$ and E, $\bar{E}$. But a nine-spring realization is possible. With some trial
and error and a little effort, the nine-spring realization of Figures 3.10(b) and (c)
can be obtained. Only nine springs are necessary because the contacts have been
arranged such that transfer contacts can be used on all three relays. ■

3.2 DIODE LOGIC

Relays are much too slow in switching speed to be used
for some digital applications, and in particular for components in the
arithmetic unit of a modern digital computer. Electronic components
such as diodes and transistors must be used. Diodes have been and are
now being used extensively in digital circuit applications.

Ideal Diode

The circuit representation for an *ideal diode* is shown in
Figure 3.11(a). If the diode is in a circuit in which the applied voltage

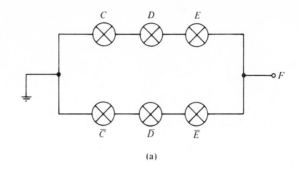

(a)

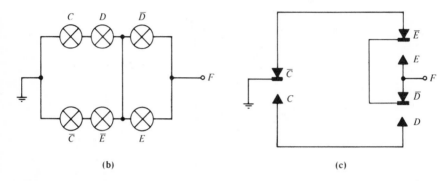

(b)   (c)

Figure 3.10 Example 3.4.

has a polarity to cause current to flow in the direction indicated by the arrow, the ideal diode acts like a closed switch, as shown in Figure 3.11(b). If the polarity is reversed, the diode becomes an open circuit, as shown in Figure 3.11(c). In other words, $v = 0$ if $i > 0$, and $i = 0$ if $v < 0$.

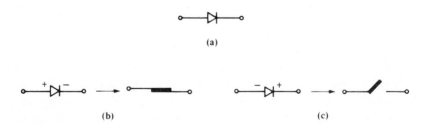

(a)

(b)   (c)

Figure 3.11 Ideal diode symbol and model.

Of course, an actual diode, which can be constructed or purchased, only partially performs like an ideal diode. For our study we will often be satisfied with considering realizations with ideal diodes. However, we should realize that physical diodes have some limitations that can have a deleterious effect on circuit performance. In this regard, we will now briefly consider a semiconductor diode which consists of a *pn* junction that, for convenience of illustration, is shown in Figure 3.12(a) as two contiguous blocks. Actually the diodes are not constructed as shown, but the details of construction are not relevant here.

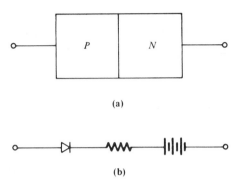

(a)

(b)

Figure 3.12 *PN* junction diode and model.

In Figure 3.12(a) the *N* and *P* refer to semiconductor materials to which impurities have been added to increase the conduction properties. The semiconductor material used in diodes is usually either germanium or silicon, both of which are valence four elements. If a valence five material such as arsenic is added (usually in very small amounts), the semiconductor material is called *n* type material. In this material the extra valence *electrons* of the added impurities are active in the conduction process. If, instead, a valence three impurity such as boron is added, the semiconductor is referred to as *p* type material. The deficiency in valence electrons, as compared to the host semiconductor material, produces what are referred to as *holes* that act very much like positive charges.

Electrons are the principal current carriers in *n* type material and are thus called the majority carriers. There will also be a few holes, which are called minority carriers. In *p* type material holes are the majority carriers and electrons the minority carriers.

The terminal connected to the *p* type material corresponds to the terminal at the arrowhead in Figure 3.11(a). This is the anode of the diode. The *n* material is the cathode.

The diode of Figure 3.12(a) is nonlinear and thus can only be approximated by an ideal diode and linear elements. For many purposes the model shown in Figure 3.12(b) suffices. This model comprises an ideal diode in series with a resistor and a voltage source. Because of the source there is no current flow until the forward-applied voltage (a forward voltage is a voltage of a polarity to produce conduction) exceeds that of the voltage source. The resistor and source produce a voltage drop corresponding to that across an actual diode when it is forward biased (a forward bias is a forward-applied voltage). For normal operation this drop is less than 1 V.

For many purposes the physical diode can be considered to be an ideal diode and thus we can use the model of Figures 3.11(b) and (c) rather than the more complex one of Figure 3.12(b). We will use the ideal model exclusively.

Up-Follower and Down-Follower

There are just two diode logic circuits: the *up-follower* and the *down-follower*. A three-input up-follower is shown in Figure 3.13(a). Not everyone calls this circuit an up-follower, but it is an appropriate name since it indicates the circuit action. That is, the output voltage at F is the up voltage or, in other words, the most positive voltage applied at the inputs, provided that this voltage is more positive

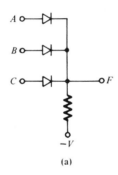

(a)

A	B	C	F
−	−	−	−
−	−	+	+
−	+	−	+
−	+	+	+
+	−	−	+
+	−	+	+
+	+	−	+
+	+	+	+

A	B	C	F
0	0	0	0
0	0	1	1
0	1	0	1
0	1	1	1
1	0	0	1
1	0	1	1
1	1	0	1
1	1	1	1

A	B	C	F
1	1	1	1
1	1	0	0
1	0	1	0
1	0	0	0
0	1	1	0
0	1	0	0
0	0	1	0
0	0	0	0

(b) Voltage truth table   (c) Positive logic table   (d) Negative logic table

Figure 3.13 Up-follower.

than $-V$. This operation is not difficult to understand since the diode with the most positive voltage applied will certainly be forward biased, assuming this voltage exceeds $-V$. When this diode conducts, the potential at F becomes this most positive potential and reverse biases all of the other diodes which then do not conduct.

Example 3.5 Determine the output voltage for the up-follower of Figure 3.13(a) if the voltages at terminals A, B, C, and $-V$ are 5, 3, -2, and -10, respectively. All voltages are with respect to ground potential.

Solution Most certainly the diode at terminal A will conduct because this 5 V is a forward bias and also it is the most positive voltage applied at the inputs. When this diode conducts, the 5 V appears at F and thus at all the diode cathodes. Since the other two diodes have anode voltages less than 5 V, they are reverse biased and do not conduct. Consequently, the output voltage is 5 V. ∎

The voltage truth table for the three-input up-follower is shown in Figure 3.13(b). This table illustrates the circuit operation voltagewise with all possible combinations of input voltages, but only of two levels. The plus sign designates the up voltage or more positive voltage and the minus sign designates the down or more negative voltage. Actually, either or both of these voltages may be positive or negative with respect to ground, but both of them should be more positive than $-V$. Figure 3.13(c) is the positive logic truth table and Figure 3.13(d) the negative logic truth table.

From the truth tables the *up-follower is obviously an OR gate* for positive logic and an AND gate for negative logic. This is true regardless of the number of inputs, and of course they can be other than three.

The other diode circuit, the down-follower, is shown in Figure 3.14(a) for three inputs. This circuit is sometimes referred to as the down-follower because the output voltage follows, or, in the ideal case, *is* the same as the most negative applied voltage, provided this voltage is more negative than $+V$. The diode with the most negative cathode voltage conducts and causes this negative voltage to appear at the anodes of the other diodes. Then these diodes are reverse biased and do not conduct.

Example 3.6 Determine the output voltage for the down-follower shown in Figure 3-14(a) if the voltages at terminals A, B, C, and $+V$ are 6, -3, 2, and 10, respectively.

Solution The diode at terminal B will certainly be forward biased, and when it conducts the -3 V appears at F and at the anodes of the other two diodes, reverse biasing these diodes. Thus the output voltage is -3 V. ∎

The voltage truth table and the positive and negative logic truth tables for the down-follower are illustrated in Figures 3.14(b), (c), and (d). From these tables it is evident that the *down-follower is an AND gate* for positive logic and an OR gate for negative logic.

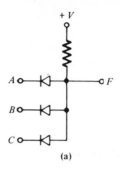

(a)

A	B	C	F
−	−	−	−
−	−	+	−
−	+	−	−
−	+	+	−
+	−	−	−
+	−	+	−
+	+	−	−
+	+	+	+

(b) Voltage truth table

A	B	C	F
0	0	0	0
0	0	1	0
0	1	0	0
0	1	1	0
1	0	0	0
1	0	1	0
1	1	0	0
1	1	1	1

(c) Positive logic table

A	B	C	F
1	1	1	1
1	1	0	1
1	0	1	1
1	0	0	1
0	1	1	1
0	1	0	1
0	0	1	1
0	0	0	0

(d) Negative logic table

Figure 3.14   Down-follower.

With just diodes and resistors, the only gates possible are AND and OR. The NOT gate cannot be obtained since for it a diode-resistor arrangement would have to provide a decreasing output voltage for an increasing input voltage, and vice versa. Such circuit action is not possible with just diodes and resistors. Thus diode logic, per se, is not sufficient for generating expressions unless complements of the variables are available. Frequently, they are.

Example 3.7   Show a two-level diode circuit for realizing $F = AC + \bar{A}\bar{C}(D + B) + \bar{A}\bar{B}$. Complements of the variables are available. Use positive logic.

Solution   The first step in the realization is the obtaining of an MPOS and an MSOP. Thus a Karnaugh map should be used, but before entries can be inserted in a map the function should be placed in SOP form for convenience: $F = AC + \overline{A}\overline{C}D + \overline{A}\overline{C}B + \overline{A}\overline{B}$. The corresponding Karnaugh map is shown in Figure 3.15(a) along with the grouping required for an MPOS and an MSOP. From this map

$$F = AC + \overline{A}\overline{B} + \overline{A}\overline{C} = (\overline{A} + C)(A + \overline{B} + \overline{C})$$

The MPOS, having fewer literals, will be realized. The realization is shown in Figure 3.15(b). ■

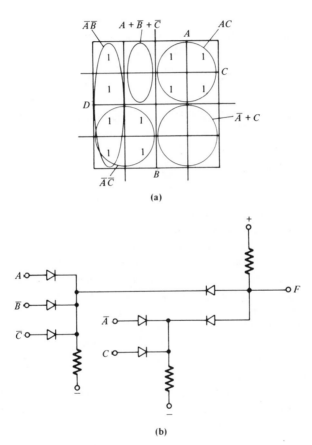

(a)

(b)

Figure 3.15 Example 3.7.

Practical Limitations

As has been mentioned, conducting diodes have voltage drops across them. Also, reverse-biased diodes conduct some current. Of course, we are now discussing actual diodes and not ideal diodes. These nonideal conditions produce deterioration of the signals. Furthermore, there are other factors, which will not be discussed, that are inherent to the diode circuits and that also produce some loss of signal. Thus a signal cannot pass through many diodes (say, more than four) and yet maintain a level for correct operation. However, if the signal passes through an OR gate and then an AND gate or vice versa, the drops in the diodes in the two gates tend to cancel and the original signal is more closely obtained at the output than if several AND or several OR gates are used in succession. Hence, for best operation, AND-OR gates should be alternated.

Since the diodes are nonideal there is incomplete isolation between the inputs, and this lack of isolation increases with the number of input diodes. Also, the reverse-biased diodes conduct some current; the greater the number of diodes the greater this reverse current. This current produces an undesirable voltage drop across the gate resistor. These and other factors limit the maximum number of diodes that can be used as inputs in order for the circuit to function properly. This limiting factor on inputs, which is called *fan-in*, is not restricted to diode logic, but is rather general. Specifically, *the fan-in capability of a circuit is the maximum number of inputs the circuit can have and yet operate correctly.*

There is also a *limitation on the number of outputs* of a gate. This limitation is called *fan-out*. Each output line requires driving power at, in this case, a fairly fixed voltage level, and for the diode circuits, and digital circuits in general, there is a limit on the load current that can be drawn if the output voltage is to stay within a specified range. Although there is some tolerance in the voltage levels corresponding to the 0's and 1's, the tolerance limits can be exceeded if too many gates are connected to the output terminal of a gate.

These limitations, as well as the important one of the lack of a complementing element, severely restrict the usefulness of purely diode logic. Amplifiers must be used to restore signals and to permit greater fan-out. Transistors are often used with diodes, as will be discussed in the next section, for an implementation called *diode-transistor logic*. The transistors correct for many of the deficiencies of the pure diode gates and, in addition, provide complementation.

3.3   TRANSISTOR LOGIC CIRCUITS

At present, the transistor is the most popular switching component. It operates at extremely rapid speeds, requires little power, is rugged, can be made extremely small, and is inexpensive. Transistors are capable of current amplification for increasing fan-out and also isolation for producing a reasonable fan-in. Some manufacturers claim that some of their transistor gates have a fan-in and fan-out capability of up to 20. However, less than 10 is more typical.

Transistors are used in several types of gates, the most popular ones of which we will study. But before commencing this study, we should consider a few properties of transistors.

Basic Transistor Characteristics

A thorough presentation of the physical nature and operation of transistors will not be presented here since it is not essential for present purposes. We will be concerned with studying transistors only to the extent necessary to obtain a qualitative understanding of the operation of transistor digital circuits.

The most common transistor, called a *bipolar transistor*, is a specially treated portion of a semiconductor crystal having three regions: *emitter, base,* and *collector*. This transistor is often represented, for ease of understanding, as in Figure 3.16(a), although transistors are not constructed in this form. However, this representation does illustrate the three regions, as mentioned, and the separation of emitter and collector by the base.

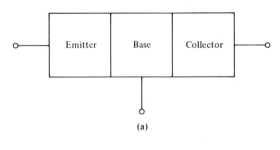

(a)

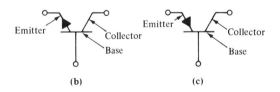

(b)   (c)

Figure 3.16 Bipolar transistor and symbols.

There are two types of these transistors: the *NPN* and the *PNP*. In an *NPN* transistor the emitter and collector are formed from n type material and the base from p type material. Electrons are the principal carriers of current in these transistors. In a *PNP* transistor the emitter and collector are p type material and the base is n type material and holes are the principal carriers of current.

The symbols for these transistors are shown in Figures 3.16(b) and (c). The arrow designating the emitter also indicates the direction of current flow in the emitter for normal operation. That is, current flow is out of the emitter of an *NPN* transistor and into the emitter of a *PNP* transistor. Also, in an *NPN* transistor current normally flows into the collector and into the base. In a *PNP* transistor current normally flows from the collector and from the base.

For many purposes the transistor can be considered as constructed of two diodes, one diode being that of the emitter and base and the other of the collector and base. However, this consideration is not strictly accurate and, instead of emitter-base diode and collector-base diode, it is more accurate to say emitter-base junction and collector-base junction, respectively.

For approximately linear operation of the transistor, the emitter-base junction is forward biased and the collector-base junction is reverse biased. Also, the emitter is usually grounded and the input applied to the base (really, between base and emitter) and the output taken from the collector (really, between collector and emitter) as illustrated in Figures 3.17(a) and (b) for the two types of circuits.

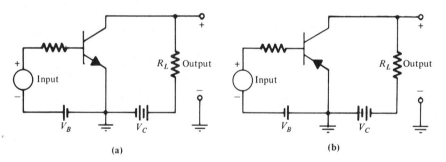

(a)   (b)

Figure 3.17 Typical transistor circuits.

An increase in positive voltage applied to the base of the *NPN* transistor, or in negative voltage applied to the base of the *PNP* transistor, causes an increase of current in the collector circuit of either transistor. This current increases the voltage signal across the load resistor R_L. In other words, variations in voltage applied to the base produce corresponding variations in collector current which in turn produce variations in voltage across the load resistor R_L. It can be shown that the signal power in the load circuit greatly exceeds that in the input circuit, and thus there is signal amplification.

For digital circuit applications, the *NPN* transistor is used almost exclusively. There are several reasons for this. The reason often given is that the conduction processes in the *NPN* transistor can operate at higher speeds than those of the *PNP* transistor, and this is true. But the difference in speeds is scarcely overwhelming: perhaps the speeds differ by a factor of 2. The principal reason NPN transistors are used so extensively in digital circuit applications is that in the types of circuits now being used so much (integrated circuits), NPN transistors are much easier to make than PNP transistors of comparable quality. Because of the extensive use of NPN transistors, our discussion and illustrations of transistors will be limited to the NPN type.

For many digital circuit applications the transistor can be considered as a switch. In digital circuits the base voltage applied for conduction is usually sufficiently positive to cause a large collector current to flow in R_L. The resulting voltage across R_L almost equals the supply voltage V_C and thus the voltage drop from collector to emitter is quite small. This drop may be only 0.05 to 0.1 V for germanium and 0.1 to 0.3 V for silicon, which is small enough for our purposes to be considered zero. In other words, the collector is almost shorted to the emitter when the transistor conducts heavily.

When the transistor is in this condition the *collector-base junction is usually forward biased*, and the transistor is said to be *saturated*. The voltage drop between base and emitter is not substantially affected by the saturation and is considerable: approximately 0.8 V for silicon and 0.6 V for germanium.

During saturation some excess charge is in the transistor. There are excess electrons in the base region and excess holes in the collector region. This excess charge slows switching speed somewhat, as will be mentioned later.

If the emitter-base junction is reverse biased or even if a small forward bias is applied, the transistor is *cut off*, which means that the collector current decreases to almost zero. For our purposes, the collector current for cutoff is small enough that it can be neglected, and thus the transistor can be considered to be an open circuit.

For most digital circuit applications the switching transistors have just two conditions of operation: cutoff and saturation. And since in cutoff the transistor acts much like an open switch, while in saturation it acts much like a closed switch, a switch model as shown in Figures 3.18(a) and (b) is often satisfactory. The closed-switch model of Figure

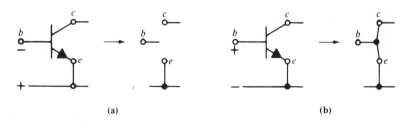

(a)   (b)

Figure 3.18 Transistor switch models.

3.18(b) is perhaps too crude since the base-to-emitter voltage is shown to be zero when actually it often cannot be neglected. But for many purposes the switch model suffices.

Before we discuss some of the transistor logic circuits we should note that a single transistor with a grounded emitter is an *inverter*, which is another name for a NOT gate. For an understanding of this, consider the transistor of Figure 3.19. There are two voltage levels: ground and a positive voltage. When the input voltage applied at A is positive, the transistor saturates, causing the output terminal at B to be grounded through the transistor. If the input is ground, the transistor is cut off and the output voltage tends toward V_C but never reaches it. Load current drawn through R_L by transistors (not shown) connected to B, prevents the voltage at B from attaining. V_C. Since a ground in results in a positive voltage out, and a positive voltage in produces ground out, the circuit is an inverter regardless of whether positive or negative logic is used. This inverter will be used in most of the following transistor logic circuits.

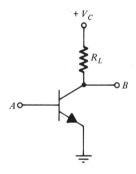

Figure 3.19   Transistor inverter.

Transistor-Resistor Logic (TRL)

In *transistor-resistor logic*, often referred to by the acronym *TRL*, resistors perform AND and OR, and transistors provide inversion. Thus the logic operations are NAND and NOR. The basic circuit is shown in   Figure 3.20 with only three inputs, for convenience, but there may be more.

The inputs A, B, and C are from transistor collectors of other gates, and the output line is connected through coupling resistors R_1 (not shown) to the bases of other transistors. These coupling resistors R_1 limit the current in each fan-out path and also provide some isolation between inputs. But the isolation is incomplete, and this can cause some problems. More specifically, a change of voltage level at, say, A is, to perhaps a significant extent, conducted back through the coupling resistor R_1 connected to, say, B and affects the potential at B. Terminal B may be connected to the inputs of other gates, which are thus also affected by the potential change at A. Of course, this situation is undesirable and may produce erroneous operation.

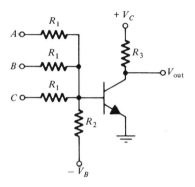

Figure 3.20 TRL circuit.

As regards values, the coupling resistors R_1 and the collector resistor R_3 are usually just a few kilohms, but the bias resistor R_2 may be much larger: say, 15 or 20 kΩ. The voltage supplies are large for transistors: of the order of 10 to 20 V. With the large voltages and with the coupling resistors R_1, a large voltage difference exists between the two voltage levels representing the 0's and 1's. These voltages may, for example, be 10 and 0 V. This large voltage difference ensures correct operation even in the presence of considerable noise. Also, because of these values, the resistors can vary considerably from their nominal values (that is, not be precision resistors) and yet the gate will function properly.

From looking at the TRL gate of Figure 3.20, one cannot determine if it is a NAND gate or a NOR gate, even if the type of logic used is known. Both the NAND and NOR gates have the same configuration. Thus the potentials and resistor values determine the type of gate.

In this regard we will determine what is required for a NAND gate. Assume positive logic and that 10 V corresponds to a logical 1 and ground to a logical 0. Then the resistor values are selected such that the voltage at the base of the transistor is negative, and thus the transistor cut off, if any input is at ground. With the transistor cut off, the output voltage goes positive. This operation is shown in Figure 3.21 (a) for the *worst case condition:* only one input at ground. If all three inputs are at 10 V, as shown in Figure 3.21 (b), the transistor base is positive and the transistor saturates. The switch model is shown for the transistor.

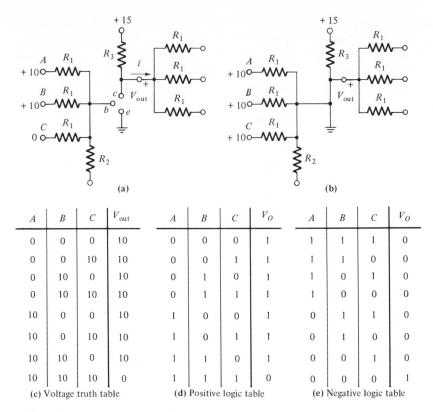

A	B	C	V_{out}	A	B	C	V_o	A	B	C	V_o
0	0	0	10	0	0	0	1	1	1	1	0
0	0	10	10	0	0	1	1	1	1	0	0
0	10	0	10	0	1	0	1	1	0	1	0
0	10	10	10	0	1	1	1	1	0	0	0
10	0	0	10	1	0	0	1	0	1	1	0
10	0	10	10	1	0	1	1	0	1	0	0
10	10	0	10	1	1	0	1	0	0	1	0
10	10	10	0	1	1	1	0	0	0	0	1
(c) Voltage truth table				(d) Positive logic table				(e) Negative logic table			

Figure 3.21   NAND TRL operation and truth tables.

With the transistor cut off, as in Figure 3.21(a), the output voltage tends to increase to the 15 V of the collector supply, but actually it does not increase much beyond 10 V because of the voltage drop across R_3 caused by the current that flows to the bases of the transistors that are connected to the output. This current flows from the positive terminal of the collector supply, through R_3, then through the R_1's of the following gates, through the bases, and to ground. If all of the input potentials are at 10 V, the transistor conducts and is saturated. Then the collector potential, which is the output terminal potential, becomes almost ground.

In Figure 3.21(c) is shown the voltage truth table of this gate, and in Figures 3.21(d) and (e) the corresponding logic truth tables for positive logic and negative logic, respectively. From the truth tables obviously this is a NAND gate for positive logic and a NOR gate for negative logic.

As mentioned, the circuit of Figure 3.20 could as well be a NOR gate for positive logic and a NAND gate for negative logic. All that is required is a different selection of resistor values such that only all inputs at ground cause the transistor to cut off, and any positive input, even only one positive input (the worst case condition), causes the transistor to saturate. The development of the truth tables for this case should be apparent and thus will not be presented here.

Example 3.8   Design a TRL circuit of two levels for realizing $F = \bar{A}(B + \bar{B}C) + \bar{B}C$. Use positive logic. Complements of the variables are available.

Solution   The first step is to obtain an MSOP and an MPOS. The function is entered on the map of Figure 3.22(a) from which obviously $F = \bar{B}C + \bar{A}B = (\bar{A} + \bar{B}) \cdot (B + C)$. Because both expressions have the same number of literals, either one may be used. With the MSOP arbitrarily selected, the realization is shown in Figure 3.22(b), NAND gates assumed.   ■

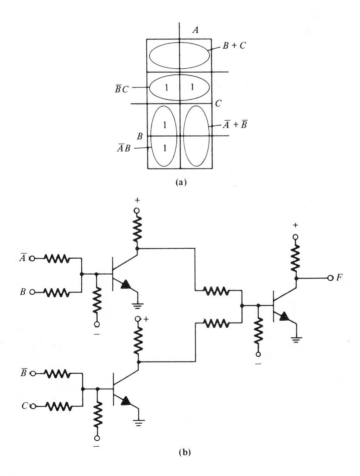

(a)

(b)

Figure 3.22   Example 3.8.

The TRL circuit has some important disadvantages. As mentioned, there is coupling between the inputs through the coupling resistors, and thus little isolation. As a consequence, the change of one input can be fed back to affect the voltage output at another input gate. This is a serious disadvantage, and there are others. If this circuit is studied in detail it will be found that the relatively large voltage excursions and also the presence of the relatively large resistors adversely affect the switching speed. The large voltages cause significant charge storage in the capacities of the lines and other elements. And the resistors prevent this charge and the excess charge in the saturated transistors from discharging rapidly when the transistors are driven to cutoff. Compared to other transistor digital circuits, this is a slow circuit, as will be seen.

The TRL circuit was developed at a time when the costs of resistors were much less than those of transistors. And this circuit, with its large number of resistors and few transistors, had a cost advantage over most other transistor circuits. Resistors now, however, have no cost advantage, especially in integrated circuits, and thus the TRL circuit is not popular.

Diode-Transistor Logic (DTL)

Diode-transistor logic (*DTL*) is similar to TRL, the principal difference being that diodes instead of resistors provide the AND and OR operations. The DTL gates, which can be considered to be AND or OR gates followed by an inverter, have the basic circuits shown in Figures 3.23(a) and (b). *Figure 3.23(a) is a positive logic NOR gate and Figure 3·23(b) a positive logic NAND gate*, as is evident from the arrangement of the diodes. Of course, there may be a different number of inputs than the three shown.

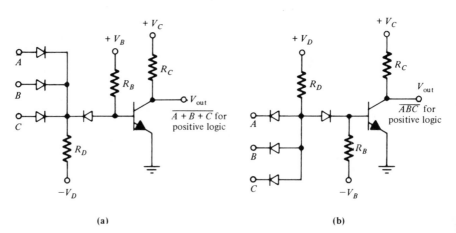

(a)   (b)

Figure 3.23   DTL circuits.

In each circuit a diode is between the up- or down-follower and the base of the transistor (sometimes two diodes are used). This diode provides a voltage drop that is opposed to, and that compensates for, the voltage drop in the diodes in the preceding follower.

If in the circuit of Figure 3.23(a) any of the inputs A, B, or C are positive, a positive voltage appears at the base of the transistor and causes the transistor to saturate and effectively short the output voltage terminal to ground. In essence, a positive voltage in produces ground out. If the three inputs are all at ground, this ground appears at the transistor base, cutting off the transistor and causing it to act effectively as an open circuit and disconnect the output terminal from ground. As a result, the output voltage tends toward V_C but never quite reaches it. Gates connected to the output terminal draw current through R_C, producing a voltage drop across it which prevents the output voltage from increasing to V_C.

The operation of the circuit of Figure 3.23(b) should be apparent. If any input is at ground, then ground appears at the transistor base, cutting off the transistor. Consequently, the output voltage tends toward V_C. But, if all inputs are positive, there is a positive potential at the transistor base, the transistor saturates, and the output voltage is essentially at ground. This positive potential may come from $+V_D$ instead of the inputs to the diodes. That is, with all inputs positive the input diodes may be cut off.

Example 3.9   Design a two-level DTL half subtractor using positive logic. Complements of the variables are available.

Solution   In the last chapter we designed a half subtractor in logic diagram form. The expression obtained was $D = \overline{X}Y + X\overline{Y}$ and $B = \overline{X}Y$, and NAND gates were used. From this, the realization is fairly obvious and is shown in Figure 3.24. If the current amplification and the isolation properties of a transistor are not needed for the B output, a transistor can be eliminated by taking the B output directly from the output of the first down-follower.   ∎

DTL was, for several years, the most popular logic, especially for medium-speed applications. But now it has lost its popularity rating to the faster TTL, described next.

Transistor-Transistor Logic (TTL)

Transistor-transistor logic (TTL or T^2L) is closely related to DTL, the principal difference being that the multidiode inputs are replaced by emitters of one or more transistors. In a circuit having discrete components, several transistors can be used, one for each input line. Or, in an integrated circuit, a single transistor with a number of

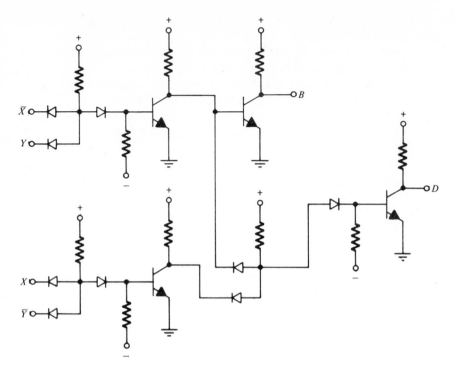

Figure 3.24   Example 3.9.

emitters can be used. We will discuss only the form having a single transistor with several emitters, as shown in Figure 3.25. This particular circuit is available from a manufacturer who states that it is designed for operation of up to 35 MHz with a power dissipation per gate of approximately 15 mW.

The transistor T_1, as shown, is a multiple-emitter transistor. It is always operated in the saturation condition, which means, of course, that it is faster in operation than a transistor that must switch from saturation to cutoff and vice versa. As mentioned, a surplus charge occurs in both the base and collector regions during saturation, and before the transistor can be cut off this excess charge must be eliminated. This elimination requires precious time. With a transistor always in saturation, this problem is obviated.

When one of the multiple emitters is down (that is, the down or the more negative voltage level is applied), there is heavy conduction in this emitter; as a result, the transistor saturates, causing the collector potential to become approximately that of the down emitter. This low collector potential cuts off transistor T_2, which is an inverter. Because of cutoff, the collector of T_2 goes more positive, turning on transistor

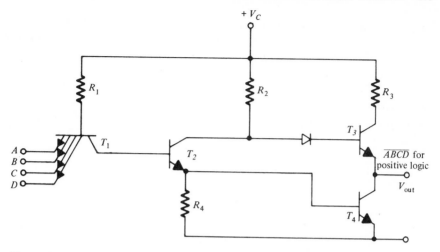

Figure 3.25 TTL circuit.

T_3, which provides current to the gates (not shown) connected to the output terminal. Transistor T_4 is cut off because its base is effectively at ground (there is no current through R_4 with transistor T_2 cut off). In this circuit condition, the output is up, which is a 1 for positive logic.

If all inputs are up, transistor T_1 still saturates even though the emitter junctions are reverse biased. This saturation occurs because the collector-base junction is forward biased by voltage supply V_C. Because of saturation, the collector potential is at a sufficiently high potential to turn on transistor T_2. With this transistor conducting, current flows in resistor R_4, and the resulting voltage drop places a positive potential on the base of transistor T_4, turning on T_4 and grounding the output terminal. At the same time, the lower collector voltage of the conducting transistor T_2 cuts off transistor T_3. With transistor T_3 off and transistor T_4 on, load current can flow into the output terminal.

From this description of the operation of the TTL gate, plainly *the circuit of Figure 3.25 is a NAND gate* for positive logic.

Because transistors T_3 and T_4 can provide large output currents in both directions, this circuit has a large fan-out and can drive large capacitive loads.

The diode should be mentioned. Its function is to provide a voltage drop to maintain T_3 in a cutoff condition when transistor T_4 is conducting.

Example 3.10   Realize $F = (A + \bar{B}\bar{C})(\bar{A} + B + \bar{C})$ using the TTL circuit of Figure 3.25. Complements of the variables are available. Use positive logic.

Solution   Since for positive logic the circuit of Figure 3.25 is a NAND gate, we need an MSOP. It is easily obtained from a Karnaugh map as $F = AB + \bar{B}\bar{C}$. Thus the realization is as shown in Figure 3.26.   ■

The TTL circuit is very popular, especially for integrated circuits because of the mentioned large fan-out feature and also because of its high operating speed. In addition it has reasonable noise insensitivity and a lower power consumption than some of the other logic circuits.

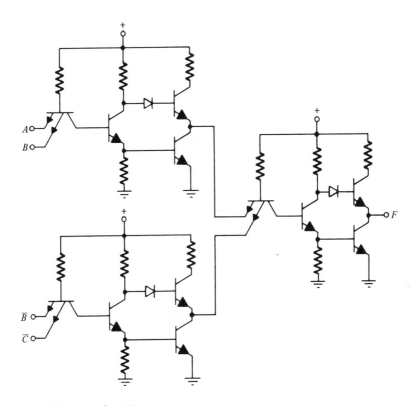

Figure 3.26   Example 3.10.

Direct-Coupled Transistor Logic (DCTL)

Direct-coupled transistor logic (*DCTL*) is almost deceptively simple; there are so few components as can be seen from the basic circuit shown in Figure 3.27. The circuit may, of course, have more than the three inputs shown. Gates like that of Figure 3.27 are interconnected with conductors, which are the only coupling elements.

If in the circuit of Figure 3.27 one or more of the inputs are positive, the corresponding transistors saturate, producing almost a short to ground for the output terminal. Of course the output voltage is actually at a little above ground; for silicon transistors the output voltage may be as little as 0.2 V.

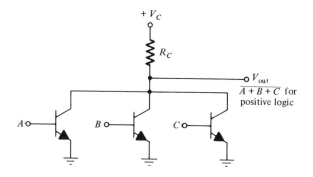

Figure 3.27   Parallel DCTL circuit.

Only when all of the inputs are down is the output voltage up, for then all of the transistors are cut off and act as open circuits. With all transistors cut off, the output voltage tends toward C_C (which may be in the range of 2 to 4 V) but never reaches it because of current flow through R_C to bases of transistors connected to the output terminal. That is, the situation shown in Figure 3.28 usually occurs when the output voltage is positive; the driven transistors become saturated and draw heavy base currents. The output voltage of the driver stage is

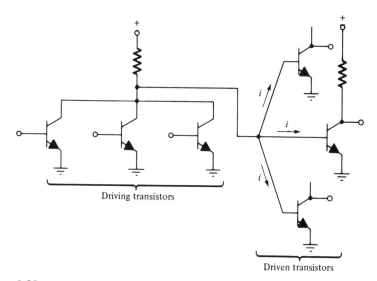

Figure 3.28   Loaded DCTL circuit.

then, obviously, the base-to-emitter voltage of the driven transistors, which voltage is usually slightly less than 1 V. From this description of the operation, it should be apparent that the circuit of Figure 3.27 is a NOR gate for positive logic.

For successful operation of the DCTL circuits, the collector-to-emitter voltage drop of the driving transistors, when they are saturated, must be sufficiently small to prevent conduction of the driven transistors. This output voltage is always positive and thus of a polarity to forward bias the emitter-base junction of the driven transistors. Consequently, cutoff condition is attained not by reverse biasing but simply by decreasing sufficiently the forward bias.

Proper operation using silicon transistors is obtained with about 0.5 V to spare: the collector-to-emitter voltage for saturated transistors may be 0.2 V and the base-to-emitter voltage required for conduction may be in excess of 0.7 V. However, at high temperatures this voltage difference can be as small as 0.1 V, and then the circuits may have errors in operation if signal noise voltages are present.

DCTL circuits have a problem—*current hogging*—that can be alleviated, but at a cost of speed. When a DCTL gate drives several transistors having different input characteristics, some of the driven transistors conduct considerably more than their share of the current available from the driving stage; they *hog* the current.

Often the current distribution is so uneven that when the output of the driving stage is up, some of the driven transistors do not receive sufficient base current to drive them into saturation, and consequently there is a failure in operation. This problem can be eliminated by inserting small current-limiting resistors (a few hundred ohms) in the base leads of the driven transistors to equalize the base currents. Although these resistors alleviate the current hogging, they also slow the switching speed.

The differences in input characteristics are caused by physical differences of the driven transistors and also by different numbers of *conducting* transistors in the gates of the driven transistors. The physical differences are often greatly significant for discrete transistors but much less so for transistors in an integrated circuit. But even if the driven transistors are identical, current hogging can occur because transistors draw different base currents if they are paralleled by different numbers of conducting transistors. These parallel transistors draw off some of the collector current from a driven transistor and thereby produce a change in its input base current.

Example 3.11   Design a two-level half subtractor using the DCTL circuit of Figure 3.27. Use negative logic. Complements of the variables are available.

Solution For negative logic the circuit of Figure 3.27 is a NAND gate. These gates were used in the implementation of a half subtractor in Example 2.33, the logic diagram for which is in Figure 2.31. Obviously, a DCTL circuit can be inserted for each NAND gate. The result is shown in Figure 3.29. ∎

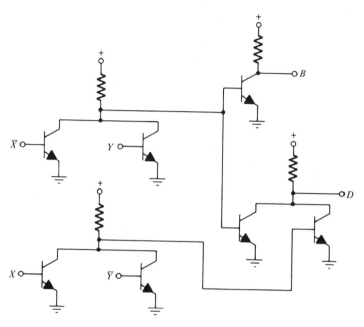

Figure 3.29 Example 3.11.

There is one other basic DCTL circuit and in it the transistors are in series (or *cascode*), as shown in Figure 3.30. In this circuit the output voltage is up if any of the input voltages are down. The output voltage is down only for the single case of all of the input voltages being up; that is, for the one case for which all of the transistors conduct. *This circuit is, obviously, a NAND gate* for positive logic.

Only a few transistors can be placed in series in the circuit of Figure 3.30, the number depending on the collector-to-emitter voltage of the transistors when they are saturated. If, for example, this voltage is 0.2 V, and the transistors in the following driven stage conduct for applied voltages greater than 0.7 V, then no more than three transistors can be placed in series for proper operation. And then a noise voltage of only 0.1 V will produce an error.

The series connection also affects the driving transistors. If there are n transistors in series, and the $n-1$ lower ones are saturated, the top driving transistor has an emitter potential above ground of $n-1$ times the collector-to-emitter voltage of a saturated transistor. Thus, for

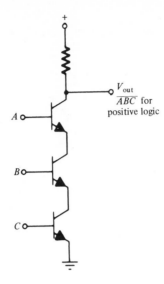

Figure 3.30 Series DCTL circuit.

saturation its base voltage must exceed that which would have to be applied if the emitter were grounded by $n - 1$ times the collector-to-emitter voltage. Of course, this voltage may not be available from the prior stage.

Example 3.12   Design a half subtractor using the DCTL circuit of Figure 3.30. Complements of the variables are available. Use positive logic.

Solution   From the work done in Example 3.11 it should be obvious that the realization is as shown in Figure 3.31.   ■

Although DCTL has some disadvantages, such as a rather limited fan-in and fan-out and more than average susceptibility to noise, it has considerable advantages. It can switch rapidly and has a low power dissipation (3 to 10 mW), and with a little care in design can function quite satisfactorily in many applications. With present technology, the switching time can be as short as 10 nsec. The low power dissipation is obviously extremely important for those digital circuit applications in which many transistors are used.

Resistor-Transistor Logic (RTL)

Resistor-transistor logic (*RTL*) is very similar to DCTL. In fact, if resistors are used in the base leads of DCTL, the circuit is

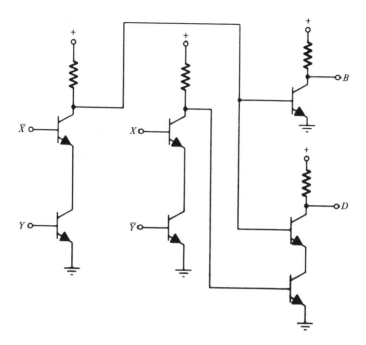

Figure 3.31 Example 3.12.

RTL. Because of this similarity, RTL will be considered only briefly. Its two basic circuits are shown in Figures 3.32(a) and (b).

If the base and collector resistors are small (less than 1000 Ω), the switching time can be short, approaching 10 nsec, with a power dissipation of approximately 12 mW. With larger resistors, the power dissipation can be significantly decreased, but then the switching time increases. Sometimes each base resistor is paralleled with a charge-compensating capacitor to obtain an increase in switching speed. Then the logic is called *RCTL* (*resistor-capacitor-transistor logic*).

Emitter-Coupled Logic (ECL)

Emitter-coupled logic (*ECL*), sometimes called current-mode logic (CML), is noted for its high switching speeds and is reputed to be the fastest transistor digital logic. The high switching speed results from operation *without saturation*. Since the transistors never saturate, they have no stored excess charge that must be eliminated before cutoff can be achieved.

As has been mentioned, when an *NPN* transistor saturates, excess electrons in the base region and also excess holes in the collector region

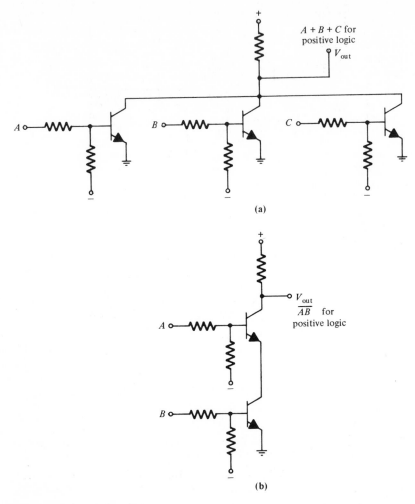

Figure 3.32   RTL circuits.

must be removed before the transistor can cut off. And, it takes time to remove this charge.

This problem is not as severe as it once was. With present transistors the excess charge is not large, and some effective techniques have been developed for removing this charge rapidly when the transistor goes to cutoff. Thus present transistors can operate in the saturation mode and still have high switching speeds. Although ECL is perhaps the fastest logic, the other logic circuits will probably be with us for some time.

In an ECL circuit, *saturation is prevented by components in the emitter circuit that limit the collector current.* This is in contrast to conventional operation in which the maximum collector current, up to the saturation current, is controlled by the base-to-emitter voltage or by the base current, depending upon the point of view. In ECL circuits, the base-to-emitter voltage still has control of whether the transistor conducts, but it has little control, within limits, over the maximum value of collector current.

One version of the ECL circuit is shown in Figure 3.33. In this circuit the resistor R_E is much larger than either of the resistors R_C, which are equal. In some circuits R_E is fifty times as great as R_C. Also, V_E has a larger magnitude than V_C—perhaps five times as large. Because of these resistor and voltage values, the current $I_E \cong V_E/R_E$ and is almost constant. With a suitable selection of values for V_E and R_E, the current I_E can be made less than the collector saturation current.

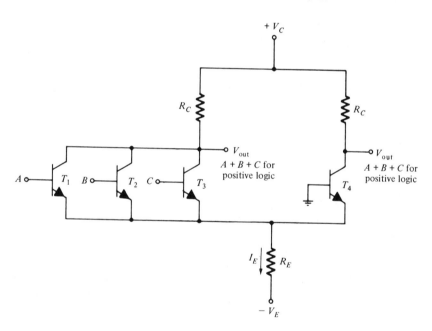

Figure 3.33 ECL circuit.

A preferred manner of considering this circuit is to think of the current I_E as being constant, as mentioned, and all of it conducted through transistor T_4 when the inputs A, B, and C are down. The down potential in this case is below ground which is the potential on the base of transistor T_4. Of course, this current also flows through the collector resistor R_C of transistor T_4. However, if one or more of the input transistors have inputs that are up (above ground), this current flows through them instead of through transistor T_4. In essence, this is a current steering circuit in which almost constant current is steered through a transistor by applying an up voltage to its base.

In ECL circuits, in general, a fixed voltage is applied to the transistor corresponding to transistor T_4 and the voltage levels for switching are above and below this fixed potential. Of course, the fixed potential need not be ground. Also, for highest speed these circuits are designed so that only a few tenths of a volt change steers the current from one transistor to another. Another feature of these circuits is complementary outputs: For positive logic, *the OR of the inputs is available at the collector of transistor T_4 and NOR is available at the junction of the other collectors.*

Because the transistors are never saturated, the collector voltages must be more positive than the base voltages. Consequently, in the circuit of Figure 3.33 both output voltages are always above ground. But if these voltages are to be input voltages for other similar ECL circuits, they must be able to vary below ground to produce switching. Another way of considering this situation is to say that in this circuit, as it stands, the output potentials corresponding to 0 and 1 are greater than those for the inputs. Obviously, the proper signal levels must be restored before these output voltages can be applied as inputs to other circuits.

One way of restoring the proper voltage levels is to pass the output voltage through a voltage-dropping circuit such as that shown in Figure 3.34(a). In this circuit the diode is a Zener diode which, when *reverse* biased to a sufficient degree, breaks down or, in other words, conducts in the reverse direction. A characteristic of this diode is that in this breakdown condition, the voltage across it is nearly constant, almost regardless of the current flow through it. For this circuit the Zener diode is selected such that the voltage drop across it cancels the increase in voltage level produced by the preceding ECL circuit. Thus the output voltages are restored to the proper levels required for the activation of other gates.

Another way of restoring voltage levels is to use *emitter followers* at the outputs as shown in Figure 3.34(b). Each *NPN* emitter follower comprises a transistor with its collector connected to the positive terminal of the supply voltage and with its emitter connected through a resistor to the negative terminal of the supply voltage. The output emitter voltage *follows* the input base voltage except for a drop of several tenths of a volt from base to emitter, which in this circuit compensates for the collector-to-base voltage drop in the ECL transistors. In addition to this compensation, the emitter followers provide increased fan-out.

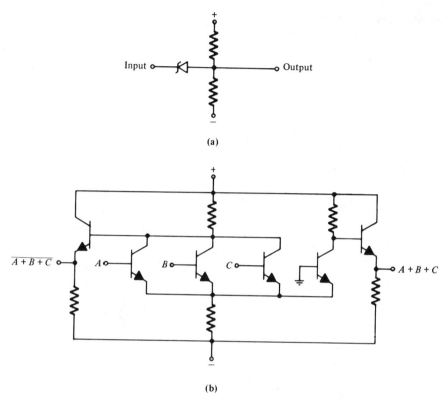

(a)

(b)

Figure 3.34   Voltage-compensation circuits.

Example 3.13   Realize $F = (A + B)(\overline{A} + \overline{B})$ with ECL circuits. Complements of the variables are available. Use positive logic.

Solution   The expression is already in MPOS form and thus need not be minimized. Of course, such a form is desired because for positive logic the basic ECL circuit is a NOR gate. The solution, which should be apparent from our prior work, is shown in Figure 3.35.   ■

Voltage-restoring circuits are not needed if one is willing to accept a high noise susceptibility. If V_C of Figure 3.33 is made small, say 0.25 V, the output voltage varies about ground. In this operation the collectors go negative with respect to the bases and thus ground. Hence the collector-base junctions are sometimes forward biased, which is the condition for the undesired saturation. But saturation does not result because the forward bias is too small to produce saturation. In this operation the voltage excursions are small, say from 0.2 to −0.2 V, causing the circuit to be susceptible to improper operation if significant noise voltages are present. This is a disadvantage, but with the lack of saturation and the small voltage excursions, the switching speed is high.

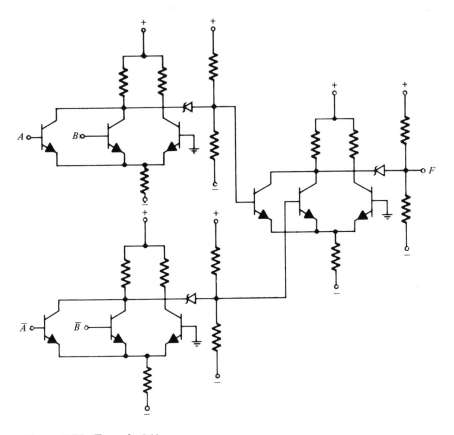

Figure 3.35 Example 3.13.

The ECL circuit has many advantages, the principal one of which is high switching speed: switching times of less than 1 nsec can be achieved. Also, it can be shown that it has a large fan-out capability. The ECL circuit has a disadvantage of requiring more components than other types of digital circuits. This is not a serious disadvantage if integrated circuits are used, since in such circuits the components are inexpensive and are small. Having more components, ECL circuits require more power than other digital circuits. Also, if ECL circuits are designed for high switching speed they are significantly sensitive to noise. At present, some circuit designers believe that the advantages far outweigh the disadvantages, and they predict that ECL circuits will soon become the most popular logic circuit.

MOS FET Logic

The transistors in the logic circuits we have discussed so far are sometimes referred to as bipolar transistors, since in them current is produced by movement of both positive and negative charge (holes and electrons). In another transistor that is becoming increasingly important in digital applications, current is produced by movement of either holes or electrons, but not both. Thus it is called a *unipolar transistor*. Another more common name is *field-effect transistor* (*FET*).

Of the various types of FET's, only one is used extensively in logic circuits: the *metal oxide semiconductor FET* or, more simply, the *MOS FET*. This transistor can be either what is called a *depletion type* or an *enhancement type*. For reasons we need not consider, the enhancement type is preferred for digital applications and so we will consider it exclusively.

A cross-sectional view of an enhancement type MOS FET is shown in Figure 3.36(a). This FET is constructed on a silicon *p* type material base called a substrate on which hundreds of other FET's may be similarly formed and interconnected to produce an integrated circuit. An insulator, usually silicon dioxide, covers the substrate except for openings through which two spaced *n* type regions have been formed. Metal electrodes are deposited on these *n* type regions and also on the insulation layer between these regions. As indicated, these three electrodes are called the *source, gate,* and *drain.*

Often the drain and source are indistinguishable except as to use: an FET is connected such that current carriers enter at the source and leave at the drain. For the illustrated *p* type substrate FET, electron flow produces current. And, since the electrons enter at the source and leave at the drain, the source must be made negative in potential with respect to the drain when the FET is placed in a circuit.

The voltage difference between gate and source controls current flow between source and drain. For a *p* type substrate FET, no flow occurs until this voltage is positive (that is, the gate is positive with respect to the source) and in fact more positive than a value called the *threshold voltage*. A voltage exceeding the threshold attracts a sufficient number of electrons to a thin surface layer of the *p* type substrate and causes the concentration of electrons there to exceed greatly that of holes. As a consequence, the principal current carriers of this layer become electrons and the layer performs like *n* type material, producing a conduction path or channel between the *n* type source and drain. In fact, this layer is called an n *channel*. The greater the gate voltage, the greater the current in this conducting channel.

The gate current is approximately zero since the gate electrode is insulated from the substrate. Actually, during changes of gate voltage,

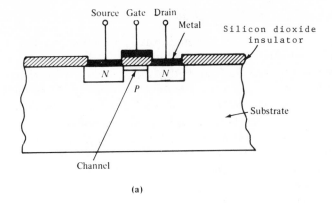

(a)

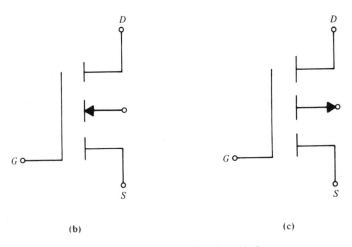

(b)   (c)

Figure 3.36 Enhancement type MOS FET and symbols.

gate currents do flow for short times to charge and discharge inter-electrode capacitances existing between the gate electrode and the source and drain electrodes. But for our purposes these transient currents need not be considered.

An enhancement type MOS FET can also be constructed from an n type substrate in which source and drain regions are formed from p type material. For this FET, holes are the current carriers. Thus, in a circuit the source is positive with respect to the drain and conduction occurs between source and drain if the gate is made sufficiently negative in potential with respect to the source. This negative gate potential causes the formation of a p *type conducting channel* extending from source to drain beneath the gate.

The circuit symbols we will use for enhancement type MOS FET's are shown in Figures 3.36(b) and (c). The symbol in Figure 3.36(b), with the arrow directed in, indicates a p type substrate, n-channel MOS FET. The symbol in Figure 3.36(c), with the arrow out, indicates an n type substrate, p-channel MOS FET. In each symbol the arrow designates the junction between the conducting channel and the substrate. Thus a connection to the arrow is a connection to the substrate.

In Figure 3.37 an MOS FET inverter circuit is illustrated in which a p-channel MOS FET is connected in series with an n-channel MOS FET. When opposite types of transistors are used in the manner shown, they form a *complementary circuit,* which in this case is a complementary inverter.

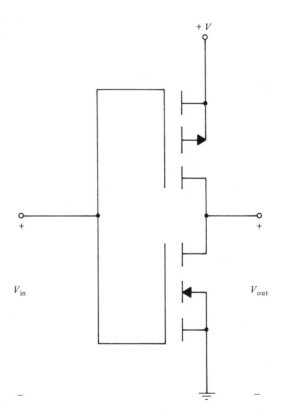

Figure 3.37 MOS FET complementary inverter.

In some MOS FET inverters, but not complementary inverters, two transistors of the same type are connected in series between a source terminal and ground. In this circuit one transistor acts as a resistor and the other transistor as a switching element.

The voltage levels for the complementary inverter are $+V$ and zero. When the input voltage is zero, the p-channel FET has a negative gate-to-source voltage that causes it to conduct. At the same time the bottom FET does not conduct since its gate-to-source potential is zero and not positive as is required for conduction. This cutoff transistor is essentially an open circuit having a source-to-drain resistance of perhaps as much as 1000 MΩ. In contrast, the conducting transistor presents a source-to-drain resistance of only 1000 Ω or less. Because the nonconducting transistor is almost an open circuit, negligible current flows. In fact, too little current flows to produce a significant source-to-drain voltage drop across the conducting transistor. Consequently, the output voltage becomes $+V$ for this input ground condition.

In the other input condition of $+V$ applied, the top p-channel transistor is nonconducting because its gate-to-source voltage is zero and not negative as is required for conduction. But this voltage produces a positive gate potential on the bottom n-channel transistor, causing it to conduct and to ground the output terminal.

During a switching operation, current may temporarily flow to the load (not shown) which presumably is one or more gates of other FET's. As has been mentioned, the gate-to-drain and gate-to-source capacitances charge or discharge during switching, thereby producing this temporary current flow. However, between switching times all currents are negligibly small and thus this complementary circuit, as do other complementary circuits, dissipates almost negligible power. Indeed, small power dissipation is perhaps the principal advantage of complementary circuits.

Two positive logic NOR gates are shown in Figures 3.38 (a) and (b). Both these gates have just three inputs but can easily be modified to have more than three inputs, as should be obvious. In the circuit of Figure 3.38 (a) all the FET's are of the n-channel type, including the top FET which with its gate connected to the positive drain terminal is in the conducting state and thus acts as a resistor. The other transistors perform switching functions.

If one of these switching transistors has a positive gate potential greater than the threshold value, it provides a conduction path between the output terminal and ground. In fact, this path exists if any one, two, or three inputs are sufficiently positive. Then the output potential tends toward ground but never reaches it because the resistance of the conducting switching transistors is not negligible in comparison with that of the resistance transistor. However, if the switching transistors are constructed such that their resistance is sufficiently small compared with that of the resistance transistor, the output potential, although not at ground, is less than the threshold voltage of the FET's (not shown) connected to the output terminal. In fact, this condition must exist for proper operation.

If all inputs are at ground potential, the three switching transistors are nonconducting and in this state prevent current flow. Without current the resistance transistor has zero voltage drop from drain to source, and the output potential becomes $+V$.

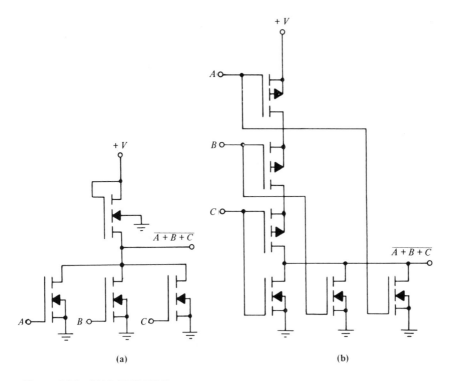

Figure 3.38   MOS FET NOR gates.

The circuit of Figure 3.38(b) is also a NOR gate for positive logic. It is a complementary circuit having three p-channel transistors connected in series between the positive voltage source terminal and three parallel-connected n-channel transistors. When one or more of the inputs is positive and greater than the threshold potential, at least one of the three parallel n-channel transistors conducts and provides a conduction path from the output terminal to ground. Also, at the same time at least one of the series p-channel transistors cuts off and opens the path between the positive terminal and the output terminal. Consequently, the output voltage goes to zero. If all three input terminals are grounded, the three series p-channel transistors provide a conduction path between the positive terminal of the source and the output terminal. Simultaneously, the three parallel n-channel transistors cut off and thereby open the path between the output terminal and ground. As a result, the output potential becomes $+V$.

From our prior work we should expect that MOS FET's can be used to form positive logic *NAND gates* such as are illustrated in Figure 3.39. The gate in Figure 3.39(a), which is constructed entirely of n-channel transistors, has one transistor that is a resistor and three other transistors that are switching elements. The other NAND gate, that of Figure 3.39(b), is obviously a complementary circuit.

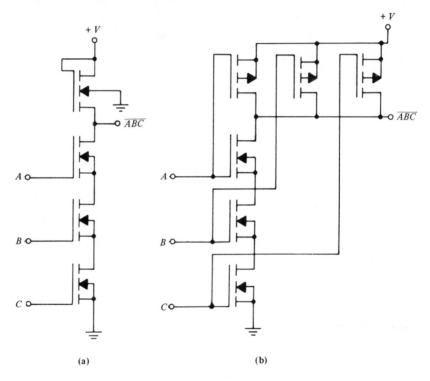

(a)   (b)

Figure 3.39 MOS FET NAND gates.

In either circuit the output terminal is connected to ground through the series n-channel transistors only if all three inputs are more positive than the threshold voltage. Then, in the Figure 3.39(a) circuit, the output voltage is small and positive and less than the threshold voltage of the load FET's (not shown) if the total resistance of the three switching transistors is sufficiently less than that of the resistance transistor. In the circuit of Figure 3.39(b), all positive inputs cut off the three p-channel parallel transistors while causing the three n-channel series transistors to conduct and ground the output terminal.

Any other set of inputs in either circuit causes at least one of the series n-channel transistors to cut off and to produce essentially an open circuit between the output terminal and ground. Then the output voltage becomes $+V$ because of the conduction path through the resistance transistor in the n-channel circuit or, in the case of the complementary circuit, because of the conduction path through at least one of the parallel p-channel transistors. This latter action occurs in the complementary circuit since a ground input potential that cuts off an n-channel series transistor simultaneously turns on a p-channel parallel transistor.

Perhaps the reader has noted the similarities between the MOS FET gates and the DCTL gates. If a person understands the interconnection of DCTL gates, he should have no trouble interconnecting MOS FET gates. For this reason we need not now consider a complete circuit example with MOS FET gates.

MOS logic circuits are generally considered slow operating in comparison with bipolar transistor logic circuits. The significant input capacitances and the rather large resistances of conducting FET's are a principal cause of frequency limitation. An FET cannot switch until its input capacitance charges or discharges through a path that invariably includes the source-to-drain resistance of one or more conducting FET's. And since the charge or discharge time is directly proportional to the product of this significantly large capacitance and resistance, these transistors are slow in switching and in the circuits shown cannot operate at frequencies much above 2 MHz. However, more sophisticated MOS FET circuits have been developed that operate up to 50 MHz. Although this frequency is considerably less than the 120 MHz obtainable with ECL, it is comparable to the operational frequencies of expensive TTL circuits.

In integrated circuits, MOS FET's have many advantages over bipolar transistors. The manufacture of conventional MOS FET integrated circuits requires only 25 steps as compared to about 150 for bipolar circuits. Even complementary MOS circuits, which use both p- and n-channel transistors, require only 50 steps. Another advantage is the close packing possible with MOS FET's. MOS transistors, unlike bipolars, are self-insulating and thus do not interact when closely spaced on a substrate. In contrast, bipolar transistors interact and consequently require an isolation region around each transistor. Also, MOS FET's dissipate such little power that close packing does not produce overheating. Finally, MOS FET's generate less noise than do bipolar transistors and, having high input capacitances and operating at greater voltages, are less susceptible to faulty operation because of noise voltages.

Not all MOS FET's require high threshold voltages—4 V or more. Some have threshold voltages of less than 2 V and these can readily be driven by bipolar circuits. The lower thresholds also permit faster operation for the same power dissipation.

PROBLEMS ━━━━━━━━━━━━━━━━━━━━━━

3.1   Show a relay circuit for producing $F = A\bar{B}\bar{C} + \bar{A}B\bar{C} + AB\bar{C}$.

Answer   See Figure 3.40.

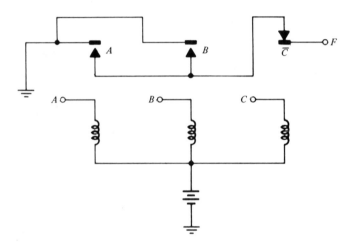

Figure 3.40   Problem 3.1.

3.2   Show two relay circuits with the same number of contacts for producing $F = \bar{A}C + AB\bar{C} + ABC$.

3.3   A lamp is controlled by four switches A, B, C, and D. The lamp is to light when three of the switches are closed. It makes no difference if the lamp is on or off when all four switches are closed. Design a relay circuit for operating the lamp.

3.4   A lamp is controlled by four switches A, B, C, and D. The lamp is to be off when three of the switches are closed. It makes no difference if the lamp is on or off when all four switches are closed. Design a relay circuit for operating the lamp.

3.5   Design a relay circuit for implementing $F = A\bar{B}\bar{C} + A\bar{B}D + \bar{A}\bar{C}D + \bar{A}BC\bar{D}$. Use no more contacts than necessary.

3.6   Repeat Problem 3.5 for $F = BCDE + A\bar{C}\bar{D}E + \bar{A}BD + \bar{A}\bar{B}\bar{D} + B\bar{D}\bar{E}$.

3.7   Design a relay circuit for realizing $F = AB\overline{C} + \overline{A}\,\overline{B}C$. Only three transfer contacts are to be used.

Answer   See Figure 3.41.

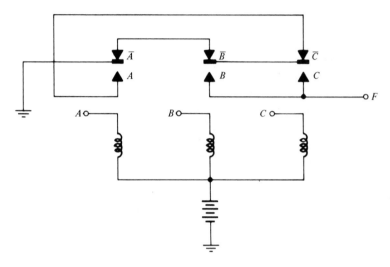

Figure 3.41   Problem 3.7.

3.8   Design a relay circuit for realizing $F = \overline{A}BC + A\overline{B}\overline{C}$. Only three transfer contacts are to be used.

3.9   Determine a POS and an SOP for the bridge of Figure 3.42.

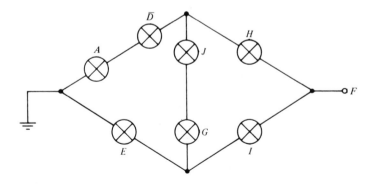

Figure 3.42   Problem 3.9.

Answer $F = (A + E)(\overline{D} + E)(A + J + I)(A + G + I)$
$(\overline{D} + J + I)(\overline{D} + G + I)(E + H + J)(E + H + G)$
$(H + I) = A\overline{D}H + A\overline{D}JGI + EI + EJGH$

3.10   Determine a POS and an SOP for the bridge of Figure 3.43

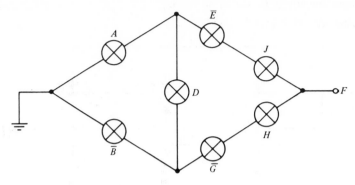

Figure 3.43   Problem 3.10.

3.11   For each of the following sets of inputs, determine the output voltage from a diode up-follower having a supply voltage of -10 V:
(a) 3, 6, and -2 V   (c) 3, 6, and -12 V
(b) -4, -5, -6, and -7 V   (d) -11, -12, and -13 V

3.12   For each of the following sets of inputs, determine the output voltage from a diode down-follower having a supply voltage of 10 V:
(a) 3, 6, and -2 V   (c) 3, 6, and 12 V
(b) -4, -5, -6, and -7 V   (d) 11, 12, and 13 V

3.13   Two diode down-followers, each having a supply voltage of 10 V, provide the only inputs to a diode up-follower having a supply voltage of -10 V. Determine the output voltage from the up-follower if the inputs to the down-followers are 10, -5, and 3 V to one and -11, -6, -8, and 6 V to the other.

Answer -5 V

3.14   Two diode up-followers, each having a supply voltage of -10 V, provide the only inputs to a diode down-follower having a supply voltage of 10 V. Determine the output voltage from the down-follower if the inputs to the up-followers are 10, -5, and 3 V to one and -11, -6, -8, and 6 V to the other.

3.15   Show two two-level and one three-level diode realizations for $F = BC + AB + AC$. Use positive logic.

3.16   Show two two-level diode realizations for $F = ABC + BC + DC + A\bar{B}C$. Assume that complements of the variables are available.

In the odd-numbered problems from 3.17 through 3.28, the function $F = ACD + A\bar{B}D + AC\bar{D} + \bar{A}\bar{B}CD$ is to be realized. And in the even-numbered problems, the function $F = (\bar{A} + \bar{C} + \bar{D})(\bar{A} + B + \bar{D})(\bar{A} + \bar{C} + D)(A + B + \bar{C} + D)$ is to be realized.

Complements of the variables are available. Positive logic is to be used in all but Problems 3.25 and 3.26. The realizations are to be of two levels with as few components as possible.

3.17 Design a TRL circuit using the basic circuit of Figure 3.20.

3.18 Repeat Problem 3.17.

3.19 Design a DTL circuit using the basic circuit of Figure 3.23(b).

3.20 Design a DTL circuit using the basic circuit of Figure 3.23(a).

3.21 Design a TTL circuit using the basic circuit of Figure 3.25.

3.22 Repeat Problem 3.21.

3.23 Design two DCTL circuits using the basic circuits of Figures 3.27 and 3.30, respectively.

3.24 Repeat Problem 3.23.

3.25 Design an ECL circuit using the basic circuit of Figure 3.33. Assume negative logic.

3.26 Repeat Problem 3.25.

3.27 Design two MOS FET circuits using the basic circuits of Figures 3.38(a) and 3.39(b), respectively.

3.28 Design two MOS FET circuits using the basic circuits of Figures 3.38(b) and 3.39(a), respectively.

In Problems 3.29 through 3.40 the function $F = C\bar{D}\bar{E} + A\bar{B}\bar{E} + \bar{B}C\bar{D}\bar{E} + C\bar{D}E + \bar{A}\bar{B}C\bar{D}\bar{E}$ with a don't care of $A\bar{B}C\bar{D}\bar{E}$ is to be realized in two levels with as few components as possible. Complements of the variables are available. Positive logic is to be used unless there is a statement to the contrary.

3.29 Design a TRL circuit using the basic circuit of Figure 3.20. Assume it is a NAND gate.

3.30 Repeat Problem 3.29 and assume the circuit of Figure 3.20 is a NOR gate.

3.31 Design a DTL circuit using the basic circuit of Figure 3.23(a).

3.32 Design a DTL circuit using the basic circuit of Figure 3.23(b).

3.33 Design a TTL circuit using the basic circuit of Figure 3.25.

3.34 Repeat Problem 3.33 but use negative logic.

3.35 Design a DCTL circuit using the basic circuit of Figure 3.27.

3.36 Design a DCTL circuit using the basic circuit of Figure 3.30.

3.37 Design an ECL circuit using the basic circuit of Figure 3.33.

3.38 Repeat Problem 3.37 but use negative logic.

3.39 Design two MOS FET circuits using the basic circuits of Figures 3.38(a) and 3.39(a), respectively.

3.40 Design two MOS FET circuits using the basic circuits of Figures 3.38(b) and 3.39(b), respectively.

3.41 If the outputs of several gates are directly joined, they are said to be connected to form the wired-OR function, sometimes also known as a dot OR or a solder OR. Figure 3.44 shows two DTL gates with a wired-OR connection. What is the output F?

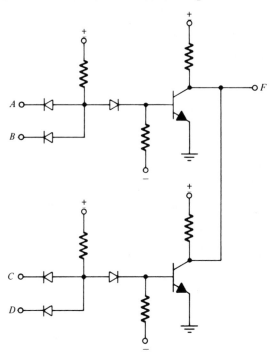

Figure 3.44 Problem 3.41.

Answer $F = \overline{AB} \cdot \overline{CD}$

3.42 Generate $F = AB + \overline{A}B + \overline{B}C$ using the type of DCTL circuit of Figure 3.30 with a wired-OR connection. The resulting circuit is to be of one level. Use positive logic.

3.43 Can wired-OR be used with the TTL circuit of Figure 3.25?

Answer No, because if two TTL circuits are wire-OR'd together and one is in the 1 state and the other is in the 0 state, a very low impedance path will exist from $+V_C$ to ground. Hence this path, which is through the two conducting output transistors for these circuits, will conduct a large destructive current.

4

Basic
Digital
Circuits

We have studied switching algebra and some of the circuits for implementing logic functions. We will now combine these two topics in a consideration of some of the most important circuits used in digital systems: adders, subtractors, registers, counters, encoders, and decoders. Again, our purpose is to study some of the general features of these circuits and not the circuit details or the optimization of designs.

4.1   HALF ADDER

A *half-adder circuit* adds two bits. It has two inputs, one for each bit, and two outputs, one for the sum bit and the other for the carry bit. A block diagram of the half adder is shown in Figure 4.1 with two inputs A and B, a sum output S, and a carry output C. Its truth table is

A	B	S	C
0	0	0	0
0	1	1	0
1	0	1	0
1	1	0	1

Figure 4.1 Half adder.

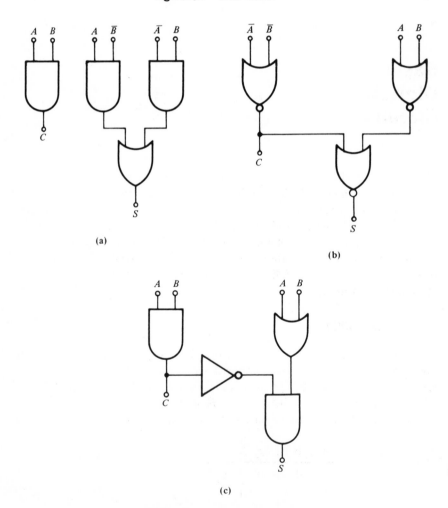

Figure 4.2 Half-adder realizations.

From this truth table it is evident that $S = \overline{A}B + A\overline{B} = (A + B)$ $(\overline{A} + \overline{B}) = A \oplus B$ and $C = AB$.

An obvious logic diagram realization is shown in Figure 4.2(a). In this realization no circuits are common to the sum and carry operations. However, fewer components are often required if circuits are shared between operations. Figure 4.2(b) is another realization, and this one has some circuits common to both outputs. A third realization, presented in Figure 4.2(c), is perhaps less obvious than some of the other realizations, but it can be readily verified.

The half adder is often used in the adders of digital computers. However, with only two inputs it cannot be the sole adder circuit. A third input is needed for carries. An adder with three inputs is a *full adder*.

4.2   FULL ADDER

In the addition of two numbers, a half adder can add the two least significant digits of the addend and augend, but a carry may be generated in this addition that must be included in the addition of the next to the least significant digits. For example, suppose in an addition the augend (A_2A_1) and addend (B_2B_1) have two bits each; then

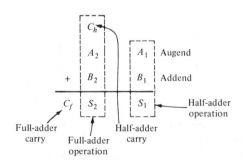

A half adder suffices for adding the A_1 and B_1 bits. But, a three-input adder is needed for adding the A_2 and B_2 bits plus the carry that may be generated in the A_1 and B_1 addition.

A block diagram of a *full adder* is shown in Figure 4.3(a). The carry from the prior addition is C_o (the *old* carry) and that generated is C_n (the *new* carry).

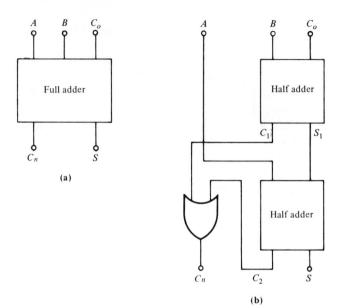

Figure 4.3 Full adder.

The truth table for the full adder is

A	B	C_o	S	C_n
0	0	0	0	0
0	0	1	1	0
0	1	0	1	0
0	1	1	0	1
1	0	0	1	0
1	0	1	0	1
1	1	0	0	1
1	1	1	1	1

From this table and the minimization techniques we have studied, the functions are $S = \bar{A}\bar{B}C_o + \bar{A}B\bar{C}_o + A\bar{B}\bar{C}_o + ABC_o = (A + B + C_o)$ $(A + \bar{B} + \bar{C}_o)(\bar{A} + B + \bar{C}_o)(\bar{A} + \bar{B} + C_o)$ and $C_n = AB + BC_o + AC_o$ $= (B + C_o)(A + B)(A + C_o)$. Although the sum-of-products and the product-of-sums expressions for the sum output are in expanded form, they cannot be minimized further.

One of the many ways to realize a full adder is by using two half adders, as is shown in Figure 4.3(b). In this arrangement the addition is performed in two steps. First, bits B and C_o are added, and then bit A is added to this sum. It should be apparent that these two steps produce the correct sum bit. A carry bit is generated by the full adder if any two (or all three) input bits are 1's. If B and C_o are 1's then their addition generates an intermediate carry C_1 that passes through the OR gate to the C_n terminal. If A and either (but not both) B and C_o are 1's, a carry C_2 is generated at the second half adder that passes through the OR gate to C_n. Thus all possibilities for the generation of a carry are obtained.

We could consider many full-adder circuits, but with the exception of the straightforward two-level implementations, which should be obvious from the sum and carry equations, they are of more than two levels and thus cannot be systematically designed with any of the methods we have studied.

4.3   HALF SUBTRACTOR

As can be surmised from our prior adder discussions, a *half subtractor* is a two-input and two-output circuit. We will call one input M to designate a digit in the minuend and the other input S, the corresponding digit in the subtrahend. The two outputs are D the difference bit and B the borrow bit. Of course, the half subtractor performs the following:

$$\begin{array}{r} M \\ -\quad S \\ \hline B \quad D \end{array}$$

A block diagram of a half subtractor is shown in Figure 4.4(a). Its truth table is

M	S	D	B
0	0	0	0
0	1	1	1
1	0	1	0
1	1	0	0

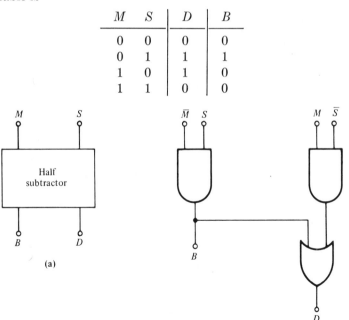

(a)

(b)

Figure 4.4   Half subtractor.

Obviously, $D = \overline{M}S + M\overline{S} = (M + S)(\overline{M} + \overline{S}) = M \oplus S$ and $B = \overline{M}S$. It should be noted that the expression for the difference bit is the EXCLUSIVE OR of the inputs, which is the same expression as for the sum bit of a half adder. One of the ways the half subtractor can be realized is shown in Figure 4.4(b).

Although the half subtractor can be used in subtractor circuits of digital computers, it does not have sufficient inputs to be the sole subtractor circuit—a third input is needed for borrows. A subtractor with three inputs is a *full substractor*.

4.4   FULL SUBTRACTOR

In the subtraction of two numbers, a half subtractor can produce the difference of the two least significant digits of the minuend and subtrahend, but a borrow may be generated that must be included in the subtraction of the next to the least significant digits. For an understanding of this possibility, consider a minuend and subtrahend of two bits each, with the minuend being larger. Then the subtraction is

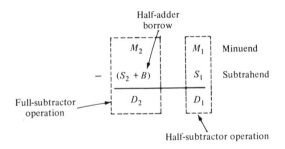

With a little thought, we see that the full subtractor (Figure 4.5) performs the operation $(M - B) - S = M - (S + B)$ in which B is

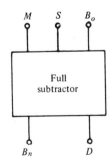

Figure 4.5   Full subtractor.

the borrow output from the first subtraction. The corresponding truth table is

M	S	B_o	D	B_n
0	0	0	0	0
0	0	1	1	1
0	1	0	1	1
0	1	1	0	1
1	0	0	1	0
1	0	1	0	0
1	1	0	0	0
1	1	1	1	1

in which B_o is the borrow from the prior stage of subtraction and B_n that generated. From this truth table and the studied minimization techniques

$$D = \overline{M}\overline{S}B_o + \overline{M}S\overline{B}_o + M\overline{S}\overline{B}_o + MSB_o$$

$$= (M + \overline{S} + \overline{B}_o)(\overline{M} + S + \overline{B}_o)(M + S + B_o)(\overline{M} + \overline{S} + B_o)$$

and

$$B_n = \overline{M}B_o + SB_o + \overline{M}S = (\overline{M} + S)(\overline{M} + B_o)(B_o + S)$$

Note that the expression for the difference bit of the full subtractor is the same as that for the sum bit of the full adder.

We could implement the difference expression and the minimized borrow expression easily enough, but a better realization can be obtained. From a glance at the truth table or the Karnaugh map, we see that the expanded expressions for the difference and borrow bits have three terms in common. Thus, in a realization of the expanded expressions, considerable components can be shared as is shown in Figure 4.6(a).

The subtractor of Figure 4.6(a) can be improved, economically speaking, by using only two NAND gates common to both outputs. This economy can be achieved by rearranging and simplifying the borrow expression: $B_n = \overline{M}\overline{S}B_o + MSB_o + (\overline{M}SB_o + \overline{M}S\overline{B}_o) = \overline{M}\overline{S}B_o + MSB_o + \overline{M}S$. The $\overline{M}S\overline{B}_o$ input is still needed for the difference bit D, but it is not needed for the borrow bit B_n and can be combined with $\overline{M}SB_o$ to simplify to $\overline{M}S$. As a result of this simplification, the final NAND gate for the borrow bit output need have only three inputs. The total saving for the improved circuit shown in Figure 4.6(b) is two inputs.

There are many other versions of the full subtractor, but they are of no consequence to us in our present study. It suffices that we know how a full subtractor functions and have some idea of the manner in which a full subtractor can be realized.

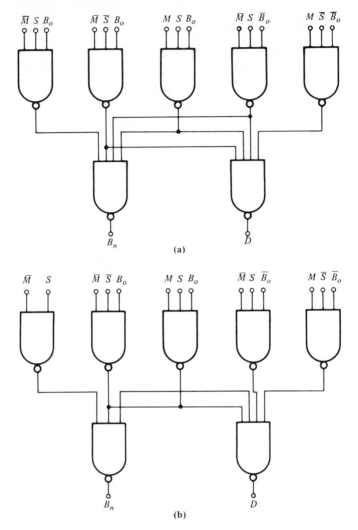

Figure 4.6 Full-subtractor realizations.

4.5 FLIP-FLOPS

Flip-flops have been mentioned but not considered in any detail. We will further study them now, but again the nuances of circuit design will not be treated.

Flip-flops can store binary quantities in the form of voltages. The binary storage of present interest is of 1's and 0's which may be considered to be either binary numbers or logic values, whichever is more convenient or pertinent.

Flip-flops have two outputs and one, two, three, or more inputs. A two-input flip-flop is shown in Figure 4.7, with output lines Y and $\overline{Y}$ The voltages on these lines are of two levels, one of which may, for example, be 0 V (ground) and the other -5 V at any one time. In the case of positive logic and the storage of a 1, line Y has the more positive voltage, here ground, and $\overline{Y}$ the more negative voltage, here -5 V. If a 0 is stored, the converse is true.

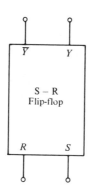

Figure 4.7   S-R flip-flop.

The contents of a flip-flop, or static conditions of operation called *states,* are often associated with a switching function variable, which is here assumed to be Y. From the description of the voltage operation, it is apparent that this flip-flop produces outputs corresponding to this variable and also its complement. Consequently, as has been assumed in much of our prior work, the variables and their complements are frequently available.

If a flip-flop is not energized at any of its inputs, it remains in a single state for as long as power is supplied to the circuit. That is, it is a *bistable* device that can remain in either the 0 or 1 state indefinitely. The state of a flip-flop is changed by voltage pulses applied at the inputs. However, voltage-level signals that we call dc voltages are often used with pulses to control flip-flop operation. Of course these dc-level signals change with time as do pulses, but the level signals are usually more like a square wave than the spikes of voltage normally associated with pulses. In some flip-flops, called dc flip-flops, these voltage levels are the only inputs.

The act of storing a 1 in the flip-flop is called *setting* the flip-flop. Putting in a 0 is called *clearing* or *resetting* the flip-flop.

We will consider the four basic types of flip-flops: the S-R (set-reset),

D, T (trigger or toggle), and J-K. We will also consider *edge-triggered* *flip-flops*.

S-R Flip-Flop

The first flip-flop we will discuss is the *S-R flip-flop*, shown in Figure 4.7. This flip-flop is also known as the S-C (set-clear) flip-flop.

If this flip-flop is in the 0 state, a voltage pulse applied to the S line causes the flip-flop to change to the 1 state, but a pulse applied to the R line produces no change—the flip-flop remains in the 0 state. Now suppose the flip-flop is in the 1 state; a pulse applied to the R line causes the flip-flop to change to the 0 state and a pulse applied to the S line produces no change—the flip-flop remains in the 1 state.

These are the normal conditions of pulsing, but there are two others. If no pulses are applied to either the R or S line, the flip-flop remains indefinitely in whatever state it is in, as has been mentioned. The final pulsing condition that could possibly occur is that of pulses applied to both the R and S lines. For this input, the operation is indeterminate. That is, there is no telling what the circuit will do; it may change state or remain in the same state. Thus this input condition is to be avoided.

Flip-flops can be constructed from any of the transistor digital circuits we have discussed. Although these transistor flip-flop circuits have some differences, they also have much in common. In general they have two transistors, the conducting states of which determine the storage of a 1 or a 0. If a 1 is stored, then one of these two transistors conducts, and is usually saturated, and the other one is cut off. If a 0 is stored, the conduction states of the transistors are reversed. In these flip-flop circuits, the output (the collector for a bipolar transistor) of each switching transistor is connected to the input of the other (the base). In essence, these two transistors are inverters connected in a loop.

A DCTL S-R flip-flop is shown in Figure 4.8 with inputs and outputs designated on the basis of positive logic and the application of positive pulses or levels (this is a dc flip-flop) for changing the state of the flip-flop. The two switching transistors are T_1 and T_2. When the flip-flop is in the 1 state, transistor T_1 is cut off and causes terminal Y to be positive, and transistor T_2 is saturated and shorts terminal $\overline{Y}$ to ground. When the flip-flop is in the 0 state, transistor T_2 is cut off and makes terminal $\overline{Y}$ positive, and transistor T_1 is saturated and shorts terminal Y to ground.

If a positive voltage is applied to terminal S while the flip-flop is in the 0 state, T_4 saturates and shorts the $\overline{Y}$ terminal to ground. This potential, which is also on the base of T_1, causes T_1 to cut off. With

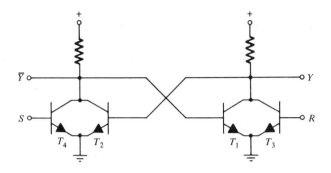

Figure 4.8 DCTL S-R flip-flop.

T_1 cut off, the potential on terminal Y and on the base of T_2 increases and T_2 saturates, thereby providing another path for shorting terminal $\bar{Y}$ to ground, which path continues after the input pulse to T_4 decreases and T_4 is no longer saturated. With the ground potential on $\bar{Y}$ conducted to the base of T_1, this transistor is maintained cut off. Thus, after a positive voltage is applied to terminal S, terminal $\bar{Y}$ is grounded, terminal Y is positive, and a 1 is stored in the flip-flop and will remain stored until a positive voltage is applied to terminal R.

If a positive voltage is applied to terminal R when the flip-flop is in the 1 state, T_3 saturates and makes the potential on the Y terminal and the base of T_2 decrease to almost ground. Then T_2 cuts off and, as a result, the potential increases on terminal $\bar{Y}$ and on the base of T_1, causing T_1 to saturate and provide another shorting path for terminal Y to ground, which path continues after the input pulse to T_3 decreases and T_3 is no longer saturated. This ground is conducted to the base of T_2 and maintains this transistor cut off. Thus, after a positive pulse is applied to terminal R, terminal Y is almost at ground and terminal $\bar{Y}$ is at a positive potential and a 0 is stored in the flip-flop and will remain stored until a positive voltage is applied to terminal S.

As has been mentioned, if no positive voltages are applied to the flip-flop of Figure 4.8, the flip-flop remains in whatever state it is in. And, if positive voltages are applied simultaneously to terminals R and S, both output terminals go to ground, with the final state of the flip-flop depending on which positive voltage is removed first. This input condition should be avoided.

Some manufacturers modify the basic circuit of Figure 4.8 by placing small resistors in the base leads. However, the operation is still that explained.

The circuit of Figure 4.8 comprises two NOR gates with the output of each gate connected to the input of the other one as shown in logic diagram form in Figure 4.9(a). An S-R flip-flop can also be constructed from NAND gates as shown in Figure 4.9(b). Although the operation of this NAND S-R flip-flop is similar to that explained for the NOR flip-flop, there are sufficient differences to justify a detailed explanation.

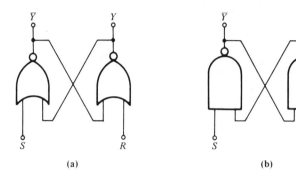

(a)   (b)

Figure 4.9   S-R flip-flop logic diagrams.

If, for the NAND flip-flop of Figure 4.9(b), the inputs S and R are both 1's, the state of the flip-flop remains unchanged. This result is apparent because a 1 into a multi-input NAND gate cannot affect the output—the NAND operation is AND followed by NOT and 1 AND anything is that anything. If the S input is 0 and the R input 1, the NAND gate with the S input then produces a 1 output on the $\bar{Y}$ line. This 1 output is conducted to an input of the other NAND gate which also has a 1 input from the R line. With two 1's in, this NAND gate produces a 0 output on the Y line. This 0 is fed back to an input of the other NAND gate so that the state of the flip-flop does not change if the S input should subsequently go to 1. If the R line input is 0 and the S line input is 1, then obviously the flip-flop operation is just opposite that which has just been explained.

If both S and R inputs are 0's (the forbidden input condition), both NAND gates produce 1's out. Then the final state of the flip-flop depends on which input line goes to 1 first. The NAND gate with this input produces a 0 output. For the very improbable input condition of both input lines changing to 1 at exactly the same time, the operation depends upon differences in construction of the two NAND gates and is, therefore, unpredictable from a logic diagram point of view.

Note that in the operation of this NAND S-R flip-flop, the 0's are the significant inputs. They, and not the 1's, are the initiators of action.

Some S-R flip-flops have a third input, CP (often referred to as T), for a clock signal, as is illustrated in Figure 4.10. The clock signal, which may be a square wave, is often used to synchronize the operations of components in a digital system, as will be explained later in this chapter. The operation with a clock input is essentially that explained except that the switching is in synchronism with the clock pulses; that is, the inputs S and R are locked out except when the clock input is a 1.

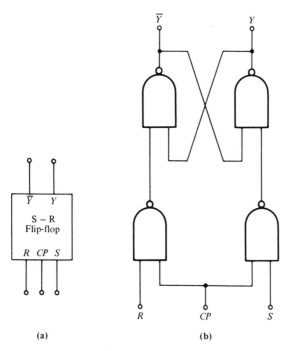

(a)

(b)

Figure 4.10 S-R flip-flop with clock input.

As can be seen in the logic diagram of Figure 4.10(b), when the CP input is 0 it produces 1 outputs from both input NAND gates regardless of the S and R inputs. However, when the clock signal is 1, the input (S or R) that is 1 produces a 0 output from an input NAND gate and this 0 determines the state of the flip-flop, as has just been explained for the NAND flip-flop of Figure 4.9(b).

Note that because of the inverter action of the two input NAND gates, the S and R inputs in Figure 4.10(b) are opposite the inputs of Figure 4.9(b). Also, with this inverter action, 1 inputs are the initiators of action for the whole flip-flop and thus two 1 inputs are to be avoided instead of two 0's.

D Flip-Flop

The next flip-flop we will discuss is the D *flip-flop*, which is shown in Figure 4.11(a) in block diagram form and in Figure 4.11(b) in logic diagram form. It has two inputs: input CP for clock pulses and input D for a dc control voltage. The operation is simple. If the voltage applied at D corresponds to a 1 when a clock pulse occurs, the flip-flop switches to or remains in the 1 state, and if the voltage applied at D corresponds to a 0 when a clock pulse occurs, the flip-flop switches to or remains in the 0 state.

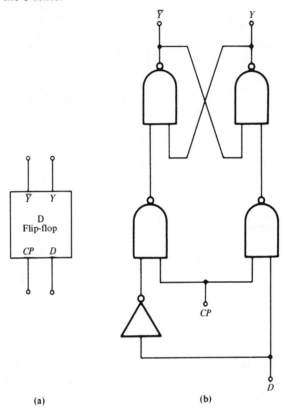

(a)   (b)

Figure 4.11   D flip-flop.

A comparison of Figures 4.10(b) and 4.11(b) shows that the D flip-flop is basically an S-R flip-flop with an inverter added to provide a second dc input. With this arrangement, the two inputs from the D line and the inverter can never by the same and thus we cannot have forbidden inputs.

T Flip-Flop

If in the S-R flip-flop of Figure 4.10(b) we connect the Y output line to the R input and the $\bar{Y}$ output line to the S input, we will have the T *flip-flop* of Figure 4.12. This flip-flop, which is called a trigger, toggle, or simply T flip-flop, has only one input. We will designate this input by T, even though in some applications clock pulses are applied to it.

If this flip-flop is in the 1 state when an input pulse occurs, then the two inputs to the left input NAND gate of Figure 4.12(b) are 1's and thus the flip-flop resets; that is, it goes to the 0 state. But if the flip-flop is initially in the 0 state, then on the occurrence of a pulse on the T input, the two inputs to the right input NAND gates are 1's and thus the flip-flop sets or, in other words, changes to the 1 state. From this explanation obviously the flip-flop complements when a pulse is applied at the T input.

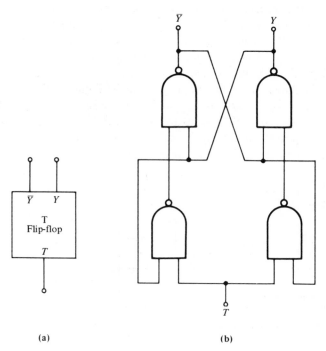

(a)

(b)

Figure 4.12   T flip-flop.

This flip-flop, being a complementing type, is not suitable for storage applications as are the storage type D and S-R flip-flops, as well as the J-K flip-flop, which we have yet to consider. That is, the contents of the T flip-flop depend upon its prior contents rather than solely on its input. This flip-flop, however, is very useful in counters, as we will see.

For proper operation the triggering pulse must be shorter in duration than the switching time of the flip-flop. Otherwise when the flip-flop changes state, the signals fed back to the input NAND gates will change and retrigger the flip-flop just like an input pulse. This retriggering will continue for the duration of the clock pulse. Thus either the clock pulses must be short in duration or other techniques, mentioned below, must be used.

One way of eliminating the self-retriggering problem is to design the T flip-flop so that it triggers on the *trailing edge* of each input pulse. This feature can be achieved using capacitors and diodes as is described in the literature. With trailing-edge triggering the input pulse is completely decayed by the time the flip-flop switches and so there is no problem with self-retriggering. However, for this action the trailing edge of the triggering pulse must be quite sharp and, in fact, so sharp that it is difficult to achieve. Reasonably shaped input pulses can be used and yet self-retriggering avoided if master-slave flip-flops are used.

A master-slave flip-flop comprises two flip-flops with the output of one flip-flop (the master) providing the inputs for the other flip-flop (the slave), as is shown in block diagram form in Figure 4.13. It suffices to show an S-R flip-flop since, as we should readily realize, this S-R flip-flop can be converted to a T flip-flop by feeding back the outputs from the second flip-flop to the inputs of the first flip-flop. Or, it can be converted to a D flip-flop with the addition of an inverter.

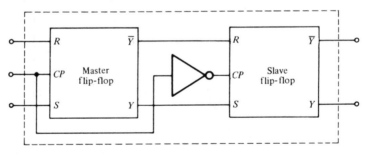

Figure 4.13 S-R master-slave flip-flop.

The operation of the master-slave flip-flop is easy to understand. On the leading edge of the clock pulse the input master flip-flop goes to the state dictated by the S and R inputs. While this input clock pulse is a 1, the inputs to the output slave flip-flop are locked out because of the 0 output of the inverter connected to the CP input. Thus the state of this slave flip-flop cannot change during the duration of the clock pulse. Therefore this master-slave flip-flop will not retrigger if it is connected as a T flip-flop.

When the clock pulse returns to 0, the inverter connected to the slave CP input produces a 1 out which activates the slave flip-flop inputs. Then the state of the slave flip-flop becomes the same as that of the master flip-flop. Note that it is on the trailing edge of the clock pulse that the output of the master-slave flip-flop, as a whole, changes to the voltages specified by the input conditions. Thus, with this circuit we have trailing-edge triggering even though the activation is dc.

J-K Flip-Flop

A very popular flip-flop, and certainly the most versatile, is the *J-K master-slave flip-flop* shown in block diagram and logic diagram forms in Figures 4.14(a) and (b), respectively. Not only can this flip-flop perform unique operations of its own, but with simple connections (and in the case of the D flip-flop an added inverter), it can perform like any of the other flip-flops we have studied. Its obvious circuit complexity is not a serious disadvantage if it is constructed in integrated circuit form.

For the purposes of explanation, assume that there is only one J and one K input terminal. Then *this J-K flip-flop is, except for one input' condition, identical in operation to the S-R flip-flop with the* J *terminal corresponding to* S *and the* K *terminal to* R. The one input condition that produces a different operation is that of 1's applied to both inputs. In the use of the S-R flip-flop we want to avoid this input because the resulting response is indeterminate. But, for the J-K flip-flop the response is known—the flip-flop changes state regardless of the original state of the flip-flop. Thus, for the J-K flip-flop a 1 applied at the J input causes the flip-flop to change to or to remain in the 1 stage when the trailing edge of the input clock pulse occurs. A 1 at the K input causes the flip-flop to change to or to remain in the 0 state. And, as mentioned, 1's applied simultaneously to both inputs cause the flip-flop to change state. Of course if 0's are applied at the two inputs, the flip-flop remains in whatever state it is in.

The multiple J and K inputs, which many manufacturers provide, give inputs of $J_1 \cdot J_2 \cdot J_3$ and $K_1 \cdot K_2 \cdot K_3$ instead of just J and K. The inputs could be OR functions instead, depending on the design. Manufacturers also provides S-R flip-flops with multiple S and R inputs.

Not all inputs for these J-K and other flip-flops will always be used. Manufacturers should specify potentials to apply to the unused inputs. But often potentials need not be applied; no connections may be necessary. As an illustration, the inputs may be to diode down-followers the lack of inputs to which may produce the same result as applied up potentials (positive logic 1's): both conditions may produce nonconduction of the input diodes. A J-K flip-flop of this type without connections to the J and K inputs becomes the equivalent of a toggle flip-flop with the clock pulse input serving as the T input.

Later in this chapter when we consider counters constructed from

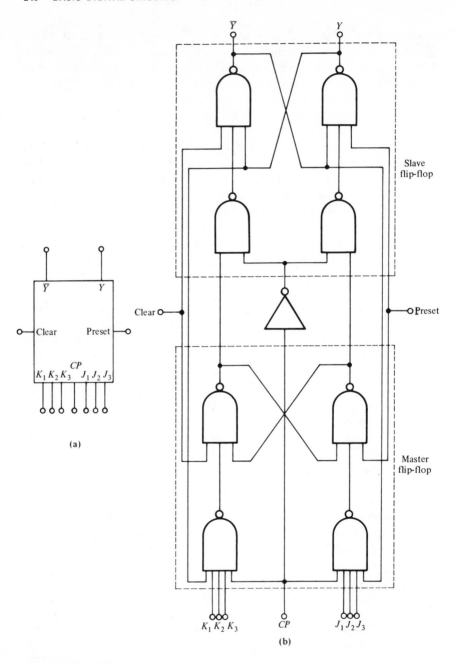

Figure 4.14   J-K flip-flop.

flip-flops, some of the flip-flop inputs are without connections. For these we will assume that the inputs are of a type that no signal in is the equivalent of an applied positive logic 1.

In Figure 4.14 the inputs, CLEAR and PRESET, permit control of the flip-flop, which control overrides that of the J, K, and clock pulse inputs. This operation is easily seen by noting that the terminals for these inputs are directly connected to the output NAND gates of both flip-flops. Hence, a 0 on the CLEAR input causes both master and slave flip-flops to be in the 0 state with a 1 on the $\overline{Y}$ line and a 0 on the Y line. And a 0 on the PRESET line sets both flip-flops, producing a 1 on the Y line and a 0 on the $\overline{Y}$ line. The CLEAR and PRESET lines should not be energized simultaneously with 0's for exactly the same reason presented for the inputs of the S-R flip-flop of Figure 4.9(b). However, 1's on these two lines are acceptable and, in fact, usually desired, for they permit the flip-flop to operate in normal J-K fashion. Incidentally, J-K flip-flops are not the only ones that can have these CLEAR and PRESET inputs. Manufacturers also provide them for the other flip-flops.

The flip-flop of Figure 4.14(b) comprises two S-R flip-flops, both of which are like the one shown in Figure 4.10(b), with an inverter connected between the clock inputs. The outputs of the slave flip-flop are conducted back to the inputs of the master flip-flop with the Y output going to a K input and the $\overline{Y}$ output going to a J input in a feedback fashion similar to that explained for the T flip-flop.

For an understanding of the operation of this flip-flop, consider the case first of 1's on all J and K inputs. With these inputs the flip-flop will have, on the occurrence of a clock pulse, a next state that is completely determined by the present state.

If the present state is 1, a 1 is conducted back from the Y output line to an input of the K NAND gate. This gate, having inputs of all 1's, produces a 0 out that clears the master flip-flop. Then after the trailing edge of the clock pulse, the output of the master flip-flop clears the slave flip-flop. During this operation, a 0 is conducted to an input of the J NAND gate from the $\overline{Y}$ output line. As a consequence, this gate produces a 1 output, which, of course, has no effect on the state of the flip-flop. In effect, the 0 input for this J NAND gate disenables this gate.

If the present state is 0, the J input NAND gate has all 1's at its inputs and therefore produces a 0 out that immediately sets the master flip-flop, the output of which then sets the slave flip-flop after the clock pulse goes to 0. The K input NAND gate with a 0 input from the Y line will be inhibited from affecting the state of the flip-flop.

From this explanation we see that when all J and K inputs are 1's, the J-K master-slave flip-flop acts just like a T flip-flop.

If all the J inputs are 1's and one or more K inputs are 0's, the J input NAND gate can possibly affect the state of the flip-flop but the K input NAND gate cannot because it is disenabled by the 0 inputs. If the state of the flip-flop is 1, the J input NAND gate will also be disenabled by a 0 conducted to one of its inputs from the $\overline{Y}$ output line. With both input NAND gates disenabled, the flip-flop will remain in the 1 state, which, of course, is exactly the condition desired.

If, with this input condition, the state of the flip-flop is 0, then the J input NAND gate will have all 1's in and will thus produce a 0 out that will set the master flip-flop on the occurrence of a clock pulse. And then the output of the master flip-flop will set the slave flip-flop after the clock pulse goes to 0. Thus, regardless of the present state of the flip-flop, all 1's on the J inputs and one or more 0's on the K inputs cause the flip-flop to go to or to remain in the 1 state.

By the same argument, if all the K inputs are 1's and one or more of the J inputs are 0's, the flip-flop will go to or remain in the 0 state after a clock pulse occurs. If some of the J inputs and some of the K inputs have 0's on them, both input AND gates are disenabled and the state of the flip-flop will not change.

Edge-Triggered Flip-Flops

The flip-flops we have considered are responsive to input changes that occur while the clock pulse is 1. Because in some applications this condition is undesirable, *edge-triggered flip-flops* have been developed that trigger on the *leading* edge of the clock puse, and that, upon triggering ,immediately *lock out the input* so that the flip-flop is unresponsive to further changes in inputs until after the clock pulse returns to zero again and another clock pulse occurs.

An edge-triggered D flip-flop composed of NAND gates is shown in Figure 4.15. In this flip-flop gates 5 and 6 are the main flip-flop gates zero inputs to which determine the state of the flip-flop. Gate 2 provides lockout of the input when the D input is initially a 1. And gate 1 provides lockout when the D input is initially a 0. Gates 3 and 4 provide the 0's for controlling the main flip-flop gates 5 and 6 when the clock input is 1, but which obviously have 1 outputs and do not affect gates 5 and 6 when the clock input is 0.

For an understanding of the operation, consider a D input of 1 immediately before the leading edge of the clock pulse. With this input and the other input from gate 3, which input is also a 1 as mentioned above, gate 1 produces a 0 out. This output, which is conducted to an input of gate 2, causes gate 2 to produce an output of 1. When the clock pulse goes to 1, the output of gate 4 changes to 0 because of its two inputs of 1, one from gate 2 and the other from the clock

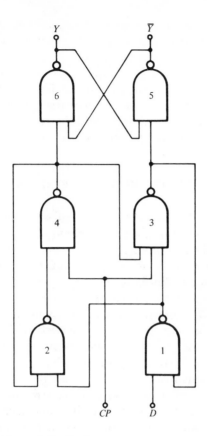

Figure 4.15 Edge-triggered D flip-flop.

input. This 0 output energizes gate 6 to produce an output of 1 and thereby set the flip-flop in the 1 state. This 0 output from gate 4 is fed back to an input of gate 2 to maintain the gate 2 output at 1 regardless of changes in the other input to gate 2. As a consequence, even though the D input changes from a 1 to a 0 while the clock pulse is 1, thereby causing the output of gate 1 to change, the flip-flop state is unaffected because the two gates 2 and 3 to which the output of gate 1 goes still produce 1's as a result of the 0 inputs from gate 4.

If the D input is 0 before the leading edge of the clock pulse, then the output of gate 1 is 1, which 1 conducted to gate 2 produces a 0 output from this gate (the other input to gate 2 is also a 1 then). When the clock pulse goes to 1 on the leading edge, the output of gate 3 changes to 0 because all the inputs to this gate are then 1's. But gate 4 still produces a 1 output because of the 0 input from gate 2. The 0 output from gate 3 forces gate 5 to produce a 1 and thus the flip-flop to go to the 0 state. Also, at the same time this 0 output from gate 3 is fed back to an input of gate 1, resulting in gate 1 producing a 1 out even if the D input changes to a 1 while the clock pulse is 1.

Regardless of the input, when the clock pulse returns to 0, both gates 3 and 4 produce 1's out and so the flip-flop is readied for the D input that occurs on the leading edge of the next clock pulse.

For simplicity, we have considered only an edge-triggered flip-flop of the D type. The other flip-flops also have edge-triggered versions.

4.6   TIMING IN DIGITAL SYSTEMS

Now that we have discussed some features of flip-flops, we should consider some of the digital circuits in which they are used. But, before doing this, we need to discuss timing in digital systems and particularly in digital computers because of the relationship between timing and the pulsing of flip-flops.

Most computers that have been constructed to date are *synchronous computers*. They are characterized by operations having steps that are allotted a specific amount of time for completion. If a step takes less than the allotted time, then some time is wasted since the computer does not begin the next step until the allotted time for the present one has expired even though the present step has been completed. If a step is not finished in the allotted time, then an error occurs. The machine designer must make certain that this situation never happens.

Timing is not a problem in another type of computer—the *asynchronous computer*. After a step is completed in an asynchronous computer, a signal is generated for initiating the next step. Thus no time is wasted and, as a consequence, asynchronous computers are inherently faster in operation than synchronous computers, other factors being the same. But, in spite of the speed advantage, few asynchronous computers have been marketed. They are too costly and difficult to design.

In a synchronous computer, a timing mechanism called a *clock* operates at a fixed frequency. It may, for example, produce a square wave for controlling the timing of the operations, which may include the gating of flip-flops, as has been mentioned. This clock signal often provides gating in conjunction with AND gates, OR gates, and dc signals, as we will now discuss. In this discussion we will assume that the more positive half cycles of the clock pulses correspond to 1's and the more negative half cycles to 0's.

If clock pulses are applied to an AND gate along with a dc signal that is a 1, as shown in Figure 4.16(a), the clock pulses appear at the output line. This action is apparent because the output is 1 whenever both inputs are 1, and with one of the inputs 1 (the dc input) then the output is 1 whenever the clock pulses are 1, which is every other half cycle.

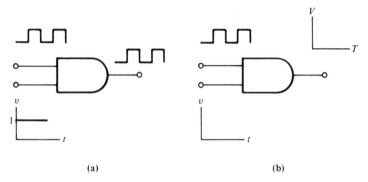

Figure 4.16 ANDing clock signal and dc signals.

There are two points of view for this operation. In one view, the application of the 1 permits the clock pulses to pass through the gate. However, from another point of view, this operation is a conversion of the 1 input dc signal into pulses.

If a 0 is applied at the dc input instead of a 1, then the output is obviously 0, as shown in Figure 4.16(b). Thus a 0 dc input blocks clock pulses from passing through the AND gate.

Clock pulses and dc signals may be applied to OR gates as shown in Figure 4.17. When the dc input signal is 1, as shown in Figure 4.17(a), it blocks the clock pulses from passing through the OR gate and produces an output of 1. Note that this output is different from that shown in Figure 4.16(b) even though clock pulses are blocked in both cases. If the dc signal is a 0, as in Figure 4.17(b), the clock pulses pass through the OR gate. This action results from the output being 1 whenever either of the inputs is 1, which occurs every half cycle for the clock pulses.

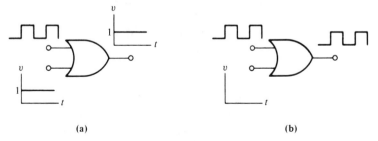

Figure 4.17 ORing clock signal and dc signals.

The foregoing discussion of gating is significant in the storing of information in flip-flops. Often, very often, the input to one flip-flop is the output from another flip-flop. And, of course, this output is dc. But, pulses are necessary for triggering flip-flops of the type having ac-coupled inputs (that is, capacitor coupled). These necessary pulses are often produced by clock pulses applied to the system of Figure 4.16 as shown in Figure 4.18 between two flip-flops A and B.

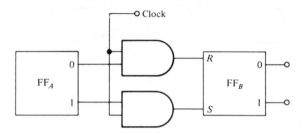

Figure 4.18   Transfer between flip-flops.

In this arrangement, the contents of FF_A (flip-flop A) are to be transferred to FF_B (flip-flop B) while at the same time being retained in FF_A. If FF_A contains a 1, then the AND gate on the S line of FF_B passes the clock pulse in accordance with Figure 4.16(a) and this pulse sets FF_B to a 1. If FF_A contains a 0, then the AND gate on the R line of FF_B passes the clock pulse, the R line is pulsed, and FF_B then contains a 0. Thus, in either case the prior (or present) contents of FF_A now reside in FF_B. This transfer technique can be employed in shift registers, which are discussed next.

Incidentally, in commercially available flip-flops, the AND gates are frequently incorporated in the flip-flop unit to form the gated flip-flops with clock inputs that we have discussed.

4.7   SHIFT REGISTERS

A *register* is a component for storing binary information such as numbers, instructions, and so on. Those registers of interest to us are constructed of flip-flops. And we will be most concerned with shift registers.

A *shift register* is an array of flip-flops that we find convenient to think of as arranged in a row, as shown in Figure 4.19 for a small shift register of only three flip-flops. Gates between the flip-flops permit shifting of bits to the right. In other registers the shifting may be to the left or either direction.

Assume for purposes of explanation that initially FF_1 contains a 1, FF_2 a 1, and FF_3 a 0. Also, assume that over a period of four clock

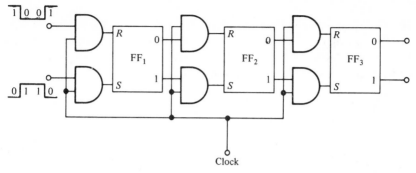

Figure 4.19 Shift register.

pulses the input to FF_1 is 0, then 1, another 1, and finally a 0. When the first clock pulse occurs, the 1 in FF_2 shifts to FF_3, the 1 in FF_1 shifts to FF_2, and the 0 input shifts into FF_1. Thus the register now contains 011. When the next clock pulse occurs, the 1 in FF_2 shifts to FF_3, the 0 in FF_1 shifts to FF_2, and the 1 input shifts into FF_1. The register now contains 101. The reader can continue with this operation to determine the register contents after the next two clock pulses. Although a register for shifting only right has been discussed, it should be apparent how this register can be modified to permit left shifts.

Gated flip-flops can be connected in a shift register arrangement without intervening AND gates. In effect, the AND gates are in the flip-flop packages.

This explanation of register operation is oversimplified. There is an excellent possibility that this circuit will not function as described because of the change of state of a flip-flop at the same time that it is providing an input for an adjacent flip-flop. This is called the *race* problem. Because of this problem, an input 1 to FF_1 can propagate through the register, changing all flip-flops to a 1 during one clock pulse. For example, suppose the register of Figure 4.19 contains 000 when a 1 is applied at the input of FF_1. At the next clock pulse, FF_1 switches to a 1. But, if it switches while the AND gates are still activated by the clock pulse, the change in FF_1 can switch FF_2 to a 1, and this switching of FF_2 can also switch FF_3, all during the same clock pulse. Thus, during only one clock pulse the register contents can change from 000 to 111 even though the desired contents are 100.

The race problem can be avoided in several ways. One way is to put in delay elements, as shown in Figure 4.20(a), that delay the signals for switching the flip-flops until after the clock pulses change from 1 to 0. Then, at the time the flip-flops switch, the AND gates are deactivated and, as a consequence, the flip-flop switching cannot propagate. Another version of this same approach is shown in Figure 4.20(b). But here the clock pulse is staggered in time by the delay elements such that the flip-flop switching starts at the rightmost flip-flop and then proceeds to the left. As a result, a pulse cannot propagate from the left to the right in the time of one clock pulse.

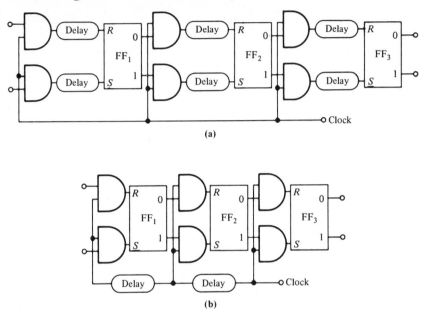

(a)

(b)

Figure 4.20   Shift register with delays.

Perhaps the simplest way of avoiding the race problem is to use edge-triggered flip-flops. Either the trailing-edge master-slave or the leading-edge triggering type is suitable. With trailing-edge triggering the slave flip-flops do not change state until after the inputs to the master flip-flops have been locked out. And, with leading-edge triggering the inputs are locked out before the flip-flops have time to change states. In either case the flip-flop switching produces no race effect.

Another solution to this race problem is the use of two arrays of flip-flops in one register, as shown for a three-flip-flop register in Figure 4.21. This may seem like an elaborate and expensive way to solve the race problem, but this register has other advantages, as will be shown in Chapter 11. In this register there is an upper array of flip-flops designated by the U subscripts and a lower array with L subscripts. The contents of the upper array are considered to be the contents of the complete register, and the lower register is used here for shifting only, but it has other uses, as will be shown in Chapter 11.

In Figure 4.21 some lines have not been completed in order to avoid unnecessary cluttering of the drawing. Thus the reader should mentally

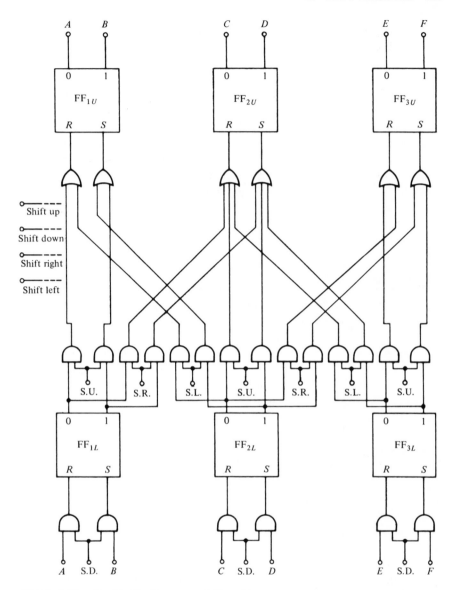

Figure 4.21 Double flip-flop array shift register.

provide some connections. For example, terminal A at the top of the figure is connected to terminal A at the bottom even though the connection line is not shown. The same is true for the corresponding terminals B through F. Also, the shift-up line at the left is understood to be connected to all terminals designated S.U. (shift up); the shift-down line is connected to all the S.D. (shift-down) terminals; the shift-right line is connected to all the S.R. (shift-right) terminals; and the shift-left line is connected to all the S.L. (shift-left) terminals.

The race problem is avoided in this register arrangement because at any one time only two flip-flops at most are connected in tandem. Consequently the contents of one flip-flop cannot transfer to more than one flip-flop. However, a disadvantage is that shifting requires two steps. For example, for a shift right, the shift-down line is first pulsed to trigger gates between flip-flops in the upper register and flip-flops in the lower register to cause the contents of each lower register flip-flop to become the same as those of the adjacent flip-flop in the upper register. Then, the shift-right line is pulsed to activate AND gates for the transfer of the contents of the lower register up and to the right into the upper register. The end result of the two shifting operations is a shift right in the upper register. That is, a shift right is achieved by a shift down followed by a shift up and to the right.

In the shift down step only one flip-flop in the lower register is connected in tandem with any one flip-flop in the upper register. Then, in the shift up and right, again no more than two flip-flops are in tandem. Thus there is no possibility of the race problem occurring.

Similarly, a shift left in the upper register is achieved by a pulse on the shift-down line followed by a pulse on the shift-left line. The contents of the upper register replace the contents of the lower register as a result of the first pulsing action. Then the second action causes the contents of the lower register to move up and left to replace the contents of the upper register.

We will consider one more type of shift register, which is the one we will use in Chapter 11 for producing timing pulses. This register, called a *ring counter*, is shown in Figure 4.22(a) with only three stages, for convenience. But, in general, there can be any number of stages. A ring counter is a shift register in which the output of the last flip-flop (here FF_3) is connected to the input of the first flip-flop (here FF_1). Thus the information contained in the circuit travels in a loop or a ring.

Normally, this information is a single 1 which can be inserted by applying a pulse on the S line of FF_1. The other flip-flops initially contain 0's. When the first clock pulse occurs after the 1 has been set into FF_1, the 1 shifts to FF_2, and FF_1 switches to 0 as a result of the 0 input from FF_3. When the next clock pulse occurs the 1 shifts to FF_3, and now this is the only flip-flop containing a 1. On the next clock pulse the 1 returns to FF_1 and the whole operation repeats.

Output terminals numbered ①, ②, and ③ are shown at the 1 side of the flip-flop outputs. When a 1 is being circulated, one and only one of these terminals is at the 1 state. The 1 switches from terminal ①, to terminal ②, to terminal ③, and back to terminal ①, and so on. The

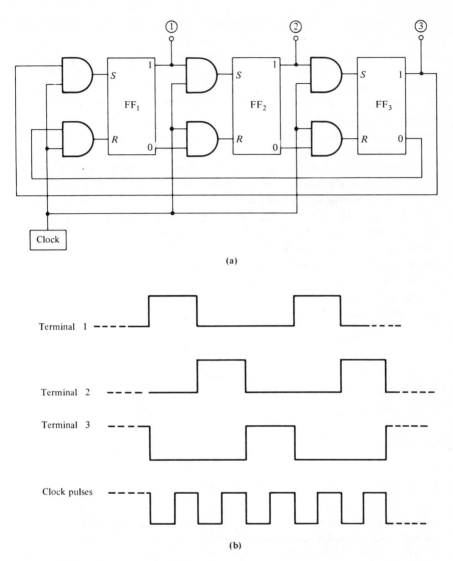

Figure 4.22 Ring counter and operation.

operation is similar to that of a distributor of a car and serves the same purpose, namely, timing, as is shown in Figure 4.22(b). The ring counter also counts the number of incoming pulses up to the number of flip-flops in the counter after which it starts counting over again. Thus this ring counter can count to three.

One last subject should be included in our discussion of shift registers and shifting: *single-line transfer*. The type of transfer that we have been employing in the illustrated shift registers is called *double-line transfer* (also called two-line jam transfer) because the two outputs from one flip-flop are connected to the two inputs of another flip-flop as, for example, shown in Figure 4.18. But transfer of signal from one flip-flop to another is possible with a single line and, strangely enough, the procedure is called *single-line transfer*. With a single line instead of two, there is a decrease by a factor of almost 2 in the number of gates needed in the transfer operations. However, this saving in hardware is at a cost of time, as will be shown.

A single-line transfer arrangement is shown in Figure 4.23 in which the contents of FF_1 are to be transferred to FF_2. In the transfer operation, FF_2 is first pulsed on the reset or R line by a reset pulse to ensure that FF_2 is in the 0 state. Then a transfer pulse is applied to the AND gate on the S line of FF_2. If FF_1 contains a 1, then FF_2 receives a pulse on its S line and is set to a 1. However, if FF_1 contains a 0, there is zero output (no pulse) from the AND gate and FF_2 does not switch—it remains in the 0 state. Consequently, after the pulsing the contents of FF_2 agree with those of FF_1 regardless of whether FF_1 contains a 1 or a 0.

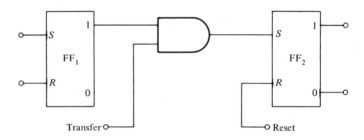

Figure 4.23   Single-line transfer with S-R flip-flops.

In single-line transfer, only one AND gate is required as compared to the two necessary for double-line transfer. Although this saving in a gate per pair of flip-flops is advantageous, there is a disadvantageous increase in the time required for switching. Switching does not occur until after two pulses are applied, while with double-line transfer switching occurs on one pulse.

The single-line transfer arrangement can be used whenever there is transfer between two registers, but not in a single-array register since the reset pulse clears the register and destroys its contents, unless the register contents are temporarily stored in delay components. But, if there are two arrays of flip-flops, as in Figure 4.21, one array can be cleared for receiving the contents of the other array. For a shift register of D flip-flops, as shown in Figure 4.24, single-line transfer is possible with one step because a D flip-flop has only one input and also because, in contrast to a T flip-flop which also has one input, the state of the flip-flop corresponds to the input.

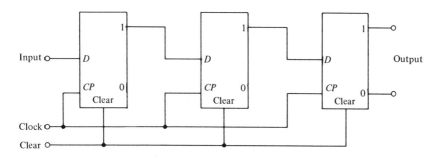

Figure 4.24 Single-line transfer with D flip-flops.

4.8 COUNTERS

We will now discuss another digital circuit that is somewhat related to the shift register: the *counter* circuit. It is similar to the shift register in that it is formed from flip-flops and the switching of a flip-flop may affect an adjacent flip-flop.

Ripple Counters

A simple *ripple counter* is shown in Figure 4.25(a) for counting pulses that may, for example, be clock pulses. The ripple feature of this counter, as we shall see, is that of the change of states of flip-flops, which changes start with FF_A on the left, then propagate to the next flip-flop (FF_B), and then to the third flip-flop (FF_C). In this operation the changes of state start from the left and occur one after another in a rippling fashion from the left to the right. This rippling is more pronounced if the counter has more than just the three flip-flops shown in Figure 4.25(a). Actually, a ripple counter can have any number of flip-flops.

Besides being a ripple counter this is also an *asynchronous counter*. That is, the internal actions do not occur synchronously nor do the final outputs (at least not all of them) appear simultaneously. This type of counter is in contrast to synchronous counters, which we will consider later, in which the flip-flops are clocked to change state simultaneously.

The counter of Figure 4.25(a) is a binary counter that counts the number of input pulses from 000 to 111 (0 to 7 decimal) and then

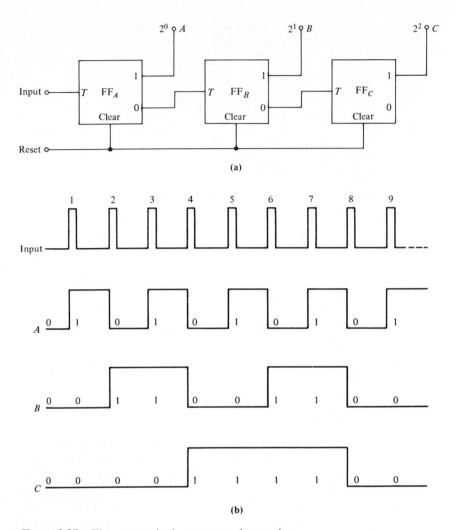

Figure 4.25 Three-stage ripple counter and operation.

starts over again at 000. It is a *modulus 8* or *MOD 8* counter, which means that it counts up to, but not including, eight and returns to zero and starts over again.

This term *modulus* is quite broad and refers to counters in general. It is a number that is one greater than the largest number (here seven) that can be contained or counted. For example, the modulus of odometers of most cars is 100,000. And for a conventional counter of n flip-flops the modulus is 2^n.

In the circuit of Figure 4.25, we will assume that the flip-flops trigger on positively going signals and that positive logic is used. Note that the signals are taken from the 1 lines but the triggering is from the 0 lines. Before the circuit can start counting, the flip-flops must be cleared or reset by a pulse on the reset line. After this pulse is applied, the three 0 lines are up in potential and the three 1 lines are down.

The circuit operation is shown in Figure 4.25(b) with the corresponding binary numbers inserted on the diagram for convenience. Whenever the input pulse goes positive, FF_A is triggered and changes state. And whenever the potential of the 1 side of FF_A goes negative, its 0 side potential goes positive and triggers FF_B. The potential on the 0 side of FF_B triggers FF_C in like fashion.

The operation should be apparent if we consider what occurs for only a few input pulses. When the first input pulse occurs, the positive leading edge triggers FF_A, causing it to switch from the 0 to the 1 state, which means that its 1 line goes up in potential and its 0 line goes down. This going down has no effect on FF_B because only positively going pulses trigger the flip-flops. The flip-flops now contain 001, or a one. When the next input pulse occurs, the leading edge again triggers FF_A and it changes from the 1 to the 0 state. In so doing, its 0 line goes from the prior down potential condition to the up condition and thus triggers FF_B to the 1 state. The flip-flops now contain 010 or two. The reader should continue with this operation on his own and check the operation diagram of Figure 4.25(b).

Note that the operation of FF_A produces an output pulse chain of half the frequency of the input pulses, and that the pulses from FF_B are at half the rate of FF_A, and so on. In other words, this is frequency-division action; in fact, one use of this counter is as a frequency divider.

The circuit of Figure 4.25 has some disadvantages, one of which is the ripple feature: the flip-flop on the right is not triggered until after the flip-flops on the left are triggered. This delay, which is caused by the trigger signals rippling through the flip-flops, can be objectionable.

For an illustration of this rippling, assume that a certain counter has eight flip-flops that at the time of interest contain 01111111. When the next input pulse occurs, the rightmost flip-flop does not receive a trigger pulse until the preceding seven flip-flops have changed state from a 1 to 0. Since the changes occur sequentially, the time required for this change may be considerable as regards time in a computer. Synchronous counters, which we will consider later, do not have this delay problem. But they usually require more components (gates).

Asynchronous Feedback Counters

A counter of the type shown in Figure 4.25 counts to some power of two, depending on the number of stages. A different count is obtainable with counters, called *feedback counters*, having feedback for advancing the count, that is, for skipping over numbers that would normally be counted.

In the design of a feedback counter, the number of flip-flops selected is the minimum number that without feedback provides a count exceeding the desired count. For example, for a count from four up to eight, three flip-flops suffice; for a counter of MOD 119, seven flip-flops are the least necessary.

Sometimes in these feedback counters the binary equivalent of the output is different from the number of pulses that have been applied. In other words, the output is coded. For example, a counter of MOD 5 may have successive outputs of 000, 001, 010, 011, and 111, with no binary equivalent of four, five, or six. In this case, a counter that was basically a MOD 8 counter was used and at a point in its counting, at what would have been 100, it was advanced by three. The output is ordinary binary except for four, which is coded (111). If this 111 output is objectionable, it can be eliminated by use of a decoder that can be designed by standard switching algebra techniques.

For an illustration of asynchronous feedback counters, we will design a MOD 5 counter from clocked J-K flip-flops that trigger on negatively going pulses. We will use positive logic. Three flip-flops are the minimum we need: one for 2^0, another for 2^1, and one for 2^2.

This being basically a MOD 8 counter it must be advanced by three sometime during the counting operation. One of the easiest ways of providing this skip is to clear the 2^2 flip-flop on the next clock pulse after the counter reaches 100, while inhibiting the 2^0 flip-flop from triggering, as has been implemented in the counter of Figure 4.26. As will be further explained later, one can easily design an asynchronous counter of MOD $2^{n-1} + 1$ with n flip-flops by using the same principle.

In the counter of Figure 4.26 flip-flops FF_C, FF_B, and FF_A produce outputs of 000, 001, 010, 011, 100, 000, and so on. To provide this output, FF_A and FF_B are connected to operate in the conventional ripple fashion, but the operation of FF_C is quite different.

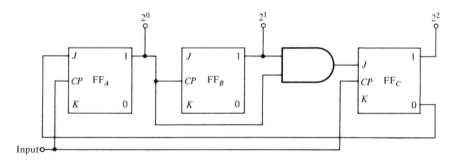

Figure 4.26   MOD 5 asynchronous counter.

FF$_C$ has pulses applied to its clock input but they have no effect until the output of the AND gate connected to the J input is 1, which condition first occurs when both FF$_B$ and FF$_A$ contain 1's. At this time the counter will be at 011. Before this time the 0 input on J prevents FF$_C$ from setting to 1 on the clock pulses. The next clock pulse after the counter goes to 011 will set FF$_C$ and will also cause FF$_B$ and FF$_A$ to reset. Then the counter contains 100. When the next clock pulse occurs, FF$_C$ resets to 0 because of the then 0 input of J and the 1 input of K. But FF$_A$ does not change state on this clock pulse since a 0, from the 0 line of FF$_C$ is fed back to the J input of FF$_A$. Thus FF$_A$ remains in the 0 state. And, of course, FF$_B$ does too because it is triggered by the output of FF$_A$. Consequently, with the resetting of FF$_C$ the counter goes from 100 to 000.

To extend this design to say a MOD 9, MOD 17, and MOD $2^{n-1} + 1$ counter, in general, one merely has to design a conventional ripple MOD 2^{n-1} counter with $n - 1$ of the flip-flops, and then for the nth flip-flop provide connections as was done for FF$_C$ in this MOD 5 counter. This is only one of several special techniques or tricks for designing asynchronous counters.

Example 4.1   Design an asynchronous MOD 10 counter using clocked J-K flip-flops that trigger on negatively going inputs. Use positive logic.

Solution   We can design this counter most simply by preceding the MOD 5 counter of Figure 4.26 with a flip flop as is shown in Figure 4.27. The first flip-flop, FF$_A$, is a two-counter that produces pulses at half the rate of the incoming pulses. Plainly, this two-counter in cascade with the five-counter produces a ten-counter or MOD 10 counter. This particular MOD 10 circuit is sometimes referred to as a biquinary counting circuit.   ∎

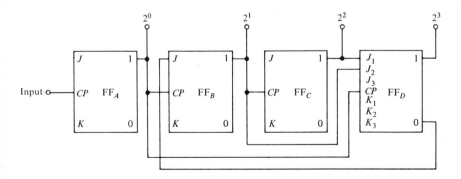

Figure 4.27   Example 4.1.

Synchronous Counters

We will now consider *synchronous counters* for which the design procedures are considerably more systematic than those we used for asynchronous counters. Synchronous counters, having all flip-flops triggered by clock pulses, can be designed such that the flip-flops are responsive only to the level outputs of the flip-flops. Because of this feature the design can be systematic.

In the systematic design of synchronous counters we determine the flip-flop inputs for producing each next state as a function of the present flip-flop outputs. In other words, we use the flip-flop outputs for a state to produce the dc input levels required to change the flip-flops to the next state when the next input pulse occurs.

For an illustration of this procedure, we will design a MOD 8 synchronous counter of T flip-flops for producing a conventional binary count. Of course three flip-flops are necessary. We will label them with letters as we have been doing.

The truth table for this counter is

C	B	A	T_C	T_B	T_A
0	0	0	0	0	1
0	0	1	0	1	1
0	1	0	0	0	1
0	1	1	1	1	1
1	0	0	0	0	1
1	0	1	0	1	1
1	1	0	0	0	1
1	1	1	1	1	1

In this truth table the input variables are the flip-flop outputs A, B, and C. The three output columns, which are headed by the flip-flop inputs T_A, T_B, T_C, have entries determinable from the present and next states of the flip-flops. To understand this, consider the state 000. Since the next state is 001, the state of FF_A, and only FF_A, must change when the next input pulse occurs. Thus, at this time the level input for T_A must be 1 to ensure that the next input pulse triggers FF_A. Similarly, the level inputs to FF_B and FF_C should be 0 because the states of these flip-flops should not change. Consequently, in the first row there is a 1 under T_A and 0's under T_B and T_C. For the next row of the truth table the counter state is 001 and the next state is 010. Since both FF_B and FF_A must change state at the next input pulse, 1's are entered under T_A and T_B, and so on for the other rows. If expressions for T_A, T_B, and T_C

are obtained from this truth table and simplified, the result is $T_A = 1$, $T_B = A$, and $T_C = AB$. The counter is shown in Figure 4.28.

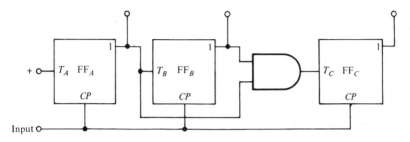

Figure 4.28 MOD 8 synchronous counter.

With the above procedure a counter can be designed to produce a binary output of any order and with any type flip-flop. Of course the gating circuits of a given synchronous counter depend upon the types of flip-flops used.

Example 4.2   Design a synchronous counter of gated J-K flip-flops to count in the following order: . . . 10, 11, 01, 10, 11, 01, . . . Use letters of the alphabet to identify the flip-flops, with FF_A on the left (the least significant digit flip-flop).

Solution   For this counter only two flip-flops are needed: FF_A and FF_B. The truth table is

B	A	J_A	K_A	J_B	K_B
0	0	Φ	Φ	Φ	Φ
0	1	Φ	1	1	Φ
1	0	1	Φ	Φ	0
1	1	Φ	0	Φ	1

The 00 row has don't-care outputs since the counter is never in the 00 state. When the counter is in the 01 state, the next state is 10. Thus on the next input clock pulse, FF_A must change from the 1 to the 0 state and FF_B from the 0 to the 1 state. Because these changes will occur if the K_A and J_B inputs are 1's, we enter 1's under the K_A and J_B columns. The other inputs J_A and K_B can be 1's or 0's and yet proper operation obtained, and so we enter don't cares in these columns. When the counter is in the 10 state, the next state is 11. Thus the state of FF_A must change from a 0 to a 1, which means that the J_A input must be 1 but it is of no consequence whether K_A is also 1. Accordingly, a 1 is entered in the J_A column and a don't care in the K_A column. Because FF_B must remain in the 1 state, K_B cannot be 1, but it would do no harm if J_B were. Therefore a 0 is entered under K_B and a don't care under J_B. Finally, if the counter is in the 11 state, the next state is 01. That is, on an input clock pulse, FF_A is to stay in the 1 state and FF_B to change from the 1 to the 0 state. Consequently, K_A cannot be 1 and J_A may, but need not be. Likewise, K_B must be 1 and it makes no difference if J_B is. Therefore we enter a don't care under J_A and J_B, a 0 under K_A, and a 1 under K_B.

From the maps for J_A, K_A, J_B, and K_B shown in Figure 4.29(a), the minimum expressions obviously are $J_A = 1$, $K_A = \bar{B}$, $J_B = 1$, and $K_B = A$. The resulting counter is shown in Figure 4.29(b).

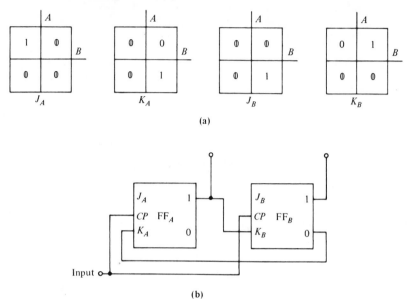

(a)

(b)

Figure 4.29 Example 4.2.

A word of caution about designing a counter in which, as in this example, not all possible states are used: *Make certain that if the counter gets into one of the unused states, say because of noise, it does not lock up* or, in other words, cycle around some or all of these unused states without progressing to a regular state. The input equations tell, of course, what states the counter goes to from these unused states; for example, in this example the counter goes to 11 from 00 on the next clock pulse. Since this counter will go to a regular state from the unused state 00, lock up is not a problem. If it had been, we would have had to change the input equations by making different assignments to the J and K entries corresponding to the unused state. ∎

In Example 4.2 the method for obtaining the J-K flip-flop inputs is the conventional one based directly on the J-K flip-flop operating characteristics. Another simpler, but more indirect, technique is due to R. E. Ruff.*

---

* "J-K Properties Ease Karnaugh Map Application," *EDN,* Vol. 15, No. 21, pp. 45–47, November 1, 1970.

The Ruff method is based on a comparison of two expressions for the next state (Q^+) of a J-K flip-flop. One expression is the right side of the difference equation $Q^+ = J\overline{Q} + \overline{K}Q$, which equation the reader can verify from his knowledge of the operation of a J-K flip-flop. The quantities on the right side of this equation are the J and K inputs and the state (Q) of the flip-flop immediately before the occurrence of a clock pulse. Another way of expressing Q^+ is, of course, in the form of an ESOP and that is the second expression used in the comparison.

For a comparison of these two expressions, we must separate the minterms of the ESOP into two groups, one of which has Q and the other $\overline{Q}$ as a factor. If these two literals are factored from the respective groups, the first group (with $\overline{Q}$ removed) must be, from a comparison with the right side of the difference equation, an expression for J and the other group (with Q removed) an expression for $\overline{K}$.

This conclusion is probably best understood from an example. Suppose that a counter has three J-K flip-flops—Q, A, and B—and assume that $Q^+ = \overline{A}BQ + A\overline{B}\overline{Q} + \overline{A}\overline{B}Q + AB\overline{Q} = (A\overline{B} + AB)\overline{Q} + (\overline{A}B + \overline{A}\overline{B})Q$. Then $J = A\overline{B} + AB = A$ and $\overline{K} = \overline{A}B + \overline{A}\overline{B} = \overline{A}$ (and $K = A$) as is evident from $Q^+ = J\overline{Q} + \overline{K}Q$.

To find J and K from Q^+ in general, one preferably makes a Karnaugh map of Q^+ and associates J with that part of the map covered by the $\overline{Q}$ variable and $\overline{K}$ with that part of the map covered by Q. The latter part of the map must, of course, be inverted to obtain the map for K. This method works regardless of the number of flip-flops in the counter, but it applies only to J-K flip-flops.

For a concrete example, consider the problem of Example 4.2. From the problem specification the maps for A^+ and B^+ (the next states of flip-flops A and B) are

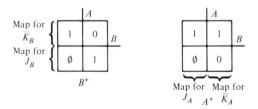

The map entries are easy to find. If, for example, the counter is at 10, then $B^+ = 1$ and $A^+ = 1$ from the specified operation of the counter that it is to go to 11 from 10. Thus the entries for the 10 squares in both maps are 1's. For the next count $B = 1$ and $A = 1$, and the counter should go to 01 upon the next clock pulse. Consequently, in the 11 square for the B^+ map the entry is 0 and for this square in the A^+ map the entry is 1. When the counter is at 01 it goes to 10 on the next clock pulse, and thus the next state for the B flip-flop is 1 and for the A flip-flop is 0. These are entered in the 01 squares of both maps. Finally, the counter is never in the 00 state which means that the next-state entries are don't cares for the 00 squares.

From these maps, obviously $J_B = 1$, $K_B = A$, $J_A = 1$, and $K_A = \bar{B}$, which are the same results obtained by the longer procedure of Example 4.2.

Note that with the Ruff technique, the maps for the J's and K's are of one less variable than for the conventional method. Also, since one does not have to be concerned about how the J-K flip-flop functions to obtain the maps, there is less chance for error in forming the maps. And, the maps are easier and quicker to obtain.

4.9   MATRIX DECODERS

In digital applications there is frequent need for a multiple-input circuit having several output lines, only one of which is energized at a time, depending upon the input energization. This circuit, called a *decoder*, is often connected to a register as is shown in Figure 4.30. Each register flip-flop provides two input lines to the decoder; that

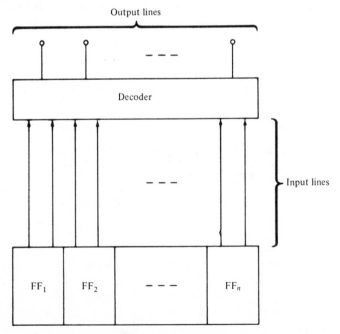

Figure 4.30   Decoder arrangement.

is, both the 0 and 1 lines are inputs to the decoder. This decoder can have as many as 2^n output lines, n being the number of flip-flops in the register.

As mentioned, only one decoder output line is energized at a time, the line depending on the contents of the register. For example, if the register contains all 0's, the arrangement may be such that the line energized is the leftmost decoder output line. If the register contains all 1's, the line energized may be the rightmost one.

We will study three decoders: the *rectangular matrix*, the *tree matrix*, and the *dual-tree matrix*.

Rectangular Matrix

A *rectangular matrix* is shown in Figure 4.31 connected to a register of three flip-flops designated as FF_A, FF_B, and FF_C. Only a three-flip-flop register and a $2^3 = 8$ output decoder are shown for convenience.

The rectangular matrix comprises AND gates connected to form all possible AND's of the register contents.

In general, for n variables the matrix has 2^n AND gates of n inputs each and thus a total of $n \cdot 2^n$ inputs. The number of inputs is important since it is usually directly related to the hardware requirements. For example, if the AND gates are diode down-followers (positive logic assumed), the number of diodes needed equals the number of inputs. A diode implementation for the matrix of Figure 4.31 is shown in Figure 4.32.

The rectangular matrix is a fast operating decoder because it is a one-level circuit. However, for any practical size decoder this matrix requires far more components than the other two decoders we will study.

Example 4.3   A decoder for providing decimal signals is required having ten light bulbs labeled 0, 1, 2, 3, 4, 5, 6, 7, 8, and 9. Only one bulb is to be lit at a time and that one corresponding to the decimal equivalent of the contents of a four flip-flop register. Design the decoder.

Solution   For convenience we will designate the four flip-flops as A, B, C, D, corresponding, respectively, to the 2^3, 2^2, 2^1, and 2^0 flip-flops. We need ten AND gates, the outputs of which operate the ten lights. The first AND gate, which has inputs of $\bar{A}$, $\bar{B}$, $\bar{C}$, and $\bar{D}$, has its output connected to the 0 light. The second AND gate, with inputs of $\bar{A}$, $\bar{B}$, $\bar{C}$, and D, has its output connected to the 1 light. And so on, until the last AND gate, which has inputs of A, $\bar{B}$, $\bar{C}$, and D and which energizes the 9 light. The circuit is shown in Figure 4.33. ∎

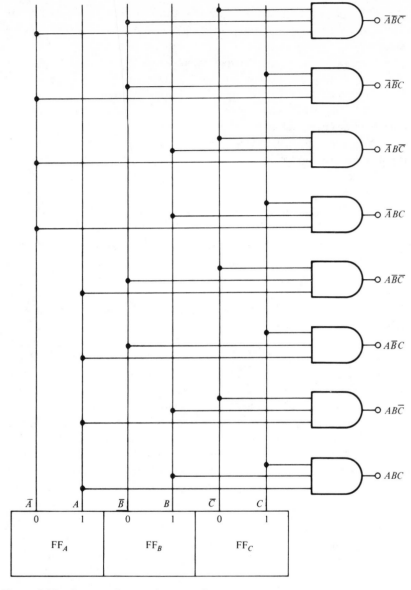

Figure 4.31   Rectangular matrix and register.

Tree Matrix

A *tree matrix decoder* is formed from AND gates, all of which have two inputs, regardless of the number of variables. It is a multilevel matrix, the number of levels of which is one less than the number of variables.

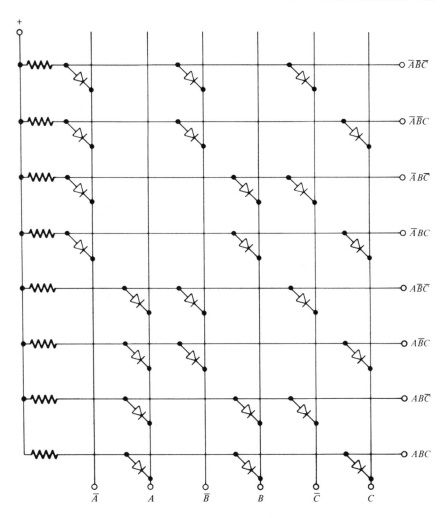

Figure 4.32 Diode rectangular matrix.

A tree matrix for three variables is shown in Figure 4.34 from which generalizations can be made for a tree matrix of n variables. At each stage a variable and its complement are introduced to all the signals from the preceding stage. Thus there are 2^2 AND gates at the second stage (the A signal and its complement are at the first stage), 2^3 AND gates at the third stage, and 2^n AND gates at the nth stage. Since each AND gate has two inputs, the total number of inputs in an n stage tree decoder is

$$2 \cdot 2^2 + 2 \cdot 2^3 + \ldots + 2 \cdot 2^n = \sum_{j=2}^{n} 2^{j+1}$$

which equals $2^{n+2} - 8$, as the reader can verify.

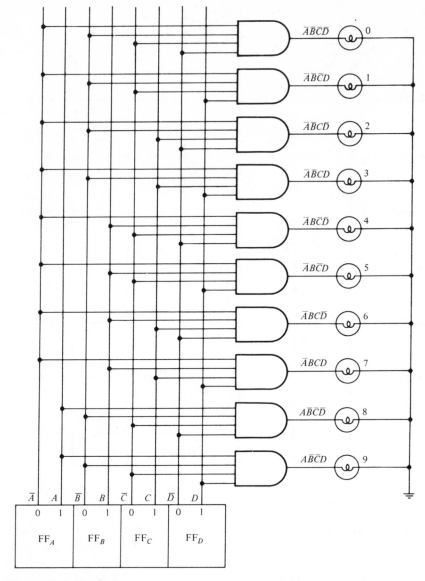

Figure 4.33 Example 4.3.

We should compare the number of inputs for the tree and rectangular matrix decoders to determine which requires more components. For three variables, the rectangular matrix has $3 \cdot 2^3 = 24$ inputs as does the tree matrix $(2^{3+2} - 8 = 24)$. For four variables the rectangular matrix has $4 \cdot 2^4 = 64$ inputs, but the tree matrix has only $2^{4+2} - 8 = 56$ inputs.

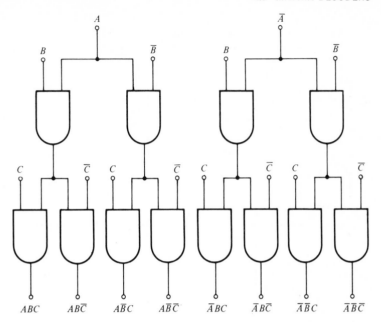

Figure 4.34 Tree matrix.

For eight variables the rectangular matrix has $8 \cdot 2^s = 2048$ inputs. However, the tree matrix has only $2^{s+2} - 8 = 1016$ inputs.

These calculations show that except for a few variables, the tree matrix requires considerably less hardware than the rectangular matrix. But of course, the tree matrix has more levels. Although the hardware advantages of the tree matrix are considerable, they are surpassed by those of the dual-tree matrix which we will study next.

Dual-Tree Matrix

The *dual-tree matrix* is rather difficult to describe in words and perhaps even more difficult to understand. Thus, in place of a description, several of these decoders will be shown and then a method will be presented for obtaining a dual-tree matrix for any number of variables.

The two-variable, dual-tree matrix is identical to the two-variable rectangular matrix and thus will not be shown. The three- and four-variable, dual-tree matrix decoders are shown in Figures 4.35(a) and (b), respectively. Two-input AND gates should be shown at each intersection of the lines in Figure 4.35(b), as in (a), but only a few representative ones have been shown for simplicity.

We will now consider the design procedure if the number of variables

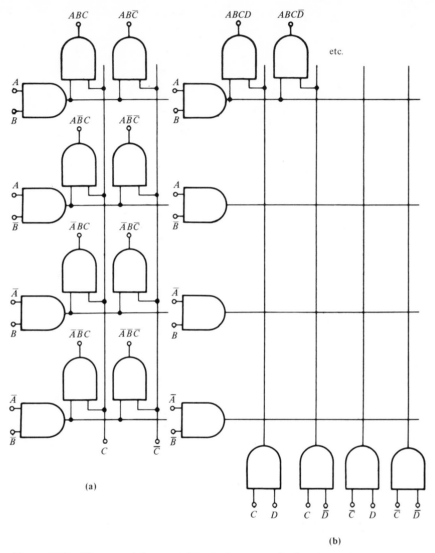

Figure 4.35   Three- and four-variable, dual-tree matrix decoders.

is more than four. This number is divided into two integers as nearly equal as possible, and then these integers are approximately halved into smaller integers, and so on, until all the results are either two, three, or four. These last integers designate two-, three-, or four-input matrices as described above. Each of the other integers represents a matrix arrangement of an intersection of lines with a two-input AND gate at each intersection.

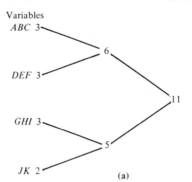

Variables

(a)

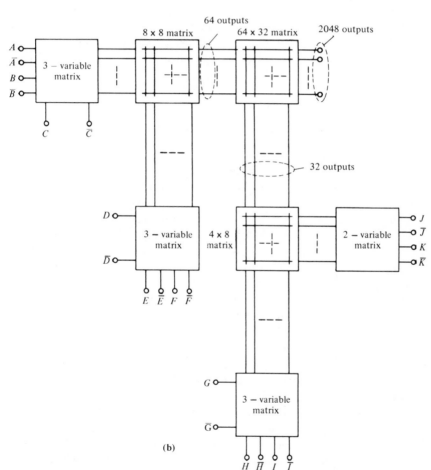

(b)

Figure 4.36 Eleven-variable, dual-tree matrix decoder realization.

This procedure is perhaps best understood from an example. If there are eleven variables, the division process is as shown in Figure 4.36(a). After the division, each number is replaced by a corresponding matrix as shown in Figure 4.36(b).

In a dual-tree matrix, the number of AND gates equals the sum of the AND gates for the various two-, three-, and four-variable matrix arrangements plus the number of intersections for the larger matrix arrangements. For the above eleven-variable case, the number of AND gates is $12 + 12 + 12 + 4 + 64 + 32 + 2048 = 2184$ for a total of $2 \cdot 2184 = 4368$ inputs. In comparison, the rectangular matrix has $11 \cdot 2^{11} = 22{,}528$ inputs and the tree matrix has $2^{11+2} - 8 = 8184$ inputs.

The hardware advantages of the dual-tree matrix are apparent from this illustration. Also, it should be noted that for any significant number of variables the dual-tree matrix decoder has fewer levels than the corresponding tree matrix decoder.

4.10   DIGITAL MULTIPLEXERS

Digital multiplexers can generate any logic function. They have other uses as well, but we will consider them only for function generation.

Multiplexers, being constructed of integrated circuits (medium-scale integration), have advantages of high speed, high reliability, less noise, lower power consumption, less space, and so on, all as compared to a design with discrete integrated circuit gates. In addition, the design procedures are simpler and less time-consuming.

A multiplexer, as shown in Figure 4.37(a), has input lines (the I's), select lines (the S's), and a single output line F. Some multiplexers have a second output line for the complement of the output.

The operation is simple. Signals on the select lines control the connection of the input lines to the output line. If both select inputs are 0's, $F = I_0$. If $S_0 = 1$ and $S_1 = 0$, $F = I_1$. If $S_0 = 0$ and $S_1 = 1$, $F = I_2$. Finally, if both select inputs are 1, $F = I_3$. In terms of switching algebra the operation is $F = \overline{S}_0\overline{S}_1I_0 + S_0\overline{S}_1I_1 + \overline{S}_0S_1I_2 + S_0S_1I_3$.

One possible gate implementation for this multiplexer is shown in Figure 4.37(b), but remember that multiplexers are purchased as single components. In general a person does not purchase discrete gates and then construct multiplexers.

Some multiplexers in a single package have eight input lines, two control lines, and two output lines. But these are just the equivalent of two of the four-input multiplexers contained in a single package with corresponding select lines interconnected.

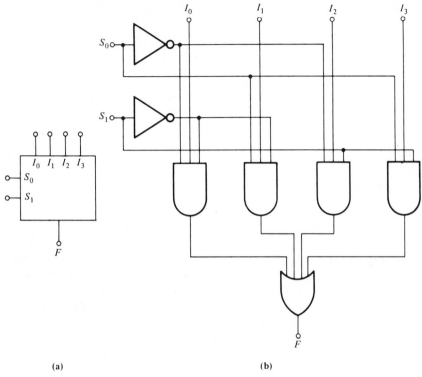

(a)   (b)

Figure 4.37   Four-input, three-variable digital multiplexer.

In general, in designing with multiplexers one needs the complement of only one of the variables. This one variable, its complement, 1's, and 0's are the I inputs. The other variables are the S inputs. Thus for a function of the variables A, B, and C, and with $\bar{A}$ available, B and C are applied to the two select lines and A, $\bar{A}$, 0, and 1 to the input lines, the particular inputs depending on the function to be generated.

For a determination of the inputs, the function of interest can be inserted on a Karnaugh map and then each input line associated with two squares of the map. The associations depend on the selection properties of the two variables connected to the S inputs. With B energizing select line S_0 and C select line S_1, the associations are as shown in Figure 4.38(a). These associations are independent of the particular function entered on the map, which function in this case is $F = A\bar{B} + \bar{A}BC$. This is the function to be generated.

Since a select input of $B = 0$, $C = 0$ selects line I_0, the area associated with I_0 covers the two squares corresponding to $B = 0$, $C = 0$. And because select line input $B = 1$, $C = 0$ connects line I_1 to the output,

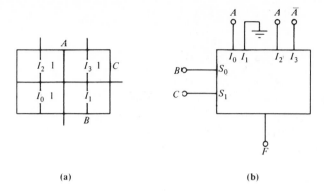

(a)   (b)

Figure 4.38   Multiplexer realization of $F = A\overline{B} + \overline{A}BC$.

I_1 is in the area of the two squares corresponding to $B = 1$ and $C = 0$, and so on.

At any one time F equals either A, $\overline{A}$, 1, or 0, depending on the B and C values. From this fact one can determine the I inputs from the Karnaugh map. For two 1's in the two squares of an I area, F equals 1 when the B and C inputs select this input. Thus a voltage corresponding to 1 should be applied to this input. Similarly, if an area contains two 0's, a 0 voltage should be applied to the input corresponding to this area. If an I area contains a 1 and a 0 and the 1 falls in the square assigned to A (then the 0 will be in the square assigned to A), the output should agree with A when the S inputs select this input line. Consequently, A should be applied to this input I line. Conversely, if the 1 falls in the area assigned to $\overline{A}$, $\overline{A}$ should be applied to this input I line.

From these rules the inputs for the function $F = A\overline{B} + \overline{A}BC$ are $I_0 = A, I_1 = 0, I_2 = A$, and $I_3 = \overline{A}$, which, assuming ground corresponds to 0, has the realization shown in Figure 4.38(b).

As shown in Figure 4.39, some multiplexers have three select lines for selecting any one of eight input lines. From the prior discussion the operation of the select inputs is as follows: For $S_0 = S_1 = S_2 = 0$, $F = I_0$; for $S_0 = 1$ and $S_1 = S_2 = 0$, $F = I_1$; for $S_0 = 0$, $S_1 = 1$, $S_2 = 0$, $F = I_2$, and so on. This multiplexer can generate any function of four variables.

Example 4.4   Using the multiplexer of Figure 4.39, generate $F = A\overline{B} + C\overline{D} + ACD + \overline{B}\overline{C}$. The variable A and its complement are available in addition to the variables B, C, and D.

Solution   With A and $\overline{A}$ available, these and 0 and 1 are the I inputs. B, C, and D should be applied to the S inputs. The map for the given function along with the areas assigned to the I's are shown in Figure 4.40(a) for B applied

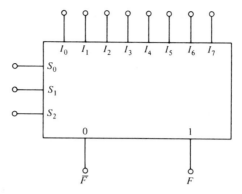

Figure 4.39 Eight-input, four-variable digital multiplexer.

to S_0, C to S_1, and D to S_2. As done here the two center columns (or rows) should be for the variable having the available complement. This way the two squares for each I area are contiguous. From the Karnaugh map obviously $I_0 = I_2 = I_3 = I_4 = 1$, $I_1 = I_5 = 0$, and $I_6 = I_7 = A$, which results in the realization of Figure 4.40(b). ■

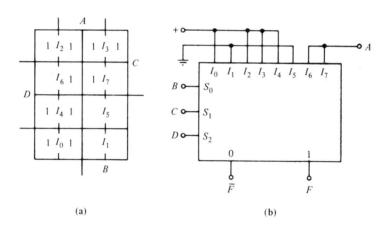

Figure 4.40 Example 4.4.

The function in Example 4.4 could have been generated without A, but with $\bar{A}$ instead. This results from the particular specified function and also from the use of a multiplexer having an output for the complement of F. The function could have been obtained by going after the complement of F and then by obtaining F from the complement output. That is, a 1 could have been applied to inputs I_1 and I_5; 0 to inputs I_0, I_2, I_3, and I_4; and $\bar{A}$ to inputs I_6 and I_7. Depending on the function, this approach can sometimes be used to generate a function without having the complement of any variable.

A function of more than four variables but less than eight can be generated with two levels of multiplexers. At the first level, functions of three and four variables are generated with a separate multiplexer generating each function. Then these functions provide inputs at the second level to a single multiplexer that has select lines at which as many as three variables can be introduced.

For an illustration, consider the six-variable function

$$Y = DF + E\overline{F}(\overline{A}B + \overline{A}\,\overline{B}\overline{C} + ABC) + \overline{D}\overline{E}\overline{F}(\overline{A}\overline{B} + C)$$
$$+ \ \overline{D}\overline{E}F(A + \overline{C}) + DE\overline{F}(AB + \overline{C}) + D\overline{E}F(\overline{A}B + \overline{C})$$

and assume that the functions of A, B, and C will be generated at the first level and then D, E, and F introduced at the second level.

For the first step the terms should be arranged so that only one term, at most, has a common D, E, and F multiplier. For this function only two terms have such a multiplier problem. Two terms have $DE\overline{F}$ multipliers. One of these terms is apparent but the other is "hidden" in the second

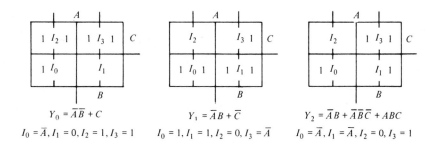

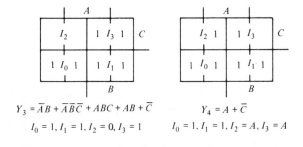

(a)

Figure 4.41a   Multiplexer realization of $Y = DF + E\overline{F}(\overline{A}B + \overline{A}\overline{B}\overline{C} + ABC) + \overline{D}\overline{E}\overline{F}(\overline{A}\overline{B} + C) + \overline{D}\overline{E}F(A + \overline{C}) + DE\overline{F}(AB + \overline{C}) + D\overline{E}F(\overline{A}B + \overline{C})$.

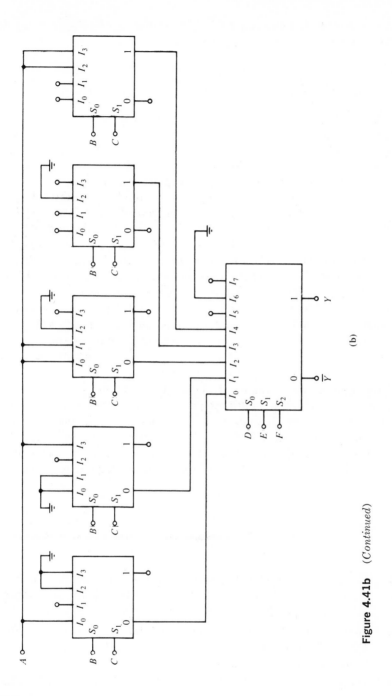

Figure 4.41b (Continued)

term, which has the multiplier $E\bar{F}$. Converting this $E\bar{F}$ to the equivalent $DE\bar{F} + \bar{D}E\bar{F}$ and rearranging terms give

$$Y = \bar{D}\bar{E}\bar{F}(\bar{A}\bar{B} + C) + D\bar{E}\bar{F}(\bar{A}B + \bar{C}) + \bar{D}E\bar{F}(\bar{A}B + \bar{A}\bar{B}C + ABC)$$
$$+ DE\bar{F}(\bar{A}B + \bar{A}\bar{B}C + ABC + AB + \bar{C}) + \bar{D}\bar{E}F(A + \bar{C}) + DF$$

At the first level five four-input multiplexers are needed for generating the five functions of A, B, and C. For a choice of A for the I inputs and B and C for the select lines S_0 and S_1, respectively, the Karnaugh maps and resulting I inputs are shown in Figure 4.41(a).

For the second-level multiplexer, Karnaugh maps are not needed to obtain the I inputs because these inputs are obvious. With D, E, and F applied to select lines S_0, S_1, and S_2, respectively, and with $Y = DF + \bar{D}\bar{E}\bar{F}Y_0 + D\bar{E}\bar{F}Y_1 + \bar{D}E\bar{F}Y_2 + DE\bar{F}Y_3 + \bar{D}\bar{E}FY_4$, obviously Y_0, the output of the leftmost multiplexer in the first level, connects to I_0, Y_1 to I_1, and so on. This leaves only the DF term to obtain. Since it is the equivalent of $D\bar{E}F + DEF$, it is necessary to apply a 1 at I_5 and I_7. Also, because the function does not have a $\bar{D}EF$ multiplier, a 0 should be applied at I_6. The result shown in Figure 4.41(b) is for a no-input connection corresponding to a 1 and a ground corresponding to a 0.

Note that by the use of the complement outputs of the first three multiplexers in the first level, the effect of $\bar{A}$ is obtained without actually applying $\bar{A}$. But this is not always possible.

From these few examples it should be apparent that any function can be generated with multiplexers. Also, the design steps are simple and do not involve minimization. The time saved in design is often more important than the few dollars worth of hardware saved by optimizing the design. Besides, with the increased use of these multiplexers, they should soon become high-volume, low-priced items.

PROBLEMS ━━━━━━━━━━━━━━━━━━━

4.1 Design a two-level half adder using the logic diagram of Figure 4.2(b). Use NPN transistors, DCTL, and negative logic. Complements of the variables are available.

4.2 Design a two-level half adder using the logic diagram of Figure 4.2(b). Use the TRL circuit of Figure 3.20 and positive logic. Complements are available.

4.3 Design a two-level half subtractor using the logic diagram of Figure 4.4(b). Use NPN transistors, DCTL, and negative logic. Complements of the variables are available.

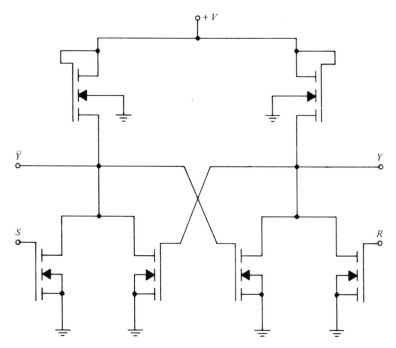

Figure 4.42 Problem 4.5.

4.4 Design a two-level half subtractor using the logic diagram of Figure 4.4(b). Use *NPN* transistors, DCTL, and positive logic. Complements of the variables are available.

4.5 Using the NOR circuit of Figure 3.38(a), make a diagram of an S-R flip-flop comprising two interconnected NOR gates.

Answer See Figure 4.42.

4.6 Using the NOR circuit of Figure 3.38(b), make a diagram of an S-R flip-flop comprising two interconnected NOR gates.

4.7 Show a logic diagram of a clocked S-R flip-flop similar to the diagram of Figure 4.10(b) but with NOR instead of NAND gates. What should be the triggering clock signal? What input condition produces indeterminate operation?

4.8 Show a logic diagram of a T flip-flop similar to that of Figure 4.12(b) but with NOR instead of NAND gates. What should be the triggering clock signal?

4.9 Show a logic diagram of a T flip-flop similar to that of Figure 4.12(b) but with provision for input clock pulses.

4.10 What connections should be removed in the J-K master-slave flip-flop of Figure 4.14(b) to make it an S-R master-slave flip-flop?

4.11   What external connections can be made to the flip-flop of Figure 4.14(b) to make it function as an unclocked S-R flip-flop?

4.12   What external connections can be made to the flip-flop of Figure 4.14(b) to make it function like a T flip-flop with the CP input serving as the T input? Is there another way of doing this? Assume that potentials must be connected to unused inputs.

4.13   Show a three-stage shift register constructed from clocked J-K flip-flops.

4.14   Design a decoder for the MOD 3 counter of Figure 4.29(b). The output of the decoder is to be a true binary representation of the count.

4.15   A counter that counts down instead of up is called a *down-counter*. Design a ripple down-counter of T flip-flops that trigger on positively going pulses. Assume positive logic. The counter is to count down from 111 to 000.

4.16   Design a MOD 9 asynchronous counter with J-K flip-flops that trigger on negatively going pulses. Use positive logic.

Answer   See Figure 4.43.

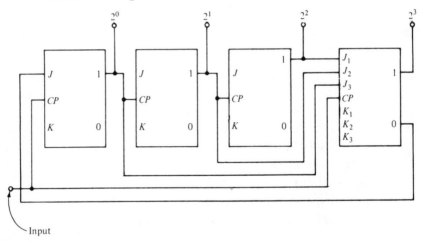

Figure 4.43   Problem 4.16.

4.17   Repeat Problem 4.16 for a MOD 18 counter.

4.18   Repeat Problem 4.16 for a MOD 17 counter.

4.19   Repeat Problem 4.16 for a MOD 34 counter.

4.20   Design a synchronous counter constructed of clocked S-R flip-flops that produce a count of . . . 110, 011, 000, 111, 100, 110, 011 . . . .

Answer   See Figure 4.44.

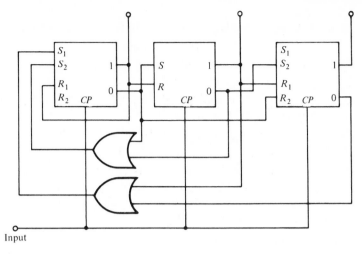

Figure 4.44   Problem 4.20.

4.21   Repeat Problem 4.20 for J-K flip-flops.

4.22   Repeat Problem 4.20 for D flip-flops.

4.23   Repeat Problem 4.20 for T flip-flops.

4.24   Design a synchronous counter constructed of clocked S-R flip-flops that produce a count of . . . 0000, 0010, 0100, 0110, 1000, 1010, 1100, 1110, 0000, 0010 . . . .

4.25   Repeat Problem 4.24 for J-K flip-flops.

4.26   Repeat Problem 4.24 for D flip-flops.

4.27   Repeat Problem 4.24 for T flip-flops.

4.28   A matrix arrangement for 13 variables is needed. Determine the number of inputs required for a
(a) rectangular matrix
(b) tree matrix
(c) dual-tree matrix
Answers   (a) 106,496;   (b) 32,760;   (c) 16,888

4.29   Repeat Problem 4.28 for 15 variables.

4.30   Repeat Problem 4.28 for 19 variables.

4.31   Make a diagram of a diode rectangular matrix for four variables: A, B, C, and D.

4.32   Using AND gates, make a diagram of a tree matrix for four variables: A, B, C, and D.

4.33   Using AND gates, make a diagram of a dual-tree matrix for five variables: A, B, C, D, and E.

4.34   Repeat Problem 4.33 for six variables: A, B, C, D, E, and F.

4.35 Make a diagram similar to Figure 4.36 for twelve variables.

4.36 Repeat Problem 4.35 for fifteen variables.

4.37 Realize $F = AB\overline{C} + BC + \overline{A}\overline{B}C$ and don't-care $A\overline{B}\overline{C}$ with a multiplexer like the one in Figure 4.37(a). Assume that A, $\overline{A}$, B, and C are the only literals available and that 0 is ground and 1 is an open circuit input. Apply B at S_0 and C at S_1.

Answer $I_0 = A$ or ground, $I_1 = A$, $I_2 = \overline{A}$, and $I_3 = 1$

4.38 Realize $F = D\overline{E} + \overline{A}BCD + AB\overline{D}E + \overline{A}\overline{B}\overline{C}E + (\overline{B}C + B\overline{C})\overline{D}E + ABC\overline{D}E + (\overline{B}C + B\overline{C} + \overline{A}C)E$ with two levels of multiplexers, each of which is like the one in Figure 4.37(a). Assume that A, $\overline{A}$, B, C, D, and E are the only literals available. Get functions of A, B, and C at the first level.

4.39 Using multiplexers of the type shown in Figure 4.37(a), implement $F = (AB\overline{C} + \overline{A}B\overline{C} + \overline{A}\overline{B}C + BC)\overline{D}\overline{E} + AB\overline{D}E + (\overline{A}B\overline{C} + \overline{A}B\overline{C} + A\overline{B}C + ABC)DE$. Use B on S_0 and C on S_1 in the first level and D on S_0 and E on S_1 in the second level. Open circuit is a 1 and ground a 0. Of course, A and $\overline{A}$ are available in addition to B, C, D, and E.

Answer   See Figure 4.45.

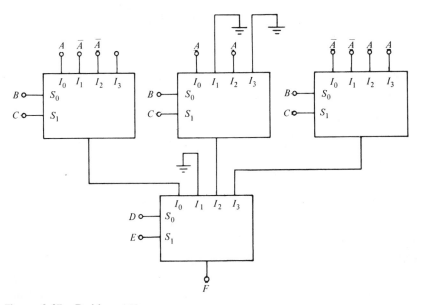

Figure 4.45   Problem 4.39.

5

Codes

In most digital computers numbers are in conventional binary form, with the possible exception of negative numbers which are often in complement form. In these computers, called *binary computers,* computations are performed in the binary number system. In another class of computers, called *decimal computers,* the computations are performed in the decimal number system. Of course, the numbers are represented by 0's and 1's as in the binary machines, but the representations are *binary-coded decimal numbers (BCD)*. That is, each decimal digit is represented by a group of bits. In this chapter we will study some of the codes that are used for decimal digits.

Even if the 0's and 1's represent binary numbers, a code may be used to permit the detection and perhaps even the correction of some errors caused by the digital system in the processing, transmission, or storage of these binary quantities. We will study some codes designed for this purpose.

In many digital applications nonbinary quantities, such as letters of the alphabet, parentheses, question marks, and so on, must also be represented by strings of binary digits. And again this representation is accomplished by codes, one of which we will briefly consider.

Codes can be classified in various ways, but for present purposes we need consider only a few classifications. Numbers can be coded in *weighted codes* in which each bit position is assigned a numerical value that in the codes we will consider is a decimal value that is usually positive but that can be negative. As an example, suppose that each decimal digit is represented by a set of four bits, the first digit of which corresponds to a decimal 5, the second bit to 2, and the last two bits to 1's. Then the decimal number 4 is coded 0111 and 8 is 1101, as one possibility. The positional values of a weighted code permit ready determination of the corresponding decimal values.

Another class of codes is *error detecting*. Errors may occur in coded information as a result of faulty circuit operation, faulty material as in the coating of magnetic tapes or in broken magnetic cores, or noise such as atmospheric disturbances in communication. It is advantageous to know when errors have occurred. Then perhaps the message can be retransmitted, or the information recomputed, or in some cases the errors can be corrected. At any rate if the operator knows of the presence of errors, he has some choices that he would not otherwise have.

Some codes are *error detecting* and *correcting*. Of course, correction implies detection since errors must be detected in order to be corrected. We would like to be able to detect and to correct all errors, but, as a practical matter, this is not possible. As we study these codes we will see that error detection and correction are obtained at a cost of added bits.

In the following discussions of specific codes we will use the term *codeword*, which is just a string of bits representing a coded number or nonnumeric quantity. For a computer, several of these codewords may be combined into a *computer word*, which, as is described in the next chapter, is a group of bits processed as a unit by the computer.

5.1   BINARY-CODED DECIMAL

Weighted Codes

The representation of the ten decimal digits requires at least four bits and ten of the sixteen different combinations of these four bits. Of the many possible codes—over a million—one of the most popular is the *8421 code* (sometimes called *NBCD*—normal binary-coded decimal) illustrated in Table 5.1. This is a weighted code in which the first bit corresponds to an 8, the next bit to a 4, the third bit to a 2, and the last bit to a 1.

Table 5.1   8421 Code

zero	0000	five	0101
one	0001	six	0110
two	0010	seven	0111
three	0011	eight	1000
four	0100	nine	1001

Example 5.1 What is the representation of the decimal number 7963 in the 8421 code?

Solution In the coding of this number each digit is replaced by the corresponding four bits from Table 5.1. The result is

7	9	6	3	decimal number
↓	↓	↓	↓	
0111	1001	0110	0011	8421 code

or 0111100101100011. ∎

In a binary-coded decimal system the digits can often be coded in more than one way. For example, in the weighted 7421 code, the number seven can be represented by 1000 or by 0111. Also, it is possible, although perhaps seldom desirable, to have a weighted code in which some of the weights are negative, such as in the $84(-2)(-1)$ weighted code of Table 5.2.

Table 5.2 $84(-2)(-1)$ Code

zero	0000	five	1011
one	0111	six	1010
two	0110	seven	1001
three	0101	eight	1000
four	0100	nine	1111

Excess-Three Code

Another popular code for decimal numbers is the *excess-three code* which can be obtained from the 8421 code by adding three to each coded digit.

Example 5.2   Code the decimal number 94623 in the excess-three code.

Solution   Each digit of the decimal number is represented by four bits that are three greater than in the 8421 code. Thus the solution is

9	4	6	2	3	decimal
↓	↓	↓	↓	↓	
1001	0100	0110	0010	0011	8421 code
↓	↓	↓	↓	↓	
1100	0111	1001	0101	0110	excess-three

or 11000111100101010110.   ∎

If binary-coded decimal arithmetic is to be performed, the excess-three code is advantageous because it is *self-complementing*.* That is, if the 1's complement of each of the codewords is taken, the result is the code for the 9's complement of the original decimal number. For example, the 1's complement of each of the characters of Example 5.2 is

0011	1000	0110	1010	1001	1's complement
↓	↓	↓	↓	↓	
0	5	3	7	6	decimal number

The decimal number 05376 is the 9's complement of 94623.

Another advantage of the excess-three code is the representation of zero, which, having 1's, can be distinguished from the no information case.

Gray Code

Gray codes are *nonweighted* codes having codewords that differ in only one bit position for successive numbers. For example, in the most common Gray code, 0110 is the code for four and 0111 is the code for five. Only the last bit differs in these coded characters. The most common version of the Gray code is shown in Table 5.3. As mentioned, adjacent entries in this table differ in only one bit.

This is called a *reflected* code because the bits in any column, except the left column, form a symmetric pattern, a mirror image, about the dotted line. For example, in the right column there is a 0 immediately above the line and another one immediately below. These are followed by two 1's above and below, and so on.

In Table 5.3 the codes for numbers greater than nine are *not* formed by using the codes for the first ten decimal digits. That is, the code

---

* For an understanding of complement arithmetic, see the Appendix.

Table 5.3 Gray Code

zero	0000
one	0001
two	0011
three	0010
four	0110
five	0111
six	0101
seven	0100
	....
eight	1100
nine	1101
ten	1111
eleven	1110
twelve	1010
thirteen	1011
fourteen	1001
fifteen	1000

for fifteen, for example, is 1000 and is not the code of one, 0001, placed beside the code of five, 0111. As a consequence, more than the shown four bits are needed for numbers larger than fifteen.

The Gray code is used extensively in mechanical analog-to-digital converters because the change in only one bit between successive numbers prevents the generation of false signals, even temporarily. This fact is not apparent now but will be when we consider the material in Chapter 12, which contains descriptions of these converters.

It is easy to convert a binary number into this common Gray code. A leading zero is placed before the most significant bit of the binary number. Then adjacent bits are EXCLUSIVE OR'd together or, in other words, are added modulo two.

Example 5.3   Determine the Gray code for 76.

Solution   First, we convert the decimal number 76 to binary or to 1001100 and insert a leading zero. Then we find the modulo two sum of adjacent bits.

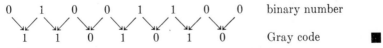

The determining of a number corresponding to a Gray codeword is slightly more difficult. In one procedure a Gray codeword is considered from left to right. The first 1 is written and repeated for every bit in the word until the next 1 occurs. Then 0's are written until the next 1 occurs. Then 1's are written, and so on. That is, after the first 1,

1's in the word indicate a *change* in what is to be written. This procedure is best understood from an example.

Example 5.4   Determine the binary number corresponding to the Gray codeword 1101010.

Solution   The first 1 is recorded. The next 1 indicates a change to a 0. The number so far is 10. The next digit in the word is a 0 and so 0 is repeated in the binary number. The result at this point is 100. The next 1 in the word designates a change: 1001. Then, another 1 is added since the following digit in the Gray codeword is a 0. At this point the partial binary number is 10011. The final 1 in the codeword indicates a change to a 0: 100110. And the final 0 indicates no change. The resulting binary number is 1001100. In decimal this is 76, the Gray code for which was obtained in Example 5.3.   ■

Example 5.5   Determine the binary number corresponding to the Gray codeword 1110001100. Then, for a check, convert the binary number into its Gray code representation.

Solution   The conversion is

1	1	1	0	0	0	1	1	0	0	Gray codeword
1	0	1	1	1	1	0	1	1	1	binary number

Now, as a check, the binary number is converted into the Gray code.

0	1	0	1	1	1	1	0	1	1	1
	1	1	1	0	0	0	1	1	0	0

■

5.2   ERROR-DETECTING AND ERROR-CORRECTING CODES

As has been mentioned it is advantageous to be able to correct errors that may occur in codewords. The numeric codes we have discussed so far have little error detection and *no* error correction capability. If errors occur in a codeword and by chance the resulting word does not agree with a valid codeword, then an error can be detected. For example, for an 8421 code, the occurrence of any of the words 1010, 1011, 1100, 1101, 1110, or 1111 indicates an error. However, most errors result in valid codewords. In this regard, the ten valid codewords each have a possibility of four single errors for a total of forty possible single errors. If these are investigated, only ten will be found that produce invalid codewords. Thus the probability of detecting a single error, assuming all single errors are equally likely, is only 25 percent. Apparently, bits need to be added to provide significant error detection and correction capability.

In error detection and correction the concept of *distance* is important. The distance between two codewords is the number of bits that must be changed in one word to make it the same as the other word. For example, to find the distance between codewords 10010 and 11100 we make the comparison

Since the second, third, and fourth bits must be changed in one word to make it the same as the other word, the distance between these two words is three.

Although the distance can differ between the various codewords of a code, it is convenient to speak of the distance of a code. The distance of a code is the minimum distance obtained by comparing all the codewords. For example, the distance of the code comprising the four codewords (111, 110, 101, and 011) is one; this is the distance between 111 and any of the other codewords. There being no smaller distance, this is the distance of the code even though there are larger distances between some of the codewords; for example, the distance between 110 and 101 is two.

The concept of distance has geometrical significance as can be seen from the cubes of Figure 5.1. The eight vertices of the cube in Figure 5.1(a) correspond to codewords arranged in the order (xyz), and the edges of the cube correspond to distances between codewords. Because the cube of Figure 5.1(a) has single edges between some pairs of the codewords, the code (000, 001, 010, 011, 100, 101, 110, 111) has a distance of one.

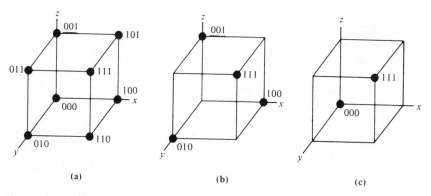

Figure 5.1 Code distance.

The code corresponding to the marked vertices in Figure 5.1(b) comprises the code (001, 010, 100, 111) which has at least two edges between any two of the vertices corresponding to the codewords. Thus this is a distance two code.

The code represented in Figure 5.1(c) is (000, 111). Because there are three edges in the shortest distance between these two codewords, this code is of distance three.

This distance feature is important in error detection. For the detection of d and *all* fewer errors, the distance of a code must be *greater* than d. If the distance is just d, then d errors can result in a codeword being changed into another valid codeword. For example, if the codeword 111 of the code illustrated in Figure 5.1(b) has two errors and becomes, say, 010, it changes into another valid codeword, and thus no error can be detected. But if in this distance two code, there is a single error in any codeword no other valid codeword can result from this error since all the other codewords are at least distance two away.

As regards error correction, c errors can be corrected if the code distance is *greater* than $2c$. Then an error codeword of c or fewer errors is closer to just one valid codeword and will be corrected to this codeword. As an illustration, if in the use of the code of Figure 5.1(c) the word 011 occurs, and if it resulted from a single error, then the codeword in which the error arose is 111 since this codeword is closer than the other codeword. This is a distance three code which permits correction of single errors. Of course if a double error occurs, "correction" is to the wrong codeword. But presumably the environment in which the code is used is such that there is little probability of more than a single error. For this distance three example, c was one and $2c$ was less than the distance. However, if the same word 011 appears with the distance two code of Figure 5.1(b) correction is not possible because more than one codeword, and in fact three (010, 111, and 001), are the same distance from this word and there is no information for ascertaining to which of the three codewords correction should be made. In this case the distance is just $2c$ but the distance must be *greater* than $2c$ for correction.

Sometimes error-detection and -correction capabilities are combined into a code. Of course with correction there is always detection, but detection is possible without correction. The number of errors that can be corrected can never be greater than the number of errors detected, that is, $d \geq c$, because an error cannot be corrected unless it is first detected. The combination of c errors can be corrected and d errors detected if the code distance is at least $c + d + 1$. The relation between c, d, and code distance, for distances up to and including five, is presented in Table 5.4.

It should be apparent from Table 5.4 that there is a trade-off between

Table 5.4   Code Arrangements

Distance	c	d
1	0	0
2	0	1
3	0	2
	1	1
4	0	3
	1	2
5	0	4
	1	3
	2	2

detection and correction—the greater the correction the less the detection and vice versa. For example, in the case of a distance four code, single, double, and triple errors can be detected if there is no correction. However, if single errors are to be corrected then triple errors cannot be detected for they would appear as single errors, correction of which would then be made to the wrong codeword. If a double error is detected, no correction will be made because several valid codewords will be within distance two of the error word and there is no way of determining to which word correction should be made.

The foregoing statement that triple errors cannot be detected requires some explanation. Actually, triple errors will be detected, but they will be interpreted as single errors and correction will be made to the wrong codeword. Thus this statement really means that a distance four single-error correcting code should not be used in an environment in which there is much probability of triple errors, for then some "corrections" will be to the wrong codewords. However, if errors are not corrected, then the code can be used to detect triple errors as well as single and double errors; that is, the code can function properly in an environment in which triple errors are likely.

Single-error Detecting Codes

One simple way to obtain single-error detection capability is to add a single bit to each codeword, the bit depending on the number of 1's in the information part of the codeword. This scheme produces a *parity code*.

There are two types of parity: *even parity* and *odd parity*. In an even-parity code the added parity bit is selected to make each codeword have an even number of 1's, including the parity bit. And, of course, for an odd-parity code the number of 1's is odd. An even-parity code is shown in Table 5.5 for a basic 4311 code. An odd-parity example for a basic 8421 code is shown in Table 5.6.

Table 5.5	An Even-Parity Code

	4	3	1	1	P
zero	0	0	0	0	0
one	0	0	0	1	1
two	0	0	1	1	0
three	0	1	0	0	1
four	1	0	0	0	1
five	0	1	1	1	1
six	1	0	1	1	1
seven	1	1	0	0	0
eight	1	1	0	1	1
nine	1	1	1	1	0

Table 5.6	An Odd-Parity Code

	P	8	4	2	1
zero	1	0	0	0	0
one	0	0	0	0	1
two	0	0	0	1	0
three	1	0	0	1	1
four	0	0	1	0	0
five	1	0	1	0	1
six	1	0	1	1	0
seven	0	0	1	1	1
eight	0	1	0	0	0
nine	1	1	0	0	1

As has been mentioned, some 1 bits are usually desired in a codeword in order that a no information case, or the loss of all 1 bits by operational failures, will not cause the error word to be detected as a zero for some codes (for example, the 4311 or 8421 codes). Thus odd parity is preferable since with it every valid codeword has at least one 1.

A double error, or any *even* number of errors, in a parity code may result in a valid codeword and thus be undetected. But one or any *odd* number of errors will always produce an invalid word since an odd number of errors produces an even number of 1's for an originally odd-parity word or an odd number of 1's for an originally even-parity word.

Although any odd number of errors can always be detected, a parity code is referred to as a single-error detecting code. The error-detecting feature of a code, or error-correcting, refers to one less than the smallest number of errors that will not always be detected, or corrected, even though a certain number of larger errors may always be detected or corrected. In parity codes some double errors cannot be detected, and thus these codes are referred to as single-error detecting codes although triple errors can always be detected.

Another single-error detecting numeric code utilizing five bits is the *2-out-of-5 code*. Actually, there are ten different 2-out-of-5 codes, one of which is shown in Table 5.7. This code, in which each codeword has two 1 bits, is easy to remember since it is a weighted code except for zero. Thus only zero need be remembered, and the other words can be determined from the weighting and the knowledge that each codeword has two and only two 1 bits.

Another single-error detecting code that has been used is the *bi-quinary* or *2-out-of-7 code*, one of which is shown in Table 5.8. This code can be pictured as having two groups of bits, one under 50 and the other under 43210. There are two 1's in each codeword, one in each

Table 5.7   A 2-out-of-5 Code

	0	7	4	2	1
zero	0	1	1	0	0
one	1	0	0	0	1
two	1	0	0	1	0
three	0	0	0	1	1
four	1	0	1	0	0
five	0	0	1	0	1
six	0	0	1	1	0
seven	1	1	0	0	0
eight	0	1	0	0	1
nine	0	1	0	1	0

Table 5.8   A Biquinary Code

	5	0	4	3	2	1	0
zero	0	1	0	0	0	0	1
one	0	1	0	0	0	1	0
two	0	1	0	0	1	0	0
three	0	1	0	1	0	0	0
four	0	1	1	0	0	0	0
five	1	0	0	0	0	0	1
six	1	0	0	0	0	1	0
seven	1	0	0	0	1	0	0
eight	1	0	0	1	0	0	0
nine	1	0	1	0	0	0	0

of the two groups, arranged such that the code is weighted. This is not an efficient code, where efficiency is defined as the ratio of information bits to the total number of bits, but it is economical to implement in terms of circuits.

Single-Error Correcting Codes

Sometimes codewords are transmitted or stored (for example, on magnetic tape) in parallel fashion such that the bits can be envisioned as being arranged in blocks. Then a parity check can be associated with each row and column (that is, *cross parity*) as in Table 5.9 for a code that is basically an 8421 code with odd parity (even parity can also be used).

Table 5.9   Cross Parity

	8	4	2	1	P_r
two	0	0	1	0	0
seven	0	1	1	1	0
nine	1	0	0	1	1
five	0	1	0	1	1
P_c	0	1	1	0	1

There are row parity bits P_r and column parity bits P_c. If a single error occurs in one codeword, then a parity check fails in the column and also in the row at the intersection of which the error occurred. Circuits can correct the error simply by changing the bit at this intersection. Suppose in the code of Table 5.9 an error occurs in the codeword seven causing it to become 01010. The result of this is an even number of 1's in row two and in column three. Thus the bit at the intersection of this column and row, which is the error bit, will be changed by circuits.

Although cross parity can best be envisioned by an array as in Table 5.9, there is no reason why the bits cannot be transmitted or stored serially and yet the cross-parity feature applied.

The *Hamming code* is another single-error correcting code. It is of distance three and has parity bits, each of which checks on a different set of bits in a manner that permits error correction.

The Hamming codeword, which can be of any length greater than two bits, is of the form

$$p_1 p_2 i_3 p_4 i_5 i_6 i_7 p_8 i_9 \ldots i_{15} p_{16} i_{17} \ldots i_{31} p_{32} i_{33} \ldots$$

wherein the p's are parity bits and the i's information bits. The subscript of a p or i indicates bit position in the codeword.

From this general codeword, plainly the positions of the p's are in bit positions 1, 2, 4, 8, 16, 32 . . . 2^n, which are all powers of two. As will become apparent in the following discussion of the determination of the values of the p bits, this placement of parity bits is such that they are independent of one another. Thus they can be evaluated simultaneously.

The information bits can be in any code. Either even or odd parity can be used.

Parity bit p_1 provides a parity check on itself, plus all information bits i whose bit positions, if expressed in binary, contain a 1 at the right in the 2^0 position—3 (1$\underline{1}$), 5 (10$\underline{1}$), 7 (11$\underline{1}$), 9 (100$\underline{1}$) . . . . This is, of course, every other bit.

Parity bit p_2 provides a parity check on itself and all information bits, the positions of which if expressed in binary have a 1 in the 2^1 position—3 ($\underline{1}$1), 6 (1$\underline{1}$0), 7 (1$\underline{1}$1), 10 (10$\underline{1}$0) . . . . An easy way to remember these positions is to start with position 2 and count it and the next one (3). Then skip two bits and take two more (6,7), skip two and take two more (10,11), and so on.

The next parity bit p_4 checks on itself and all information bits, the positions of which if expressed in binary have a 1 in the 2^2 position. These are positions 4, 5, 6, 7 and 12, 13, 14, 15 and 20, 21, 22, 23, and so on. A mnemonic aid here is to take four positions starting with position four, then skip four, take four, and so on.

The information bits that p_8, p_{16}, and so on provide parity checks for are similarly determined.

The number of parity bits needed depends, of course, on the number of information bits. For four information bits, three parity bits are needed. For five to eleven information bits, four parity bits are needed. In general, the parity bits must be sufficient in number to indicate the position of an error in either the information or the parity bits. Also, the parity bits must be capable of indicating a no error condition. Consequently, if n is the number of information bits and p the number of parity bits, p must be great enough to satisfy $2^p \geq p + n + 1$.

In the correction of a possible error in a codeword, a check is made of the positions corresponding to the parity bits p_1, p_2, and so on. Then a binary number is formed relating the positions checked. If parity holds for the positions covered by the p_1 bit, a 0 is entered into the 2^0 position of this binary number; otherwise a 1 is inserted. If the parity holds for the positions covered by the p_2 bit, a 0 is entered into the 2^1 position of this binary number. Otherwise, a 1 is entered. This process is continued. When it is finished, the binary number gives the position of the bit that is in error.

We will now consider an example in which the information bits are in the 8421 code and the number 7 is to be coded. Then the basic form of the coded word is $p_1 \, p_2 \, 0 \, p_4 \, 1 \, 1 \, 1$. If odd parity is used, p_1 should be 1 since the information bits in positions having a 1 in the 2^0 position (3, 5, and 7) contain two 1's, an even number of 1's. Similarly, the 2^1 position parity bit p_2 must be a 1 for there to be an odd number of 1's in positions 2, 3, 6, and 7. Finally, p_4 is made a 0 because positions 5, 6, and 7 contain three 1's. The resulting coded word is **1100111**.

Now assume that as a result of an error the word becomes **1000111**; that is, there is an error in position two. A parity check is made of positions 1, 3, 5, and 7. Since there are an odd number of 1's, a 0 is recorded. Then positions 2, 3, 6, and 7 are checked. They have an even number of 1's. Thus the parity check fails and a 1 is recorded. The result so far is 10. Finally, positions 4, 5, 6, and 7 are checked. They contain an odd number of 1's and so a zero is recorded. The resulting binary number 010 indicates that bit two is in error. Note that errors in parity bits are detected and corrected as well as errors in information bits.

5.3   DATA REPRESENTATION

Up to this point we have considered only codes for numbers. Of course in some applications there is need for representations of letters of the alphabet and printing symbols, such as commas, periods, or equal signs. No single code is universally accepted for general data representation and the codes vary somewhat with the computers.

In Table 5.10 is a list of a few of the codewords of the *extended binary-coded decimal interchange code* (*EBCDIC*) used in the IBM System/360 computers. With eight bits per codeword, this code can represent 256 different characters. Among the characters coded are upper and lower case letters of the alphabet; decimal digits; special characters

Table 5.10   EBCDIC Code

Data	Codeword	Data	Codeword
@	01111100	a	10000001
#	01111011	b	10000010
$	01011011	e	10000101
%	01101100	k	10010010
(	01001101	l	10010011
)	01011101	m	10010100
—	01101101	A	11000001
+	01001110	B	11000010
=	01111110	E	11000101
''	01111111	2	11110010
'	01111101	7	11110111
?	01101111	9	11111001

such as parentheses, brackets, and plus and minus signs; and control characters as, for example, space, backspace, and horizontal tab.

Example 5.6   Assume a 32-bit computer word and the use of the code of Table 5.10 and show the representation for the word *Bake*.

Solution   From Table 5.10 the codewords for upper case B and lower case a, k, and e are selected; then these codewords are combined into a single computer word. The result is

$$11000010100000011001001010000101 \qquad \blacksquare$$

PROBLEMS

5.1   Code the decimal numbers 954, 672, 1394, and 67,942 in the following codes:

(a) 8421   (b) 84(−2)(−1)

(c) the excess-three code

Answers   (a) 100101010100, 011001110010, 0001001110010100, 01100111100101000010;   (b) 111110110100, 101010010110, 0111010111110100, 10101001111101000110;   (c) 110010000111, 100110100101, 0100011011000111, 10011010110001110101

5.2   Repeat Problem 5.1 for the decimal numbers 876, 4594, and 43,298.

5.3   Determine the Gray codewords for the decimal numbers

(a) 23   (b) 426   (c) 2134

Answers   (a) 11100;   (b) 101111111;   (c) 110001111101

5.4   Repeat Problem 5.3 for
   (a) 45   (b) 562   (c) 6752

5.5   Determine the binary numbers corresponding to the Gray codewords
   (a) 1101011   (b) 1011101101   (c) 1101110110101
   Answers   (a) 1001101;   (b) 1101001001;   (c) 1001011011001

5.6   Repeat Problem 5.5 for
   (a) 101101   (b) 110110111   (c) 10001110101001

5.7   Determine the distance between the following pairs of codewords:
   (a) 101101 and 111111
   (b) 1001100111 and 1111100000
   (c) 1100010100101 and 1011110001101

5.8   Repeat Problem 5.7 for
   (a) 1000101 and 0000000
   (b) 110101110011 and 000000111111
   (c) 11010111001011001 and 10110010110111000

5.9   Determine the distances of the following codes:
   (a) {000, 101, 011}
   (b) {0000, 1101, 0101, 1011}
   (c) {00000, 01011, 11111, 11100, 10010}
   Answers   (a) two;   (b) one;   (c) two

5.10 Repeat Problem 5.9 for
   (a) {101, 011, 101, 000}
   (b) {1011, 0100, 0011}
   (c) {11001, 00100, 10010, 10111}

5.11 If s is the distance of a code and d the number of errors detected
   determine the number of errors that can be corrected if
   (a) $s = 6, d = 4$ (d) $s = 7, d = 4$
   (b) $s = 6, d = 3$ (e) $s = 7, d = 5$
   (c) $s = 6, d = 5$ (f) $s = 9, d = 6$
   Answers   (a) single;   (b) double;   (c) none;   (d) double;
             (e) single;   (f) double

5.12 Repeat Problem 5.11 for
   (a) $s = 7, d = 3$ (d) $s = 8, d = 4$
   (b) $s = 7, d = 6$ (e) $s = 8, d = 6$
   (c) $s = 8, d = 5$ (f) $s = 9, d = 4$

5.13 Using even parity and conventional binary representation, determine the Hamming codewords for the decimal numbers
   (a) 15   (b) 45   (c) 223
   Answers   (a) 1111111;   (b) 0010011101;   (c) 101110101111

5.14 Using odd parity and the 8421 code, determine the Hamming codewords for the decimal numbers
   (a) 18   (b) 53   (c) 426

5.15 Each of the following Hamming codewords has a single error. Correct the error and determine the decimal equivalent of the corrected information bits if the information bits are in conventional binary representation. Assume odd parity.

(a) 010111001   (b) 11101110110   (c) 0111110000000

Answers   (a) 011111001, 29;   (b) 11101111110, 126;
              (c) 0111110010000, 464

5.16 Repeat Problem 5.15 for
(a) 1010000100
(b) 011110011011
(c) 01100010010100100

5.17 Assuming a 32-bit computer word and the code of Table 5.10, code
(a) Bale   (b) lake   (c) 2 + 7 =

Answers   (a) 11000010100000011001001110000101
            (b) 10010011100000011001001010000101
            (c) 11110010010011101111011101111110

5.18 Repeat Problem 5.17 for
(a) meal   (b) BEAm   (c) (2%)

6

Introduction
To Digital
Computers

6.1 DIGITAL COMPUTER FEATURES

Almost all digital computers are primarily *electronic* systems since electrical components best satisfy computer requirements of high operating speeds, along with reliability, compactness, lightness, low power consumption, and low cost per component. Indeed, digital computers are so often thought of as electronic systems that the acronym *EDP* (*electronic data processor*) is often used as a synonym for digital computer.

In digital computers the physical quantities operated on or processed represent numerical digits. A digital computer "understands" numbers and only numbers. These numbers may, of course, correspond to nonnumerical quantities, such as letters of the alphabet, but everything operated on or processed by a digital computer must be coded into numbers.

These numbers are seldom represented by the same physical quantities throughout all parts of a digital computer. In a part called the *memory*, magnetic flux is most often used, and in another part, the *arithmetic unit,* voltages are most often used. Since different physical quantities can be and are used for the digits, we will often prefer to imagine digital computers as operating directly on numbers rather than on physical quantities, even though the latter is actually what occurs.

Digital computers perform relatively simple operations. For example, the only arithmetic operation performed may be addition, and only the addition of two numbers at a time.

Although digital computer operations are not sophisticated, they are performed at great speeds. It is this tremendous speed of operation that has resulted in the great popularity and use of the digital computer. Digital computers can solve problems in hours that a person would require a lifetime to do. And the digital computer, if it has been debugged and is free of faulty components, will make considerably fewer errors.

Even when error free, digital computers, in normal use, do not produce exceptionally accurate results. Much, much, less expensive desk calculators are often as accurate. A digital computer costing several million dollars may begin arithmetic operations with numbers that if expressed in decimal are accurate to seven or eight decimal places. After the operations, the results may be accurate to only four or five decimal places. In contrast, a desk calculator, costing only hundreds, may start with numbers accurate to 12 decimal places and then provide results several places less accurate. Digital computers are often operated in a special mode, called double precision, in which the accuracy is increased. However, this increased accuracy is obtained at the expense of speed.

The statements above should not be taken to mean that desk calculators are inherently more accurate than digital computers. They are not. But they can be more accurate if initially given more significant digits to work with. In arithmetic operations both digital computers and desk calculators produce progressively significant errors. But these errors result from the nature of the arithmetic operations and not from the particular implementation used to obtain these operations.

The digital computer should be distinguished from another type of computer—the *analog computer.* A digital computer operates on *discrete* quantities and an analog computer on *continuous* quantities. If, for example, voltages represent numbers in both a digital computer and an analog computer, the digital computer has only two acceptable voltage levels for representing the digits. These levels, for example, may be 0 and 2 V, with some permissible deviations from these values. But in the analog computer, acceptable voltages exist over a complete range that often is −100 to 100 V.

Another distinction between digital and analog computers, in normal use, is the manner in which problems are solved. A digital computer solves problems in a step-by-step manner, in serial fashion, in which the first step is completed before the second step is begun. In an analog computer the steps, if they can be called steps, are performed essentially simultaneously; that is, problem-solving is executed in a parallel manner. Also, in a digital computer many of the same components are involved in the execution of different steps, but in an analog computer each "step" may be executed or performed by a different component.

In analog computers integration is performed directly, but in digital computers integration must be performed indirectly by numerical approximation methods in which addition is used. An analog computer can usually integrate much faster than a digital computer.

Since an analog computer can perform some operations better than a digital computer, and a digital computer can perform other operations better, some computing systems, called *hybrid computers*, have a digital computer connected to operate with an analog computer. In such a system, each computer performs the operations it does better.

Digital computers should also be distinguished from *desk calculators*. Although a conventional desk calculator and a digital computer are both digital machines, they have distinguishing characteristics. A digital computer has a memory unit, not present in a desk calculator, in which numbers and a set of instructions, called a program, can be stored or "remembered." By means of these instructions, operations are performed on the numbers or data without intervention by an operator, who needs only to start the process. However, in a desk calculator there is no memory and thus no stored instructions. Instead, for each addition or other arithmetic operation, the operator must intervene by inserting numbers and then initiating execution of the pertinent arithmetic operation. Thus, in the operation of a desk calculator the human element is required for each arithmetic step, while with a digital computer, human intervention is required only once and then only to initiate execution of the program. Because of the greater human intervention, more time is required to use a desk calculator than a digital computer if there are many operations.

The foregoing distinctions between digital computers and desk calculators have their greatest validity for mechanical calculators. Some electronic machines now being marketed as calculators are much more difficult and perhaps impossible to distinguish from digital computers. Some of these calculators have memories for storing data numbers and some can even store instructions. Since in the operation of these machines, human intervention is not required for each step, perhaps they should be referred to as digital computers instead of electronic calculators.

6.2 BASIC DIGITAL COMPUTER COMPONENTS

The basic components or units of a digital computer are shown in Figure 6.1. The *input-output (I/O) components* are the man-computer interface or, in other words, the equipment with which an operator communicates with the computer. The input components may take many forms: card readers, typewriter terminals, paper tape readers, magnetic tape units, and so on. With this equipment, an operator can insert data and instructions into the computer by means of cards, paper tape, magnetic tape, keys, and even buttons. The output components may include printers, card punches, paper tape punches, typewriter terminals, and magnetic tape units. Although the results may be in various forms, they are usually printed.

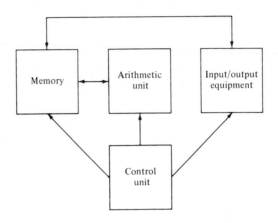

Figure 6.1   Basic computer components.

As has been mentioned, the *memory* stores numbers. Some of these numbers are data and also intermediate results, while others correspond to the instructions that are being executed. Because the computer "understands" numbers only, everything, including instructions, data, and letters of the alphabet, must be coded into numbers. All of these numbers can be stored in the memory from which they can be removed for reference or to be operated upon.

The *arithmetic unit* is the part of the computer in which the operations on the numbers are performed. As has been mentioned, the basic arithmetic operation is usually addition, but this really includes subtraction since complement arithmetic can be used to obtain subtraction from addition. In some computers the basic mathematical operation is subtraction, and then addition is performed by complementation. By either of these operations both multiplication and division can be obtained, as will be explained. Other operations are also performed upon numbers in the arithmetic unit. More will be said about this matter in other chapters.

The *control unit* supervises the operations. It initiates the various operations such as that of input and output, and it also controls the arithmetic operations. It decodes the instructions to determine if they are add, subtract, multiply, or some other operation, and it ensures that an operation is not initiated until the preceding one is completed. At the beginning of operation it causes the input program to be read from the I/O equipment and written into or stored in the memory. After this storage is completed, the control unit initiates execution of the program. Then after the program has been executed, the control unit causes the results to be read from the memory and channeled to the proper output equipment.

These four units are basic to digital computers in general. However, they are seldom distinct since the arithmetic and control units often have a considerable overlapping of components. Also, the four units can differ considerably in different computers. In the following chapters we will discuss each unit and show some details of each.

6.3   CLASSIFICATION OF DIGITAL COMPUTERS

Digital computers can be classified as either *special purpose* or *general purpose*. Some digital computers are designed for a very special purpose with all their components dedicated and designed for the accomplishment of one specific function. Some of these computers are used for missile guidance, others for fire control applications in airplanes, and so on.

A computer designed for one specific purpose can usually be made cheaper, smaller, and lighter than a computer that must perform different functions. Also, these special-purpose computers often have wired-in programs and thus need input equipment only for data. Usually the output equipment is not extensive; in fact, the output is often just control signals. In general, unless extensively modified, these computers cannot be used for purposes other than those for which they were specifically designed.

A general-purpose computer is designed to do many different types of jobs. The large computers that are so popular are general-purpose computers. These computers are typically large, fast, and expensive, and often have considerable input-output equipment of different types.

Digital computers are also classed as either *parallel* or *serial*. This classification is based on the transmission of bits and also operations on the bits, as in addition. In a parallel computer the bits to be transmitted, say between registers, are transmitted simultaneously. Also, in an addition operation, all the bits of the augend are simultaneously added to those of the addend. In contrast, in a serial computer the bits are transmitted one at a time, one after the other. And, in an addition operation only one bit of the augend is added, at a time, to one bit of the addend. Obviously, a parallel computer is much faster in operation than a serial computer. However, the increase in speed is at a cost of components; that is, there is a trade-off between speed and number of components. Thus the faster parallel computer has, in general, many more components than the slower serial computer.

Computers are classified in other ways. Some computers are designed especially for solving scientific problems. These problems usually have relatively little data but require a great number of operations on these data. In these computers the arithmetic unit must perform rapidly in order that the large number of calculations can be accomplished in a reasonable time.

Some computers are designed for controlling manufacturing processes. Such a computer might, for example, monitor temperature sensors positioned in furnaces. In response to signals from these sensors and in accordance with a stored program, the computer could initiate signals for controlling fuel flow into the furnaces. Typically, these computers have many inputs and outputs. Converters are often associated with these computers for converting the input signals, which are generally in analog form, into digital form. Also, there may be converters at the outputs for converting the output digital signals into analog signals. These computers need not be nearly as fast in operation as the scientific problem-solving computers.

Some computers perform a few relatively simple operations over and over again on an enormous amount of data. Examples of such use are bookkeeping in banks and compiling grade reports in large universities. This function is called *data processing*. The instruction repertoire for a data-processing computer need not be as extensive as that for a scientific computer. Also, these computers are often smaller than the computers used for problem-solving. Although a high-speed printer is often associated with these computers, the input-output equipment is usually less extensive and the memory not as large as in a scientific computer.

One of the most recent developments in computer systems is *time-sharing*. A time-sharing system has many sets of input-output equipment, called terminals, remotely situated from the processing unit of the computer. There is no limit to the distance that the terminals can be located from the processing unit. The only requirement is for communication channels, often just telephone lines, between the terminals and the processing unit. These terminals, which may be as small as typewriters, can be located in homes or in offices, sometimes thousands of miles from the processing unit. The number of terminals varies with the computers but usually ranges from thirty to over a hundred. Operators at the terminals use the computer apparently independently of one another and simultaneously, or apparently simultaneously. In some installations an operator may have some time delays, often just fractions of a minute, in the insertion and execution of his program. In these delays an operator is waiting his turn to use the computer.

Time-sharing has many advantages. Almost the full capability of a very large computer can be brought into an office or even into a home, and at relatively little cost since the total cost is shared by all terminal users. Also, a person can insert a program into a computer at a terminal, which is usually located conveniently, and can obtain results almost instantly. This use is in distinction to conventional use in which a person must travel to a computing center or location where a computer is located, hand his program to the operator, and then wait hours for the results. At present, time-sharing systems are increasing at a great rate, and companies are making terminal facilities available to subscribers throughout the country.

Another computer that is becoming increasingly important and popular is the *minicomputer*. This computer is difficult to define, especially so since the general understanding of what it is changes significantly with time. But, in general, a minicomputer is a physically small, general-purpose computer that costs in the range of $3,000 to $20,000. The low price, which is the most significant feature as regards the "mini" of minicomputer, is sufficiently low that these computers are generally purchased outright rather than leased, as usually are the large general-purpose computers.

The classes of computers that have been mentioned are not, in general, mutually exclusive. A computer designed for data processing or one designed for process control can be used for problem-solving. Also, time-sharing computers are usually the scientific problem-solving type of computer. Some companies offer computers that are presented as being approximately equally suited for performing most of these functions.

Even though digital computers can be classified as to various types, the structures of all digital computers have much in common. In fact, the basic features of digital computers can be studied with little regard for classification. Thus most of the material presented in the following chapters is not directed to specific computers.

7

Computer
Words

7.1 DEFINITION OF A WORD

A *word* is the basic group of digits that are treated as
a unit by a digital computer. Actually, in some computers even a word is subdivided into parts, sometimes
called *bytes,* that may be operated on and treated as a
unit. Also, words may be combined into units of double-
word length. Thus any definition of a word must be
vague and loose if it is to apply to digital computers in
general. Of course, the instruction manual for any particular computer contains a specification of the word
for that computer.

In some computers the word length is as short as
12 bits and in others as long as 64 bits, with perhaps
a number of bits in the thirties being most common. In
the popular IBM System/360 computers the basic word
length is 32 bits. It is 36 bits in the older IBM 7094
computer. Minicomputers have word lengths of usually
eight, twelve, or sixteen bits, with eight bits being perhaps the most common.

In a first study of digital computers it is convenient

to think of a word as being a fixed number of digits, with perhaps several parts, that is always operated on as a single unit by the digital computer. These are the only words that we will consider.

There are two basic types of words: *instruction words* and *data words*, both of which are numbers that are distinguishable solely in the way they are used in a computer. If a person instructs a computer to execute an instruction that is actually a data number, the computer will do something, and no telling what, unless the number, by chance, coincides with an instruction. Also, instructions can be added, subtracted, and so on like any other numbers.

Instructions

The instruction words "tell" the computer what operations to perform: whether to add, subtract, multiply, jump over an instruction, and so on. Only part of the instruction word contains the operation code. Some instructions have as few as three operation code bits and others as many as twelve or more. Although 4096 different instructions can be coded in twelve bits, the complete instruction repertoire of a large computer may total only 400 or fewer different instructions. Hence the full capacity of the operation code bits may not be used.

Since only a part of the instruction word designates the pertinent instruction, bits are available for other purposes, and these are usually considered as grouped into one or more parts. Many instructions have a part called the *address* that provides the location in memory of a number that is to be an operand. Of course, some instructions do not produce operations on numbers, and for them there is no part of the word corresponding to an address. An example of such an instruction is one that stores zeros in a specific register. Another one is the instruction that halts computer operations.

In regard to addresses, something should be said about the memory. For present purposes, the memory can be thought of as an array of "pigeon holes," like the ones at post offices, each of which has a location number for identification. These location numbers should not be confused with the numbers that can be stored in the pigeon holes. For example, pigeon hole 17 may contain the number 3286 or any other number within the range of the computer. The instruction words and the data words are the numbers stored in the pigeon holes, and the addresses of instructions specify the location numbers of pigeon holes.

As mentioned, the address of an instruction provides the location in memory in which an operand is located, at least for those instructions causing operations to be performed on numbers. Of course, in each of these operations there is another operand, unless the operation is very simple, such as shifting or complementing. In some computers the second operand is in a known location in the arithmetic unit. However, in other computers the second operand may not be, at least initially, in the arithmetic unit and may still be in the memory. In this case the instruction may have two addresses for specifying the memory locations of the two operands.

Instructions may have more than two addresses. A third address may be needed to specify the location of the instruction to be executed next. This third address is usually unnecessary since in many computers the instructions are executed in the order in which they are located in memory. That is, the system that loads the programs in memory may position, for example, a program with 100 instructions in locations or pigeon holes 0 to 99. Then the computer first executes the instruction in location 0, and then the instruction in location 1, and so on. In these computers, the location of the instruction to be executed next does not have to be specified in the instructions; it is determinable from the sequential feature of the operation. However, some computers do not have this feature and in them the location of the instruction to be executed next must be specified along with the locations of the operands.

For a complete treatment of instructions, all of the various types should be considered. However, since in the following chapters we will use only single-address instructions, we will limit our discussion to them. This is not an unreasonable restriction since they are used extensively in minicomputers and in many large computers.

The operation code and the address seldom require all the bits of an instruction word and thus bits are available for other purposes. If, for example, a word comprises 36 bits with 12 bits used for the operation code and 15 bits for the address, then nine bits are available for other purposes. These extra bits have many possible uses, such as modifying an instruction during the execution of a program, or counting the number of times an instruction is executed. More will be said about these extra bits in a subsequent section.

Data

As mentioned, data words are indistinguishable from instruction words, except as regards use, and even in use sometimes instructions are operated on as if they were ordinary numbers. The data words we normally think of are those containing numbers that are operands, but there are other types of data words. Some data words may, for example, contain coded letters of the alphabet. For the present, we will consider only data words for operands that are conventional numbers.

Data words corresponding to ordinary numbers have two different forms: *fixed-point numbers* and *floating-point* or so-called *real numbers*.

Fixed-point numbers have the form of numbers as we ordinarily think of them: one bit indicates the sign and the remainder of the bits designate the magnitude. In the use of these numbers the operator or programmer must keep track of the binary point. In doing this he may conveniently consider the binary point as being to the extreme right of the digits, in which case the number is an integer. But he may consider the binary point as being between any two bits of the number.

If a computer word comprises, for example, 36 bits, and one bit is used for the sign, then 35 bits remain for the magnitude. The largest number containable in this word is $2^{35} - 1$, which is 34,359,738,367. This may seem like a large number, but in scientific applications numbers may greatly exceed this. Also, this type of number is inconvenient for fractions, especially small magnitude fractions. For example, this number is grossly inadequate for a number such as 1.6×10^{-19}—the charge of an electron in coulombs. Thus for numbers that are fractions or that have extremely large magnitudes, this fixed-point format is not suitable. In these cases floating-point numbers are preferred.

In floating-point numbers one bit of the word is for the sign, a part of the word is for an exponent, and the remainder of the word is for a multiplier. With the exponentiation of a floating-point number, fractions and widely varying magnitudes of numbers can be readily manipulated. However, since part of the word is used for an exponent, less of the word is available for significant digits. Thus there is less precision than with fixed-point numbers for the same word size.

7.2 TYPES OF INSTRUCTIONS

Instructions can be classified in various ways. One way is according to the operations performed. For example, some instructions may be for fixed-point numbers and others for floating-point numbers. And there are other operations that we are not now prepared to appreciate but that are presented in Chapter 10.

Instructions can also be classified according to the arrangement of bits in the instruction words. One type of instruction may, for example, have the operation code in the first twelve bits of the word. Another may have the operation code in the first three bits. Or some of the operation code bits may be at the beginning of the word and some at the end. Also some instructions may have no address. Large computers may have a dozen or more different types of instructions.

For our present purposes we need only two different instruction formats, and the corresponding instructions will be referred to as *type 1 instructions* and *type 2 instructions*. For purposes of explanation we will be specific about the number of bits in the words—all the words contain 36 bits.

The format for the type 1 instructions is illustrated in Figure 7.1(a). As indicated, the first 12 bits identify the operation; that is, whether it is add, subtract, or something else. In 12 bits the number of possible different combinations of 0's and 1's is 4096, which is far more than the number of instructions needed. However, some of these 12 bits may be used to identify the type instruction. For example, type 1 instructions might be designated by zeros in the second and third bit positions. Of course, each different type of instruction must have its characteristic features in order that the various pieces of information that have been coded into the instruction word can be properly identified.

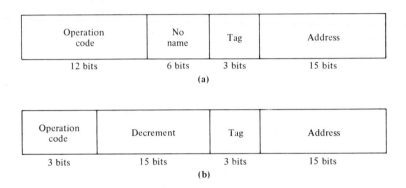

Figure 7.1 Instruction formats.

In the type 1 instruction the six bits after the operation code are not used; they are not needed. But since the word has a specific number of bits, all bits must be provided for. The next three bits are the *tag* which designates parts of the computer called index registers that are discussed in Chapter 10. The last 15 bits comprise the address, which, as mentioned, may specify the location in memory of an operand that takes part in the particular operation specified by the operation code. The address has other functions, but in any event, it specifies a location in memory. Having 15 bits, the address can specify 32,768 different memory locations.

A few instructions we will consider have the format shown in Figure 7.1(b), and will be called type 2 instructions. The operation code for each type 2 instruction is just three bits, which means only eight different instructions can have this format, assuming none of the code bits designates the type of instruction. The 15 bits adjacent the operation code are the decrement, the purpose of which will be described in Chapter 10. The tag and the address serve the same function as in the type 1 instructions.

7.3   TYPES OF DATA

The data words of most interest to us are those corresponding to numbers to be used in arithmetic operations, but there are other data words. For example, nonnumeric characters can be coded into data words. These include letters of the alphabet, decimal numbers, and various characters such as a dollar sign, plus and minus signs, a comma, or a period.

For more than 32 and less than 65 of these characters, six bits are required for coding each character. With six bits per character, six characters can be coded into a 36-bit word. For an illustration, assume the word CHECK is to be coded, and the codes are 010011 for C, 011000 for H, 010101 for E, 100010 for K, and 110000 for a blank. Then the coded word CHECK is 010011011000010101010011100010110000. A blank has been placed on the right since CHECK has only five letters but the computer word has space for six coded characters.

We will not have reason in the present chapter to consider further data words other than those for fixed-point or integer numbers and for floating-point or real number words.

Fixed-Point Words

In a 36-bit word a fixed-point number word comprises a sign bit followed by 35 bits for the magnitude, as shown in Figure 7.2. In the sign bit either a 1 or a 0 can represent the positive sign. Often a 0 is used for a plus sign and 1 for a minus sign, and this is what we will use.

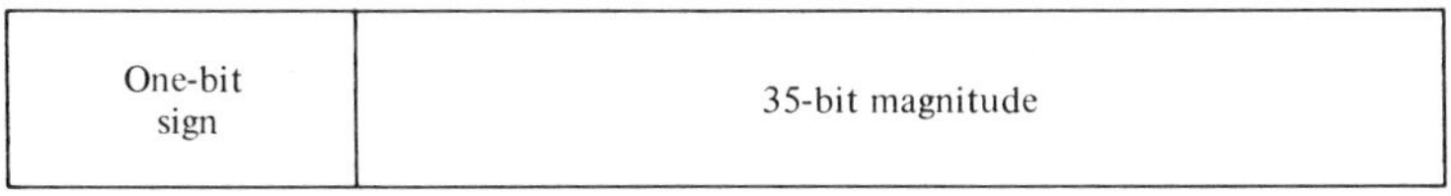

One-bit sign	35-bit magnitude

Figure 7.2   Fixed-point word format.

For an example of a fixed-point integer, the binary equivalent of 66 decimal will be shown. If the binary point is assumed to be at the extreme right, this number is 000000000000000000000000000001000010. An octal or hexadecimal shorthand is often used for writing and printing words. For our purposes, an octal shorthand is better because the parts of the words of interest are all multiples of three bits. In the use of this octal shorthand, a little "cheating" is done on the first three bits; the sign is shown and then the second and third bits are used for the first octal digit. Normally, of course, three bits correspond to each octal digit. With this convention, the first octal digit cannot be more than three, that being the maximum octal number that can be obtained from just two bits. The octal shorthand for the word corresponding to the decimal number 66 is +000000000102.

For another example, consider the decimal number −134. The corresponding fixed-point word in binary is

$$10000000000000000000000000010000110$$

for which the octal shorthand is −000000000206.

In some computers each negative number is represented as a complement of the corresponding positive number. This matter is discussed in Chapter 8. For our present purposes, we need consider just the case in which the negative numbers differ from the corresponding positive numbers in the sign bit only.

If fixed-point numbers are used for fractions or mixed numbers, the programmer must keep track of the location of the binary point. He must, for example, be certain in adding two fixed-point numbers that the binary points are located between the same bits of both numbers, that is, the binary points must be aligned. Of course, there is no designation in the word for the binary point, that is, the location of the binary point is purely a conceptual matter.

If a certain mixed number has its binary point between the second and third rightmost bits, then before a second number can be added to it, the bits of the second number must be shifted such that the binary point is also between the second and third rightmost bits. Alternatively, the first number could be shifted such that its binary point is in the same position as the binary point of the second number.

Keeping track of the location of binary points is a difficult task, especially if a program has many arithmetic operations. Although in some small computers this work is necessary, large computers usually have a floating-point feature that eliminates the binary point problem while providing an extensive range of numbers.

Floating-Point Words

In solving scientific problems a digital computer must be capable of handling numbers such as 1.6×10^{-19}, 9×10^{-31}, 3×10^{8}, and so on, of very small or very large magnitudes that are extremely difficult to represent and to manipulate in fixed-point form. Many digital computers conveniently represent and manipulate such numbers in a normalized floating-point form that is really a type of exponentiation. Floating-point numbers provide the tremendous range of magnitudes needed for scientific problems, as will be shown. Also, the form of these numbers is such that binary point location requirements can be automatically satisfied by action of the computer.

Not all digital computers have a built-in, floating-point capability. That is, many of the small computers do not have circuits designed to include operations on floating-point numbers. The large digital computers usually do. Even in the small computers, floating-point numbers can be used by a programmer if he writes his program to include the steps that would be performed by floating-point circuits in a large computer. Of course, this program is more difficult to write than one containing floating-point instructions and requires more computer time to run. As a practical matter, the programmer may need not be concerned about including instructions for converting from fixed- to floating-point because often small computer installations have a program stored in auxiliary memory for performing this conversion.

Floating-point numbers correspond to numbers such as AR^B. In digital computers the multiplier A is in binary as is the exponent B. The radix R, which is not represented directly, need not be the binary base 10 (two decimal), but frequently it is. Although R is not represented directly in the computer, the value for B depends on the R selected. Except for a brief discussion of floating-point words in the IBM System/360 computers, we will select R as the binary base 2. Also, we will be considering normalized floating-point numbers. These have a value of B such that the binary point is considered to be at the left of the most significant digit of A.

In floating-point number words, part of the word is used for the sign of the floating-point number, part for the multiplier A, and part for the representation of the exponent B. There is a fixed number of bits to be divided between parts A and B, and the number used for each part is a matter of compromise. The more bits used for A, the greater the precision but the fewer the bits remaining for B, which means that the range of possible magnitudes is decreased, and vice versa.

For purposes of discussion, a specific selection will be made, which is, for a 36-bit word, one bit for the sign, eight bits for the exponent, and 27 bits for the multiplier, as shown in Figure 7.3. The group of eight bits corresponding to the exponent is called the *characteristic* and the group of 27 bits for the multiplier is called the *fraction* or *mantissa*.

One-bit sign	Eight-bit characteristic	27-bit fraction

Figure 7.3   Floating-point word format.

As has been mentioned, the multiplier is often a proper fraction, in which case the binary point is considered to be at the immediate left of the 27 bits of the fraction. The process of placing the binary point to the left of the leftmost bit is called *normalization*.

Example 7.1 Normalize the binary number 1100.011.

Solution The integer has four bits. Thus for normalization the binary point must be shifted four places to the left. Then, to avoid changing the number we must multiply this fraction by two raised to a power equal to the number of positions shifted. That is, the normalized number is, in binary, 0.1100011×2^4. ∎

Example 7.2 Normalize the binary number 0.0011101.

Solution Because the number is a fraction less than one-half, the binary point must be shifted right until it is immediately to the left of the most significant one bit. For this number we obviously must shift the binary point two places to the right. At the same time we must introduce a multiplier of 2^{-2} to compensate for this shift. Thus, the normalized number is 0.11101×2^{-2}. ∎

In the normalized floating-point word the fraction part of the word contains the proper fraction part of the normalized number. In the case of the 27-bit fraction and, say, the number 11011.111011, the fraction is 110111110110000000000000000. For the binary number 0.000110111101, the fraction is 110111101000000000000000000.

As has been mentioned, the characteristic part of the word contains the representation for the exponent of the normalized number. The exponent could be placed directly in the characteristic, in which case a sign bit would have to be included for distinguishing positive and negative exponents. It is more customary, however, to use a *biased characteristic*, in which case a sign bit is not necessary.

A biased characteristic is obtained by adding the exponent, resulting from the normalization, to a fixed number, which is usually approximately half the range of the characteristic. Negative exponents, when added, decrease the characteristic and of course positive exponents increase it. A bias number midway in the range allows the magnitude of permissible negative exponents to be approximately equal to that for positive exponents.

In the specific case of the word of Figure 7.3, the number in the characteristic can range between 0 and 255 (decimal). Since 128 is approximately in the middle of this range, it should be the bias. Then, if the exponent from normalization is positive, we will add it to 128, and if it is negative we will subtract its magnitude from 128. The most negative acceptable exponent is -128, and the maximum positive exponent is 127. Of course, the characteristic is really in binary rather than decimal and has a bias of 10000000, which is 200 in the octal shorthand.

Example 7.3 Convert -73.5 (decimal) to floating-point form.

Solution First, we find the binary equivalent; it is -1001001.10. Then, we normalize the number: -0.100100110×2^7. We add the exponent, which is in decimal, to 128 and convert the result to binary: $128 + 7 = 135$ or 10000111_2. Finally, we place the fraction in 27-bit form by adding trailing zeros and then precede it with the sign and characteristic as indicated in Figure 7.3. The result is 1100001111001001100000000000000000000. In octal shorthand this result is -207446000000. ■

Example 7.4 Convert 7/64 (decimal) to floating-point form.

Solution The binary equivalent is 0.000111. We can normalize it by shifting the binary point three places to the right and multiplying the result by the base two raised to the -3: 0.111×2^{-3}. Then we add the exponent to 128 and convert the result to binary: $128 - 3 = 125$ or 1111101_2. We need to place this binary number in eight-bit form or 01111101 since eight bits are needed for the characteristic. Finally, we place the fraction in 27-bit form and then precede it with the sign and characteristic. The result is 001111110111100000000000000000000000000, which is $+175700000000$ in the octal shorthand. ■

For the floating-point word format of Figure 7.3 the magnitudes of the numbers that can be represented are between approximately 2^{-128} and 2^{127} (approximately 10^{-39} and 10^{39}, decimal). Also, zero can be represented (36 0's). Of course, a number can be too small or too large in magnitude to be represented. For example, if two numbers of almost equal value are subtracted, the result may be too small to be within the range of the computer. In particular, if the difference were, say, $1.2 \times (10)^{-41}$ (decimal), the computer could not place this difference in floating-point form. Likewise, too large a number frequently occurs. Perhaps the most common error in this regard is the division of a number by zero. Thus even with floating-point numbers some care is required to make certain that all the results of the calculations are within the range of the computer.

Some numbers are nonterminating in binary and can only be approximately represented in floating-point form. For example, consider the decimal number $\frac{1}{10}$. In binary it is 0.0001100110011001100110011001100-11001100 . . . , which is a nonterminating fraction. There are two ways of forming a floating-point word from such a number: *truncating* and *rounding-off*. In truncating a number, the computer simply disregards the bits that do not fit into the floating-point word. However, in rounding off, it adds a 1 to the least significant bit that will fit into the word, provided the first bit that does not fit is a 1. Otherwise, the computer leaves the number in truncated form.

The IBM System/360 computers have two floating-point forms: single precision and double precision, both of which have a sign bit and a seven-bit characteristic. The fraction for the single-precision form is 24 bits and that for the double-precision form is 56 bits.

In these computers the radix R is not two as we have been considering but is 16. That is, the exponents of interest are powers of 16. Since the characteristic has seven bits, the bias, which is the midrange, is 1000000 or 64 in decimal (40 in hexadecimal). Consequently, the exponents can range from $+63$ to -64 and the range in magnitudes is approximately 16^{63} to 16^{-64} or in decimal approximately 10^{76} to 10^{-78}. Note that this is a much larger range than for the other floating-point word we considered even though the characteristic has one less bit.

This increased range is obtained at the cost of a slight decrease in precision that results from the floating-point 360 words being normalized in hexadecimal rather than in binary. With hexadecimal normalization, the fractions can have as many as three leading zeros and thus three fewer bits for the significant digits.

To convert a decimal number to IBM System/360 floating-point form, we can work entirely in hexadecimal and then as a last step convert the hexadecimal number into a binary number.

Example 7.5   Convert the decimal number 462.35 to IBM System/360 single-precision, floating-point form.

Solution   The decimal number must be converted to hexadecimal. In this conversion six hexadecimal digits suffice because there is no room for more digits; that is, six digits times four bits per digit yields 24 bits, which is the size of the fraction. The corresponding approximate hexadecimal number is 1CE.59A (rounded off), which normalized in hexadecimal is $0.1CE59A \times 16^3$. The exponent 3 added to the bias 40 yields a characteristic of 43. Thus the floating-point word is $+431CE59A$ in hexadecimal or 01000011000111001110010110011010 in the binary format of the computer. Note that the fraction, which begins with the ninth bit, contains three leading zeros and is thus not normalized in binary.   ■

PROBLEMS ━━━━━━━━━━━━━━━

7.1   A certain computer has a 40-bit word size. Show the fixed-point representations in binary and in hexadecimal for the following decimal integers:

(a) -642

(b) 10^3

(c) -10^4

(d) 542,768

(e) 10^{30}

7.2 Normalize the following binary numbers:
(a) 1011.1   (b) 11011100.001   (c) 0.000110111

Answers   (a) 0.10111×2^4;   (b) 0.11011100001×2^8;
           (c) 0.110111×2^{-3}

7.3 Normalize the following binary numbers:
(a) 11011.01   (b) 11100111001   (c) 0.0001001011

7.4 Use the 36-bit floating-point word format of this chapter and convert the following decimal numbers to floating-point form:
(a) $\frac{3}{8}$ (c) $-\frac{1}{3}$
(b) 762.625   (d) 0.000926

Answers   (a) 001111111111000000000000000000000000
          (b) 010001010101111101010100000000000000
          (c) 101111111101010101010101010101010101
          (d) 001110110111100101011111011001110111
            (rounded off)

7.5 Repeat Problem 7.4 for
(a) $\frac{1}{4}$ (c) $-\frac{1}{10}$
(b) -8962.875 (d) -0.006352

7.6 Repeat Problem 7.4 for
(a) $\frac{3}{7}$ (c) 3.1416
(b) -10^4 (d) 3×10^8

7.7 Use the IBM System/360 single-precision, floating-point word format and convert the following decimal numbers to floating-point form:
(a) $\frac{3}{8}$ (c) $-\frac{1}{3}$
(b) 762.625   (d) 0.000926

Answers   (a) 01000000011000000000000000000000
          (b) 01000011001011111010101000000000
          (c) 11000000010101010101010101010101
          (d) 00111110001111001010111110110100 (rounded off)

7.8 Repeat Problem 7.7 for
(a) $\frac{1}{4}$ (c) $-\frac{1}{10}$
(b) -8962.875 (d) -0.006352

7.9 Repeat Problem 7.7 for
(a) $\frac{3}{7}$ (c) 3.1416
(b) -10^4 (d) 3×10^8

7.10 A certain computer has 40-bit floating-point words with 10-bit characteristics. The exponentiation has a binary base.
(a) What is the bias?
(b) What is the approximate range in decimal of the numbers that can be represented?

(c) Approximately what is the number of significant *decimal* digits that the representation corresponds to; that is, what is the number of decimal digits corresponding to the fraction?

Answers   (a) 1000000000_2;   (b) 10^{153} to 10^{-154} and zero;
(c) almost nine

7.11   Repeat Problem 7.10 for a 45-bit word with a 12-bit characteristic and an exponentiation with an octal base.

7.12   Repeat Problem 7.10 for a 50-bit word with a 14-bit characteristic and an exponentiation with a binary base.

7.13   A certain computer has 20-bit floating-point words with 5-bit characteristics. The exponentiation has an octal base. Assume round-off and that the words are arranged with the sign bit first, then the characteristic, and last the fraction. Determine what the representations are, in binary, for the following decimal numbers:

(a) 324.5   (c) 1362.78
(b) −69.42   (d) −0.00324

Answers   (a) 01001110100010010000
(b) 11001100100010101101
(c) 01010001010101001011
(d) 10111000110101000101

7.14   Repeat Problem 7.13 for
(a) 628.5   (c) −177.77
(b) 32,768.875   (d) −0.000654

7.15   Repeat Problem 7.13 for
(a) 1728.6   (c) −9872.645
(b) −0.0463   (d) 10^{-3}

8

Arithmetic
Operations
And Units

In this chapter we will discuss the various forms binary numbers can have in digital computers and the arithmetic operations with these forms. We will also consider two adder units. A knowlege of complement arithmetic for the binary number system to the extent presented in the Appendix is essential for an understanding of the material of this chapter.

8.1 REPRESENTATION AND ADDITION OF SIGNED FIXED-POINT BINARY NUMBERS

Three forms of signed binary numbers are popular: *signed magnitude, signed 1's complement,* and *signed 2's complement.* We will first consider these three forms as related to integer-type or fixed-point numbers in which the first bit in a number word is the sign bit and each binary point is assumed to be immediately to the right of the least significant digit even though it could be elsewhere.

In the following treatment of number systems, the

computers referred to are assumed to have adders and no subtractors, and the basic arithmetic operation is addition. Of course, some computers have subtractors instead. Because the rules for subtraction follow rather obviously from our addition discussion, we will not consider operations with subtractors.

Signed-Magnitude Number System

In the *signed-magnitude form*, a positive or negative number is represented by a sign bit followed by the magnitude in binary. For example, in a five-bit word the number 13 is 01101 and −5 is 10101, with, as is conventional, a 0 bit for a plus sign and a 1 bit for a minus sign. Also, there is a plus zero and a minus zero, which for five bits are 00000 and 10000, respectively.

In adding signed-magnitude numbers of the same sign, a computer adds the magnitude bits and makes the sign bit of the sum agree with that of the numbers. If the numbers have different signs, one of the numbers is complemented before the addition. This complement in a parallel machine is often the 1's complement, *which is the one used in the following discussion*.

After the complement is taken, the magnitude of the uncomplemented number is added to the magnitude of this complement. If there is an overflow, called an end-around carry, it is added to the least significant digit of the sum and the computer makes the sign of the sum the same as the sign of the number that was not complemented. But if there is *no* end-around carry, the sum is complemented and the computer makes the sign bit of the sum the same as that of the number that was complemented.

Often the register containing the number that was complemented will, after the addition, contain the sum. That is, the sum replaces the complemented number. Then, if there is no end-around carry, the sign bit of this register is left unchanged. Otherwise, it is changed. This register is often referred to as the *accumulator*, or just the *AC*, for short.

Example 8.1   Explain how a computer adds 13 and −5 in a five bit word machine in which the numbers are represented in signed-magnitude form.

Solution   The operation is 01101 + 10101. Because the signs are different, one number, say the second, is complemented, and then the addition is performed:

```
      1  1  0  1
 +    1  0  1  0
   ┌ 1  0  1  1  1
   └───────► +  1      end-around carry
      1  0  0  0
```

Since there is an end-around carry, the sign bit of the sum is that of the number that was *not* complemented. The result is 01000. ■

Example 8.2 Explain how a computer adds 5 and -13 in a five-bit word machine in which the numbers are represented in signed-magnitude form.

Solution The operation is $00101 + 11101$. With the signs different, the magnitude of one number, say the second, is complemented, and then the addition is performed:

$$
\begin{array}{r}
0 \quad 1 \quad 0 \quad 1 \\
+ \quad 0 \quad 0 \quad 1 \quad 0 \\
\hline
0 \quad 1 \quad 1 \quad 1
\end{array}
$$

Because there is no end-around carry, the result is complemented to 1000, and the sign bit of the complemented number is used. Thus the sum is 11000. ■

In subtracting, the computer changes the sign of the number that is the subtrahend and then proceeds with the addition operation as explained above. That is, except for the change of the sign bit of the subtrahend, the operations of addition and subtraction are identical. This similarity is also true for the two other number systems.

The basis for the rules for addition of numbers of like sign should be obvious, but the rules in the case of unlike signs are not so apparent and require consideration. In particular, we will consider the addition of two numbers having magnitudes N_1 and N_2 in a system having a modulus M. If these numbers have different signs, then the complement of one of the numbers, say that with magnitude N_2, is added to the other number:

$$
\begin{array}{r}
N_1 \\
+ \quad M - N_2 - 1 \\
\hline
M + N_1 - N_2 - 1
\end{array}
$$

If N_1 is greater than N_2, the sum is equal to or greater than M and an end-around carry is generated that is similar to an overflow but which is really the modulus M. When this carry is added to the least significant digit, it cancels the -1.

$$
\begin{array}{rl}
N_1 - N_2 - 1 & \\
+ \, 1 & \quad \text{from } M \\
\hline
N_1 - N_2 &
\end{array}
$$

Obviously, the sign of the sum should be that having magnitude N_1, the number that was *not* complemented.

If N_2 is greater than N_1, then $M + N_1 - N_2 - 1$ is less than M, and the sum fits into the specified number of bits without an overflow or end-around carry being generated. If this sum is complemented, the result is

$$M - (M + N_1 - N_2 - 1) - 1 = N_2 - N_1$$

and the correct sign for this result is that of the complemented number.

The final possibility is that N_2 and N_1 are equal. Then $M + N_1 - N_2 - 1 = M - 1$ (all 1's), and the sum fits into the register as it does for the N_2 greater than N_1 case. After the computer complements this result, the sum is all 0's except possibly for the sign bit. Whether the sum is plus or minus zero depends on which number was complemented. As mentioned, the register containing the number that was complemented may contain the sum after the addition. In this case the sum is negative if the number complemented was the negative number and is positive if the number complemented was the positive number.

It is possible, of course, to have an overflow when two positive numbers or two negative numbers are added. This is a true overflow and should not be confused with the end-around carry that may occur if the signs of the numbers differ.

Signed 1's Complement Number System

Positive numbers in the *signed 1's complement system* are the same as in the signed-magnitude number system, but negative numbers differ for they are represented in 1's complement form. For example, the 1's complement of -13 for a five-bit word is 10010. Also, since plus zero is 00000, minus zero is 11111.

The sign bits of 1's complement numbers are often considered as magnitude bits for purposes of addition, and they are so considered in the following discussion. That is, the sign bits are added as if they were magnitude bits.

The method for adding two 1's complement positive numbers should be evident except for one point that should be mentioned. When an overflow occurs in the addition of two positive numbers, it is indicated by a 1 bit in the sign bit of the sum. That is, the overflow goes over into the sign position. Of course, a computer has circuits for detecting this condition.

If two negative numbers are added, an end-around carry always occurs which is produced by the two 1 sign bits of the numbers being added. And this carry is added into the least significant bit position. Also, if the sum is within the range of the system, another carry goes into the sign position of the sum from the magnitude positions and provides the 1 sign bit. For example, if -3 and -7 are added in a five-bit system, the process is

$$
\begin{array}{ccccccl}
  & 1 & 1 & 1 & 0 & 0 & (-3) \\
+ & 1 & 1 & 0 & 0 & 0 & (-7) \\
\end{array}
$$

```
    1 1 1 0 0    (−3)
 +  1 1 0 0 0    (−7)
 ┌1 1 0 1 0 0
 └──────────→ + 1
    1 0 1 0 1    (−10)
```

But, if −7 and −11 are added in the same system, an overflow should occur since the sum exceeds the system range.

```
    1 1 0 0 0    (−7)
 +  1 0 1 0 0    (−11)
 ┌1 0 1 1 0 0
 └──────────→ + 1
    0 1 1 0 1    (+13)
```

This positive erroneous sum can be detected by the lack of a carry from the magnitude positions into the sign position.

If numbers of unlike signs are added and the positive number is larger, an end-around carry occurs that must be added to the least significant digit. There is no such carry if the sum is negative. For example, consider the addition of 13 and −5 in a five-bit system.

```
    0 1 1 0 1    (13)
 +  1 1 0 1 0    (−5)
 ┌1 0 0 1 1 1
 └──────────→ + 1
    0 1 0 0 0    (8)
```

Not until after the end-around carry has been added is the sum correct. Now, consider the addition of 5 and −13.

```
    0 0 1 0 1    (5)
 +  1 0 0 1 0    (−13)
    1 0 1 1 1    (−8)
```

No end-around carry was generated, but it was not needed.

We should summarize addition in the 1's complement system. A most important point is that the sign bits are added along with the magnitude bits. Also, any end-around carry is always added to the least significant digit. But this carry occurs only in the addition of two negative numbers or of a positive and a negative number when the positive number is larger. If the magnitude bits produce a carry into the sign bit when both numbers are positive, this carry is actually an overflow and, as a result, the sum is incorrect. Also, if in the addition of two negative numbers the result is positive, then, of course, there is an error—the result exceeds the system range.

We will now consider justifications for these rules for adding two numbers in the signed 1's complement number system. The adding of two positive numbers is so obvious that the rule requires no justification. But the rules for negative numbers do. We need to justify the rules for adding a positive number and a negative number for all cases—the negative number having the larger magnitude, the smaller magnitude, and both numbers having equal magnitudes. Then we must justify the rule for adding two negative numbers.

Before justifying these rules we need to consider the form of the negative numbers in more detail. In the signed 1's complement number system a negative number of magnitude N has the form of $2M - N - 1$, wherein M is the modulus. One of these two M's is for the sign bit, which is, of course, in the 2^n position, n being the number of bits in the magnitude (counting the sign bit, the total number of bits is $n + 1$). The other M comes from $M - N - 1$, the 1's complement of the magnitude of the number. In an addition involving a negative number we must consider all of $2M - N - 1$ since the sign bit is equivalent to a magnitude bit in the addition process.

If a positive number with magnitude N_1 is added to a negative number of magnitude N_2, the first step of the addition is

$$\begin{array}{r} N_1 \\ +\quad 2M - N_2 - 1 \\ \hline 2M + N_1 - N_2 - 1 \end{array}$$

Now, if N_1 is greater than N_2, the sum is equal to or greater than $2M$ and hence the addition generates an end-around carry from a 1 in the 2^{n+1} position. When this carry, which is the $2M$, is added to the least significant digit, it cancels the -1.

$$\begin{array}{r} N_1 - N_2 - 1 \\ +\ 1 \qquad \text{from } 2M \\ \hline N_1 - N_2 \end{array}$$

The sign bit is 0, as it should be, because the positive number is larger.

If the negative number has the larger magnitude, that is, if N_2 is greater than N_1, then $2M + N_1 - N_2 - 1$ is less than $2M$ and the sum fits into the $n + 1$ bits; a carry is not generated. This result, when written as $2M - (N_2 - N_1) - 1$, is seen to be the 1's complement of $N_2 - N_1$ (with minus sign). Thus the rules provide the correct results when one of the two numbers being added is positive and the other is negative regardless of which has the larger magnitude. If both numbers have the same magnitude, the sum is $2M - 1$ (all 1's), which is negative zero.

Now, consider the addition of two negative numbers having magnitudes N_1 and N_2.

$$\begin{array}{r} 2M - N_2 - 1 \\ + \; 2M - N_1 - 1 \\ \hline 4M - (N_2 + N_1) - 2 \end{array}$$

In this partial result, $2M$ of the $4M$ produces an end-around carry that, when added to the remainder produces

$$\begin{array}{r} 2M - (N_2 + N_1) - 2 \\ + \; 1 \qquad \text{from } 2M \\ \hline 2M - (N_2 + N_1) - 1 \end{array}$$

This $2M - (N_2 + N_1) - 1$ is just the 1's complement of $N_2 + N_1$ (with minus sign) and hence is the correct result. We have now considered all possible cases of addition involving negative numbers.

As mentioned, the 1's complement form is popular in parallel computers. In these computers a 1's complement can be formed so readily either by pulsing the trigger inputs of the flip-flops of a register or by taking the output from the 0 lines of these flip-flops.

Signed 2's Complement Number System

Positive numbers in the *signed 2's complement system* are the same as in the other two systems. However, negative numbers are in 2's complement form. For example, -14 in a five-bit word is 10010. In this system there is only one zero, positive zero, or 00000, which can be determined by adding two numbers of the same magnitude but of opposite signs. Also, in the addition of 2's complement numbers, as with 1's complement numbers, the sign bit is often treated as a magnitude bit for addition, and it will be so treated in the following discussion.

The addition of two positive numbers will not be discussed because this addition is the same as in the 1's complement system. However, the addition of positive and negative numbers or of two negative numbers is different, the principal difference being that *carries are ignored*. For example, when a positive number is added to a negative number, a carry is generated if the result is positive. But this carry is ignored. If the sum is negative, there is no carry. Following are some examples:

$$\begin{array}{cccccc} & 1 & 1 & 0 & 1 & 0 & (-6) \\ + & 0 & 1 & 0 & 0 & 0 & (8) \\ \hline 1 & 0 & 0 & 0 & 1 & 0 & (2) \end{array} \qquad \begin{array}{cccccc} & 1 & 0 & 1 & 1 & 1 & (-9) \\ + & 0 & 0 & 1 & 1 & 0 & (6) \\ \hline & 1 & 1 & 1 & 0 & 1 & (-3) \end{array}$$

disregard

If two negative numbers are added, there is a carry that must be disregarded. Also, if the sum is in the range of the system, a carry is produced from the magnitude bits into the sign bit of the sum and forms the necessary 1 bit for the negative sign of the sum. However, if the sum exceeds the range of the system, there is no carry from the magnitude bits, although, of course, there still is from the sign bits.

Some examples follow:

$$
\begin{array}{lllll}
  & 1 & 1 & 0 & 1 & 0 \\
+ & 1 & 1 & 1 & 0 & 1 \\
\hline
1 & 1 & 0 & 1 & 1 & 1
\end{array}
\quad
\begin{array}{l}
(-6) \\
(-3) \\
(-9)
\end{array}
\qquad
\begin{array}{lllll}
  & 1 & 0 & 1 & 1 & 1 \\
+ & 1 & 0 & 1 & 1 & 0 \\
\hline
1 & 0 & 1 & 1 & 0 & 1
\end{array}
\quad
\begin{array}{l}
(-9) \\
(-10) \\
\text{error}
\end{array}
$$

disregard ⌐   ⌐disregard

We will now summarize the rules for adding numbers in 2's complement form. In all cases, each sign bit enters the addition as if it were a magnitude bit. Also, any carries are always disregarded. The addition of two positive numbers is obvious, but it should be mentioned that with these numbers any carry into the sign bit of the sum is an overflow and, of course, then the sum is in error. The addition of a positive and a negative number is no problem. It happens that the sign bits generate a carry when the sum is positive but do not when the sum is negative. But these facts are not necessary to remember. When two negative numbers are added, their sign bits produce a carry that is disregarded. And, if the negative sum is within the range of the system, there is a carry from the magnitude bits into the sign bit. Really, all that must be remembered about addition of 2's complement numbers is that carries are ignored and that overflow occurs if a sum is positive when two negative numbers are added or is negative when two positive numbers are added.

We need to justify the rules for addition with negative numbers. From the 1's complement it should be obvious that a negative number of magnitude N has the form $2M - N$ in the 2's complement number system. One M of the $2M$ is the minus sign and the other M is for $M - N$, the 2's complement of N.

If a positive number of magnitude N_1 is added to a negative number of magnitude N_2, the result is

$$
\begin{array}{r}
N_1 \\
+ \; 2M - N_2 \\
\hline
2M + N_1 - N_2
\end{array}
$$

If N_1 is greater than N_2, this sum is greater than $2M$, in which case only $N_1 - N_2$ appears in the register containing the sum because there is no room for the bit that represents $2M$—this is the carry that is ignored. The resulting sum $N_1 + N_2$ is, of course, the correct result.

If the magnitudes N_1 and N_2 are equal, the sum is just $2M$, which is the carry that is ignored. What is left (all 0's) is positive zero, the only zero in this system.

If N_2 has the larger magnitude, then $2M + N_1 - N_2$ is less than $2M$ and the sum fits into the $n + 1$ bits; no carry is generated. This result, when rearranged as $2M - (N_2 - N_1)$, is seen to be the 2's complement of $N_2 - N_1$ with minus sign, which is the correct result. Thus the rules provide the correct result when one of the two numbers being added is positive and the other negative, regardless of the relative magnitudes of the two numbers.

In the addition of two negative numbers having magnitudes N_1 and N_2, we have

$$\begin{array}{r} 2M - N_2 \\ + \ 2M - N_1 \\ \hline 4M - (N_2 + N_1) \end{array}$$

In the sum, $2M$ of the $4M$ produces a carry that is ignored. The remaining $2M - (N_2 + N_1)$ is the 2's complement of $N_2 + N_1$, the correct

Table 8.1 Signed Number System Comparison

	Number System		
Topic	Signed Magnitude	Signed 1's Complement	Signed 2's Complement
Negative numbers in complement form?	No	Yes	Yes
Sign bit involved in addition or subtraction?	No	Yes	Yes
Form of zeros	Plus (00 . . .) Minus (100 . . .)	Plus (00 . . .) Minus (111 . . .)	Plus (00 . . .) No minus zero
Use end-around carry?	Yes, if 1's complement used when numbers have different signs; no, if 2's complement used	Yes	No
Method for detecting overflow in adding two positive numbers	Carry from magnitude bits	Negative sum	Negative sum
Method for detecting overflow in adding two negative numbers	Carry from magnitude bits	Positive sum	Positive sum

result. We have now considered all possible cases of addition with negative numbers in the 2's complement number system.

The 2's complement representation is popular for serial computers. One reason for this popularity is the lack of need for end-around carries. End-around carries are cumbersome for serial adders since they are not generated until after the least significant digits are added and thus cannot enter into this addition.

For ready reference, some important comparisons for the three number systems are presented in Table 8.1.

8.2   FIXED-POINT ADDERS

There are various forms of adders. Some add serially and others in a parallel fashion. Adders also differ depending on the number representation. For convenience, we will consider only two adders, one for parallel addition with 1's complement numbers and the other for serial addition with 2's complement numbers.

Parallel Adder

A *parallel adder* for adding two four-bit numbers, including the sign bits, is shown in Figure 8.1. The two numbers added are $x_0x_1x_2x_3$ and $y_0y_1y_2y_3$ and the sum is $s_0s_1s_2s_3$. In these numbers x_0, y_0, and s_0 are the sign bits; x_1, y_1, and s_1 are the most significant digits; and x_3, y_3, and s_3 are the least significant digits.

In Figure 8.1 all of the adders are full adders since each has three inputs. One of the three inputs for the rightmost adder FA_3 is the end-around carry. However, if 2's complement representation is used instead of 1's complement, there is no end-around carry and this last adder, which then need have only two inputs, can be a half adder.

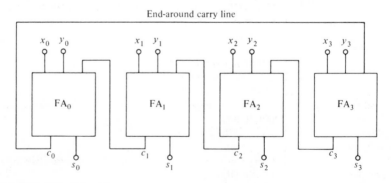

Figure 8.1   Parallel adder.

The operation of this parallel adder should be apparent from Figure 8.1. Each adder adds two corresponding bits of the numbers to any carry from the prior adder stage.

This method of adding carries can cause significant delays, as can best be seen by adding 1111 (negative zero) to 0001. The sum is, of course, 0001 as shown below.

$$
\begin{array}{r}
1\ \ 1\ \ 1\ \ 1 \\
+\ \ 0\ \ 0\ \ 0\ \ 1 \\
\hline
{}^{-1}\ 0\ \ 0\ \ 0\ \ 0 \\
\longrightarrow +\ \ \ 1 \\
\hline
0\ \ 0\ \ 0\ \ 1
\end{array}
$$

Some delay occurs in the generation of this sum because of the carry initiated at the rightmost adder, although to a lesser extent it is caused by all carries. In this addition, this rightmost carry must ripple through all the other adders before the sum is formed. That is, a 1 generated in the adder at the right must propagate through all the adders before the result is available. Of course, this is an extreme case, but it does illustrate that in this parallel adder the sum does not appear instantly nor simultaneously on all the output sum lines; time must be allowed for the effects of carries to propagate through the adders. And, with many adders the delay is considerable. There are techniques for decreasing this time delay, but we will not discuss them. For our purposes it is sufficient to note that this carry ripple problem exists and it has been at least partially solved.

Serial Adder

The hardware requirements for an adder system can be considerably reduced if a *serial adder* is used instead of a parallel adder. Unfortunately, the savings in hardware are accompanied by a corresponding increase in the time required for adding.

A serial adder is shown in Figure 8.2 for adding two six-bit numbers that are in 2's complement form. In these numbers the least significant bits occur at time t_1 and the sign bits at time t_6, which is five bit times later than t_1. A delay element is needed for delaying the carry generated at one time to make it coincident with input number bits that occur one bit time later. The carry generated at time t_6 has no effect on the sum, for, as has been mentioned, what would be end-around carries in other systems are disregarded in the 2's complement system.

To understand the operation of this adder, consider the addition of the two numbers shown. At time t_1 the 1 bit in the addend is added to two 0 bits—one from the augend and the other from the delay element

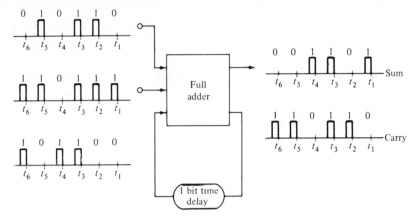

Figure 8.2 Serial adder.

output. This output is 0 if any prior inputs to the delay element occurred more than one bit time previously, which condition is necessary for proper operation. With these inputs, the adder produces (if it has negligible delay) a sum output at t_1 of $1 + 0 + 0 = 1$ and a carry output of 0.

At time t_2 the 0 bit from the delay element and the two 1 bits from the augend and addend are added to produce a sum bit of 0 and a carry bit of 1. With this 1 bit input at t_2, the delay element produces an output of 1 at t_3. This 1 added to the 1 bits of the augend and addend, that also occur at t_3, produces a 1 sum bit and also a 1 carry bit from the adder at this time.

The remainder of the operation of this adder should be apparent from the figure without further explanation.

The savings in hardware for the serial adder are apparent. There is only one full adder regardless of the number of bits in the addend or augend. In contrast, in the parallel adder there is an adder for every bit in the addend or augend.

8.3   FIXED-POINT MULTIPLICATION

Multiplication, like addition, differs slightly in parallel and serial machines. Even though the difference is slight, it is sufficiently significant to warrant separate discussions for the two machines.

Parallel Multiplication

Three registers are used in multiplicaton. One, the *SR* (*storage register*), holds the multiplicand. Another, the *MQ* (*multiplier-quotient*), contains the multiplier initially and the least significant digits of the product after the multiplication. The third register, the AC (*accumulator*), holds the most significant digits of the product. The names of these registers are not nearly as important as the fact that three registers are used in multiplication. However, since these names are used with many computers, we will use them here and in other chapters.

In the following discussion of multiplication we will treat only signed-magnitude numbers without sign bits. Nor will we show registers having flip-flops for sign bits. The sign bits need not be considered since they have no effect on the multiplication process except for the sign bit of the product. This operation is simple: If the sign bits of the numbers being multiplied are the same, the computer makes the sign bit of the product positive. Otherwise, it makes this sign bit negative.

In the multiplication process we are considering, a multiplier or multiplicand that is originally negative and in either the 1's or 2's complement forms, is converted to signed-magnitude form before the start of the multiplication process. Thus, in effect, only the magnitudes of the numbers are directly involved in the multiplication.

For an understanding of multiplication, consider the following multiplication of two four-bit magnitude numbers as it would be done by hand.

$$
\begin{array}{r}
1\ 0\ 1\ 1 \\
\times\ 1\ 1\ 0\ 1 \\
\hline
1\ 0\ 1\ 1 \\
0\ 0\ 0\ 0 \\
1\ 0\ 1\ 1 \\
1\ 0\ 1\ 1 \\
\hline
1\ 0\ 0\ 0\ 1\ 1\ 1\ 1
\end{array}
\qquad
\begin{array}{l}
\text{multiplicand} \\
\text{multiplier} \\
\\
\\
\\
\\
\text{product}
\end{array}
$$

This example illustrates the fact that, in general, the product contains *twice* the number of bits of either the multiplier or multiplicand. Thus, in a computer the product may extend over two registers. Another fact gleaned from this illustration is that the product is the result of the addition of numbers that are simply shifted multiplicands. For each 1 in the multiplier, the multiplicand is included in shifted form, and for each zero in the multiplier there is only a shift.

In the multiplication process we will consider, the computer performs the multiplication in a slightly different manner than just shown. The computer adds only two numbers at a time to form a running sum. Also, it shifts the running sum *right* after each addition; there is no left shift. But a right shift of this sum is equivalent to a left shift of the multiplicand, when it is added to the running sum. One other matter. The AC register in which each sum is formed must have a flip-flop for overflows that often occur in the additions. These overflows are normal and do not indicate errors. Since each addition is followed by a shift right, this overflow flip-flop contains an overflow bit only temporarily.

For our discussion of multiplication we will consider the multiplication of the two four-bit numbers that was just presented. The components for performing this multiplication are shown in Figure 8.3 with contents at the beginning of multiplication.

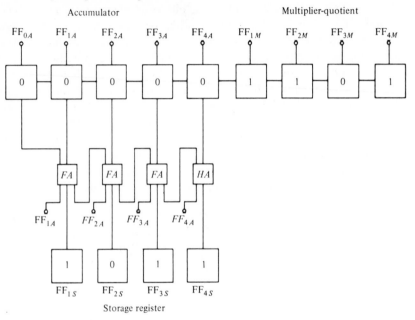

Figure 8.3   Parallel multiplier.

Several features of this multiplier should be mentioned. The AC and MQ are connected as one large shift register with flip-flop FF_{0A} of the accumulator being the overflow flip-flop that was just mentioned. The adders, which add the contents of the accumulator to that of the storage register, include a half adder at the right. A full adder is not needed here since there will be no end-around carries (the addition is that of positive numbers). However, as a practical matter it may be a full adder because this adder may be needed for other operations. Finally, note that the accumulator is cleared initially.

In the addition process, the computer first senses the least significant digit of the number in the MQ (the contents of FF_{4M}). It is initially a 1, so the computer adds the contents of the AC and SR

$$
\begin{array}{ccccc}
 & 0 & 0 & 0 & 0 & 0 \\
+ & & 1 & 0 & 1 & 1 \\
\hline
 & 0 & 1 & 0 & 1 & 1 \\
\end{array}
$$
AC
SR
AC

and then shifts the contents of the AC and MQ right. In this shifting the least significant digit in the AC moves into the most significant bit position in the MQ. The registers then contain

$$
\begin{array}{cc}
\text{AC} & \text{MQ} \\
0\ \ 0\ \ 1\ \ 0\ \ 1 & 1\ \ 1\ \ 1\ \ 0 \\
\text{SR} & \\
1\ \ 0\ \ 1\ \ 1 &
\end{array}
$$

The computer again detects the least significant digit of the number in the MQ. Because this time it is a 0, there is no addition, but only a shift right in the AC and MQ.

$$
\begin{array}{cc}
\text{AC} & \text{MQ} \\
0\ \ 0\ \ 0\ \ 1\ \ 0 & 1\ \ 1\ \ 1\ \ 1 \\
\text{SR} & \\
1\ \ 0\ \ 1\ \ 1 &
\end{array}
$$

Again, the least significant MQ bit is detected, which is a 1. As a result, the contents of the AC and SR are added.

$$
\begin{array}{rl}
0\ \ 0\ \ 0\ \ 1\ \ 0 & \text{AC} \\
+\ \ \ \ 1\ \ 0\ \ 1\ \ 1 & \text{SR} \\
\hline
0\ \ 1\ \ 1\ \ 0\ \ 1 & \text{AC}
\end{array}
$$

And the AC and MQ are shifted right.

$$
\begin{array}{cc}
\text{AC} & \text{MQ} \\
0\ \ 0\ \ 1\ \ 1\ \ 0 & 1\ \ 1\ \ 1\ \ 1 \\
\text{SR} & \\
1\ \ 0\ \ 1\ \ 1 &
\end{array}
$$

The least significant digit of the MQ contents is detected for the last time. Since it is a 1, the contents of the SR and AC are added.

$$
\begin{array}{rl}
0\ \ 0\ \ 1\ \ 1\ \ 0 & \text{AC} \\
+\ \ \ \ 1\ \ 0\ \ 1\ \ 1 & \text{SR} \\
\hline
1\ \ 0\ \ 0\ \ 0\ \ 1 & \text{AC}
\end{array}
$$

⌞ overflow

And then the AC and MQ contents are shifted right. The final result is

$$
\begin{array}{cc}
\text{AC} & \text{MQ} \\
0\ \ 1\ \ 0\ \ 0\ \ 0 & 1\ \ 1\ \ 1\ \ 1 \\
\text{SR} & \\
1\ \ 0\ \ 1\ \ 1 &
\end{array}
$$

with the product being contained in the combined AC and MQ. After the multiplication is completed, the computer inserts the sign bit of the product in the sign bit flip-flops (not shown) of the AC and MQ.

The total number of add and shift right or just shift right operations (depending on the last bit in the MQ) was four in this case and in general equals the number of bits in the basic number, exclusive of the sign bit.

Serial Multiplication

Serial and parallel multipliers have many similarities. Three registers are needed for both, and for both the multiplication processes are add and shift right for ones in the multiplier and just shift right for zeros. However, a *serial multiplier* has only one adder. And, of course, with only one adder it is considerably slower in operation than a parallel multiplier.

For an understanding of serial multiplication, we will first consider recirculating registers since they are used in serial multipliers. A *recirculating register* is a register having only one output and also only one input with the output connected to the input as shown in Figure 8.4. The binary data move in serial fashion through the register to the right, in this case. As the data move, bits emerge from the output, one at a time, and are conducted to the input for recirculation. This register can be a conventional shift register that is triggered by clock pulses for movement of the data. Or, it can be a delay line in which the bits are in constant motion, with a pulse-shaper circuit in the feedback path.

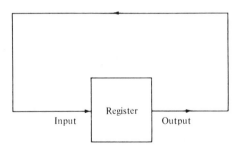

Figure 8.4   Recirculating register.

If a shift register is used, it need not be operated in the recirculation mode. That is, the bits can be held statically in the register and then shifted out one at a time as needed. For these registers, a one-bit right shift, as is needed in multiplication, is produced by applying a single clock pulse. However, if the register is in the recirculation mode, a one-bit right shift is produced by applying one clock pulse more than is needed to shift the bits through the register.

A delay line must be operated in the recirculation mode. And, in this mode a right shift is obtained by shortening the delay by one bit time. Shortening is necessary since for a right shift the bits occur one bit time sooner than they would without the shift.

Figure 8.5 shows a serial multiplier set for multiplying 1011 by 1101. Again, the sign bits are omitted because they have no effect on the multiplication process. The operation and the register contents during the multiplication process are identical to the parallel case and thus need not be repeated here. However, a few aspects of the multiplier should be mentioned. First, the output of the AC is shown connected to two components: the adder and the MQ. Actually, a gating action produced by a gate that is not shown causes the AC to be connected to the adder during an add and to the MQ during a shift right. Then, assuming the registers are of the shift register type, when a 0 is the last bit in the MQ, the AC contents are shifted right one bit and are not circulated through the adder. In this shift right, the least significant digit of the AC shifts out of the AC into the most significant bit position of the MQ. The other actions are the same as that explained for the parallel multiplier.

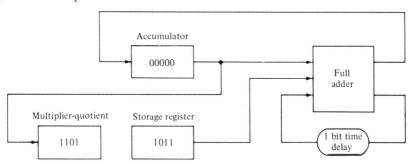

Figure 8.5 Serial multiplier.

8.4   FIXED-POINT DIVISION

Division is considerably more difficult and time-consuming than multiplication because of the necessary trial subtractions. A computer cannot look ahead in the dividend, as a person can, and know just how many digits of the dividend to take for a successful subtraction. Instead, the computer must try each subtraction, called a *trial subtraction*, that may be successful in general. If one of these subtractions produces a negative result, it is unsuccessful and hence the subtracted divisor must be restored to the dividend (at least in one division process) and then another trial subtraction made with the divisor shifted with respect to the dividend.

For example, if 11 is divided into 10101, a computer first subtracts 11 from the first two digits (from the left) of the dividend. With subtracting by adding the 2's complement of the divisor, this subtraction is

$$
\begin{array}{ccccc}
1 & 0 & 1 & 0 & 1 \\
+ \ 0 & 1 & & & \\
\hline
1 & 1 & 1 & 0 & 1
\end{array}
\qquad
\begin{array}{l}
\text{dividend} \\
\text{2's complement of the divisor} \\
\\
\end{array}
$$

Since this subtraction produces a negative result, as is evidenced by the lack of a carry, this trial subtraction is unsuccessful. Not only was time wasted in this unsuccessful subtraction but also the dividend was destroyed. Thus the divisor must be added back to the result to restore the dividend.

$$
\begin{array}{cccccc}
& 1 & 1 & 1 & 0 & 1 \\
+ & 1 & 1 & & & \\
\hline
1 & 1 & 0 & 1 & 0 & 1
\end{array}
\qquad \text{restored dividend}
$$

disregard

A typical division, having many such unsuccessful subtractions and subsequent restorations, is a time-consuming, as well as relatively difficult, operation.

We will now consider a few general matters about division. In binary arithmetic, the arithmetic used in most digital computers, the quantity subtracted is always the divisor. Of course, in decimal arithmetic this is not the case. Also, in a computer each subtraction may be performed by adding the complement of the divisor instead of directly subtracting the divisor. In the division method we will discuss, only the magnitudes of the numbers are used, and these numbers must be in signed-magnitude form. After division, separate circuits insert a positive quotient sign (0) if the divisor and dividend have like signs and a negative sign (1) if they have unlike signs.

This division method is similar, really almost identical, to that which we would perform be hand: a 1 is entered into the quotient for each successful subtraction and a 0 for each failure. However, after each subtraction the dividend is shifted *left* rather than the divisor *right* as is done by the hand method.

Perhaps the easiest approach to understanding division is from an example. In our example we will consider numbers of five bits each, exclusive of the sign bits. The dividend can be ten bits because a five-bit divisor into a ten-bit dividend can yield a five-bit quotient. This dividend extends over two registers, the AC and MQ, with the most significant five bits of the dividend being loaded into the AC and the other five bits into the MQ. However, if the dividend is five bits or less, it is loaded into the MQ and 0's are placed in the AC. The five-bit divisor is placed in the SR.

The MQ also serves as the quotient register. As the bits in the AC and MQ are shifted left, as explained below, quotient bits come into the right end of the MQ into the bit positions vacated by the shifting dividend.

As will become apparent in the following discussion, the circuit of Figure 8.3, which has been described as a multiplier, can be used as a divider as well.

In our example, 11010 will be divided into 1001001100. At the beginning of division, the contents of the three pertinent registers are, exclusive of the sign bits

AC	MQ	SR
1 0 0 1 0	0 1 1 0 0	1 1 0 1 0

In the division process the computer first tries to subtract the divisor from the leftmost five bits of the dividend. This subtraction should not yield a positive result if the quotient is to fit into a five-bit register. If it does, the computer may indicate an error and terminate the division.

With this first subtraction, plus those following the left shifts of the dividend, the total number of required subtractions is one greater than the number of bits in the MQ, or six for this example.

Assuming the subtraction is the result of adding the 2's complement of the divisor, the result is

```
  1 0 0 1 0 0 1 1 0 0              1 0 0 1 0 0 1 1 0 0
−     1 1 0 1 0          or   +      0 0 1 1 0
————————————————————         ——————————————————————
                                    1 1 0 0 0 0 1 1 0 0
```

As is the case with hand operations, only the leftmost bits of the dividend, the contents of the AC, are involved in the subtraction. Thus only these bits will be shown in the following subtractions.

If in the addition of the 2's complement of the divisor there is no carry into the sixth bit position, the result is negative, the subtraction is unsuccessful, and the divisor must be restored (at least in this division method). If there is a carry, the result is positive and the subtraction was successful. Since in this case there is no carry, the result is negative and it is necessary to restore the dividend to its original state:

```
      1 1 0 0 0
+     1 1 0 1 0
——————————————
    1 1 0 0 1 0
    ↑
    └─disregard
```

Then the quotient bits and the dividend bits are shifted left one bit place. Due to this left shift the dividend is increased by a *factor* of 2. That is, if it has a value of x before the shift, it has a value of $2x$ after the shift. This fact is not of special pertinence in this division process, but it is of significance in at least one other division process. Also note that the AC register must have an extra flip-flop to accommodate the leftmost bit of the dividend after a left shift. At this point the register contents are

$$
\begin{array}{cc}
\text{AC} & \text{MQ} \\
1\ 0\ 0\ 1\ 0\ 0 & 1\ 1\ 0\ 0\ 0
\end{array}
$$

After this shift, another subtraction is performed. The result is

$$
\begin{array}{ccc}
\begin{array}{r}
1\ 0\ 0\ 1\ 0\ 0 \\
-\ \ \ 1\ 1\ 0\ 1\ 0 \\
\hline
\end{array}
& \text{or} &
\begin{array}{r}
1\ 0\ 0\ 1\ 0\ 0 \\
+\ \ \ 0\ 0\ 1\ 1\ 0 \\
\hline
1\ 0\ 1\ 0\ 1\ 0
\end{array}
\end{array}
$$

The presence of the carry indicates a positive result and hence a successful subtraction. Because of this success, the rightmost bit of the MQ is made a 1 and both the contents of this register and of the AC register are shifted left. Note that the last bit of the MQ register is changed *before* the left shift. The contents of the AC and MQ registers at this step are

$$
\begin{array}{cc}
\text{AC} & \text{MQ} \\
0\ 1\ 0\ 1\ 0\ 1 & 1\ 0\ 0\ 1\ 0
\end{array}
$$

Another trial subtraction is made.

$$
\begin{array}{r}
1\ 0\ 1\ 0\ 1 \\
+\ \ 0\ 0\ 1\ 1\ 0 \\
\hline
1\ 1\ 0\ 1\ 1
\end{array}
$$

With no carry, the result is negative. Consequently, the contents of the AC must be restored:

$$
\begin{array}{r}
1\ 1\ 0\ 1\ 1 \\
+\ \ 1\ 1\ 0\ 1\ 0 \\
\hline
1\ 1\ 0\ 1\ 0\ 1
\end{array}
$$

└ disregard

Then, the contents of the AC and MQ registers are shifted left.

$$
\begin{array}{cc}
\text{AC} & \text{MQ} \\
1\ 0\ 1\ 0\ 1\ 1 & 0\ 0\ 1\ 0\ 0
\end{array}
$$

Again, a trial subtraction is made.

$$
\begin{array}{r}
1\ 0\ 1\ 0\ 1\ 1 \\
+\quad 0\ 0\ 1\ 1\ 0 \\
\hline
1\ 1\ 0\ 0\ 0\ 1
\end{array}
$$

Since the result is positive, the last bit of the quotient is made a 1 and then the AC and MQ bits are shifted left.

AC	MQ
1 0 0 0 1 0	0 1 0 1 0

Another trial subtraction is made.

$$
\begin{array}{r}
1\ 0\ 0\ 0\ 1\ 0 \\
+\quad 0\ 0\ 1\ 1\ 0 \\
\hline
1\ 0\ 1\ 0\ 0\ 0
\end{array}
$$

Again, there is a carry, and so the last bit in the MQ is made a 1, and then the contents of the AC and MQ registers are shifted left.

AC	MQ
0 1 0 0 0 0	1 0 1 1 0

A final subtraction is made.

$$
\begin{array}{r}
1\ 0\ 0\ 0\ 0 \\
+\ 0\ 0\ 1\ 1\ 0 \\
\hline
1\ 0\ 1\ 1\ 0
\end{array}
$$

Because there is no carry the result is negative and restoration must be made.

$$
\begin{array}{r}
1\ 0\ 1\ 1\ 0 \\
+\ 1\ 1\ 0\ 1\ 0 \\
\hline
1\ 1\ 0\ 0\ 0\ 0
\end{array}
$$

disregard⤴

The final register contents are

AC	MQ	SR
0 1 0 0 0 0	1 0 1 1 0	1 1 0 1 0

with the quotient in the MQ and the remainder in the AC.

The reader might be interested in trying this division method with the 1's complement of the divisor instead of the 2's complement. The 1's complement approach is straightforward except when the result of a subtraction is negative zero, in which case there is no carry even though the subtraction is successful. Consequently, with 1's complements the absence of a carry does not always indicate an unsuccessful subtraction and something else must be done other than merely to use carries as indicators of successful subtractions. The 2's complement method does not have this disadvantage.

8.5 FLOATING-POINT ADDITION

Floating-point arithmetic is quite different from fixed-point arithmetic because of the differences in format of the two types of numbers. As has been mentioned, each floating-point number comprises, in addition to a sign bit, a characteristic part and a fraction part. The characteristic is a biased exponent of some radix which is often two (we will use two for the radix), and the fraction is the part remaining after the specified number is normalized.

We will be assuming in all four of our floating-point arithmetic discussions a word size of only ten bits. Of these, one bit is for the sign, four bits for the characteristic, and the remaining five bits are for the fraction. The sizes of these parts are purely for convenience of explanation and should not be presumed to be realistic since usually the number of bits in the characteristic is closer to approximately one-fourth of the total.

With four bits for the characteristic, the bias is preferably 1000_2, and that is what we will use.

We will also be assuming in our floating-point discussions that immediately preceding the arithmetic operations, the floating-point numbers involved are normalized; that is, the fraction of each has a 1 in the most significant bit position.

In the *addition of floating-point numbers*, as in the addition of numbers represented in decimal exponential form, such as $3.56 \times 10^7 + 14.2 \times 10^5$, the exponents must be the same before addition can be performed. The corresponding requirement with floating-point numbers is for them to have equal characteristics. In the above decimal example, we can produce agreement by changing either the smaller or the larger exponent:

$$3.560 \times 10^7 + 0.142 \times 10^7 = 3.702 \times 10^7$$

or

$$356.0 \times 10^5 + 14.2 \times 10^5 = 370.2 \times 10^5$$

In a digital computer the number with the smaller characteristic is usually changed such that its characteristic agrees with that of the larger number. More particularly, before addition one of the two numbers to be added is loaded into the AC and the other into the SR and the MQ is cleared, often automatically. The computer checks to determine which number has the smaller characteristic. If it is the number in the AC, this number remains in the AC. But, if the smaller number is in the SR, the computer interchanges the contents of the AC and SR so that the number with the smaller characteristic is in the AC. If both numbers have the same characteristic there is no interchange.

With the number having the smaller characteristic in the AC, the AC fraction is shifted right. With each shift the AC characteristic is increased by one. This shifting continues until the two characteristics are the same. As the bits shift out of the right end of the AC, they go into the left of the fraction part of the MQ. In this way these bits are retained.

The MQ characteristic should, of course, correspond to the significance of the bits in the MQ fraction. Thus the MQ characteristic is made, in this case, five less than the AC characteristic. In general, the difference in AC and MQ characteristics equals the number of bits in the AC fraction.

Example 8.3   Decimal numbers 9.50 and 0.125 are to be added. The first number, in binary, has been loaded into the AC and the second into the SR. Show the contents of the AC, MQ, and SR after the shifting and before the addition, assuming the ten-bit floating-point format that has been described.

Solution   With the floating-point format we have been discussing, 9.50 in floating point is 0   1100   10011 and 0.125 is 0   0110   10000. Initially, the contents of the three registers are

AC	MQ	SR
0 1100 10011	0 0000 00000	0 0110 10000

Since the characteristic of the number in the SR is less than that of the number in the AC, the two numbers are interchanged. At this step the registers contain

AC	MQ	SR
0 0110 10000	0 0000 00000	0 1100 10011

Then, the fraction of the AC number is shifted right a number of bits equal to the difference in characteristics: $1100 - 110 = 110$ or six decimal. These bits go into the fraction part of the MQ. The characteristic in the AC is then made equal to that of the number in the SR, and the characteristic of the MQ is made five less, or 0111. The final result before addition is

AC	MQ	SR
0 1100 00000	0 0111 01000	0 1100 10011 ■

After the numbers have been shifted and the characteristics in the AC and SR are the same, the addition can be accomplished. We will consider a method of addition in which the numbers must be in signed-magnitude form. In this addition the fractions in the AC and SR are added, and the sum extends over the AC and MQ which act together as a single register.

If in this addition the signs of the numbers in the AC and SR are the same, that is, either both positive or both negative, the SR fraction is added to the AC fraction without any complementing. In fact, the signs of the numbers are not used in this addition. If an overflow occurs into the characteristic of the AC, this characteristic is increased by 1 and the AC and MQ fractions are shifted right one bit, which shifting makes this overflow bit the most significant bit in the AC fraction. Of course, the MQ characteristic is also increased by 1 to maintain a constant difference between the AC and MQ characteristics. Also, the sign bit in the AC is retained and the MQ bit is made to agree with it.

Example 8.4   Explain the manner in which the computer adds −14 and −6 with the ten-bit, floating-point format we have been discussing.

Solution   In floating-point form −14 is 1   1100   11100 and −6 is 1   1011   11000. Regardless of how these numbers are loaded into the arithmetic section of the computer, the computer places the larger number in the SR and the smaller one in the AC and clears the MQ.

AC	MQ	SR
1 1011 11000	0 0000 00000	1 1100 11100

Since the AC characteristic is one less than the SR characteristic, the AC fraction bits are shifted one bit to the right, the AC characteristic is made the same as that of the SR, and the MQ characteristic is made five less. Also, the MQ sign bit is made the same as that of the AC.

AC	MQ	SR
1 1100 01100	1 0111 00000	1 1100 11100

Then the AC fraction is added to the SR fraction.

$$
\begin{array}{ccccccc}
  & 0 & 1 & 1 & 0 & 0 \\
+ & 1 & 1 & 1 & 0 & 0 \\
\hline
1 & 0 & 1 & 0 & 0 & 0 \\
\end{array}
$$

overflow ⤴

This sum replaces the contents of the AC. Because of this overflow, the AC and MQ characteristics are increased by one and the AC and MQ fractions are shifted right one bit. The final result is

AC	MQ	SR
1 1101 10100	1 1000 00000	1 1100 11100 ∎

In the floating-point addition method we are discussing, little complexity is introduced if the numbers to be added have different signs.

Then, the 1's complement of the AC fraction is added to the SR fraction and the sum replaces the contents of the AC and MQ fractions.

This procedure is slightly modified in the case of the magnitude of the SR fraction being greater than that of the AC fraction and the MQ fraction being other than zero as a result of the right shift of the original AC contents. Then the MQ fraction should not remain the same after the addition. For the correct result in both AC and MQ, the difference of the AC and SR fractions *minus one* is placed in the AC and the 2's complement of the MQ fraction replaces the MQ fraction.

The one taken from the difference in the AC can be viewed as providing a number from which the MQ fraction is subtracted. This one, being in the significant position it is, corresponds to a modulus for the MQ fraction, and, of course, the subtraction of a number from a modulus is the same as taking the 2's complement of the number. Thus, although there is no direct subtraction of the MQ fraction, the final result is the same as if there were.

In the addition of numbers of unlike signs, an end-around carry often occurs since the AC fraction magnitude is usually smaller than the SR fraction magnitude. But this is not always the case. Since an interchange of AC and SR register contents is made only if the AC characteristic is larger than the SR characteristic, the AC number could have the same characteristic as the SR number and yet be larger. Hence the AC number is usually, but not always, smaller.

If an end-around carry occurs, then the original AC fraction magnitude was smaller, and thus the AC and MQ sign bits must be changed to agree with that of the SR. If there is no end-around carry, then the sum in the AC is in complement form and must be recomplemented to be in signed-magnitude form. Also, the lack of an end-around carry indicates that the original AC fraction magnitude was larger than the SR fraction magnitude and, in this case, the sign bits of the AC and MQ are left unchanged.

Finally, if the resultant sum is not in normalized form, that is, the AC fraction has leading zeros, then the AC and MQ fractions are shifted left and the AC and MQ characteristics reduced accordingly until the sum is in normalized form.

Example 8.5 Explain the addition of decimal numbers 6 and −7. Assume that at the time of addition the binary representation for −7 is in the AC and that for 6 is in the SR. Use the discussed ten-bit, floating-point format.

Solution At the time of addition, the contents of the SR, AC, and MQ are

AC	MQ	SR
1 1011 11100	1 0110 00000	0 1011 11000

With the AC and SR characteristics the same, no interchange occurs even though the AC number has the larger magnitude. As a result of the different signs in the AC and SR, the 1's complement of the AC fraction is added to the SR fraction.

$$
\begin{array}{r}
0 \ \ 0 \ \ 0 \ \ 1 \ \ 1 \\
+ \ \ 1 \ \ 1 \ \ 0 \ \ 0 \ \ 0 \\
\hline
1 \ \ 1 \ \ 0 \ \ 1 \ \ 1
\end{array}
$$

Because there is no end-around carry, the computer takes the 1's complement of the sum and obtains an AC fraction of 00100. Thus, temporarily, the contents of the AC are 1 1011 00100. This number is not normalized, there being two leading zeros in the fraction. Consequently, the AC and MQ fractions are shifted left two places and the AC and MQ characteristics decreased by two. The signs in the AC and MQ are not changed because the lack of an end-around carry is an indication to the computer that the original number in the AC had a larger magnitude than the number in the SR. The final result is

AC	MQ	SR	
1 1001 10000	1 0100 00000	0 1011 11000	■

Example 8.6   Explain how the computer adds the decimal numbers −29 and 13 in the ten-bit, binary floating-point format we have been discussing. Assume that at the time of addition the binary representation for 13 is in the AC and that for −29 is in the SR.

Solution   Immediately after the final loading, the contents of the three registers are

AC	MQ	SR
0 1100 11010	0 0000 00000	1 1101 11101

The AC characteristic, being one less than the SR characteristic, is increased by one and the AC fraction is shifted right one place. Also, the MQ characteristic is made five less than the AC characteristic. The result is

AC	MQ	SR
0 1101 01101	0 1000 00000	1 1101 11101

Since the AC and SR numbers have different signs, the 1's complement of the AC fraction is added to the SR fraction.

$$
\begin{array}{r}
1 \ \ 0 \ \ 0 \ \ 1 \ \ 0 \\
+ \ \ 1 \ \ 1 \ \ 1 \ \ 0 \ \ 1 \\
\hline
1 \ \ 0 \ \ 1 \ \ 1 \ \ 1 \ \ 1 \\
+ \ \ 1 \\
\hline
1 \ \ 0 \ \ 0 \ \ 0 \ \ 0
\end{array}
$$

The end-around carry indicates that the number in the SR was of larger magnitude than the original number in the AC. Thus the sign of the SR is used for the sum and is inserted into the sign bit positions of the AC and MQ. The answer is

AC	MQ	SR
1 1101 10000	1 1000 00000	1 1101 11101 ■

It is not necessary to consider subtraction as a separate case because the rules for floating-point subtraction are the same as those for addition with one exception: In subtraction, the sign of the SR is changed before the addition is started. Otherwise, the subtraction and addition operations are identical.

8.6   FLOATING-POINT MULTIPLICATION

In *floating-point multiplication*, as in fixed-point, the multiplier is loaded into the MQ and the multiplicand into the SR. Also, after the operation the product extends over the AC and MQ. However, in floating-point multiplication the most important part of the product is in the AC, even for a small product. This result is a consequence of normalization, or, in other words, the left adjustment of the product bits until the most significant 1 bit is in the most significant bit position of the AC. Then the MQ can possibly, but does not necessarily, contain all zeros. In contrast, in fixed-point multiplication, the important half of a product is in the MQ if the product is sufficiently small that it fits into one register. Then the AC contains all zeros except possibly for the sign bit.

There are other differences between the two multiplications. In floating-point multiplication only the fractions in and not the entire contents of the MQ and SR are multiplied. Also, as bits shift right out of the AC, they move into the top end of only the fraction part of the MQ. If the product is not normalized after multiplication, the MQ and AC fractions are shifted left until the number in the AC is normalized. During this normalization, the characteristics of the AC and MQ are decreased in number equal to the number of shifts.

In floating-point multiplication, the characteristics are added since they are biased exponents; that is, in multiplication, exponents are added. From this sum, the constant bias is subtracted because the sum contains two of these constants, one from each characteristic, and thus one of these must be cancelled.

The sign of the product is determined in the same manner as in fixed-point multiplication.

Example 8.7   Explain how the computer multiplies −7 by 6 in the ten-bit, floating-point format we have been discussing.

Solution   At the time of multiplication, the multiplier 6 is in the MQ and the multiplicand −7 is in the SR, and the AC is cleared. The contents of the registers are

AC	MQ	SR
0 0000 00000	0 1011 11000	1 1011 11100

The MQ and SR characteristics are added.

$$
\begin{array}{cccc}
 & 1 & 0 & 1 & 1 \\
+ & 1 & 0 & 1 & 1 \\
\hline
1 & 0 & 1 & 1 & 0
\end{array}
$$

And, the bias is subtracted from this sum.

$$
\begin{array}{cccc}
1 & 0 & 1 & 1 & 0 \\
- & 1 & 0 & 0 & 0 \\
\hline
 & 1 & 1 & 1 & 0
\end{array}
$$

This new characteristic (1110) is inserted into the AC and this characteristic minus five (1001) is inserted into the MQ.

In the multiplication of the SR fraction by the MQ fraction, the three trailing zeros in the MQ fraction produce a three-place right shift in the MQ and AC fractions, but not in the characteristics. Then, assuming the new characteristics have been inserted, the register contents at this point in the multiplication are

AC	MQ	SR
0 1110 00000	0 1001 00011	1 1011 11100

Next, the rightmost 1 in the MQ produces an addition of the SR and AC fractions. The resulting sum replaces the contents of the AC fraction (not the characteristic) and then the AC and MQ fractions are shifted right one place.

$$
\begin{array}{ccccc}
 & 0 & 0 & 0 & 0 & 0 \\
+ & 1 & 1 & 1 & 0 & 0 \\
\hline
 & 1 & 1 & 1 & 0 & 0
\end{array}
\quad \xrightarrow[\text{shift}]{\text{right}} \quad 0 \; 1 \; 1 \; 1 \; 0
$$

The result so far is

AC	MQ	SR
0 1110 01110	0 1001 00001	1 1011 11100

The 1 in the right bit of the MQ causes another addition of the SR and AC fractions. This addition is followed by a shift right of the AC and MQ fractions.

$$
\begin{array}{ccccc}
 & 0 & 1 & 1 & 1 & 0 \\
+ & 1 & 1 & 1 & 0 & 0 \\
\hline
1 & 0 & 1 & 0 & 1 & 0
\end{array}
\quad \xrightarrow[\text{shift}]{\text{right}} \quad 1 \; 0 \; 1 \; 0 \; 1
$$

As a final step, the computer checks the sign bits of the SR and AC. Since they are different, the computer makes the sign bits in the AC and MQ negative. The final result is

AC	MQ	SR
1 1110 10101	1 1001 00000	1 1011 11100

The product in the AC is $-0.10101 \times 2^6 = -101010_2$, which is -42_{10}. ∎

8.7 FLOATING-POINT DIVISION

Floating-point division is similar to fixed-point division. Of course, only the fraction part of the words are involved in the division and the characteristics must be considered separately, but the actual division of the divisor fraction into the dividend fraction is the same as in fixed-point division.

The dividend can be two words long, as in fixed-point division, and can extend over two registers that for our purposes are the AC and MQ. Before dividing, the computer places the most significant half of the dividend fraction in the AC and the other half in the MQ. Naturally, the characteristics in the AC and MQ correspond to the significance of the fraction digit positions in the respective registers. The divisor is loaded into the SR. After division the quotient appears in the MQ and the remainder in the AC.

The characteristic of the quotient is obtained by subtracting the characteristic of the divisor from that of the dividend. This operation is not too surprising since these characteristics correspond to exponents and in division the difference in exponents is taken. In this subtraction the characteristic bias is cancelled and must be restored. Thus the computer adds the bias to this result.

There is one other significant difference between fixed-point and floating-point division and it relates to the first trial subtraction. If this subtraction is successful, the quotient will not be normalized. Thus, after a successful first subtraction, the computer restores the dividend and then shifts the AC and MQ fractions right by one bit. Also, it increases the AC and MQ characteristics by one to compensate for this shift. That is, the computer denormalizes the dividend to ensure that the quotient will be normalized. Note that if this first trial subtraction is successful, the number of subtractions is increased by one and becomes two more than the number of bits in the fraction of the divisor.

Example 8.8 Explain how the computer performs the division: 13.25 ÷ 2.875 (decimal). Assume the ten-bit, floating-point format of our discussions.

Solution The decimal number 13.25 is 1101.01 in binary. This number cannot fit into a single ten-bit, floating-point word since if it is normalized it becomes 0   1100   110101, a total of eleven bits. But this word can extend over the AC and MQ registers with the most significant five bits of the fraction in the AC and the remaining single bit in the MQ. The divisor, the decimal number 2.875, is 0   1010   10111 in the floating-point format and, of course, is in the SR.

In the following explanation we will assume that the computer first operates on the fractions and then on the characteristics.

At the beginning of division the registers contain

AC	MQ	SR
0 1100 11010	0 0111 10000	0 1010 10111

A trial subtraction is made by adding the AC fraction to the 2's complement of the SR fraction

$$
\begin{array}{cccccc}
  & 1 & 1 & 0 & 1 & 0 \\
+ & 0 & 1 & 0 & 0 & 1 \\
\hline
1 & 0 & 0 & 0 & 1 & 1 \\
\end{array}
$$

Since the result is positive, as evidenced by the carry, restoration is made and the AC and MQ fractions are shifted right one bit while the characteristics are increased by one. The registers then contain

AC	MQ	SR
0 1101 01101	0 1000 01000	0 1010 10111

Another trial subtraction is made. The result is

$$
\begin{array}{ccccc}
  & 0 & 1 & 1 & 0 & 1 \\
+ & 0 & 1 & 0 & 0 & 1 \\
\hline
1 & 0 & 1 & 1 & 0 \\
\end{array}
$$

The subtraction is unsuccessful, that is, a negative difference is obtained. Thus restoration is made and the AC and MQ fractions are shifted left.

AC	MQ
0 1101 11010	0 1000 10000

This second subtraction will always be unsuccessful when it follows a first subtraction that produces a positive result as in this case. The right shift following the first subtraction denormalizes the dividend and so, of course, the subtraction of the normalized divisor from the denormalized dividend is unsuccessful. The end result of these first two subtractions is simply an increase of one in the AC and MQ characteristics and the insertion of a zero in the rightmost bit of the MQ. Thus, for added speed, circuits could be provided for omitting the first subtraction if the circuits inserted a zero in the bottom end of the MQ and increased the characteristics by one. In any event, this second subtraction serves no purpose in this case. A third trial subtraction is made.

$$
\begin{array}{cccccc}
  & 1 & 1 & 0 & 1 & 0 \\
+ & 0 & 1 & 0 & 0 & 1 \\
\hline
1 & 0 & 0 & 0 & 1 & 1 \\
\end{array}
$$

This subtraction being successful, the last bit in the MQ is made a 1 and then the AC and MQ fractions are shifted left.

AC	MQ
0 1101 00111	0 1000 00010

A fourth trial subtraction is made.

$$
\begin{array}{ccccc}
  & 0 & 0 & 1 & 1 & 1 \\
+ & 0 & 1 & 0 & 0 & 1 \\
\hline
  & 1 & 0 & 0 & 0 & 0 \\
\end{array}
$$

Since the trial is unsuccessful, the AC is restored and then the AC and MQ fractions are shifted left. The AC and MQ registers now contain

AC	MQ
0 1101 01110	0 1000 00100

A fifth trial subtraction is made

$$
\begin{array}{ccccc}
  & 0 & 1 & 1 & 1 & 0 \\
+ & 0 & 1 & 0 & 0 & 1 \\
\hline
  & 1 & 0 & 1 & 1 & 1 \\
\end{array}
$$

Again, the trial is unsuccessful, and so the AC and MQ fractions are shifted left

AC	MQ
0 1101 11100	0 1000 01000

A sixth trial subtraction is made

$$
\begin{array}{ccccc}
  & 1 & 1 & 1 & 0 & 0 \\
+ & 0 & 1 & 0 & 0 & 1 \\
\hline
  & 1 & 0 & 0 & 1 & 0 & 1 \\
\end{array}
$$

The subtraction is successful and so the last bit in the MQ is made a 1 and then the AC and MQ fractions are shifted left. The AC and MQ registers are now

AC	MQ
0 1101 01010	0 1000 10010

The seventh and final subtraction is made.

$$
\begin{array}{ccccc}
  & 0 & 1 & 0 & 1 & 0 \\
+ & 0 & 1 & 0 & 0 & 1 \\
\hline
  & 1 & 0 & 0 & 1 & 1 \\
\end{array}
$$

Because the trial was not successful, the AC is restored. Next, the characteristic of the SR is subtracted from that of the AC and the bias 1000 is added to the difference.

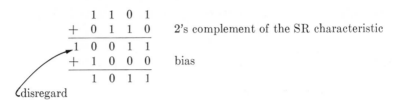

```
      1  1  0  1
   +  0  1  1  0        2's complement of the SR characteristic
      1  0  0  1  1
   +  1  0  0  0        bias
      1  0  1  1
```
disregard

This characteristic 1011 now becomes the characteristic of the MQ since the quotient is contained in the MQ. And the characteristic of the AC, being that of the remainder, is made five less than its initial value after the denormalization step. The final result is

AC	MQ	SR
0 1000 01010	0 1011 10010	0 1010 10111 ∎

PROBLEMS ▬▬▬▬▬▬▬▬▬▬▬▬▬▬▬▬▬▬▬

8.1 Determine the decimal equivalents of the following binary numbers in each of the three representations: signed magnitude, 1's complement, and 2's complement.

(a) 101010   (d) 101101
(b) 111111   (e) 111100
(c) 100000   (f) 110011

Answers (a) −10, −21, −22; (b) −31, −0, −1; (c) −0, −31, −32; (d) −13, −18, −19; (e) −28, −3, −4; (f) −19, −12, −13

8.2 Repeat Problem 8.1 for

(a) 1101111   (d) 1000000
(b) 0000000   (e) 1110111
(c) 1111111   (f) 1110100

8.3 Repeat Problem 8.1 for

(a) 1110000   (d) 1010101
(b) 1000111   (e) 1100110
(c) 1000001   (f) 1011111

8.4 Repeat Problem 8.1 for

(a) 10000000   (d) 10101010
(b) 11111111   (e) 10011111
(c) 10000011   (f) 10110111

8.5 Use seven bits to show the three binary representations of signed magnitude, 1's complement, and 2's complement for the decimal numbers

(a) −23   (c) −0   (e) −54
(b) +0   (d) −64   (f) −37

Answers **(a)** 1010111, 1101000, 1101001; **(b)** 0000000, 0000000, 0000000; **(c)** 1000000, 1111111, 0000000; **(d)** none, none, 1000000; **(e)** 1110110, 1001001, 1001010; **(f)** 1100101, 1011010, 1011011

8.6 Repeat Problem 8.5 for
    (a) -63 **(c)** -3 **(e)** -65
    (b) -18 **(d)** -60 **(f)** -34

8.7 Repeat Problem 8.5 for
    (a) -1 **(c)** -41 **(e)** -58
    (b) -19 **(d)** -62 **(f)** -11

8.8 Explain how the following numbers, shown in decimal, are added in a seven-bit word machine in which the numbers are represented in fixed-point, signed-magnitude form. Work each addition two ways, complementing a different number in each way.
    (a) $63, -28$ **(c)** $-63, 1$
    (b) $-59, 34$ **(d)** $-6, 6$
    (e) $24, -12$ **(f)** $-37, 54$ **(g)** $-29, 62$

8.9 Repeat Problem 8.8 for
    (a) $58, -23$ **(c)** $-62, 38$
    (b) $4, -47$ **(d)** $53, -26$
    (e) $39, -51$ **(f)** $61, -41$ **(g)** $-39, 46$

8.10 Repeat Problem 8.8 for an eight-bit word machine and for
    (a) $127, -83$ **(c)** $-124, 118$
    (b) $-99, 72$ **(d)** $-77, 88$
    (e) $-100, 99$ **(f)** $-117, 105$ **(g)** $-121, 63$

8.11 Explain how the following numbers, shown in decimal, are added in an eight-bit word computer that uses the fixed-point signed 1's complement number system.
    (a) $-93, 24$ **(c)** $-24, -43$
    (b) $73, -26$ **(d)** $10, -10$
    (e) $-93, -22$ **(f)** $123, -36$ **(g)** $-6, 7$

8.12 Repeat Problem 8.11 for
    (a) $-26, -27$ **(c)** $77, -85$
    (b) $43, -120$ **(d)** $-115, 28$
    (e) $113, -47$ **(f)** $-119, 108$ **(g)** $-61, -55$

8.13 Repeat Problem 8.11 but for a nine-bit word computer and for
    (a) $131, -68$ **(c)** $232, -112$
    (b) $-111, -110$ **(d)** $-245, 67$
    (e) $-161, 78$ **(f)** $-171, -87$ **(g)** $-171, 87$

8.14 Repeat Problem 8.11 but for the 2's complement number system.

8.15 Repeat Problem 8.12 but for the 2's complement number system.

8.16 Repeat Problem 8.13 but for the 2's complement number system.

8.17 Make bit-time diagrams for a serial adder as shown in Figure 8.2 for the fixed-point addition of 17 and −13 (decimal).

8.18 Repeat Problem 8.17 for −24 and −14.

8.19 Repeat Problem 8.17 for 23 and −15.

8.20 In the fixed-point multiplication of 1001 by 0111, what are the contents of the AC, MQ, and SR immediately after the second step in the multiplication process?

Answers   00110, 1101, 1001

8.21 Repeat Problem 8.20 for the multiplication of 11011 by 11101.

8.22 In the fixed-point multiplication of 1101 by 0111, what are the contents of the AC, MQ, and SR immediately after the third step in the multiplication process?

8.23 Repeat Problem 8.22 for the multiplication of 111011 by 101111.

8.24 Assume five flip-flop MQ and SR registers and a six flip-flop (one for overflow) AC. Determine the contents of these registers immediately after the shift of the third step in the fixed-point division of 10111 into 1011001101.

Answers   01110, 10111, 101001

8.25 Repeat Problem 8.24 but for the division of 11001 into 110110111.

8.26 Repeat Problem 8.24 but for the division of 11110 into 1110110100.

8.27 Decimal numbers 11.5 and 3.875 are to be added. The first number, in binary, has been loaded into the AC and the second into the SR. Show the contents of the AC, MQ, and SR after the shifting and before the addition, assuming the ten-bit, floating-point format of this chapter.

Answers   0 1100 00111, 0 0111 11000, 0 1100 10111

8.28 Repeat Problem 8.27 but for decimal numbers 13.5 and 2.375.

8.29 Repeat Problem 8.27 but for decimal numbers 21.0 and 0.125.

8.30 Show the contents of the AC, MQ, and SR registers after (a) the third step, and (b) the final step of the floating-point multiplication of 2.5 by 4.75 (decimal). Use the ten-bit, floating-point format of this chapter and assume the characteristics are processed before the third step.

Answers   (a) 0 1101 00111, 0 1000 10010, 0 1010 10100
          (b) 0 1100 10111, 0 0111 11000, 0 1010 10100

8.31 Repeat Problem 8.30 for −3.5 by 4.25.

8.32 Repeat Problem 8.30 for 6.625 by 2.5.

8.33 Show the contents of the AC, MQ, and SR registers after (a) the third step, and (b) the final step of the floating-point division of

11.875 by 4.75 (decimal). Use the ten-bit, floating-point format of this chapter and assume the characteristics are processed before the third step.

Answers   (a) 0 1000 01001, 0 1010 10010, 0 1011 10011
           (b) 0 1000 00000, 0 1010 10100, 0 1011 10011

8.34 Repeat Problem 8.33 for the division of 14.875 by 4.25.

8.35 Repeat Problem 8.33 for the division of 16.5625 by 2.5.

9

Memories

Both registers and memories store words or parts of words. Since in this chapter we will be discussing memories and not registers, we should have some appreciation for the differences between these two storage systems.

A memory can store a large number of words—typically, many thousands of words. In contrast, a register usually stores only one word or a part of one word. Thus capacities are significantly different.

There are other differences. Registers, at least in the large, fast computers, usually have components capable of faster switching than those of memories. Registers may contain flip-flops that can switch in a few nanoseconds. But memories usually contain switches of magnetic material that require more than 100 nsec for switching.

Although registers and memories can often be distinguished in speed of operation, this is not true in all computers. In some computers the registers and the memory are different portions of the same component, for example, a magnetic drum. But even in these systems the read and write mechanisms for the registers may be faster acting than those for the memory. Also, in some new computers with small memories, the memory elements as well as the register elements are composed of flip-flops. But even in these computers, registers are a little faster acting.

Registers and memories can also be distinguished by use. Registers, being faster acting, are for transitory storage, while memories are for more permanent storage.

From what has been said it should be apparent that registers and memories can usually be distinguished, but in some applications the distinctions are not very pronounced.

At present, memories of large- and even medium-sized computers are usually constructed of magnetic material, which may continue to be used for some time. However, interest is increasing in other memories such as *semiconductor memories*, which are presently being used for some small auxiliary memories, called *scratch-pad memories*, and even for memories of several thousand-word capacity. Perhaps in five or ten years they will be used extensively for large main memories. Because of the present extensive use of magnetic memories, our discussion in this chapter will be limited principally to them with only a brief mention of semiconductor memories.

Two types of magnetic memories are used in computers. One is called the *inner memory* and the other the *auxiliary memory*. The inner memory, much the faster of the two, stores the instructions, data, results, and so on, for the running of a program. In the large scientific computers this memory is usually constructed of *ferrite cores* with one core per bit of storage. In slower computers the inner memory may be a *magnetic drum*.

Auxiliary memories are usually either *magnetic tape, disk,* or *data cell* memories that are much slower in operation than inner memories. However, auxiliary memories can usually store considerably more bits, and they also have a significant cost advantage per bit of storage.

Auxiliary memories have many uses. They can be backup storage for inner memories: in them subroutines and complete programs can be stored for future use. Also, in time-sharing systems, the various programs being processed may reside in auxiliary storage until the specific times for their running when they are brought into inner memory in preparation for execution.

Most of our study of memories will be directed to the ferrite-core memory, which, at present, is popular as an inner memory. Ferrite-core memories are not new; they have been used for years even though they are far from completely satisfactory. They are not particularly fast in operation, and constant efforts are being made to increase their switching speeds.

Although ferrite-core memories are far from outstanding as regards speed of operation and of cost, nothing else is superior for large memories when all factors are considered. Thus they continue to be used.

In the following study of ferrite-core memories, we will first study the physical characteristics of the cores, and then we will study the configurations and systems in which they are used.

9.1   FERRITE CORES

A single *ferrite-core* memory element is shown in Figure 9.1 with only one wire or line passing through its hole; actually two or more wires are necessary for operation. This toroidally shaped core is formed from a ferrite material that is a magnetic ceramic made by processes similar to those for making ordinary ceramics. Because ferrites have a high resistivity, the cores have negligible eddy current loss even though they are not laminated. For fastest switching speeds these cores are made very small: 18 or 22 mils, or less, outer diameter.

Figure 9.1   Ferrite-core memory element.

Logic 1's and 0's are stored in these cores as directions of residual flux. If the flux is directed counterclockwise then, say, a 1 is stored, and if clockwise a 0 is stored or vice versa.

Considerable time is required for switching the direction of flux in a core—more than 100 nsec. This time is often of critical importance in a digital computer because in the execution of a typical instruction, cores may be switched four times. With the flip-flops and other electronic circuits in the arithmetic unit having much faster switching speeds than these cores, the operational speed of a digital computer may be closely related to the operational speed of the inner memory.

The ferrite material of these cores has nearly a square hysteresis loop, as shown in Figure 9.2, in which flux density B is plotted as a function of wire current I. When the current I is zero, the flux density in the core is either $+B_r$ corresponding to a counterclockwise flux, or $-B_r$ corresponding to a clockwise flux, depending upon the history of the past energization. The $+B_r$ and $-B_r$ are residual flux densities that represent the logic 1 and 0. We will arbitrarily assign $+B_r$ to 1 and $-B_r$ to 0.

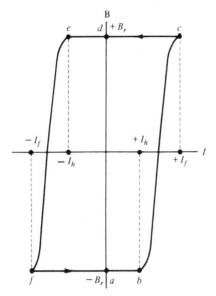

Figure 9.2 Hysteresis loop for a ferrite core.

We must understand the manner in which the core switches. With the core in the 0 state $(-B_r)$, a current pulse of $+I_h$ (see Figure 9.2) moves the point of operation on the hysteresis curve from point a to b and then back to a after the pulse decays, as shown in Figure 9.3(a). The resultant small, almost negligible, temporary change of flux density is

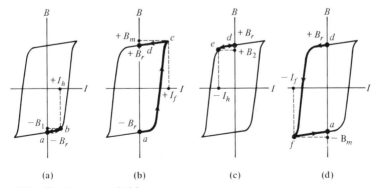

(a)   (b)   (c)   (d)

Figure 9.3 Ferrite-core switching.

from $-B_r$ to $-B_1$. This current pulse of $+I_h$ is not of sufficient magnitude to produce switching; the core was in the 0 state before the pulse was applied and remains in the 0 state after the pulse decays.

A current pulse of peak value $+I_f$, twice the peak value of $+I_h$, can move the point of operation from point a, in Figure 9.3(b), to c and then to d, in the direction of the arrows. In this change, the flux density decreases to zero, reverses to the counterclockwise direction, and then increases to a peak value of $+B_m$ when $I = +I_f$. When the pulse decays, the flux decreases slightly to $+B_r$ and remains at this value until the next current pulse is applied. The core has switched: before the $+I_f$ pulse was applied, the core was in the 0 state and after the application of the pulse, it is in the 1 state. Although a positive current produces switching from the 0 to the 1 state, being positive is not enough. In addition, the peak value has to be approximately twice $+I_h$.

When a core is in the 1 state $(+B_r)$, a negative current pulse of peak $-I_h$ moves the point of operation along the hysteresis curve from point d and e and then back to approximately d, as shown in Figure 9.3(c). The flux density changes only slightly: from $+B_r$ to B_2 and then back to $+B_r$. This change is only temporary; the core does not switch.

A current pulse of peak value $-I_f$ moves the point of operation from point d to f and finally to a, as shown in Figure 9.3(d). The corresponding flux-density change is from $+B_r$ to zero and then in the opposite direction to a peak value of $-B_m$. Finally, the flux density decreases slightly to $-B_r$, at which value it remains until another current pulse is applied. Thus the core switches. It is important to note that a current pulse of $-I_h$ peak value is not sufficient to produce switching from 1 to 0; a negative pulse $-I_f$ of nearly twice the magnitude of $-I_h$ is required.

If the core is in the 0 state $(-B_r)$, a $-I_f$ current pulse changes the flux density to $-B_m$ and then back to $-B_r$; the core does not switch. Similarly, if the core is in the 1 state $(+B_r)$, a $+I_f$ current, which changes the flux density to $+B_m$ and then back to $+B_r$, does not switch the core.

For emphasis, we will summarize the switching operation.

1. For a core in the 0 state $(-B_r)$, a $+I_f$ current pulse switches it to the 1 state $(+B_r)$. A $+I_h$ pulse cannot switch the core.
2. For a core in the 1 state, a $-I_f$ current pulse switches it to the 0 state. A $-I_h$ pulse cannot switch the core.
3. A core in the 1 state is not switched by a positive current pulse, either $+I_h$ or $+I_f$.
4. A core in the 0 state is not switched by a negative current pulse, either $-I_h$ or $-I_f$.

For representation of magnetic cores, the illustration of Figure 9.1 is inconvenient. It is tedious to draw for small diagrams and is not at all practical for memory core arrays having many cores. The straight line representations shown in Figures 9.4(a) and (b) are preferable. These lines are placed at either 45° from the horizontal or 135°, depending on how the lines are threaded through the cores.

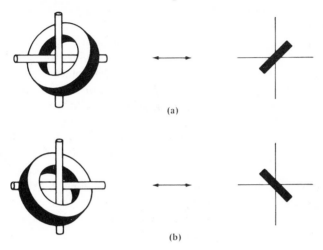

(a)

(b)

Figure 9.4   Core symbols.

9.2   2D CORE MEMORY

The simplest standard memory system for cores (it is applicable to other memory elements as well) is the 2D (*two-dimensional*) *memory* also called the *linear select system*. In it the cores are arranged, at least conceptually, in a two-dimensional array, as shown in Figure 9.5, for a very small memory that can store only four words of three bits each.

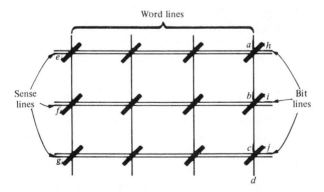

Figure 9.5   2D memory core array.

Three lines pass through each core: a *bit line*, a *sense line* parallel to the bit line, and a *word line* orthogonal to these other two lines. This orthogonal arrangement reduces magnetic and capacitive coupling between the word and sense lines. Cores for storing a single word are arranged in a column; for example, cores a, b, and c store the three bits of a single word.

Bit lines and word lines are used in the *writing process,* that is in the storing of a word in memory. If a 1 is to be stored in core a, a 0 in core b, and a 1 in core c, the computer places this word in a register, not shown, called a *memory information register* or just *MIR*, that contains a flip-flop for each bit of a word (three flip-flops here) for controlling the energization of the three bit lines. In addition to loading the MIR, the computer sets cores a, b, c to the 0 state by applying a $-I_f$ pulse on word line d. Then the computer applies $+I_h$ current pulses to word line d and also to bit lines h and j as determined by the MIR flip-flops containing 1's. By coincidence action two $+I_h$ pulses or a total of $+I_f$ energize cores a and c, switching them from the 0 to the 1 state. Core b, which is energized only by the single $+I_h$ pulse on word line d, remains in the 0 state. The word 101 is now stored in cores a, b, and c.

The currents $+I_h$ are called *half-select currents* because by themselves they cannot produce switching. But two of these currents can, by *coincidence* action, switch a core.

When the word stored in cores a, b, and c is to be *read* or, in other words, obtained from the memory, the computer applies a current pulse of $-I_f$ to word line d, causing cores a and c to switch from 1 to 0 and their flux densities to change from $+B_r$ to $-B_r$. The changes of flux induce voltages on sense lines e and g, which voltages are amplified by components not shown and then stored as 1's in the MIR.

After the read operation, cores a, b, and c are all in the 0 state. This *destructive read-out* is almost always followed by a write cycle for restoring the contents of the cores. Thus, whether the primary purpose is reading or writing, both a *read cycle* and a *write cycle* are necessary. When the primary purpose is reading, the read cycle is followed by a write cycle for restoring the contents of the memory location. And when the primary purpose is writing, an initial read cycle is necessary for setting cores at the addressed location to 0 to permit writing. However, in this reading the voltages induced on the sense lines are not used, for if they were, they would change the contents of the MIR and thereby destroy the word to be written into the location.

Since the sense and bit lines are not used at the same time, each pair of these lines can be replaced by a single line that is used for both bit driving and sensing. But then more sophisticated driving and sensing circuits are required.

Figure 9.6 is a block diagram of a 2D memory system having M bit lines, M sense lines, and N word lines. Obviously, the number of cores is $N \cdot M$, and the storage capacity is N words of M bits each. Sense amplifiers are provided for amplifying the small voltages induced on the sense windings during read cycles. Outputs from these amplifiers trigger MIR flip-flops to the 1 state. Of course, there is a sense amplifier for each sense line—a total of M sense amplifiers—and an MIR flip-flop for each sense amplifier.

These MIR flip-flops, in conjunction with a signal on a write line, control bit-line drivers. When a bit driver is energized by a write pulse and by the output of an MIR flip-flop containing a 1, the driver generates a $+I_h$ pulse on the bit line to which it is connected.

The contents of the MAR (*memory address register*) determine the selection of the word line energized during a read and write cycle. This register contains X flip-flops, where $2^X \geq N$, the total number of words.

The outputs of these flip-flops are decoded by a decoder having N output lines, each corresponding to a different memory location. Only one line is energized at a time, with the line selected depending on

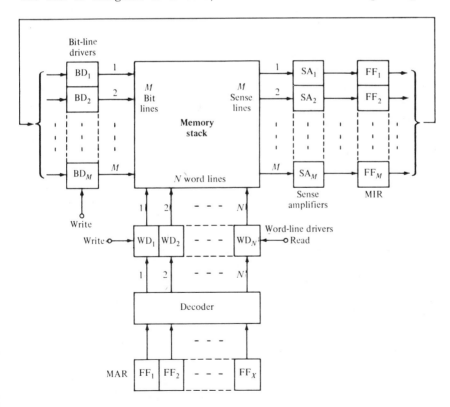

Figure 9.6 2D memory system.

the address in the MAR. A voltage on the selected line with pulses on read and write lines control the operation of N word-line drivers. When a read pulse is applied, the driver energized by the decoder output generates a $-I_f$ current pulse on the word line specified by the address in the MAR. However, if a write pulse is applied, this driver produces a $+I_h$ pulse on this word line. Thus these drivers must be capable of providing bidirectional currents.

For a memory with many word lines, an excessive number of word-line drivers is required for the system of Figure 9.6. As a consequence, the word lines are usually connected in a matrix arrangement which reduces the number of drivers needed to $2N^{1/2}$. However, this saving in drivers is at the expense of diodes for the matrix.

In the writing of a word into memory, the computer loads the MAR with the address at which the word is to be stored. After this address is decoded and the corresponding line from the decoder energized, the computer applies a read pulse to the word-line drivers. In response to this activation and the energized line from the decoder, the selected word-line driver generates a $-I_f$ current pulse on the word line corresponding to the address in the MAR. This pulse sets to 0 any cores on this word line that were previously in the 1 state, but of course, does not disturb any cores in the 0 state. When the cores in the 1 state switch, voltages are induced on some of the sense lines. However, these voltages have no effect because they are not amplified by the sense amplifiers, all of which are biased to cutoff so they will not disturb the contents of the MIR.

During these operations, the word to be stored has been loaded into the MIR. With 0's in the specified location and the word to be stored in the MIR, the read cycle is completed and the write cycle can commence.

During the write cycle, a write pulse is applied to both the word-line drivers and the bit-line drivers. The bit-line drivers energized by MIR flip-flops containing 1's produce $+I_h$ current pulses on the respective bit lines. At the same time, the selected word-line driver produces a $+I_h$ current pulse on the word line corresponding to the address in the MAR. Then by coincident current action, the cores at the intersections of the energized bit lines and this word line switch to the 1 state. As a result, the word in the MIR, which is still in the MIR, is now also stored in the specified memory location.

If the principal objective is reading from a storage location, the operations are almost the same as those for writing. The only difference is that the MIR is cleared (its flip-flops set to the 0 state) before the read pulse is applied. And, of course, the sense amplifiers now amplify the voltages induced on the sense lines, which voltages are applied to the corresponding MIR flip-flops, triggering them to the 1 state. As a consequence, the word that was in the memory location specified by the address in the MAR is now in the MIR, and the contents of this memory location are zero. This read cycle is followed by a write cycle for restoring the contents of this location. This is a conventional write cycle which has already been described.

The 2D memory has advantages and disadvantages in comparison with other memory systems. Its principal advantage is perhaps that of speed; the read cycle can be shortened significantly by increasing the magnitude of the read current pulse. This pulse was described as having a peak value of $-I_f$ but actually the peak magnitude can be much greater than I_f for driving the cores harder and thereby causing them to switch faster.

Unfortunately, the cores cannot be similarly overdriven during the write cycle, although it is possible to overdrive them a little if one is willing to use bidirectional current drivers for the bit lines. Overdriving during the write cycle with a current pulse greater than $+I_f$ applied to a word line sets *all* cores on that line to 1's. However, if the bit-line drivers can provide negative current pulses as well as positive current pulses, negative pulses can be applied to the bit lines for which the cores are to remain in the 0 state to prevent these cores from switching. But, even with this modification. any overdrive during the write cycle must be considerably less than $2I_f$. Thus, with overdrive, the read cycle is shorter than the write cycle because the overdrive read pulse can be considerably greater in magnitude than the overdrive write pulse.

Another advantage of the 2D memory is fewer lines through the cores than in other memory systems. As mentioned, only two lines are necessary, although three lines are sometimes used.

The 2D system has a disadvantage of requiring considerably more components than other memory systems. More word-line drivers are necessary. Also, the decoder has more components. For many core memory applications the disadvantages outweigh the advantages and other memory systems are used. However, the 2D system is used extensively in magnetic film and semiconductor memories.

9.3   3D CORE MEMORY

The most popular inner memory for large computers—the *3D* (*three-dimensional*) *core memory*—has cores arranged in a three-dimensional array. The cores are in planes called *bit planes* that are stacked into a three-dimensional array called a *core stack*. An 8×8 bit plane is shown in Figure 9.7(a) and a core stack in Figure 9.7(b). In practice, the planes are often 32×32 or 64×64.

As can be seen from Figure 9.7(a), four lines pass through each core.

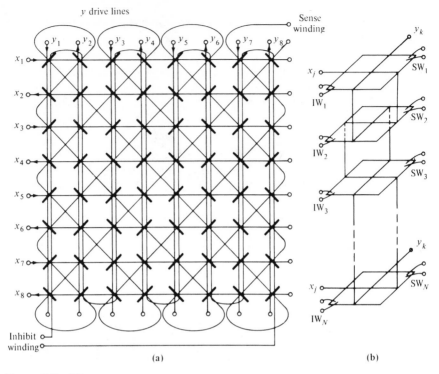

Figure 9.7   3D core memory.

Two of these lines, an x drive line and a y drive line, combine to give word selection by coincident current action. If, for example, the core at the intersection of the x_2 and y_3 lines is to be switched from the 0 to the 1 state, a $+I_h$ current pulse is applied to line x_2 and to y_3. Then the total current through this one core $(I_h + I_h = I_f)$ is sufficient to switch it. Of course, the other cores on the x_2 and y_3 lines are energized, but only by a current pulse of $+I_h$, which is insufficient for switching. These cores are said to be *half selected*.

The number of x lines and the number of y lines should each be some power of two for a most economical array, as will be seen. Thus in a bit plane the number of cores which equals the number of x lines times the number of y lines is almost always a power of two.

In a single memory stack, each location has one, and only one, core per bit plane. Thus the number of bit planes in a stack equals the number of bits in a computer word. The cores for a single location are arranged vertically in the stack, one above the other.

As is illustrated in Figure 9.7(b), the corresponding x lines in the planes of a stack are connected in series. For example, the x_9 line in the top bit plane is in series with the x_9 line in the second plane, and these are in series with the x_9 line in the third plane, and so on. Likewise, corresponding y lines are in series.

Because of these series connections if, say, one x_3 line and one y_4 line conduct a $+I_h$ current pulse, all the x_3 and y_4 lines conduct the $+I_h$ pulses with the result that all the cores at the x_3, y_4 line intersections are in the 1 state after the pulse decays. These cores, which store the bits of one word, have received, by *coincident current action*, an energization of $I_h + I_h = +I_f$, which is of sufficient magnitude to produce switching to the 1 state.

Each bit plane has a single winding, called an *inhibit winding*, that passes through all the cores. As shown in Figure 9.8, it has a configuration such that it can be arranged parallel to either the x lines or the y lines. It is shown parallel to the y lines in Figure 9.7(a) but could as well be parallel to the x lines. When this winding is energized, a pulse of I_h magnitude flows through it in a direction opposite to the write current of the y line for the addressed location, cancelling the effect of the y line current. Then only the $+I_h$ current on an x line has an effect but is insufficient to switch a core.

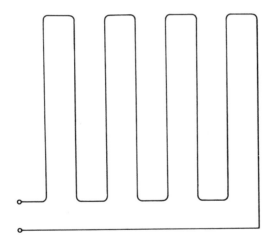

Figure 9.8 Inhibit winding.

In the 3D memory, as in the 2D memory, the cores of the selected location are set to 0 by a read cycle in preparation for a write cycle. Then 1's and 0's are stored by switching the cores that are to store the 1's and by not disturbing the cores that are to store the 0's since they are already in the 0 state. A current pulse I_h is applied to the inhibit winding of a bit plane during the write cycle if the core in the plane for the addressed location is to contain a 0. If the core is to be switched to a 1, then the inhibit winding is not energized.

As can be seen from Figure 9.7(a), the write currents in adjacent y lines must flow in opposite directions for the inhibit current to produce cancellation, that is, in order for the I_h pulse in the inhibit winding to oppose the write currents in all y lines. Also, the write currents in adjacent x lines must flow in opposite directions for coincident current action between the x and y line currents. The arrows on the x and y lines of Figure 9.7(a) indicate the direction of current flow for writing. Of course, the read currents in both the x and y lines are in opposite directions from the arrows.

The fourth winding in each bit plane is the *sense winding*. It also passes through all cores in the plane. One suitable configuration is shown in Figure 9.9 and also in Figure 9.7(a).

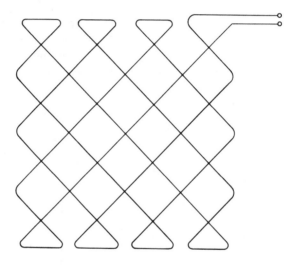

Figure 9.9   Sense winding.

During a read cycle, a sense winding has a significant voltage induced in it if the core for the addressed location is switched from the 1 to the 0 state. In general, sense windings serve exactly the same function as the sense lines of the 2D memory of Figure 9.6.

Something must be said about the sense-winding configuration. Each sense winding is wound through the cores of a plane in a snake-like fashion such that voltages induced by adjacent cores are opposed; that is, induced voltages produced by flux changes in adjacent cores tend to cancel. This cancellation is essential because of *half-select voltages* induced in the sense winding, as we shall now consider.

As has been mentioned, during a read cycle all the cores on the energized y line are energized by a pulse of $-I_h$ except the selected core which receives a $-I_f$ pulse. Although $-I_h$ is insufficient current to produce switching, it does produce a small flux change that induces in the sense winding a small voltage called a *half-select voltage*. Each of the half-select voltages is negligible, but their sum may exceed the voltage induced by the switching of the core receiving the full-select current. Of course, this situation is undesirable and can lead, for example, to the false reading of a 1. With the sense winding wound such that adjacent voltages are induced in opposite directions, the half-select voltages tend to cancel, thereby permitting the signal voltage from the switched core to predominate.

Another reason for threading the sense winding as in Figures 9.7 (a) and 9.9 is to place it at a 45° angle with respect to the x and y lines. With this placement, less electromagnetic and electrostatic coupling exists between these lines and the sense winding than if the sense winding were parallel to one of them. This coupling is undesirable because induced noise voltages result from it.

A 3D memory system is shown in Figure 9.10 with some obvious details omitted for the sake of simplicity. For example, the x lines and the y lines are not shown in the bit planes. But these lines have already been considered in Figure 9.7 (a) and so their omission should not prevent an understanding of the system.

The system has N bit planes and thus N bits per word. It has M x lines and also M y lines and hence a storage capacity of $M \cdot M$ words. The bit planes are square arrays as is usually the case.

N sense amplifiers, one for each sense winding, control N flip-flops in the MIR. In turn, the MIR flip-flops control the operation of N inhibit drivers, one for each inhibit winding. These drivers are also controlled by a write pulse.

The MAR has two sections: an x section for selecting an x line and a y section for selecting a y line. Because of the equal number of x and y lines, the number of flip-flops in the x and y sections are the same, R, where R is such that $2^R = M$.

Two decoders, one for each section, along with read and write pulses, control the operation of the x line drivers and y line drivers. As shown, each x and y line has a driver, for a total of $2M$ drivers. However, if the x lines are arranged in a matrix and the y lines in another matrix, the number of drivers can be reduced from $2M$ to $4M^{1/2}$. Of course, diodes are necessary for each matrix, but they are less expensive than drivers.

When a word is to be written into a memory location, the computer places this word in the MIR and the desired address in the MAR. Also, the computer generates a read pulse on the read line inputs at both the x and y line drivers. In response to these pulses and the address in the MAR, an x driver and a y driver generate $-I_h$ pulses on the selected x and y lines. By coincident current action, these pulses combine

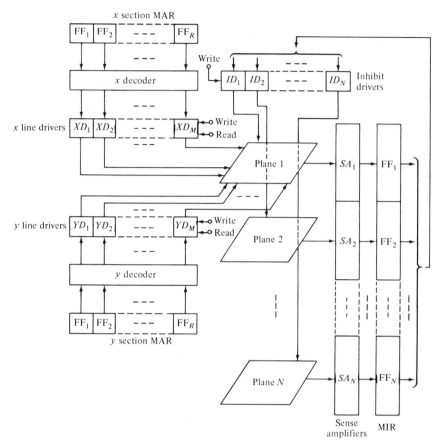

Figure 9.10   3D memory system.

to produce a net current pulse of $-I_f$ through the cores at the selected location, causing all of them to switch to or remain in the 0 state. During this read cycle the sense amplifiers are cut off to ensure that the contents of the MIR, the bits to be stored, are not changed.

In the subsequent write cycle, the computer generates a write pulse on the write inputs of the x and y line drivers and of the inhibit drivers. These inhibit drivers are also controlled by the MIR flip-flop outputs such that the only drivers energized are those corresponding to flip-flops containing 0's. Then, in response to the write pulse, these drivers generate I_h current pulses in the corresponding inhibit windings.

At the same time, or a little later, the x driver and y driver for the selected location generate $+I_h$ pulses on the selected x and y lines. If it were not for the inhibit-winding current, all the cores at the selected location would then switch to the 1 state because of the coincidence of the x and y line currents. But each core that is to remain in the 0 state also receives an inhibit current pulse that cancels the y line current pulse and prevents switching. The other cores in the location do switch, and thus the word in the MIR becomes stored in the selected location.

If a word is to be read from a memory location, the address of this word is placed in the MAR and the MIR is cleared. Then the computer generates a read pulse on the read inputs of the x and y line drivers, which are also energized by the x and y decoder outputs. In response to these inputs, the drivers generate $-I_h$ pulses on the corresponding x and y lines. Through coincident current action, the cores at the selected location receive a net current pulse of $-I_f$ that switches those in the 1 state to the 0 state.

This switching induces voltages in the sense winding on which these switched cores are threaded, and these voltages, after being amplified by sense amplifiers, trigger corresponding MIR flip-flops to the 1 state. Thus the MIR flip-flops that correspond to the cores that were in the 1 state are now in the 1 state, but the other MIR flip-flops remain in the 0 state. Although the desired word is in the MIR, all the cores at the selected location are now in the 0 state; the readout is *destructive*. Since the word that was read may be used again, it must be restored to the memory by a write cycle, as has been described.

During a read cycle each sense winding has a considerable noise voltage, a large portion of which is caused by electromagnetic and electrostatic coupling between the sense winding and the x and y drive lines of the same bit plane. This noise voltage occurs whether or not a core switches in the plane, but it occurs slightly in advance of the voltage from switching. Thus if the corresponding sense amplifier is turned on or *strobed* only at the particular time the signal voltage from switching would occur, then the noise voltage has little effect on the sense amplifier.

The two voltages induced in the sense winding for the switching and nonswitching cases are shown in Figure 9.11, in which time is measured from the initiation of the drive line pulses. If the core being read from initially contains a 0, and thus does not switch, the induced voltage decays rather rapidly. But, as can be seen, if this core contains a 1 and thus switches, the voltage increases to a peak at a time t_p and then decays.

By the time t_p, the noise voltages have decayed to almost zero as is evident from a comparison of the two voltage curves. Hence, if the pertinent sense amplifier is strobed for a short interval centered around the time t_p, the signal from the switched core is amplified, but there is almost no danger of a significant noise signal being amplified. If a noise voltage was amplified, it could cause triggering of an MIR flip-flop to the 1 state

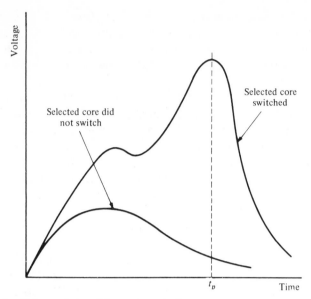

Figure 9.11   Voltages induced in a sense winding.

when the flip-flop should remain in the 0 state. Strobing of the sense amplifiers at time t_p is a common practice.

We should compare the 2D and 3D systems that we have studied. For the same capacity memory, the 3D system has fewer electronic components in the decoders, matrix arrangements, and line drivers. To show this, we will consider a memory for storing 2^K words of N bits each. If we assume diode rectangular-matrix arrangements for the decoders, the single decoder of the 2D system has 2^K outputs and K inputs and thus a total of $K \cdot 2^K$ diodes. In contrast, in the 3D system each of the two decoders has $2^{K/2}$ outputs and $K/2$ inputs. Hence the total number of diodes in the two decoders is $2 \cdot (K/2) \cdot 2^{K/2}$. Obviously, the $K \cdot 2^{K/2}$ diodes for the 3D decoders are much fewer than $K \cdot 2^K$ diodes for the 2D decoder. Similarly, the matrix arrangement for the drivers in the 2D system has considerably more diodes than the two matrix arrangements for the 3D systems.

The 3D system also requires fewer line drivers. Consider a memory for storing M^2 words. If the lines are not connected in a matrix, the 2D system requires M^2 line drivers but the 3D system requires only $2M$ line drivers. With a matrix arrangement, the number of line drivers in the 2D system is reduced to $2M$. In the 3D system, if a matrix is used for the y lines and another matrix for the x lines, the number of line drivers is reduced to $4M^{1/2}$. Thus the 3D system requires fewer line drivers. The line drivers in both systems must be bidirectional, that is, capable of providing positive and negative current pulses.

Although the 2D system requires more components, it can operate at higher speeds because a large read pulse can be used, and thus the read cycle time shortened. This overdrive is not possible in the 3D system, at least not to the extent as is possible in the 2D system.

9.4 $2\frac{1}{2}$D CORE MEMORY

The *$2\frac{1}{2}$D memory system* has features of both the 2D and the 3D memory systems. In it, parallel drive lines, that we will call x lines, are connected in series with corresponding lines in the other bit planes as in a 3D system. Other drive lines, that we will call y lines, are orthogonal to the x lines but are not interconnected between planes. Consequently separate y line drivers are needed for each plane.

In the $2\frac{1}{2}$D system, as in the 3D system, the number of cores in each plane equals the number of computer words. However, the bit planes are not square as they usually are in a 3D system; typically, the number of x lines is eight or sixteen times the number of y lines per plane. Because of the separate y line drivers for each plane, inhibit windings are not needed, but each plane has a sense winding. Thus the $2\frac{1}{2}$D system is basically a three-wire system as contrasted to the four-wire 3D system.

A $2\frac{1}{2}$D memory system shown in Figure 9.12 has details of the N bit planes omitted for convenience. We will assume that each bit plane has M x lines and L y lines with, as mentioned, M usually being eight or sixteen times L. Having N bit planes and M x lines and L y lines in each plane, this system can store $M \cdot L$ words of N bits each. The N bits of each word are distributed through the N planes as in a 3D system. Obviously, the number of x line drivers is M and of y line drivers is $L \cdot N$. Of course, the number of drivers can be reduced by arranging them in matrix form.

The sense amplifier and MIR arrangements are the same as in a 3D system. That is, there are N sense amplifiers, one for each plane, and N MIR flip-flops, each controlled by the output of a different sense amplifier. During the write cycle, the outputs of these flip-flops partially control the activation of the y line drivers. This activation is also partially controlled by a portion of the MAR flip-flops, S of them, in which $2^S = L$, the number of y lines. Only one y line driver in each bit plane is activated at a time, the particular driver depending upon the contents of this y section of the MAR. The outputs of this section are decoded by a decoder having output lines connected to all the y line driver inputs such that corresponding y line drivers are activated in each plane, for example, all YD_2 line drivers might be activated at a time, or all YD_3 line drivers. Of course, these drivers are also controlled by pulses applied to read and write inputs.

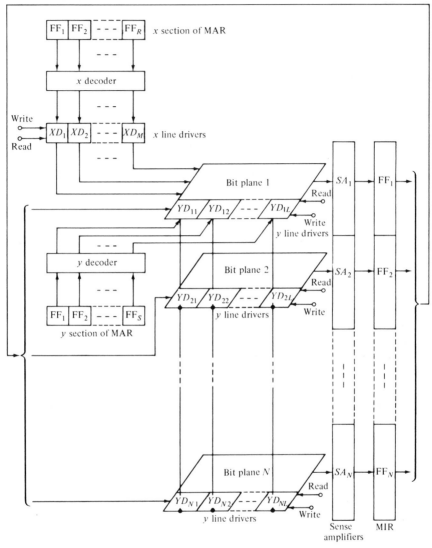

Figure 9.12 $2\frac{1}{2}$D memory system.

Most of the MAR flip-flops control the x line driver activation. R of these flip-flops are in the X section of the MAR, wherein the number R is such that $2^R = M$, the number of x lines. The x line drivers are also controlled by pulses applied to the read and write inputs of these drivers. These drivers are *not* controlled by the MIR flip-flop outputs.

When a word is to be read from a $2\frac{1}{2}$D memory, the computer loads the pertinent address into the MAR, clears the MIR, and then generates a pulse on the read inputs of the x and y line drivers. The x decoder activates only one x line driver, but the y decoder activates N of the y line drivers, one in each plane. For example, XD_3 and all the YD_4 line drivers could be activated. In response to the read pulses and the decoder signals, each activated x line driver and y line driver generates a $-I_h$ pulse on the drive line to which it is connected. Then, by coincidence current action, each core at the selected location receives a net pulse of $-I_f$ and thus either remains in or is switched to the 0 state. Those cores that switch induce voltages in the sense windings on which they are threaded, which voltages, after amplification by sense amplifiers, trigger MIR flip-flops to the 1 state. In this way the word is read from the selected location and placed in the MIR. Because of the destructive readout, a write cycle usually immediately follows for restoration of the word to the memory.

The write cycle in the 2½D system, as in the 3D system, must be preceded by a read cycle for setting the cores at the selected location to 0. If this prior read cycle is used to obtain the contents of the selected memory location, the sense amplifiers *are strobed* during the read cycle. But, if the purpose of the read cycle is only to clear the cores at the selected location, the sense amplifiers *are not strobed*.

Whatever the purpose of the read cycle, assume it has been accomplished, and that the word to be written into the memory location is in the MIR, and that the address of the location is in the MAR. Then in the following write cycle, the computer applies a pulse to the write inputs of the x line and y line drivers. In response to this pulse and the output of the x decoder, one x line driver is activated to generate a $+I_h$ pulse on the x line of the selected location. At the same time, the y line drivers corresponding to the selected location are partially activated by the write pulse and the outputs of the y decoder. But only those drivers that are also activated by MIR flip-flops containing 1's are completely activated and generate $+I_h$ pulses on the corresponding y lines. Then, by coincident current action, the cores corresponding to 1's in the MIR flip-flops switch to the 1 state and cause the word in the MIR to be stored in the memory.

For the same storage capacity, the 2½D system requires considerably more electronic components than the 3D system but less than the 2D system. It is most important to compare the 2½D and 3D core systems since they are both popular. The 2½D system has a greater number of electronic components, but since its drivers have less load, they can be simpler and less expensive. Also, it can be shown that the 2½D system has shorter delays and faster recovery from current pulses. There are other factors, all of which permit a faster cycle time.

Of course, the three wires of a 2½D system are cheaper to string than the four wires of a 3D system. And, with fewer wires, the 2½D system can have smaller cores with faster switching times. Cost comparisons between $2\frac{1}{2}$D and 3D systems for large memories show that the $2\frac{1}{2}$D system has a cost advantage (cost per bit) for the storage of short words and the 3D system for long words.

9.5   MAGNETIC FILM MEMORIES

Planar Thin Film

We should not limit our study of magnetic memories to core types. Improvements are being made in other memories to the extent that soon they may be preferred for many of the applications in which core memories are presently used. In particular, the magnetic *planar thin-film memory* is becoming increasingly competitive with core memories and so should be considered.

A planar thin-film memory has a very thin film (approximately 1000 Å) of a nickel-iron alloy that is deposited as dots or as a sheet on glass, aluminum, or some other smooth material in the presence of a magnetic field. The individual memory elements can be spaced dots or just regions of the sheet of the alloy material. This fabrication produces material having different magnetic characteristics along two orthogonal axes called the *easy axis* and the *hard axis*.

The hysteresis loops for these two axes are shown in **Figure 9.13**. The hysteresis loop along the easy axis is the familiar almost rectangular-shaped loop having considerable residual magnetism that can be used for the storage of 0's and 1's. The hard axis has substantially zero residual magnetic flux and flux along this axis is used only in switching flux along the easy axis.

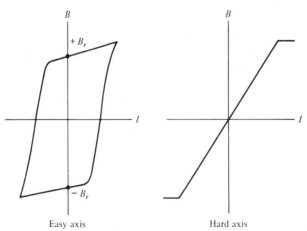

Easy axis   Hard axis

Figure 9.13   Thin-film hysteresis loops.

In Figure 9.14 four thin-film elements are shown, each of which contains two spaced rectangular spots of films. Between each pair of spots are horizontal sense and bit lines and a single vertical word line, all of which are deposited strips of conductor material. Two bit lines are used per element instead of a single bit line, but both of these lines carry the same current. A single bit line could be used but the currents in the split lines produce a more uniform magnetizing effect on the spots than current in a single line.

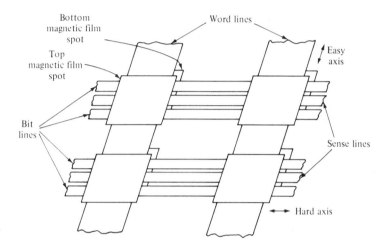

Figure 9.14 Planar thin-film elements.

Flux has opposite directions in the two spots of a pair. The flux directions in the following description are for the bottom spot.

Flux direction along the easy axis determines the storage of a 1 or a 0. We will assign the up direction of flux for the storage of a 1, as in Figure 9.15(a), and, of course, the down direction, as shown in Figure 9.15(b), for the storage of a 0. With the two face-to-face spots in each element this easy-axis flux has a path that is entirely in magnetic material except for two small air gaps at the ends.

In each word line current flows in only one direction, which we will arbitrarily designate as down. Word current in this direction establishes a magnetic field along the hard axis to the right, as in Figure 9.15(c).

Both right-directed and left-directed bit-line currents are required. Bit current to the right produces a magnetic field up and along the easy axis [Figure 9.15(a)] and bit current flow to the left produces a magnetic field that is down as in Figure 9.15(b).

A 1 is stored by first applying a word-line current and then a right-directed bit current. Together they produce a net magnetic field and

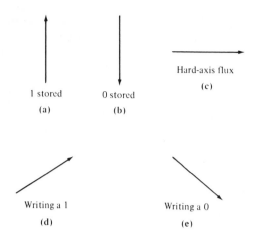

1 stored   0 stored
(a)   (b)

Hard-axis flux
(c)

Writing a 1   Writing a 0
(d)   (e)

Figure 9.15   Directions of magnetic field and flux.

thus a direction of flux that is up and to the right as in Figure 9.15(d). Then the word-line current is decreased to zero and, as a consequence, the direction of flux spins to the nearest easy axis, which is up. Finally, the bit current is decreased to zero, but the direction of flux remains up as in Figure 9.15(a) because of residual magnetism.

The procedure for storing a 0 is the same except that the direction of bit current is to the left instead of the right, and the resultant residual flux is directed down instead of up.

The above procedure is used for writing regardless of the original magnetic states of the elements. Note that flux direction is reversed by spinning the direction of flux as contrasted to direct reversal. Spinning produces faster switching.

A practical memory has many rows and columns of the basic elements of Figure 9.14 arranged in a configuration similar to that of Figure 9.5, which is for cores in a 2D system. In fact, these thin-film elements are used in a 2D system similar to that of Figure 9.6. Since we have already discussed the 2D core system, we will not completely consider the 2D thin-film system. Instead, only those operations that are different will be mentioned.

In the thin-film system the sense amplifiers are preferably responsive to positive *and* negative voltages, because, as will be discussed, the storage of one state is indicated by a positively induced voltage in a sense line and that of the other state by a negatively induced voltage. That is, the polarity of the voltage distinguishes whether the stored bit is a 1 or a 0 rather than the presence or absence of a voltage as in a core system. Another difference from the core systems is the word-line drivers; they need be capable only of producing current flow in one direction. But, the bit-line drivers must provide bidirectional currents.

The read and write cycles are also different. In the read cycle, a word current is generated in the selected word line and maintained on. This current causes the direction of magnetic flux to spin to the right, as in Figure 9.15(c), for all the elements along the selected word line. If a 1 is stored in an element, this spin is clockwise and induces a voltage of one polarity in the sense line. But if a 0 is stored, the spin is in the counterclockwise direction and induces a voltage of the opposite polarity in the sense line. The induced voltages are amplified by sense amplifiers to set respective MIR flip-flops to 1's or 0's, depending upon whether the induced voltages are positive or negative. Of course, the read-out is destructive.

For restoring the word to memory, the word-line current is maintained flowing after the voltages have been sensed. Then the bit-line drivers are activated. For each MIR flip-flop in the 1 state, the corresponding bit-line driver produces current to the right in the bit line to which it is connected. However, if an MIR flip-flop is in the 0 state, then the corresponding bit-line driver produces current flow to the left. Thus the magnetic fluxes in the various selected elements rotate either to the direction shown in Figure 9.15(d) or (e). Next, as has been explained, the word current and then the bit-line currents are reduced to zero. The word that was read is now restored to the memory location.

The advocates of thin-film memories predict that in the near future these memories will, in general, have a cost advantage as well as a speed advantage over the core memories. Also, the thin-film memories are obviously well suited to batch fabrication processes. At present, the films have a slight speed advantage over cores and, in some cases, a cost advantage (price per bit), especially for the storage of medium to long words in memories having large storage capacity. The principal disadvantage appears to be that of higher cost per bit for the popular-sized memories.

Cylindrical Film

Another film memory that is becoming increasingly popular is the *cylindrical-film or plated-wire memory*, a section of which is shown in Figure 9.16. This is basically a two-wire memory having bit or digit lines that also serve as sense lines. These sense-bit lines, which are parallel to each other, are encircled by hairpin-shaped word lines that are parallel to one another and approximately perpendicular to the sense-bit lines.

The sense-bit lines are actually wires that in one memory have a diameter of 5 mils and a spacing of 30 mils. They have a magnetic

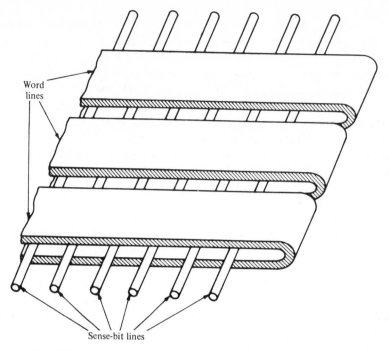

Word
lines

Sense-bit lines

Figure 9.16   Cylindrical-film memory.

alloy coating of typically 30 μin. thick which forms the film of the cylindrical-film memory. During the manufacturing process this film is made magnetically anisotropic with an easy magnetization axis around the wire and a hard axis along the wire, as shown in Figure 9.17. The bit elements are on these sense-bit lines under the word lines with one element at each sense-bit and word-line intersection.

The word lines, sometimes referred to as *straps,* are 40 mils or so wide and approximately 20 mils apart. These dimensions restrict the bit packing density to typically 16 to 22 bits per inch of sense-bit line. The spread of the word field around each word line prevents closer packing. However, higher packing densities can be obtained by placing magnetic strips on the word lines. These strips inhibit the word-line field from spreading while also increasing the flux beneath the word lines.

At the beginning of a read operation a selected word line receives a current pulse that causes the direction of flux of each element beneath the energized word line to spin from the easy circumferential axis toward the hard longitudinal axis. However, this word current is not of sufficient amplitude to produce alignment of the flux along the hard axis; a significant circumferential component remains.

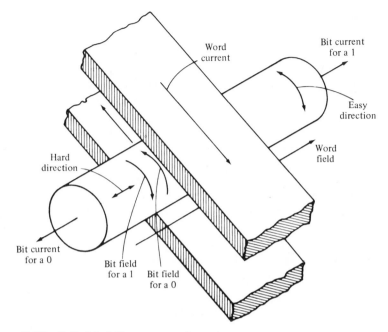

Figure 9.17 Cylindrical-film memory element.

The flux spin in any one element induces a voltage of perhaps 10 mV in the sense-bit line on which the element is located. The polarity of this voltage depends upon the direction of the original circumferential flux, which as can be seen from Figure 9.17, is one direction for a 1 and the opposite direction for a 0.

When the word current decays to zero the direction of flux in each element beneath the word line returns to the original circumferential direction without appreciable demagnetization. Thus this is *nondestructive readout (NDRO)*. Although, the read operation does not have to be NDRO, there are significant advantages to it, as will be mentioned. Of course, the induced voltages are amplified to set flip-flops in a memory information register, as has been explained in discussions of other memories.

In a write operation a selected word line is energized in the same manner as in a read operation. That is, word current flows in the same direction and with the same magnitude for reading and writing. After the word current is established and the flux in each bit element beneath the energized word line spins toward the longitudinal hard axis, selected sense-bit lines are energized. If this is a 2D memory all of the sense-bit lines are energized but in a 2½D memory only certain ones are energized, which are, of course, the lines having bit elements in which we want to write.

In the writing, the *direction* of the bit currents determines whether 1's or 0's are written, as is evident from Figure 9.17. These bit currents are produced by drivers that in turn are controlled by MIR flip-flops. For any one element the combined word-line and sense-bit-line fields cause the flux to have the desired circumferential component so that when the word current is cut off, which occurs in the next step, the flux spins to the circumferential easy axis in the desired direction. Finally, the bit current is cut off and the writing is complete.

One of the principal advantages of the cylindrical film memory is nondestructive readout. With NDRO two independent read operations can be completed in approximately the same time required for a single read operation in a *destructive readout (DRO)* memory. The elimination of write following read produces a speed increase of approximately 67 percent. For this increase we are assuming a typical computer use of approximately four read instructions for each write instruction. In a DRO memory, these five instructions require ten operations—five read-write pairs. But in an NDRO memory they require only four read operations plus a single clear-write pair, or a total of six operations. The ratio of the ten operations to the six gives the speed increase of 67 percent.

Although the planar thin-film and cylindrical-film memories have many common features, NDRO, at present, is practical only for the cylindrical-film memories, at least for mass production versions of these two memories. Planar thin-film memory elements in an NDRO environment tend to demagnetize because of the open flux paths at their ends unless the elements are constructed from material having a high coercive force. But such material requires more drive current and also it is magnetostrictive; that is, it changes size when magnetized. This varying of size adversely affects the assembly, mounting, and packaging of these memories.

Cylindrical-film systems are suitable for either 2D or $2\frac{1}{2}$D memories. A 2D version is shown in Figure 9.18. Its operation should be apparent from our prior discussions. Also, a $2\frac{1}{2}$D implementation should be obvious from prior considerations.

Cylindrical-film memories are replacing core memories for some applications. In fact, advocates predict that in three or four years these memories may comprise 10 to 20 percent of the total random access memory production in the United States. There is no denying that cylindrical-film memories have advantages of faster operation and less power consumption than comparable core memories and apparently they are cost competitive. And, of course, they have the NDRO feature. The relatively low bit density is the principal disadvantage.

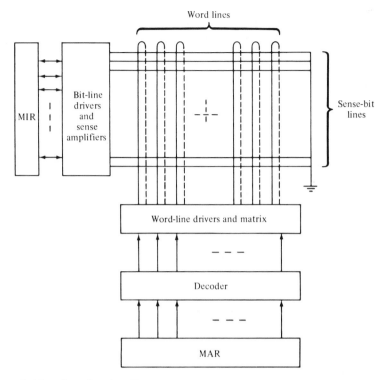

Figure 9.18   2D cylindrical-film memory.

9.6   MAGNETIC DRUM MEMORY

The memories we have discussed up to this point have been *static* and *random access,* and, except for cylindrical-film memories and some versions of thin-film memories, have had individual memory elements, such as cores, for storage of the bits. These memories are static since they have no moving parts. They are random access in that any memory location can be accessed without sequencing through other memory locations. Also, the time required for accessing any location is the same as that for any other location. Although these memories are fast operating, they are costly.

Some computers do not require high-speed memories, and even those that do usually have auxiliary storage units operating at slower speeds. These auxiliary units typically have a larger storage capacity than the core storage and invariably have a cost per bit of storage that is much less. There are several types of such storage units. Of these, we will consider the *magnetic drum, magnetic disk, magnetic tape,* and *data cell memories.*

The drum of a *magnetic drum memory* is actually a rotating cylinder, as shown in Figure 9.19, the surface of which is coated with magnetic material having a square-loop hysteresis characteristic similar to that for cores. These drums come in various sizes and operate at different speeds. Usually, the larger the diameter the slower the speed of rotation. Some drums are in the size range of 12 in. in diameter and 8 in. in length and have rotational speeds of a few thousand revolutions per minute.

In a drum memory stationary read-write *heads* are positioned along the drum surface, as shown in Figure 9.19. Read and write operations may be performed by the same heads or there may be separate heads for reading and writing. During a write operation, the heads magnetize annular regions called *tracks* that may number in the hundreds and even thousands, each having one or more recording heads. The heads do not physically contact the drum but are positioned just a few thousandths of an inch away from the surface.

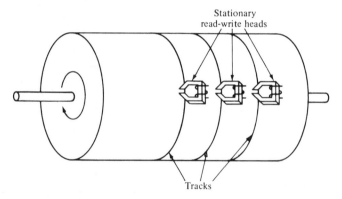

Figure 9.19   Magnetic drum.

As can be seen better in Figure 9.20, each head is a partially closed core of magnetic material encircled by a winding. A gap in the core near the drum surface provides a high reluctance path. Often a shim of paramagnetic material is inserted in the gap for increasing the reluctance. Current in the winding produces flux that, as a result of the high reluctance of the gap, links with the drum surface and magnetizes a small region called a memory cell that stores a bit. The packing density of the stored bits is usually several hundred bits per inch.

During reading, which is NDRO, the magnetized areas passing under a head produce a changing flux that induces in the winding voltages that are amplified and then stored in a register. For a drum having a speed of 3600 rev/min, a bit density of 500 bits per inch, and a diameter of 12 in., the rate of reading is approximately one-half million

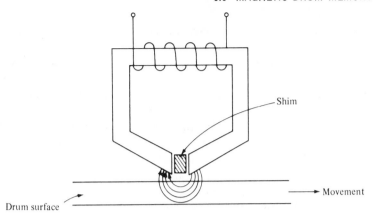

Figure 9.20   Magnetic head.

bits per second. Thus, during actual reading, the rate of bit transmission is high. The reputed slowness of the drum is not the result of the rate at which the bits are read, but rather the considerable time, sometimes several milliseconds, that elapses after the accessing starts and before the desired word passes under the heads.

Words can be recorded on a drum in several ways. For example, words are arranged serially around the tracks, with all the bits of any word on a single track. For this arrangement and a drum circumference of, say, 36 in., a packing density of 300 bits per inch, and words of 30 bits each, each track contains 360 words. The part of the track containing a word is called a *sector*. With this arrangement the bits are obviously read and written serially.

The bits of a word can also be arranged in parallel fashion with one bit per track, all the bits being in the same positions in the tracks so that they pass under recording heads at the same time. Then the memory cells of a word are said to be in a *slot*. In this parallel mode, all bits of a word are read or written at the same time.

In another mode of operation, a combination of the serial and parallel modes, the bits of a word extend over several tracks, often four tracks, as in the parallel mode. Also, each stored word has more than one bit per track as in the serial mode. Thus several bits of a word are read or written at a time, but not all the bits.

In any of these modes of operation a word must pass under the read head or heads before it can be read. The time from the start of the command to read until the word is actually read is a variable called the *access time*.

In the worst case, the word to be read will have just passed under the read head or heads at the beginning of the read command, in which case the word cannot be read until the time for a complete revolution has elapsed, assuming one head per track. This maximum access time depends on the speed of revolution of the drum, but in general, being in the range of milliseconds, it is of the order of a thousand times greater than the access time for core storage. On the other hand, the word to be read may be approaching the read head or heads at the beginning of the read command, in which case the access time is approximately zero. For only one read head per track the average access time is the time required for half a revolution of the drum. Obviously, this time can be decreased by using several read heads per track.

One track of the drum is often used for the generation of clock pulses. This track, in which 1's are stored at the specified packing density, provides clock pulses for controlling the reading or writing of bits in all the tracks so that the bits in the various tracks are grouped in parallel fashion in slots at the specified packing density. Clock pulses can also be used for a slot counter that is reset to zero once each drum revolution. From the contents of this counter the computer can determine what slot is beneath the heads at any time.

For serial operation a timing track may be provided having a bit at the beginning of each sector. Another timing track may contain the addresses of the sectors that will next appear under the recording heads. Then when the address in the MAR and the address in this track are the same, a read or write operation can be initiated and the correct sector read from or written into. For parallel operation there is no need for the sector and address tracks since the words are coincident with the clock bits.

A block diagram of a serially operated drum memory system is shown in Figure 9.21. To have something specific to discuss, we will assume the drum has 64 tracks, not counting the timing tracks, and 128 sectors per track. Then six bits are required to select a head and seven bits to select a sector. Consequently, the addresses must be 13 bits each, and the MAR must have 13 flip-flops for storing the addresses. In Figure 9.21 the MAR is shown in two sections, one of which has six flip-flops for selecting the head and the other seven flip-flops for selecting the sector.

If the operation is that of writing, the word to be written is loaded into the MIR which is a shift register that is shifted by clock pulses during actual writing. In response to the head section of the MAR, a switch selects the correct head. The correct sector is selected by comparing the contents of the sector section of the MAR and the contents of a modulo 128 counter that is triggered by pulses from a sector track. This counter provides the address of the sector that is under the heads at any particular time. When the contents of this counter and those of the sector section of the MAR agree, this comparator produces a gating signal that permits the clock pulses to shift the contents of the

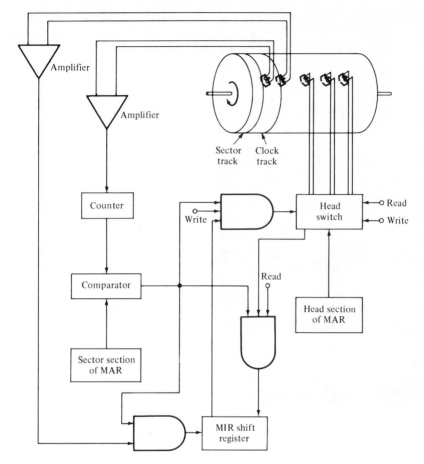

Figure 9.21 Serially-operated drum memory system.

MIR out and into the head switch, which, in turn, directs the signals to the correct head. Then the contents of the MIR are written onto the drum. A read operation is substantially the same as regards selection of head and sector. But, of course, the command read signal causes reading instead of writing.

A typical commercial drum storage system is shown in Figure 9.22.

9.7 DISK, TAPE, AND DATA CELL MEMORIES

Disk Memory

The *magnetic disk memory* is another popular, relatively inexpensive, large-capacity storage system. In general, it is slower in operation than the drum, has a greater storage capacity, and is less expensive per bit of storage.

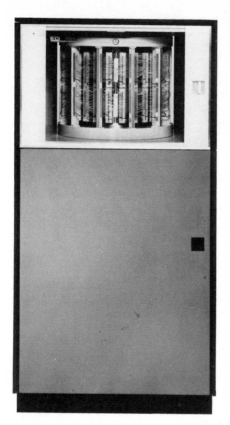

Figure 9.22 Drum storage system (courtesy of International Business Machines Corporation).

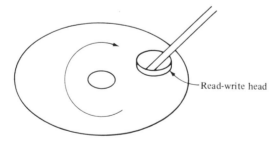

Read-write head

Figure 9.23 Disk and read-write head.

A single disk, shown in Figure 9.23, looks much like a record for a record player, but it may be considerably larger and the speed of revolution is considerably greater—typically of the order of 1000 rev/min. Also, the tracks are concentric circles instead of spirals. Hundreds of such tracks may be on a side of a disk. Frequently both surfaces of the disk are coated with magnetic material so that both sides can be used for storage. The recording density is in hundreds of bits per track inch.

A read-write head does not make contact with a disk but usually rides over it on a thin cushion of air produced by the disk rotation.

For reading or writing on different tracks a read-write head is moved radially. This mechanical motion of the head is relatively time-consuming and, of course, the placement of the head is quite critical. For increased speed of operation, two heads may be used, one for accessing the inner tracks and another for accessing the outer tracks.

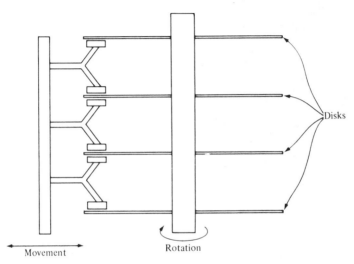

Movement   Rotation

Figure 9.24   Disk stack.

Figure 9.25   Disk pack (courtesy of International Business Machines Corporation).

In a disk memory system many disks are arranged in a stack, as shown in Figure 9.24. There may be a read-write head for each surface, as shown, or a single head that in addition to moving radially also moves vertically for insertion between different pairs of disks. These disks are not removable in some memories but in others they are. The removable disks may be arranged in a set called a *disk pack,* one of which is shown in Figure 9.25. A complete disk storage drive with disk pack is shown in Figure 9.26.

Figure 9.26   Disk storage drive (courtesy of Control Data Corporation).

Tape Memory

Another large storage capacity, inexpensive, and relatively slow memory system is that using *magnetic tape.* The tape is usually flexible plastic with a coating or a layer of magnetic material. The width is often approximately one inch and the length can be from hundreds to several thousand feet. The tracks or channels extend along the length of the tape with a density of approximately seven tracks per one-half inch of width. The bit density for each track is usually either 200, 556 or 800 bits per inch.

Magnetic tape is run over recording heads, one for each track, in magnetic tape units, as shown in Figure 9.27, from reels that can be interchanged easily and quickly.

For reasonable access times, some tapes move at rates of several hundred inches per second. The potential problem of necessary fast starts and stops with components having significant inertia has been eliminated to a great extent. The tape drive mechanism is continuously rotating and so does not start and stop for each tape movement. Instead, when the tape is to be moved, it is pressed against the tape drive mechanism. The reels have a separate drive mechanism that need be only sufficiently

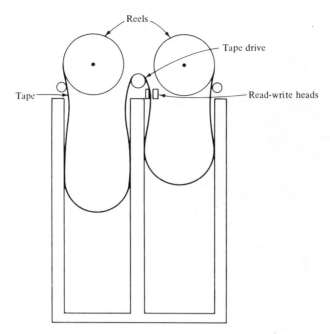

Figure 9.27   Magnetic tape unit.

fast acting to maintain buffer lengths of tapes on both sides of the tape drive as shown in Figure 9.27.

A commercial magnetic tape unit is shown in Figure 9.28.

Data Cell Memory

The data cell (or, more completely, *data cell drive*) is another large storage capacity, slow, and relatively inexpensive memory. We will discuss a particular one: the IBM 2321 Data Cell Drive. In it the bits are stored on strips of tape, as shown in Figure 9.29(a), that have a coating of magnetic material. Each strip is $2\frac{1}{4}$ in. wide. 13 in. long, and about three times as thick as magnetic tape. A strip has 100 vertically arranged tracks, each of which can store about 16,000 bits. These strips are mounted in groups called subcells, with ten strips per subcell. The subcells are mounted in pie-shaped cells with twenty subcells per cell. Ten cells form the cylinder of the data cell drive as shown in Figure 9.29(b).

In a read or write operation, the cylindrical array of cells rotates until the subcell containing the strip to be processed is under a drum mechanism positioned over the cylinder. Then separation fingers on this mechanism push back the index tabs of the strips adjacent the selected

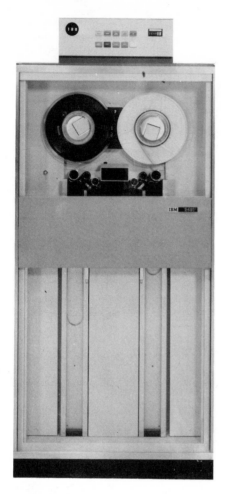

Figure 9.28 Commercial magnetic tape unit (courtesy of International Business Machines Corporation).

strip to isolate the selected strip. After this strip is exposed, a pickup head drops down and latches through the hole in the top of the strip. The strip is drawn up and wrapped around the drum and rotated past 20 read-write heads, one for every fifth track. The heads can be moved, as a unit, horizontally into five different positions to provide access to all 100 tracks of a strip.

The strip remains wrapped on the rotating drum until another strip is selected, or a command to restore, or 800 msec have elapsed since the strip was selected. In restoring the strip, the drum reverses its direction of rotation and drops the strip back into the subcell between the separated strips.

For the operation of the data cell drive, 75 to 225 msec is required for rotating the array to place the selected subcell under the drum mecha-

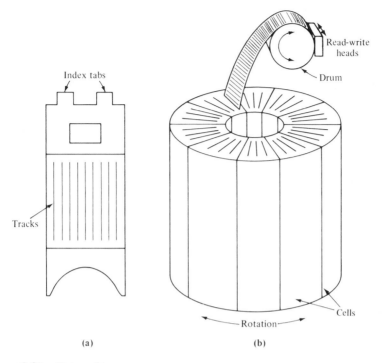

Figure 9.29 Data cell memory.

Figure 9.30 IBM 2321 Data Cell Drive (courtesy of International Business Machines Corporation).

nism. Another 175 msec is necessary for picking up a strip. Movement of the read-write heads takes another 95 msec. And 200 msec is required for restoring a strip. The average access time for the array, assuming the previous strip has been restored, is 350 msec.

The IBM 2321 Data Cell Drive is shown in Figure 9.30.

9.8 MAGNETIC SURFACE RECORDING TECHNIQUES

We will now consider how bits are stored on the magnetic surfaces of drums, disks, and tapes. Since the two recording techniques *return-to-zero* (*RZ*) and *nonreturn-to-zero* (*NRZ*) do not depend on the type of surface, we will not refer to any specific surfaces in our discussion.

Return-to-Zero

A return-to-zero recording is illustrated in Figure 9-31. A positive current pulse applied to a recording head winding produces a magnetized region with flux in one direction. The resulting flux pattern, which represents a 1 bit, is not the rectangular shape that might be expected from a rectangular current pulse, but is distorted by the fringing of flux about the gap in the recording head. The magnitudes of the current pulses are preferably sufficient to produce flux saturation in the recording surface. Then some variation in write currents can occur without attendant variations in the flux patterns. Of course, uniform intensity flux patterns are desired to avoid voltage pickup variations.

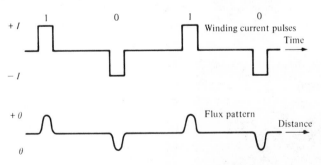

Figure 9.31   Return-to-zero recording technique.

A 0 bit is recorded by applying a negative current pulse to the recording head winding to reverse the direction of flux. Between each pair of recorded bits is a guard zone of zero flux produced by the zero return of the winding current. Of course, the different flux patterns for the 1's and 0's induce different voltages in the read head.

The return-to-zero recording technique has the disadvantage that in a rewrite over a track the newly written bits must be exactly on top of the regions on which the prior bits were stored. Otherwise, portions of the flux patterns of the prior bits remain to produce erroneous pickup voltage signals. This exact bit placement is possible on a drum having a timing track from which timing pulses control the bit placement. Although this return-to-zero technique is satisfactory for drums, it is rarely used with other surfaces.

This disadvantage of the return-to-zero technique can be eliminated by using a modified technique shown in Figure 9.32. We classify this technique with RZ, but it is really a return to a reference rather than to zero. That is, the flux is not returned to zero in the guard zone but is preferably returned to the negative saturation level. During writing, negative current flows in the winding of the head except at times at which 1 bits are to be recorded. Then the current jumps up to a level preferably sufficient to produce positive flux saturation. During reading, voltages are induced in the winding only for 1 bits. The presence of a 0 is indicated by the absence of an induced voltage at a bit time interval.

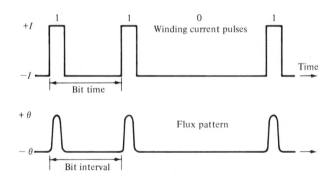

Figure 9.32   Return-to-reference recording technique.

With this technique, rewriting over a track is not critical because the negative flux of the guard zones causes all prior bits to be written over even if there is a displacement between successive recordings. This reference technique also has two other advantages over RZ. The flux changes, being twice as great, induce approximately twice the voltage magnitudes during reading. And the read amplifiers need not amplify bipolar signals as they must for RZ.

Nonreturn-to-Zero

Packing density can be doubled over that of RZ with nonreturn-to-zero (NRZ) techniques illustrated in Figure 9.33. Only the head-winding currents are shown, as the resulting flux patterns should be apparent from our RZ discussion.

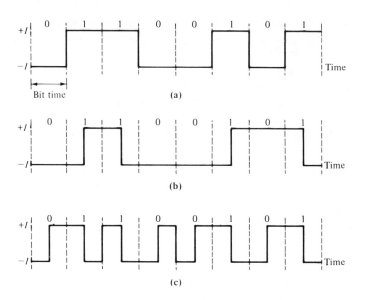

Figure 9.33   Nonreturn-to-zero recording technique.

In the first NRZ technique shown in Figure 9.33(a), the winding current is negative for the entire bit time of recording a 0 and positive for the entire bit time of recording a 1. There are no guard zones, and for several 1's in succession or several 0's, the winding current does not change. A current change and also a flux change occur only when a 1 is followed by a 0 or vice versa. Consequently, during reading, an induced voltage does not indicate a 0 or a 1 but only a change in bits. In fact, no voltages are induced in the reading of successive 1's or 0's. The required output voltages for 0's and 1's can be produced by a flip-flop that is triggered to change states by voltages induced in the head winding.

In the second NRZ technique shown in Figure 9.33(b), the winding current reverses halfway through the bit time for writing a 1 but does not reverse for a 0. During reading, an induced voltage in the winding indicates a 1 and the absence of an induced voltage during the bit time indicates a 0. The induced voltages are of both polarities.

A third method of NRZ recording illustrated in Figure 9.33(c) has various names: *Manchester, Ferranti,* and *phase recording.* In the writing of a 0, winding current is negative for the first half of the bit time and positive for the second half. It is opposite for a 1: positive for the first half of the bit interval and negative for the second half.

The highest frequency of operation is *only twice* that of the lowest frequency. The highest frequency occurs for all 1's or all 0's, in which case there is a single pulse per bit time. The lowest frequency occurs for alternate 0's and 1's. Then there is only one pulse for every two bit times. In contrast, the frequencies of the two other discussed NRZ techniques vary from zero or dc up to one pulse per two bit times. The restricted frequency range of the phase recording method permits the use of simpler amplifiers.

9.9   SEMICONDUCTOR MEMORY

Semiconductor memories are seriously challenging the supremacy of magnetic core memories. In general, semiconductor memories are somewhat faster acting. and they are excellently suited for implementation in integrated circuit form. Also, their select, read, and write circuits are considerably simpler than those for core memories. At present, semiconductor memories are cost competitive with core memories for small memories up to $4K$ ($K = 1024$) bits. And each year the cost competitive size increases.

A semiconductor memory is constructed of transistorized flip-flops, which are the memory cells, and transistorized selection, reading, and writing circuits. With present technology, FET's are preferred for the flip-flops and bipolar transistors for the selection, reading, and writing circuits. Of course, integrated circuits must be used since the cost of individual transistors is prohibitive, at least for the memory cells.

There are several reasons why FET's are preferred for memory cells. For one thing, bipolar transistors are more expensive. They need approximately 20 percent more slice area because of isolation regions *not* needed by FET's, and they also need more masking and diffusion steps. This more complex processing for bipolar transistors results in lower yields. Another important consideration is power. Bipolar transistors require considerably more power than FET's. In fact, the power required by bipolar transistors is so great that if they were used in a memory array, severe problems would occur in bringing in the required high currents and in removing heat from the cells.

Because of speed considerations, bipolar transistors should be used for the external driving, sensing, and selection circuits. If FET's are used throughout, the memory cycle time is of the order of 1 μsec. But if bipolar transistors are used in these external circuits with FET's for the memory cells, the cycle time can be as low as 100 nsec.

In the past, p-channel FET's have been preferred because the impurities that contaminate semiconductor material are more of a problem with n-channel FET's. However, new processing techniques have been developed for overcoming these difficulties and, as a result, n-channel FET's are becoming increasingly popular. They have the advantage of faster operation since their electron current carriers are more mobile than the holes of the p-channel FET's.

Semiconductor memories are usually 2D or, in other words, *word organized*. A 3D or *bit-organized* semiconductor memory has a serious disadvantage in that each of its memory cells is approximately 20 percent larger in area then a cell for a word-organized memory because of extra components and an extra line. The total increase in area when all memory cells are considered is considerably greater than the area required for a bipolar transistor word-selection switch for a word-organized memory. Thus bit organization is more costly than word organization.

A block diagram of a 2D semiconductor memory system is shown in Figure 9.34 with only a single flip-flop memory cell illustrated for convenience. The general operation should be apparent from the discussion of the 2D core memory system of Figure 9.6, with the exception of a few differences. In Figure 9.34 the read and write lines for the word-line drivers can be a single line since the word operation for writing is the same as for reading, namely, the grounding of the selected word line. Also, the bit lines are different; there are two bit lines instead of one for each bit. One of these lines corresponds to the stored bit and the other to its complement.

In the single illustrated flip-flop, T_1 and T_2 are the switching or inverter FET's, T_3 and T_4 are load resistors, and FET's T_5 and T_6 are gating transistors that, in response to ground on the word line, gate the bit lines to the flip-flop.

For a read operation, word line w_i is grounded by word-line driver WD_i, which grounding turns on T_5 and T_6. If a 1 is stored, and positive logic used, then bit line b_i is raised positive because of the conduction path to the positive voltage supply through conducting transistor T_1 and gate transistor T_5. After sensing and amplification, this positive potential sets MIR flip-flop FF_i to a 1. But if a 0 is stored, then T_2 is in the conduction state and bit line $\bar{b}_i$ goes positive as a result of the conduction path to the positive voltage supply through transistors T_2 and T_6. After amplification this voltage sets MIR flip-flop FF_i to 0. Note that read-out does not disturb the contents of the memory cell; it is nondestructive read-out. Hence, a read operation does not have to be followed by a write operation.

If a 1 is to be written into this cell, bit driver BD_i makes bit line b_i

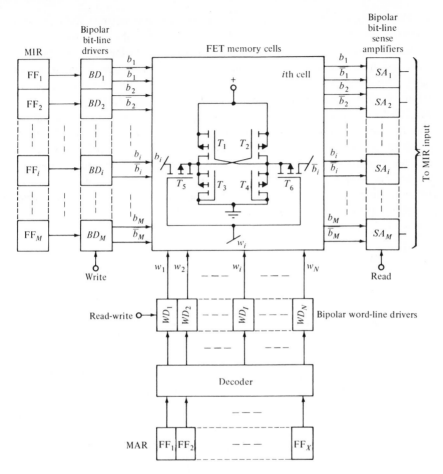

Figure 9.34   Semiconductor memory.

positive. At the same time, word-line driver WD_i grounds word line w_i, thereby enabling T_5 and T_6. The positive potential on bit line b_i conducts through T_5 to the gate of T_2 and turns T_2 off, which action turns T_1 on. Then when T_5 and T_6 are cut off by the removal of the ground on word line w_i, the flip-flop remains in this 1 state with T_1 conducting and T_2 cut off until a 0 is written or the power supply is interrupted. For the writing of a 0 the input conditions are reversed: T_1 cuts off and turns T_2 on, as should be obvious.

Semiconductor memories are usually constructed from modules with, typically, thousands of bits per module. These modules, which are interconnected to form the memory, often contain not only the memory cells but also a complete set of driver and detector circuits. Sometimes registers and timing circuits are included.

Figure 9.35 shows cost versus memory-size comparisons for core and semiconductor memories. The costs include not only the costs of the switching elements but also those of the peripheral electronic equipment such as the drivers and sense amplifiers. From this graph we see that core memories decrease significantly in cost per bit with increase in memory size. This decrease results from certain electronic costs that are, within limits, almost independent of memory size. Thus the larger the memory the more these costs can be spread over the bits. In contrast, semiconductor memories are constructed of electronic modules of fixed size in which most of the electronics is either self-contained or directly related to memory size. An increase in memory size is obtained primarily by including more modules. Hence the electronics cost per bit is almost constant regardless of memory size.

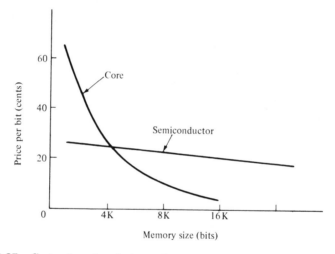

Figure 9.35 Costs of semiconductor and core memories.

At the present time, the crossover point in Figure 9.35 is at about 25 cents per bit for a 4K-bit memory size. That is, generally speaking, semiconductor memories are cheaper for memory sizes less than $4K$ bits and core memories are cheaper for memory sizes greater than $4K$ bits. But each year the almost flat semiconductor curve lowers as improvements are made in integrated circuits, and thus the crossover point moves toward larger and more economical memories.

9.10 READ-ONLY MEMORY

As its name implies, a *read-only memory* (*ROM*) has information stored in permanent or semipermanent form. The stored information cannot be altered by electrical means in normal use. Thus ROM's *cannot* be written into, and read-out is nondestructive.

In some ROM's the storing of information, or programming, must be done in the manufacturing process and cannot be altered by the user. Others, however, are programmable by the user. This programming may be a simple mechanical act such as the punching of holes in cards.

One of the main advantages of ROM's as compared to conventional core memories is operating speed. Information can be accessed in less than 100 nsec in some semiconductor ROM's. Comprising arrays of identical cells and thus being a natural for large-scale integration and batch-fabrication methods, these semiconductor ROM's also have advantages in size, cost, and power dissipation. In addition they are easy to check out for errors during manufacture and they are highly reliable in operation.

An ROM is basically a combinational circuit that is usually constructed in a matrix array to take advantage of large-scale integration techniques, at least for semiconductor ROM's. These semiconductor ROM's are now mass producible with large capacities (several thousand bits) and good yields.

One application of ROM's is as a trigonometric function generator. The input (the address) can be the argument x. And the output word can be $\sin x$ with both input and output encoded in binary, of course. Likewise, ROM's can be used to calculate roots, powers, and logarithms. Another application is as a code converter: the input may be, for example, an 8421 coded decimal digit and the output may be the corresponding Gray code. ROM's can also be used to store mathematical constants and other fixed quantities and even programs such as parts of, or entire, compilers and assemblers, which are described in the next chapter.

ROM's can be used for combinational circuits. For this application the bits of the address are variable values and the bits in the word read out are values of functions. ROM's can even be the principal components of sequential circuits in which some or all of the bits in the output word are fed back to provide bits for the address. These and other applications for ROM's have resulted in their use in most digital computers, computer peripherals, data handling systems, as well as in special-purpose digital machines.

In the ROM embodiment of Figure 9.36 the memory is 2D or word organized with electrical elements providing coupling between the word lines and selected bit lines. Almost any type of electrical component can be and has been used for coupling elements: resistors, capacitors, inductors, transformers, diodes, bipolar transistors, MOS FET's. The MAR, MIR, decoder, and sense amplifiers are conventional components that function in the usual manner.

During a read operation a coupling element at a bit location produces a 1 for the corresponding bit of the addressed word. In the absence of coupling, the bit is 0. Thus words 0, 1, 2, and 3 are, respectively, 10101, 01110, 11001, and 10111.

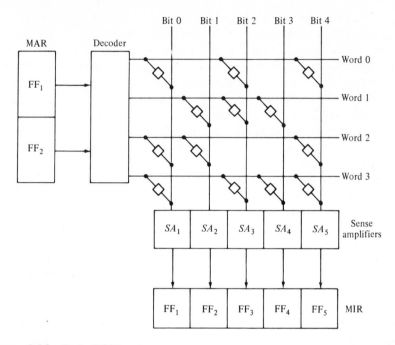

Figure 9.36 Basic ROM system.

The MAR, of course, stores the address which is decoded by the decoder to energize one word line, the particular word line depending on the address. The coupling elements connected to this word line couple the signal to bit lines and then sense amplifiers amplify the coupled signals and produce signals for setting corresponding flip-flops in the MIR. Only these MIR flip-flops will contain 1's. Since all the MIR flip-flops will have been cleared before the beginning of the read operation, the other MIR flip-flops will contain zeros. In this way, the word at the selected location is read into the MIR.

Typically, the manufacturer provides a coupling element at each intersection of the word and bit lines, that is, the matrices are *fully populated*. Then either as a step in the manufacturing process or later as an act performed by the user, selected coupling elements, corresponding to the information to be stored, are either activated or deactivated.

As an illustration, in the manufacture of ROM's constructed with MOS FET's as the coupling element, as is shown in Figure 9.37, the customer informs the manufacturer of the contents of the ROM. Then the manufacturer uses this information in one, and only one, manufacturing step, which may be gate metalization; the other steps are the same for all ROM's. If a 1 is to be stored at a location, a gate electrode is provided for the MOS FET at that location so that a gate voltage can open a conduction path between the source and drain of the transistor. If, however, a 0 is to be stored, the manufacturer omits that gate during the gate metalization.

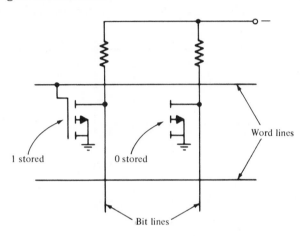

Figure 9.37   Storing of a 1 and a 0 with MOS FET's.

Some ROM's can be programmed by the user. The coupling elements each may be in series with a fusable link that can be selectively burned open by the user to store a 0 or left closed to store a 1. This act is called *field programming*. Some other ROM's that are field programmable have part or all of the coupling components on cards that may be of the size and shape of typical programming cards. By punching holes at selected locations in the card, a user changes the information stored in the ROM. Such a hole may, for example, break a lead to a resistor or to a diode at an intersection of a bit and word line and thereby produce a 0. Or the card can be metallic and grounded in use when inserted between the plates of a matrix array of capacitors. A hole punched in this card permits a capacitor to be at an intersection to provide a 1. Often cards are so constructed that no special equipment is required for punching. A conventional card punch, as is described in Chapter 12, can be used.

Example 9.1   Design an array for an ROM that converts 8421 coded decimal digits to the Gray code.

Solution   The MAR and MIR should each have four flip-flops for holding, respectively, the four bits of the 8421 coded numbers and the four bits of the Gray coded numbers. The decoder will have ten output lines, the word lines, corresponding to the numbers 0000, 0001, . . . , 1001. Regarding coupling elements between the ten word lines and the four bit lines, since 0000 in the 8421 code converts to 0000 in the Gray code, word line 0000 has no coupling elements connected to it. With 0001 converting to 0001, a coupling element must be connected between the second word line and the fourth bit line. Number 0010 converts to 0011 and so a coupling element should be between the third word line and the third bit line and another element between this word line and the fourth bit line. Continuing on with this procedure we obtain the array of Figure 9.38. ■

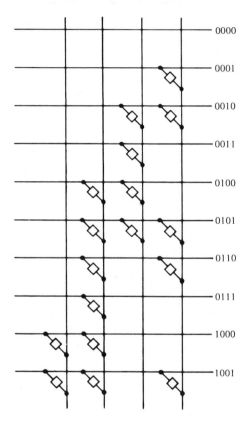

Figure 9.38   Example 9.1.

For logic applications the address is a set of variable values and each output bit line can correspond to a different function of these variables. In the realization procedure the minimization step is omitted because minimum functions provide *no* advantages. With the matrices being fully populated anyway, the minimization step will not save components. Consequently, the functions are realized in expanded form.

Each address is actually a minterm (it could be a maxterm as well) that causes the energization of one word line. If this minterm is in the function, then a coupling element is inserted between that word line and the bit line corresponding to the function. If the minterm is not present, the coupling element is omitted.

Example 9.2 Show the ROM array that provides the two functions $f_1 = A\bar{B} + BC$ and $f_2 = ABC + \bar{B}C + \bar{A}\bar{B}$.

Solution Converting the two functions to expanded form, we obtain $f_1 = A\bar{B}C + A\bar{B}\bar{C} + ABC + \bar{A}BC$ and $f_2 = ABC + A\bar{B}C + \bar{A}BC + \bar{A}\bar{B}\bar{C}$. Because of the six different minterms in the two functions, the array will have just six word lines to which elements are coupled. For the two functions we need only two bit lines. By connecting coupling elements to bit lines if the minterm corresponding to the word line is present in the function, we obtain the array of Figure 9.39. ∎

ROM's can be used in many other ways than the few we have discussed. Instead of having just one word line energized at a time, several word lines can be energized to provide additional logic. Further, ROM's can be cascaded to save components. Also, if the output is coupled back to the input, a ROM can function like a sequential circuit. And there

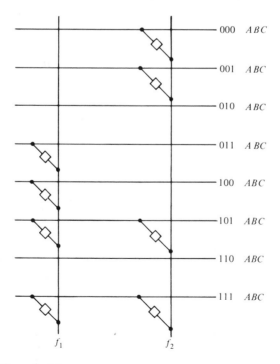

Figure 9.39 Example 9.2.

are many other applications. Obviously, with its great versatility and suitability for implementation with large-scale integration techniques that are becoming increasingly important, ROM's may have a great impact on the logic design field.

PROBLEMS ▬▬▬▬▬▬▬▬▬▬▬▬▬▬▬▬▬▬▬▬

9.1 A 2D core memory system can store 8192 words of 30 bits each. Determine the numbers of the following components:

(**a**) word lines   (**d**) MIR flip-flops
(**b**) bit lines   (**e**) MAR flip-flops
(**c**) sense amplifiers   (**f**) cores

Answers   (**a**) 8192; (**b**) 30; (**c**) 30; (**d**) 30; (**e**) 13;
          (**f**) 245,760

9.2 Repeat Problem 9.1 for a 2D core memory system for storing 32,768 words of 36 bits each.

9.3 Repeat Problem 9.1 for a 2D core memory system for storing 65,536 words of 40 bits each.

9.4 A 3D core memory system has one stack for storing 16,384 words of 30 bits each. Determine the numbers of the following components:

(**a**) x lines   (**c**) sense windings   (**e**) core planes
(**b**) y lines   (**d**) inhibit windings   (**f**) cores
(**g**) MAR flip-flops   (**h**) MIR flip-flops

Answers   (**a**) 128; (**b**) 128; (**c**) 30; (**d**) 30; (**e**) 30;
          (**f**) 491,520; (**g**) 14; (**h**) 30

9.5 Repeat Problem 9.4 for a 3D core memory system for storing 65,536 words of 36 bits each.

9.6 Repeat Problem 9.4 for a 3D core memory system for storing 32,768 words of 40 bits each.

Answers   (**a**) 128 or 256; (**b**) 256 or 128; (**c**) 40; (**d**) 40;
          (**e**) 40; (**f**) 1,310,720; (**g**) 15; (**h**) 40

9.7 A $2\frac{1}{2}$D core memory system can store 4096 words of 30 bits each. If each bit plane has a line ratio of 16 to 1, determine the numbers of the following components:

(**a**) x lines
(**b**) y lines per plane
(**c**) flip-flops in the x section of the MAR
(**d**) flip-flops in the y section of the MAR
(**e**) MIR flip-flops
(**f**) cores in each bit plane

Answers   (**a**) 256; (**b**) 16; (**c**) 8; (**d**) 4; (**e**) 30; (**f**) 4096

9.8 Repeat Problem 9.7 for a $2\frac{1}{2}$D core memory system for storing 16,384 words of 36 bits each.

9.9 Repeat Problem 9.7 for a $2\frac{1}{2}$D core memory system for storing 64,536 words of 40 bits each.

9.10 If the cycle time for the inner memory where instructions are stored is 1 μsec, how can computers with such memories execute some instructions in less time than 1 μsec?

9.11 How many cores are in a $64K$ memory of a computer having a word size of 32 bits?

Answer 2,097,152

9.12 A 3D, three-wire core memory has been proposed in which coincident current techniques are used. What are the three windings? In what directions are they wound?

9.13 In the writing operation in a thin-film memory system, why is the word current started before the bit current, and why is it terminated before the bit current?

9.14 A magnetic drum has a 12-in. diameter, a bit density of 300 bits per inch, 64 tracks, and a rotational speed of 3600 rev./min.
(a) Approximately what is the total number of bits that can be stored?
(b) At approximately what rate are the bits read from the drum?
(c) If there is one read-write head per track, what is the average access time?
(d) If there are four read-write heads per track, what is the average access time?

Answers (a) 723,000; (b) 678,000 bits per sec; (c) $\frac{1}{120}$ sec; (d) $\frac{1}{480}$ sec

9.15 Repeat Problem 9.14 for a magnetic drum with a 15-in. diameter, a bit density of 200 bits per inch, 70 tracks, and a rotational speed of 1800 rev./min.

9.16 Repeat Problem 9.14 for a magnetic drum with a 10-in. diameter, a bit density of 400 bits per inch, 128 tracks, and a rotational speed of 900 rev./min.

9.17 In a computer installation having a drum memory, the drum is often maintained in rotation on weekends when no one is using the computer. What problem concerning this drum would occur on Monday if this was not done?

9.18 In the sector track, why is the address read at any one time that of the next sector to appear under a certain read-write head rather than the address of the present sector that is under this head?

9.19 A certain drum system has 128 tracks and 256 sectors per track. How many bits must be in each address?

9.20 How many bits can be stored in the IBM 2321 Data Cell Drive?

9.21 Explain in your own words why the return-to-zero recording technique is practically limited to drum applications.

9.22 If the bit time is 1 μsec, what is the greatest frequency and the lowest frequency for voltages induced in the read-write head if the recording technique is
(a) the return-to-reference of Figure 9.32?
(b) the NRZ of Figure 9.33(a)?
(c) the NRZ of Figure 9.33(b)?
(d) phase recording?

9.23 Repeat Problem 9.22 for a bit time of 100 nsec.

9.24 Why are scratch-pad memories constructed of transistors? What are some of the considerations in deciding to use FET's or bipolar transistors in scratch-pad memories?

9.25 Why are complementary FET circuits attractive for semiconductor memories? Some memory authorities are *not* seriously considering these circuits for memory applications for the near future. Can you give some reasons for this decision?

9.26 Semiconductor memories are *volatile*. That is, if the power supply is interrupted for even a short time, the stored information is destroyed. Have we considered any other volatile memories? Can you think of a simple practical power backup unit for maintaining power for several hours if there is a main power supply interrupt?

9.27 In what memories we have considered
(a) must the sense amplifiers distinguish different voltage polarities?
(b) must the word drivers be capable of providing bidirectional currents?

9.28 Show ROM arrays for converting to the Gray code from
(a) the $84(-2)(-1)$ code.
(b) the excess-three code.

9.29 Show ROM arrays for converting to the 8421 code from
(a) the 4311 code.
(b) the biquinary code of Table 5.8.

9.30 Show an ROM array that provides the functions $f_1 = A\bar{B}\bar{C} + \bar{A}B + ABC$ and $f_2 = \bar{A}C + BC$.

9.31 Repeat Problem 9.30 for $f_1 \stackrel{.}{=} \bar{A}\bar{B}\bar{D} + A\bar{B}C + \bar{B}C\bar{D} + ABCD + \bar{A}B\bar{C}D$; $f_2 = A\bar{B} + \bar{B}C$; and $f_3 = AD + B\bar{C}D + A\bar{B}D$.

10

Instructions and
Digital Computer
Operations

In this chapter the emphasis is on *programming*. Some knowledge of programming is essential for an understanding of digital computer designs. It is as essential for an engineer in digital computers to know programming as it is for an automobile engineer to know how to drive. In both cases the design and operation of the systems are closely related. Thus in this chapter we will study programming—not with the intent of becoming adept at programming, but rather to obtain a better understanding of the operation of digital computers.

10.1 LANGUAGES

To begin our study of programming we should define what a *program* is. For our purposes a program can be considered as a list of statements for directing a computer to perform some tasks. These statements can take various forms, depending upon the pertinent programming language.

A *programming language* includes the acceptable symbols that can be used in the statements, the rules for combining the symbols, and the meaning the computer associates with each statement. Although they often differ with computers, languages possess some common elements that permit classification.

One language class, or type, is *machine language*. This, the most basic language, contains the form of instructions executed by computers. Consequently, *it is highly machine dependent,* that is, it varies considerably with different computers. For an example of machine language, the calculation of $Y = 3 + 4$ might be,

$$00010100000000000000001000000001100$$
$$00010000000000000000001000000001101$$
$$00011000000100000000001000000001110$$

or, in octal

$$+050000010014$$
$$+040000010015$$
$$+060100010016$$

In the octal shorthand, $+050000010014$ is an instruction for placing the contents of location 10014 into the arithmetic unit, and $+040000010015$ instructs the computer to add the number in location 10015 to the number in the arithmetic unit. Presumably, numbers 3 and 4 are in locations 10014 and 10015 in core memory. The last statement $+060100010016$ instructs the computer to store the sum in memory location 10016, which has been assigned to Y.

In the above example and in the remainder of the chapter, octal, decimal, and binary numbers are usually not distinguished by subscripts since the numbers are almost always apparent from the context in which they are used.

Although a digital computer must operate in machine language, this language is not required for programming. Programmers would be very unhappy if they had to program in machine language, for then they would have to remember all of the operation codes and the numbers of all the locations in core memory they are using. And it would be an unpleasant chore, and one prone to errors, to write out all the numbers. Also, machine-language programming is not similar to natural problem formulation. As a result, and because it is not necessary, very little programming in the United States is done in machine language.

Programmers write in more convenient languages, the most basic of which is an *assembly language*. This language is converted into machine language by a program called a translator or, more specifically, an *assembler* or *assembly program*. That is, the computer is used to convert a program that is convenient for the programmer into a program that can be executed by the computer. The program written by the programmer is called a *source program* and the corresponding machine-language program is called an *object program*.

In general, a *one-to-one correspondence* exists between the statements in the assembly program and the corresponding instructions in the resulting machine-language program. For example, the previous illustration of Y = 3 + 4 in assembly language might be

$$\text{CLA} \quad \text{A}$$
$$\text{ADD} \quad \text{B}$$
$$\text{STO} \quad \text{Y}$$

Each of these three assembly-language instructions, which correspond directly to the three machine-language instructions, have two parts, one of which is the *mnemonic operation code* (CLA, ADD, and STO) and the other is the symbol for a memory location (A, B, and Y).

In the translation of this program, the assembler makes two passes over the statements. In the first pass it forms a *symbol table* in which each symbol is assigned a memory location. For our example the pertinent portion of the symbol table is

Symbol	Location
A	10014
B	10015
Y	10016

Another table available to the assembler, called an *operation-code table*, contains the correspondences between the mnemonic operation-code names such as ADD and the corresponding operation codes. For this example the pertinent portion of the operation-code table is

Mnemonic Code	Operation Code
CLA	+0500
ADD	+0400
STO	+0601

In the second pass over the assembly program the assembler substitutes in the pertinent operation code and location for each instruction such that, for example, CLA A becomes +050000010014.

Programming in an assembly language is much more convenient than in a machine language. The mnemonic operation codes of an assembly language are easier to remember than the corresponding operation code numbers; for example, ADD is easier to remember than +0400. Also, location symbols are much more convenient than location numbers, especially if the symbols or names are indicative of the contents of the locations in memory. In our example the symbol THREE could be used instead of A, FOUR instead of B, and SUM instead of Y.

These names or symbols usually have some restrictions. For example, they may be limited to six or fewer characters and perhaps may have to include one nonnumeric character. For the remainder of this chapter we will assume that we have these restrictions.

Although programming in an assembly language is considerably more convenient than in a machine language, it is more difficult than necessary for most, but not all, programming. One disadvantage is the form of an assembly program: it is not similar to the form in which problems are usually placed when solved by hand techniques. Also, in order to learn and to use an assembly language, a programmer must know and be very familiar with many components of the computer. For most problems a programmer should not have to be concerned with the inner workings of a computer. To this end, additional programming languages have been developed, some of which are called *general-purpose languages*. FORTRAN and ALGOL are examples of general-purpose languages.

The translator for converting a general-purpose language program or source program into an object program is called a *compiler*. The resulting object program is often, but not always, a machine-language program. Of course, before execution there must be conversion to a machine-language program. But an assembly-language program may be an intermediate step.

In a general-purpose language the acceptable statements are mathematically oriented and, in many cases, are the same as in ordinary mathematics. In the example we have been considering, the corresponding statement in a general-purpose language might be

$$Y = THREE + FOUR$$

For our purposes, a study of a compiler language is not useful since the detailed operation of a computer, which is of interest to us, is completely hidden by the language. One can program effectively in, say, FORTRAN and yet be almost completely ignorant of the inner workings of a computer. As a consequence, we will be more concerned with an assembly language and will not further consider a general-purpose language.

10.2   BLOCK DIAGRAM OF A DIGITAL COMPUTER

In our study of an assembly language we will need more knowledge of some of the components of a digital computer. Figure 10.1 shows sufficient components for our present purposes. In this figure, the *accumulator register*, the *multiplier-quotient register*, the *storage register*, the *index registers*, the *memory address register*, the *memory information register*, and the *instruction register* all store words or parts of words.

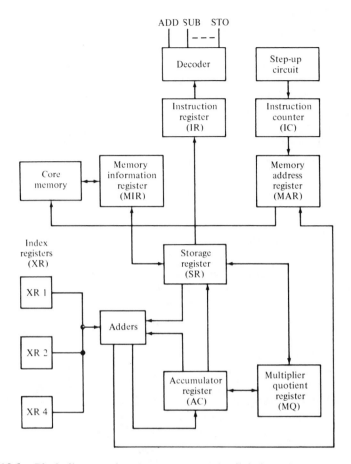

Figure 10.1 Block diagram of some components of a digital computer.

For convenience, we will often refer to these registers as the AC, MQ, SR, XR, MAR, MIR, and IR, respectively.

Although these registers can be formed from various types of electrical components, for fastest operation they are constructed of flip-flops. Recall that numbers can be read from flip-flop registers without altering their contents, that is, read-out is nondestructive. Of course, when a number is stored in a register the prior contents of that register are destroyed.

For the computer of Figure 10.1 we will assume a core memory of 32,768 locations. Because accessing this number of locations requires a minimum of 15 bits for the instruction addresses, all registers relating to addressing must contain 15-flip-flops. These include the instruction counter, the memory address register, and the index registers.

The IR must be capable of storing any operation code, the largest of which for our purposes have 12 bits. Consequently, the IR must have 12 flip-flops.

We will be considering 36-bit words. Thus the MIR, the SR, and the MQ, which all must be capable of storing complete words, each comprise 36 flip-flops. However, the AC, which holds the sums from additions, comprises 37 flip-flops, with the extra flip-flop required for a possible overflow bit.

We will prescribe parallel transmission of the bits of a word which means that all bits of a word or part of a word are transmitted at the same time. As a consequence, each transmission line of Figure 10.1 represents many lines and possibly as many as 36 or even 72 lines.

It may be an aid to the understanding of the block diagram of Figure 10.1 to consider briefly the execution of the first instruction in a program. At the beginning of the execution of a program, the computer sets the instruction counter (the contents of which determine the location of the instruction that will be executed next) to the location of the first instruction. We will assume this is location 00000, but it could be some other location. This location number is transmitted from the IC to the MAR which energizes lines to the core memory for reading the word at location 00000 into the MIR. After being read, this word is transmitted to the SR and, assuming the read-out was destructive, it is also restored to memory location 00000 for possible future use.

From the SR the operation code part of the instruction is transmitted to the IR which stores it for reference. This storing is essential since the contents of the SR will probably change as a result of the execution of the instruction. A decoder is provided having a number of outputs, each of which we will assume corresponds to a different instruction. Of course, the particular line energized by the decoder depends upon the contents of the IR.

This group of operations completes the *instruction cycle* part of the execution of an instruction. During this cycle an instruction is brought from memory into the arithmetic unit and decoded, while also being restored to the memory. This cycle is followed by an *execution cycle*, during which the operation corresponding to the instruction is performed.

At the beginning of the execution cycle, the address of the instruction is transmitted from the storage register through adders to the MAR. The passage through the adders permits incrementing or decrementing the address by the contents of one, two, or all three index registers. As we will see, this feature is important, for example, for looping; that is, for using the same instructions over and over again.

The address, perhaps modified and now residing in the MAR, causes energization of lines for reading the contents of the memory location corresponding to this address. These contents are an operand for the instruction being executed if this instruction is of the type such as add, subtract, and so on, for which there are operands. We will assume this is the case. This operand is read into the MIR and then transferred to the SR, where it replaces the instruction. Of course, the operand is also restored to the memory. If the original instruction is arithmetic, this operand will have some effect on the contents of the AC and MQ registers since these registers are used in adding, subtracting, multiplying, and so on. Toward the end of the specified operation, a step-up circuit triggers the IC to 00001 in preparation for the execution of the next instruction. With the execution cycle now complete, the computer starts on the instruction cycle of the instruction in location 00001.

Although we could spend considerably more time on the block diagram of Figure 10.1, this brief introduction suffices for the introduction of the internal components of a computer needed for the discussion of programming that follows. Actually, these parts and their functions will be better understood as we use them in our study of an assembly language.

10.3   INSTRUCTIONS FOR MOVING WORDS

The five instructions described in this section are all type 1 instructions as defined in Chapter 7; that is, they have a *12-bit operation code* followed by 6 bits that are not used. Then there is a *3-bit tag* for designating one or more index registers, and finally a *15-bit address*. Since almost all of the instructions we will study are of this type, this type instruction should always be assumed unless there are statements to the contrary.

In the discussion that follows, an abbreviated notation is used for convenience: $C(X)$ means *contents of location X*. $C(AC)$ means *contents of the accumulator,* and so on. Also, the arrow in $C(AC) \rightarrow C(Y)$ indicates that the contents of the AC are transmitted to the memory to replace the prior contents of location Y. Of course, when a word is transmitted to a location in memory or to a register, it destroys the prior contents. However, in the transmission of a word *from* a location or a register, the contents of that location or of that register are not altered since the word will be written back into the core memory (there is destructive read-out from a core memory) and the registers are usually made of flip-flops which can be read from without an alteration of their contents. Thus, for example, after $C(X) \rightarrow C(Y)$, locations X and Y contain the same word.

The first instruction we will consider is *clear and add* having mnemonic code CLA and operation code +0500 or 000101000000. In an assembly program the instruction CLA X produces $C(X) \to C(AC)$. For convenience here and in the following discussions, the symbol X will always correspond to location 12345. With this address, CLA X is, in machine language, $+050000012345$.

The name clear and add results from the manner in which a word is normally inserted into the AC; the word must pass through the adders to get into the AC. In effect, the prior contents of the AC are added to the number coming in and the sum replaces the contents of the AC. If the AC is first cleared (set to zero), then zero is added to the incoming number and the resulting sum is just this number. That is, the AC is structured such that its input is from the adders. Consequently, to insert a number into the AC, the computer adds this number to zero.

The next instruction is *store*, which has a mnemonic code *STO* and an operation code $+0601$ or 000110000001. The instruction STO X, which is $+060100012345$ in machine language, causes $C(AC) \to C(X)$.

At this point we have an instruction for inserting a word from memory into the AC and another instruction for inserting a word from the AC into the memory. We will now consider instructions for performing the same operations with the MQ. The instruction for *load MQ* is *LDQ* $(+0560)$, and LDQ X $(+056000012345)$ causes $C(X) \to C(MQ)$. The instruction for storing from the MQ into the memory, that is, *store MQ*, is *STQ* (-0600). Thus STQ X (-060000012345) causes $C(MQ) \to C(X)$.

It is sometimes desirable to *exchange AC and MQ*. The code for this is XCA $(+0131)$. The instruction XCA $(+013100000000)$ produces $C(AC) \leftrightarrow C(MQ)$ and also the setting of the overflow bit of the AC to zero. This is the first instruction we have considered for which there is no specified address. But none is needed since there is no operand.

All of the instructions so far have been for moving words. No distinction has been made regarding the type of word. The words can be fixed-point numbers, instructions, and so on. In the next section the instructions are restricted to fixed-point number words.

10.4   FIXED-POINT ARITHMETIC INSTRUCTIONS

In the following discussions of arithmetic instructions, we will assume that the numbers are in signed-magnitude representation.

For a fixed-point *add* the code is *ADD* $(+0400)$. The instruction ADD X $(+040000012345)$ produces $C(X) + C(AC) \to C(AC)$. That is, the contents of location X are added to the contents of the AC with the sum replacing the prior contents of the AC.

Fixed-point *subtract* has the code *SUB* $(+0402)$ and SUB X $(+040200012345)$ causes $C(AC) - C(X) \to C(AC)$. In other words, the contents of location X are subtracted from the contents of the AC and the difference replaces the prior contents of the AC.

In the diagram of Figure 10.1 only adders are shown for performing arithmetic operations; there are no subtractors. Thus the computer must use complement arithmetic and subtract by adding complements.

Basically, the operations of ADD and SUB are almost identical. In fact, the execution of SUB differs from that of ADD in only one respect: After the subtrahend is read into the SR from memory, the sign bit of the SR is changed. Then the procedure is exactly the same as with ADD. This similarity of operations should not be surprising since the adding of two numbers with different signs is tantamount to subtracting one positive number from another. And the subtracting of a negative number from a positive number is the same as adding two positive numbers.

If, for example, ADD X is to be executed and the sign of the number in location X differs from the sign of the number in the AC, the complement (say, the 1's complement) is taken of the number in the AC. Then this complement is added to the number from location X. If no overflow occurs, which is the case when the original number in the AC has the larger magnitude, the sum is not the correct difference. In this case, the computer complements the sum in the AC while retaining the AC sign bit. However, if there is overflow in the addition, then the result in the AC has the correct magnitude, but the AC sign bit must be changed since in this case the sign bit of the result differs from the sign of the original number in the AC.

Example 10.1   The number $+012345673765$ is in the AC and the number -124673244231 in location Y (location 46752). Show how the instruction ADD Y ($+040000046752$ in machine language) is executed.

Solution   The computer detects the difference in sign between the C(AC) and the C(Y) and, as a consequence, forms the 1's complement of C(AC) or $+765432104012$. Then the magnitude of the C(Y) is added to the magnitude of this number:

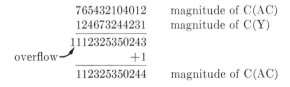

	765432104012	magnitude of C(AC)
	124673244231	magnitude of C(Y)
	1112325350243	
overflow	+1	
	112325350244	magnitude of C(AC)

Because there is an overflow, the C(AC), exclusive of the overflow bit, is correct in magnitude but the sign bit is incorrect and must be changed by the computer.

The mnemonic code for fixed-point *multiply* is *MPY* and the operation code is +0200. The assembly language instruction MPY X generates the machine language instruction +020000012345, which upon execution causes $C(X) \times C(MQ) \rightarrow C(AC$ and $MQ)$. Naturally, the sign bit in the AC and also in the MQ is set to the algebraic sign of the product. The AC overflow bit is zero after the multiplication.

The computer must provide sufficient bits for a product of 70 bits because such a sized product is possible if the multiplier and the multiplicand each have 35-bit magnitudes with no leading zeros. Although such a product exceeds the word size, it may still be practical. For example, the multiply instruction that produces this product might be immediately followed by a divide instruction for which the 70-bit product is the dividend. The resulting quotient can be word size.

The most significant 35 bits of the product reside in the AC and the least significant 35 bits in the MQ. In general, we will be interested only in the product bits in the MQ. In our work the 35 bits for the magnitude of the multiplier and multiplicand will each have a considerable number of leading zeros, so many in fact that the nonleading zero part of the product will be less than 36 bits. Thus after a multiply operation, the MQ will hold the product digits of interest and the AC. apart from the sign bit, will have only zeros.

Example 10.2   The number +000000003245 is in location X in memory and the number −000000000125 is in the MQ. What are the contents of the AC and MQ after the execution of MPY X?

Solution   The computer takes the product of the two numbers. The result is

$$(11010100101) \times (1010101) = 100011010011001001.$$

Since this product fits into the MQ, the contents of the AC, except for the sign bit, are zeros. That is, after the multiplication

$$C(AC) = 100000000000000000000000000000000000000$$

sign bit   overflow bit

and

$$C(MQ) = 100000000000000000100011010011001001.$$

sign bit   ∎

The last fixed-point arithmetic instruction we will consider is fixed-point divide which has a code *DVH* (+0220) that stands for *divide or halt*. Division occurs if the quotient does *not* exceed 35 bits in magnitude, as is determined by the first trial subtraction. Otherwise, the computer stops and usually an indicator light turns on to indicate a possible error. If there is division, the instruction DVH X (+022000012345) causes C(AC and MQ)/C(X) → C(MQ) and the remainder to be in the AC. Since a 35-bit quotient can result from the division of a 70-bit number by a 35-bit number, the contents of the AC and MQ registers are treated together as a 70-bit dividend.

In our work we will not have 70-bit dividends. In fact, all of them will be less than 35 bits. Thus, for proper operation we must, before dividing, place the dividend in the MQ and insert zeros in the AC if zeros are not already there.

Not being concerned with the remainder, we will use only the quotient appearing in the MQ.

The selection of the name for the multiplier-quotient register can now be appreciated, since from the foregoing discussions it is evident that the multiplier is placed in this register before a multiplication operation and the quotient appears in this register after a division operation. Note that this placement is in agreement with our study of computer mathematical operations in Chapter 8.

We will now consider a portion of a program in order to better understand what has just been presented.

Example 10.3   Assume that fixed-point integers 7, 13, 9, and 5 are stored in memory locations 07162, 04327, 07472, and 01623, respectively, to which the symbols A, C, D, and E correspond. Write a portion of a program for calculating $(7 \times 13 - 9)/5$ and storing the result in location 07624 (RES). Assemble this portion with the first instruction assigned to location 00144.

Solution   The pertinent portion of the source program is, with comments

LDQ	A	puts 7 in the MQ
MPY	C	the product $7 \times 13 = 91$ is now in the MQ and zeros are in the AC
XCA		moves the product into the AC in preparation for the subtraction; zeros move to MQ
SUB	D	the numerator $91 - 9 = 82$ is now in the AC
XCA		numerator moves to MQ and zeros to AC; with zeros in the AC, division is the next step
DVH	E	MQ contains the quotient 16 and the AC contains the remainder 2
STQ	RES	the integer part of the result is stored in location 07624

The assembled program is shown below to the left of the corresponding source program.

Assembled Program		Corresponding Source Statements
LOCATION	CONTENTS	
00144	+056000007162	LDQ A
00145	+020000004237	MPY C
00146	+013100000000	XCA
00147	+040200007472	SUB D
00150	+013100000000	XCA
00151	+022000001623	DVH E
00152	−060000007624	STQ RES

10.5   TRANSFER INSTRUCTIONS

The contents of the instruction counter, which determine the location of the instruction that will be executed next, are normally increased by one during the execution of an instruction, with the result that the instructions are executed in sequence. Sometimes, as will be shown, it is desirable to alter the normal sequence of instruction executions. Transfer instructions are used for this purpose.

One transfer instruction, when executed, always sets the contents of the IC. This is an unconditional transfer instruction. Other transfer instructions may or may not alter the number in the IC, depending upon events that occur during execution of a program. These are called conditional transfer instructions.

The unconditional *transfer* instruction has a code TRA ($+0020$), and TRA X ($+002000012345$) causes $X \to C(IC)$. Note that X, here 12345, and *not* the contents of X, replaces the contents of the IC *after* the latter is stepped up by one. Thus the instruction in location **12345** is executed next.

We will consider four conditional transfer instructions, all of which may produce a transfer depending upon the contents of the AC. These instructions have codes TPL ($+0120$), TMI (-0120), TOV ($+0140$), and TZE ($+0100$). TPL is *transfer on plus*, TMI is *transfer on minus*, TOV is *transfer on overflow*, and TZE is *transfer on zero*.

TPL X ($+012000012345$) replaces the contents of the IC with **12345** if the sign bit of the AC is positive (0). If this bit is negative (1), the transfer does not take place and the next instruction executed is that following the TPL instruction. TMI is similar to the TPL instruction except that the transfer is conditioned on the AC sign bit being negative instead of positive.

The instruction TOV X ($+014000012345$) replaces the contents of the IC with **12345** if the AC overflow bit is 1. Otherwise there is no change and the next instruction executed is the one following TOV X.

TZE X (+010000012345) replaces the contents of the IC with 12345 if the AC contains all 0's. This test includes the overflow bit but not the sign bit.

The last transfer instruction we will consider is the only instruction of interest to us having a type 2 format. This instruction, which is a conditional transfer instruction, has a mnemonic code *TIX* representing *transfer on index* and an operation code of +2. In the execution of this instruction, one, two, or all three index registers are used, depending on the contents of the part of the instruction called the *tag*. Since for our purposes we will not have cause to use more than one index register, only one XR will be specified in this instruction. It is also necessary to specify a *decrement* as will be explained.

For an understanding of this instruction we will consider a specific example.

$$\text{TIX} \qquad \text{X, 1, 36} \qquad\qquad (+200044112345)$$

$$\text{address} \qquad \text{tag} \qquad \text{decrement}$$

If the number in the specified index register (here XR1) *is less than or equal to the decrement* (here 36_{10}), the computer executes the next sequential instruction. But if the number in the specified index register *exceeds the number in the decrement*, then the number in this index register is decreased by an amount equal to the number in the decrement and the address 12345 replaces the contents of the IC. Consequently, the instruction executed next is in location 12345.

The TIX instruction is very useful in *looping*—for using the same instructions repeatedly. In a practical program many instructions are executed hundreds and even thousands of times. Indeed, if each instruction were executed only once, the time required to prepare a computer program would probably be greater than that required to solve the problem by hand or with a calculator.

An example with the TIX instruction will be presented, but before doing this we should consider at least one instruction for inserting numbers into the index registers. We will use *AXT* (+0774) which represents *address to index true*. As an example, the instruction AXT 23,2 causes the number 23_{10} to be stored in XR2.

Example 10.4 Write a portion of a program for obtaining $1 + 2 +, \ldots , + 500$ without using the TIX instruction, and then write another portion using this instruction. Assemble both of these. Assume that the first instruction is in location 00144, symbol ONE is assigned to location 01262 which contains a fixed-point one, symbol C5 is for location 01263 which contains fixed-point 500_{10}, and the sum is to be stored in SUM (location 01264).

Solution   For this problem we will need a variable corresponding to a term. We will call this variable N and assume it corresponds to location 01265. This problem is sufficiently sophisticated to necessitate *diagramming*, that is, the making of a plan (see Figure 10.2). The first program is, with comments,

	CLA	ONE	1 is brought into the AC
	STO	N	
			N and SUM are set to the initial values of 1
	STO	SUM	
BACK	CLA	N	BACK is the symbol corresponding to the location of the CLA N instruction
	ADD	ONE	
	STO	N	N is increased by 1
	ADD	SUM	
	STO	SUM	N is added to the SUM
	CLA	N	checking to see if we have looped a sufficient number of times
	SUB	C5	
	TZE	OUT	when the subtraction yields zero, the looping should be terminated
	TRA	BACK	then the TRA instruction will be skipped over
OUT			continuation of program

The pertinent portion of the object program is shown below:

Assembled Program		Corresponding Source Statements		
LOCATION	CONTENTS			
00144	+050000001262		CLA	ONE
00145	+060100001265		STO	N
00146	+060100001264		STO	SUM
00147	+050000001265	BACK	CLA	N
00150	+040000001262		ADD	ONE
00151	+060100001265		STO	N
00152	+040000001264		ADD	SUM
00153	+060100001264		STO	SUM
00154	+050000001265		CLA	N
00155	+040200001263		SUB	C5
00156	+010000000160		TZE	OUT
00157	+002000000147		TRA	BACK
00160	continuation of program	OUT		

The diagram of Figure 10.2 is almost equally suitable for the example in which TIX is used. The only exception is that a step is needed for loading an

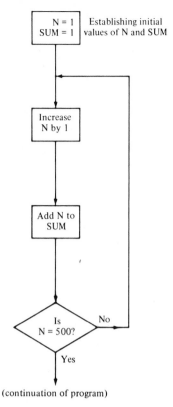

Figure 10.2 Example 10.4.

index register. Incidentally, because an error of one in loading an index register is easily made, each reader should carefully consider why in the following statements XR1 is loaded with 499 rather than 500.

Source Statements			Object Statements	
			LOCATION	CONTENTS
	CLA	ONE	00144	+050000001262
	STO	N	00145	+060100001265
	STO	SUM	00146	+060100001264
	AXT	499,1	00147	+077400100763
BACK	CLA	N	00150	+050000001265
	ADD	ONE	00151	+040000001262
	STO	N	00152	+060100001265
	ADD	SUM	00153	+040000001264
	STO	SUM	00154	+060100001264
	TIX	BACK,1,1	00155	+200001100150
continuation of program				

In this second approach the contents of XR1 are decreased by one each time, but the last, that the TIX instruction is executed. After N has been increased to 500 the contents of XR1 will be just 1, the same as the number in the decrement of the TIX instruction. Then, when this instruction is executed, there is no transfer back and the instruction executed next is the one in location 00156 (not shown) following the TIX instruction. ■

This example does not really make evident the power of the TIX instruction; there was a saving of perhaps only two words, including C5, which is not needed in the second approach. However, this example does illustrate one use of the index registers; they can be used to keep count of the number of times the instructions in a loop are executed. They have other uses, as will be shown in subsequent sections.

This example has our first illustration of indicating to the assembler that a symbol is to be assigned to a certain location: We assigned the symbol BACK to the memory location containing the CLA N instruction.

If cards are used to insert a program into a computer with one statement to a card, then the locations of the portions of the statements in the columns on the cards determine the significance that the assembler assigns to these portions. For example, symbol assignments might have to begin in column 2, mnemonic codes in column 8, and addresses in column 16.

Somewhere in the program *all names of locations must be assigned* by, for example, beginning them in column 2, as was done with BACK. This matter should become clearer after the study of pseudoinstructions in the next section.

10.6   PSEUDOINSTRUCTIONS

Pseudoinstructions in the source program instruct the *assembly program* to do something. Because these instructions do *not* appear in the object program, they do *not* have corresponding operation codes. We will consider only two pseudoinstructions, one of which relates to the insertion of data and the other to the termination of a program.

We have not yet discussed a method for inserting data into the computer for use with a program. There are several ways of doing this but for our purposes one will suffice. If we want to instruct the assembly program to place the integer, say, 29 in a location assigned to X, then we use *DEC* as in

$$X \qquad DEC \qquad 29$$

in which case X might be punched in column 2 of a card, DEC beginning in column 8, and 29 beginning in column 16.

DEC is a pseudoinstruction having an address in decimal that causes the assembly program to do two things: (1) assign the symbol X to the next sequential memory location available to the assembler, and (2) load this location with 000000000000000000000000000000011101, which is 29 in decimal and 35 in octal.

A floating-point number instead of a fixed-point number is inserted if we include a decimal point with the number. For example,

$$X \quad DEC \quad 29.$$

causes +205720000000 to be placed in the memory location corresponding to X.

It is necessary to indicate the end of the program to the assembler. This is accomplished by placing the pseudoinstruction *END* at the end.

10.7   FLOATING-POINT INSTRUCTIONS

No feature of floating-point numbers enables the computer to distinguish them from fixed-point numbers. In fact, even a person, if shown a binary number of 36 bits, cannot in general determine from the number alone whether it is fixed-point or floating-point or neither: it could be an instruction. The point is that words cannot be distinguished from their appearance, and thus if we want to instruct the computer to, say, add two floating-point numbers, which addition is different from fixed-point addition, we must inform the computer that these are floating-point numbers. This information is supplied by the type of arithmetic instructions used. We will now consider floating-point instructions for adding, subtracting, multiplying, and dividing.

The *floating add* instruction has a mnemonic code *FAD* and an operation code +0300. FAD X (+030000012345) causes C(AC) + C(X) → C(AC and MQ). The most significant part of the sum is in the AC and the least significant part in the MQ. Since the floating-point numbers are normalized, the most significant part of the sum is the part of interest, that is, *the desired sum is in the AC*. This situation is different from that of a fixed-point number extending over these two registers after a multiply operation. Since the fixed-point numbers are not normalized, a product of less than 36 bits is contained in the least significant digits, which are in the MQ. For our purposes, we will consider the floating-point sum to be entirely in the AC. However, if increased accuracy were of interest, then the portion in the MQ register would be used also.

The *floating subtract* instruction is *FSB* (+0302), and FSB X (+030200012345) causes C(AC) − C(X) → C(AC and MQ). This instruction is almost identical to FAD in execution, the only difference being that in the execution of FSB the sign bit of the number in X is changed when this number is brought into the SR.

Floating multiply has the code *FMP* (+0260). FMP X (+026000012345) causes $C(X) \times C(MQ) \to C(AC \text{ and } MQ)$. Note that the multiplier must be placed in the MQ before the multiply instruction is executed, but the most significant digits of the product, which are the digits of interest, appear in the AC.

The floating-point divide instruction is *FDH* (+0240) which represents *floating divide or halt*. FDH X (+024000012345) results in $C(AC \text{ and } MQ)/C(X) \to C(MQ)$ with the remainder in the AC. Thus, the dividend must be placed in the AC and MQ before division and then the quotient appears in the MQ after division. The computer will halt and not divide if the C(X) have a zero fraction. The reader should, on his own, study the differences between this divide instruction and that for fixed-point numbers.

Example 10.5 Write and assemble a portion of a program for calculating, in floating-point, $(7 \times 13 - 9)/5$. The result is to be stored in RES.

Solution We must instruct the assembler to generate the needed numbers if these numbers are not inserted in the computer in another manner, and we will assume this is the case. Also, we must reserve or really designate a memory location for RES. Thus, in a portion of the program that is apart from the list of instructions, we include

A	DEC	7.
B	DEC	13.
C	DEC	9.
D	DEC	5.
RES	DEC	0

These pseudoinstructions cannot be included with the ordinary instructions for then the contents of the corresponding locations will be executed as if they were instructions. Assuming the assembler assigns A to location 11234, the corresponding portion of the assembled program is

Assembled Program		Corresponding Source Statements		
LOCATION	CONTENTS			
11234	+203700000000	A	DEC	7.
11235	+204640000000	B	DEC	13.
11236	+204440000000	C	DEC	9.
11237	+203500000000	D	DEC	5.
11240	+000000000000	RES	DEC	0

The pertinent instructions are

LDQ	A	puts 7 in the MQ
FMP	B	$7 \times 13 = 91$ is now in the AC
FSB	C	$91 - 9 = 82$ is now in the AC
FDH	D	$82/5 = 16.4$ (approximately) is in the MQ
STQ	RES	the result is stored

If the first instruction of this portion of the program is placed in, say, location 01672, then this portion assembles to

Assembled Program		Corresponding Source Statements	
Location	Contents		
01672	+056000011234	LDQ	A
01673	+026000011235	FMP	B
01674	+030200011236	FSB	C
01675	+024000011237	FDH	D
01676	−060000011240	STQ	RES

10.8   ADDRESS MODIFICATION USING INDEX REGISTERS

Sometimes automatic modification of an instruction address is desired. For example, the memory may contain a block of data in 1000 sequential locations that must be brought one at a time into the AC. These 1000 operations can be obtained from a single CLA instruction if the address is changed each time the instruction is executed. Actually, the instruction itself does not have to be modified, but rather its address can be modified while passing through the adders during the execution cycle.

At the beginning of this cycle, the address of the instruction is transmitted to the MAR in preparation for the reading of the operator from a memory location. In being transmitted, the address passes through the adders where it can be modified by the contents of one or more of the index registers.

To so modify an address, the programmer must *tag* the instruction. For example, for

CLA   A, 1

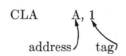

address   tag

the contents of XR1 modify the address (the number corresponding to A) as it passes through the adders on its way to the MAR. This modification is a subtraction; that is, the contents of the specified index register are subtracted from the address. Of course there is no direct subtraction. Instead, the complement of the number in the specified index register is taken to the adders and added to the address. For a change in the modification, the contents of the index register can be changed by, for example, a TIX instruction.

Not all instructions can be address modified. Instructions that use the tag in loading index registers or testing or modifying their contents do not have address modification because the tag cannot be used for two different purposes. Thus, for example, the TIX instruction and the AXT instructions do not have this feature.

Example 10.6   Five unrelated fixed-point numbers are in memory locations 01234, 01235, 01236, 01237, and 01240 that we will access by a symbol BLOC assigned to memory location 01241. Write and assemble a portion of a program for obtaining the sum of these numbers. This sum is to be stored in SUM (01245). Assume that a zero is in ZERO (01246), and that the first instruction is loaded into location 00144.

Solution   We will use looping and address modification as follows:

	AXT	5,1	this places 5 in XR1
	CLA	ZERO	ensures that C(AC) are zero initially
BACK	ADD	BLOC,1	
	TIX	BACK,1,1	explained below
	STO	SUM	

In the first execution of the ADD instruction, its address is modified to 01241 − 5 = 01234, the location of the first of the five numbers. Thus this number is added to the zero that was in the AC. When the TIX instruction is executed for the first time, the contents of XR1 are decreased by 1 to 4. Also there is a transfer back to the ADD instruction. When the ADD instruction is executed a second time the effective address is 01241 − 4 = 01235, and the second number of the group is added to the first number that was in the AC. This process continues. On the fourth execution of the TIX instruction the contents of XR1 are reduced to 1. Then when the ADD instruction is executed, the effective address is 01241 − 1 = 01240 and the fifth number is added to the sum of the other four numbers. The subsequent execution of the TIX instruction does not cause a transfer because the contents of XR1 do not exceed the decrement 1 of the TIX instruction. Thus the next instruction executed is the STO SUM instruction. The assembled program is

Assembled Program		Corresponding Source Statements
LOCATION	CONTENTS	
00144	+077400100005	AXT 5,1
00145	+050000001246	CLA ZERO
00146	+040000101241	BACK ADD BLOC,1
00147	+200001100146	TIX BACK,1,1
00150	+060100001245	STO SUM

10.9   COMPREHENSIVE EXAMPLE

An example is presented below that is complete except for the lack of instructions for making the results available in, for example, printed form to the programmer. These instructions are beyond the scope of the present study.

There is an additional instruction in this program that we have not yet discussed. It is *halt*, *HLT* (00000). It stops the computer.

Example 10.7   Approximate e^x for $x = 1, 2, 6$, and 7 using a series.

Solution   The series expression for e^x is $1 + x + x^2/2! + \ldots + x^n/n! + \ldots$. Four locations will be provided for the four sums, but they will not have individual names. Instead, they will be loaded by using one symbol TERM and address modification. For each addition a *running sum* will be formed which is a sum to which we continually add until we obtain the desired result. The different terms that are added to each running sum will be obtained by modifying a number in location TERM. A single location used for the different values of x will be named X. We will need a number which is continually modified, to aid in the formation of the denominator of each term. We will specify N for the location symbol of this number. Finally, because the calculation of each series cannot continue indefinitely, we will terminate calculations when a term becomes less than 10^{-8}, for then, we will assume, that the accuracy of the computer is exceeded. This 10^{-8} will be stored in CHECK.

This problem is sufficiently sophisticated to justify a diagram as shown in Figure 10.3. The corresponding program is

```
          AXT    4,1        XR1 is used to differentiate
                            the calculations for the four
                            sums
NEWX      CLA    X,1
          STO    X          establish correct value of X
          CLA    ONE
          STO    N          make initial values of N and
                            TERM both 1
          STO    TERM
```

```
NXRUN  CLA  TERM
       FAD  TERM,1        add TERM to pertinent
                          sum
       STO  TERM,1
       LDQ  TERM
       FMP  X
       FDH  N             new TERM = old TERM
                          times X/N
       STQ  TERM
       CLA  N
       FAD  ONE           increment N
       STO  N
       CLA  TERM
       FSB  CHECK         is this sum finished?
       TMI  NEXT
       TRA  NXRUN
NEXT   TIX  NEWX,1,1      go back if other sums are to
                          be calculated
       HLT
ONE    DEC  1.
       DEC  2.
       DEC  6.
       DEC  7.
X      DEC  0
       DEC  0 ⎫
       DEC  0 ⎪          locations reserved for the
       DEC  0 ⎬          four sums
       DEC  0 ⎭
TERM   DEC  0
CHECK  DEC  .00000001
N      DEC  0
       END
```

With the instructions separated from the data by the HLT instruction, there is no danger that the computer might execute a data word as if it were an instruction.

In the assembly process the computer makes two passes over this program. During the first pass the symbol table is formed. This is a necessary first step since, for example, the statement STO X cannot be translated to machine language until the location number corresponding to X is determined. In this first pass the computer keeps track of the number of statements and assigns location numbers to the symbols. For example, the first named statement (NEWX) is the second statement. Thus the symbol table has a first entry of

NEWX   0001

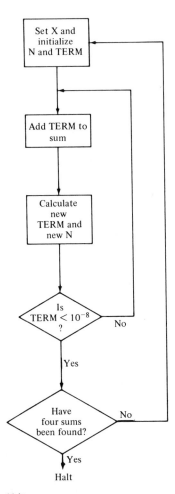

Figure 10.3 Example 10.7.

The first location 00000 is reserved for AXT 4,1, the first instruction, but of course there is no entry in the symbol table for it since it is not named. The next named instruction NXRUN, being the symbol for the seventh instruction, is assigned the location number 00006. Similarly, the other entries for the symbol table are obtained:

Symbol	Location
NEWX	00001
NXRUN	00006
NEXT	00024
ONE	00026
X	00032
TERM	00037
CHECK	00040
N	00041

In the next pass the computer uses, in addition to this symbol table, an operation-code table containing the correspondences between the mnemonic codes and the operation codes. The assembled program is

Assembled Program		**Corresponding Source Statements**		
LOCATION	INSTRUCTION			
00000	+077400100004		AXT	4,1
00001	+050000100032	NEWX	CLA	X,1
00002	+060100000032		STO	X
00003	+050000000026		CLA	ONE
00004	+060100000041		STO	N
00005	+060100000037		STO	TERM
00006	+050000000037	NXRUN	CLA	TERM
00007	+030000100037		FAD	TERM,1
00010	+060100100037		STO	TERM,1
00011	+056000000037		LDQ	TERM
00012	+026000000032		FMP	X
00013	+024000000041		FDH	N
00014	−060000000037		STQ	TERM
00015	+050000000041		CLA	N
00016	+030000000026		FAD	ONE
00017	+060100000041		STO	N
00020	+050000000037		CLA	TERM
00021	+030200000040		FSB	CHECK
00022	−012000000024		TMI	NEXT
00023	+002000000006		TRA	NXRUN
00024	+200001100001	NEXT	TIX	NEWX,1,1
00025	+000000000000		HLT	
00026	+201400000000	ONE	DEC	1.
00027	+202400000000		DEC	2.
00030	+203600000000		DEC	6.
00031	+203700000000		DEC	7.
00032	+000000000000	X	DEC	0
00033	+000000000000		DEC	0
00034	+000000000000		DEC	0
00035	+000000000000		DEC	0
00036	+000000000000		DEC	0
00037	+000000000000	TERM	DEC	0
00040	+146527461670	CHECK	DEC	.00000001
00041	+000000000000	N	DEC	0
			END	

The indicated locations for the instructions and data in this example may not be the ones used in the executed program because at the time of loading into the memory for execution, the object program may be relocated. That is, the first instruction, here AXT 4,1, may not be put into location 00000, but may, for example, be placed in location 00144

Table 10.1 Instruction List

Title	Code	Instruction	Result
Clear and Add	CLA $+0500$	CLA X	$C(X) \rightarrow C(AC)$
Store	STO $+0601$	STO X	$C(AC) \rightarrow C(X)$
Load MQ	LDQ $+0560$	LDQ X	$C(X) \rightarrow C(MQ)$
Store MQ	STQ -0600	STQ X	$C(MQ) \rightarrow C(X)$
Exchange AC and MQ	XCA $+0131$	XCA	$C(AC) \leftrightarrow C(MQ)$
Add (fixed point)	ADD $+0400$	ADD X	$C(AC) + C(X) \rightarrow C(AC)$
Subtract (fixed point)	SUB $+0402$	SUB X	$C(AC) - C(X) \rightarrow C(AC)$
Multiply (fixed point)	MPY $+0200$	MPY X	$C(X) \times C(MQ) \rightarrow C(AC$ and $MQ)$ (if the product is word size, it will be in the MQ and the AC will be cleared)
Divide or Halt (fixed point)	DVH $+0220$	DVH X	$C(AC$ and $MQ)/C(X) \rightarrow C(MQ)$ and the remainder in AC if division occurs (if the dividend is word size, then place it in the MQ and clear the AC before dividing)
Transfer	TRA $+0020$	TRA X	$X \rightarrow C(IC)$
Transfer on Plus	TPL $+0120$	TPL X	$X \rightarrow C(IC)$ if AC sign bit is 0
Transfer on Minus	TMI -0120	TMI X	$X \rightarrow C(IC)$ if AC sign bit is 1
Transfer on Overflow	TOV $+0140$	TOV X	$X \rightarrow C(IC)$ if AC overflow bit is 1
Transfer on Zero	TZE $+0100$	TZE X	$X \rightarrow C(IC)$ if $C(AC)$ is zero, exclusive of the sign bit
Transfer on Index	TIX $+2$	TIX X,T,D	$X \rightarrow C(IC)$ and $C(XR$ $T)$ reduced by D if $C(XR$ $T) > D$
Address to Index True	AXT $+0774$	AXT X,T	$X \rightarrow C(XR$ $T)$
Floating Add	FAD $+0300$	FAD X	$C(AC) + C(X) \rightarrow C(AC$ and $MQ)$ (the part of the sum of interest is in the AC)
Floating Subtract	FSB $+0302$	FSB X	$C(AC) - C(X) \rightarrow C(AC$ and $MQ)$ (the part of the difference of interest is in the AC)
Floating Multiply	FMP $+0260$	FMP X	$C(AC) \times C(MQ) \rightarrow C(AC$ and $MQ)$ (the part of the product of interest is in the AC)
Floating Divide or Halt	FDH $+0240$	FDH X	$C(AC$ and $MQ)/C(X) \rightarrow C(MQ)$ and remainder in AC if division occurs (if dividend is of word size, then place it in the AC before dividing)

and the remainder of the program loaded in consecutive locations following this one. Since all the addresses defined by variables (not absolute addresses as in AXT 4,1) will then be too small by 144_8, the loading program compensates for this relocation by adding 144 to these addresses. Consequently, while his program is running, a person may have no idea of the exact locations in memory in which the various instructions of his program are located.

10.10   SUMMARY

Some features of assembly-language programming have been presented in this chapter. Of course, because assembly languages differ with computers, the language presented here should not be considered a general language. Our purpose of studying an assembly language, in the detail in which we have, is to obtain a better understanding of the use and operation of some computer components. We were particularly concerned with the components shown in Figure 10.1, and in fact little was said about programming that was not directly related to these components.

In the discussion of programming we saw that the two most important registers, the accumulator and the multiplier-quotient, are involved in all arithmetic instructions. Another register, the storage register, holds all words coming from the core memory into the arithmetic unit. Also, it retains the instruction word during the instruction cycle and an operand during the execution cycle. The instruction register retains the operation code during the execution cycle to ensure that the correct line is activated from the decoder even when the contents of the storage register change. The index registers operating through the adders can be used to modify addresses on their way to the memory address register which determines the location that is accessed in the core memory. Index registers are also useful in looping.

In the next chapter we will consider these and other computer components in a more detailed presentation of a digital computer.

For the reader's convenience in working the following problems, the instructions of this chapter, exclusive of the pseudoinstructions are listed in Table 10.1.

PROBLEMS ▬▬▬▬▬▬▬▬▬▬▬▬▬▬▬▬▬▬▬▬▬▬▬▬▬▬

10.1 True or false:

(a) There is a standardized machine language for most digital computers.

(**b**) FORTRAN is an assembly language.
(**c**) The program executed by a computer is the source program.
(**d**) A FORTRAN program is an object program.
(**e**) Most assemblers are about the size of a portable TV set.
(**f**) There is a one-to-one correspondence between FORTRAN statements and instructions in the corresponding machine language program.

10.2 A certain computer has a 64K memory and a word size of 40 bits. All instructions have an operation code of 9 bits. Determine the number of flip-flops for the AC, MQ, SR, IR, MAR, MIR, and the XR's.

Answers   41, 40, 40, 9, 16, 40, 16

10.3 Repeat Problem 10.2 for a computer having a 16K memory, a word size of 32 bits, and instructions with 10-bit operation codes.

10.4 Repeat Problem 10.2 for a computer having an 8K memory, a word size of 38 bits, and instructions with 8-bit operation codes.

10.5 If the three index registers in Figure 10.1 are numbered XR1, XR2, and XR4 so that each is designated by one 1 bit, what is the tag for indicating
(**a**) Both XR1 and XR2?   (**c**) Both XR2 and XR4?
(**b**) Both XR1 and XR4?   (**d**) All three XR1, XR2, and XR4?

10.6 Assemble the following portion of a program. Assume that the location numbers for A, B, C, and D are, respectively, 10016, 10020, 11131, and 14672. The location of the first instruction is 01246.

CLA	A
ADD	B
SUB	C
STO	D

Answers	Location	Contents
	01246	+050000010016
	01247	+040000010020
	01250	+040200011131
	01251	+060100014672

10.7 Assemble the following portion of a program. Assume that the location numbers for ONE, SIX, FOUR, DEN, NUM, and X are, respectively, 10017, 10020, 10021, 10022, 10023, and 10024. The first instruction is loaded into location 20057.

```
CLA   ONE
ADD   SIX
ADD   FOUR
STO   DEN
LDQ   FOUR
MPY   SIX
STQ   NUM
DVH   DEN
STQ   X
```

10.8 Assemble the following portion of a program. Assume that the location numbers for W, X, Y, Z, TERM, and DEN are, respectively, 16423, 15276, 14322, 17777, 32642, and 32602. The location of the first instruction is 44567.

```
LDQ   W
MPY   X
STQ   DEN
LDQ   Y
MPY   Z
STQ   TERM
XCA
CLA   W
ADD   X
SUB   TERM
XCA
DVH   DEN
STQ   W
```

10.9 Show the expressions corresponding to the program portions for Problems 10.6, 10.7, and 10.8.

10.10 Following is a portion of a program for calculating $F = (X \cdot Y - Z)/(X \cdot Y \cdot Z)$ that contains several errors. Find all errors. Locations X, Y, and Z contain fixed-point numbers.

```
CLA   X
MPY   Y
SUB   Z
STO   F
LDQ   X
MPY   Y
MPY   Z
STO   Z
LDQ   F
DVH   Z
STO   F
```

10.11 Following is a portion of a program for calculating F = (D · E − A · B)/(B · C + D) that contains one error. Find this error. Locations A, B, C, D, and E contain fixed-point numbers.

```
LDQ  B
MPY  C
XCA
ADD  D
STO  C
LDQ  B
MPY  A
STQ  A
LDQ  D
MPY  E
XCA
SUB  A
DVH  C
STQ  F
```

10.12 Following is a portion of a program for calculating F = (A · B)/ (C − D) + C · D that contains two errors. Find these errors. Locations A, B, C, and D contain fixed-point numbers.

```
LDQ  C
MPY  D
STO  F
CLA  C
SUB  D
STO  D
LDQ  A
MPY  B
DVH  D
ADD  F
STO  F
```

10.13 Write a portion of a program for calculating F = (A · B − C · D)/ (A · D − C · D) using as few instructions as possible. Assume that all quantities are fixed point.

10.14 Repeat Problem 10.13 for

$$F = [(A · B)/(C − D) + C · D]/(A · B · C).$$

10.15 Repeat Problem 10.13 for

$$[(A · C − B) · D + (B · D − A · C)/(C · D)]/(B · D)$$

10.16 Given the following portion of a program, what are the contents of locations ONE, TWO, THREE, and FOUR after this portion is executed? Assume that initially C(ONE) = 1, C(TWO) = 2, C(THREE) = 3, and C(FOUR) = 4, all in fixed point.

```
LDQ   THREE
MPY   TWO
XCA
SUB   FOUR
STO   THREE
LDQ   TWO
MPY   FOUR
STQ   TWO
XCA
SUB   ONE
STO   ONE
XCA
DVH   THREE
STO   THREE
STQ   FOUR
```

Answers   7, 8, 1, 3

10.17 Given the following portion of a program, what are the contents of locations DEN, THREE, FOUR, FIVE, and SIX after this portion is executed? Initially, C(DEN) = 0, C(THREE) = 3, C(FOUR) = 4, C(FIVE) = 5, and C(SIX) = 6, all in fixed point.

```
LDQ   THREE
MPY   FOUR
XCA
SUB   FIVE
STO   DEN
CLA   FIVE
SUB   FOUR
STO   FOUR
CLA   THREE
ADD   FIVE
SUB   SIX
XCA
MPY   FOUR
DVH   DEN
STO   FIVE
STQ   SIX
```

10.18   Given the following program, what are the contents of locations
TWO, THREE, FOUR, and FIVE after this program is executed?

```
              LDQ   THREE
              MPY   FOUR
              XCA
              SUB   FIVE
              XCA
              DVH   TWO
              STQ   FIVE
              LDQ   FOUR
              MPY   TWO
              XCA
              SUB   FOUR
              XCA
              DVH   FOUR
              XCA
              STO   THREE
              STQ   TWO
              ADD   FIVE
              STO   FIVE
              HLT
TWO           DEC   2
THREE         DEC   3
FOUR          DEC   4
FIVE          DEC   5
              END
```

10.19   What are the contents of location X after the following program
is executed? Rewrite this program using a TIX instruction instead
of a TZE instruction.

```
BACK          LDQ   X
              MPY   THREE
              STQ   X
              CLA   CHECK
              SUB   ONE
              STO   CHECK
              TZE   OUT
              TRA   BACK
OUT           HLT
X             DEC   1
THREE         DEC   3
CHECK         DEC   25
ONE           DEC   1
              END
```

10.20 What are the contents of A, B, C, and D, in octal, after the following program is executed?

```
            LDQ   A
            FMP   B
            FSB   C
            STO   A
            STQ   B
            FDH   D
            STO   C
            STQ   D
            HLT
      A     DEC   3.
      B     DEC   4.
      C     DEC   2.
      D     DEC   6.
            END
```

Answers   +204500000000,   +151000000000,   +151400000000,
          +201652525252

10.21 Assemble the program of Problem 10.20. Assume that the first instruction is loaded into location 46523.

10.22 What are the contents of TWO, FOUR, SIX, and SEVEN, in octal, after the following program is executed? Assemble this program, assuming that the first instruction is loaded into location 00144. Show what is being calculated here.

```
            LDQ   TWO
            FMP   FOUR
            FSB   SIX
            STO   TWO
            FDH   SEVEN
            STO   SEVEN
            LDQ   SIX
            FMP   FOUR
            FAD   SEVEN
            STO   FOUR
            HLT
      TWO   DEC   2.
      FOUR  DEC   4.
      SIX   DEC   6.
      SEVEN DEC   7.
            END
```

10.23 Write a program for calculating, in floating point, $X - X^3/3! + X^5/5! - X^7/7! + \ldots$ for $X = 1$, 3, and 10. Terminate the series when a term is less than 10^{-8} in magnitude.

10.24 Repeat Problem 10.23 for the series $1 - X^2/2! + X^4/4! - X^6/6! + \ldots$.

10.25 Write a program using the TIX instruction for obtaining $2 \cdot 3 + 4 \cdot 5 + 6 \cdot 7 + \ldots + 998 \cdot 999 + 1000 \cdot 1001$ in fixed point. Assemble the program, assuming that the first instruction will be loaded into location 12345.

10.26 What calculation does the following program perform? Assemble this program assuming that the first instruction is loaded into location 01500.

	AXT	4,1
BACK	CLA	ZERO
UP	FAD	A
	STO	ZERO
	CLA	UP
	ADD	ONE
	STO	UP
	TIX	BACK,1,1
	HLT	
A	DEC	3.
B	DEC	4.
C	DEC	−5.
D	DEC	7.
ONE	DEC	1
ZERO	DEC	0
	END	

10.27 One thousand floating-point numbers are in consecutive locations in memory. The symbol BLOCK is assigned to the location of these thousand having the largest location number. Write a program without using index registers for finding the sum of these numbers. That is, modify instruction addresses directly by using ADD or SUB instead of by using index registers. Then rework the problem using an index register and the TIX instruction.

11

Arithmetic
And Control
Sections

We have studied many components used in digital computers and have considered some aspects of an assembly language. Now we will combine much of what we have learned about these components and the assembly language in a consideration of the design of the arithmetic and control sections of a small digital computer.

This digital computer, which is a parallel machine, is purely theoretical; it has never been constructed. And, it cannot do much. It has no floating-point features, no division or even subtraction capability, and the word size for numbers is too small to be practical. However, by studying the arithmetic and control sections of this impractical and relatively simple computer we can readily grasp some basic principles of these sections that apply to digital computers in general.

As mentioned, only the arithmetic and control sections will be studied. Input-output units and the memory are omitted, for convenience, but these components are not neglected in our study. Input-output units are presented in the next chapter. And, of course, we have studied memories in Chapter 9. The memory has been excluded in order to simplify some block diagrams and not because of any other difficulty. Actually, some lines to the memory are shown, and the remainder of the lines should be apparent from our study of Chapter 9.

For simplification, we will restrict word size to eleven bits that for instruction words are divided into a four-bit operation code and a seven-bit address. With this arrangement, the number of different instructions is limited to sixteen (2^4) and the number of memory locations cannot exceed 128 (2^7). None of the instructions has a tag or decrement. Thus our little computer does not have index registers.

Each data word is a fixed-point number having four leading zeros followed by seven magnitude bits, which means that the arithmetic section need be capable only of operating on seven-bit numbers. Since there is no sign bit, the numbers are considered to be positive. Using only part of the word for fixed-point numbers is unconventional but the few number of magnitude bits allows us to simplify considerably some of the arithmetic components, as will be seen.

11.1   AC, MQ, SR, AND ADDER ARRANGEMENT

The arrangement of the AC, MQ, SR, and adders is shown in Figure 11.1. The AC and MQ each have an upper and lower set of registers that function as a single shift register as described in the discussion of Figure 4.21, with the upper register contents being those normally associated with the registers. In the designations for the flip-flops, L represents lower and U represents upper. Of the eight flip-flops in the upper and also in the lower AC, one is for overflow and the other seven are for magnitude bits. The upper and lower MQ each have only seven flip-flops but the SR has eleven since it must have a sufficient number of flip-flops to hold a complete word. In Figure 11.1 only seven of the eleven SR flip-flops are shown, and these are the ones for holding the number part of a data word exclusive of the four leading zeros.

For a number to go from the SR into the AC, and really into the lower AC, it must pass through seven adders. That is, an addition must be performed to transfer a number from the SR to the AC, as has been mentioned in the prior chapter. Six of these adders must be full adders, but the least significant one can be a half adder because we will not implement this computer with subtraction and thus will not have an end-around carry.

Most of the details of the first two stages of the AC, shown in Figure 11.2, have already been shown in Figure 4.21. But there are a few changes. One line has been added; it is a CLEAR line connected to each OR gate on the R sides of the upper AC flip-flops. Another line,

Accumulator and MQ general layout

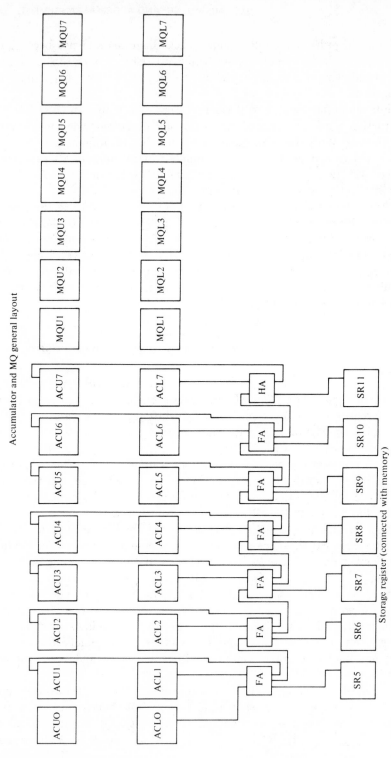

Storage register (connected with memory)

Figure 11.1   Register arrangements.

346

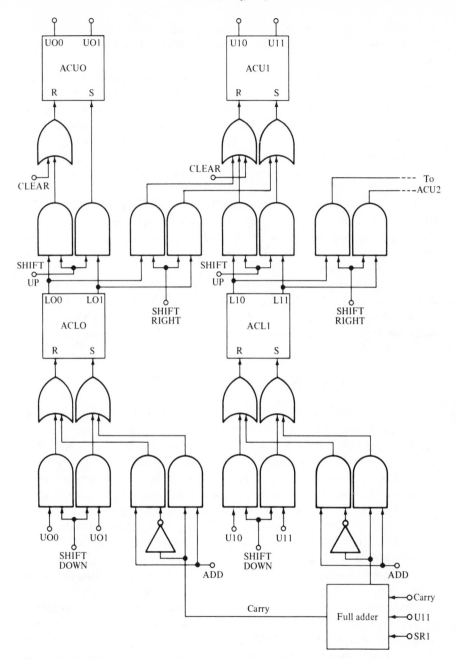

Figure 11.2 First two stages of accumulator with adder.

the SHIFT LEFT line, has been deleted because for the instructions we will consider, the shift left capability is not needed. Of course, it is needed in general.

The adders continuously add the contents of the upper AC to those of the SR, even when addition is not desired. This addition does no harm, and additional circuits would be necessary if addition were limited to actual addition instructions. However, the outputs of the adders have no effect except when an ADD line is pulsed. Then, for each adder, the sum bit and its complement, the latter provided by a NOT gate, pass through AND gates to trigger the lower AC flip-flop connected to the adder.

The AC has five control lines: SHIFT UP, SHIFT DOWN, SHIFT RIGHT, CLEAR, and ADD, each of which is connected to all the correspondingly marked terminals in the AC. For example, the single ADD line is connected to all the ADD terminals even though the actual connections are not shown.

The MQ need have only three control lines: SHIFT DOWN, SHIFT RIGHT, and CLEAR. No ADD line is needed because the MQ is not connected to the adders, and no SHIFT UP line because for the instructions we will consider there will never be a shift up in the MQ.

11.2   MULTIPLY CONTROL UNIT

The computer multiply control unit (MCU), which is shown in Figure 11.3, provides control signals for multiplying two numbers. Recall from Chapter 8 that before multiplying fixed-point numbers, the computer places the multiplier in the MQ, the multiplicand in the SR, and clears the AC. Then, for each low order MQ bit of 1, the computer adds the contents of the AC and SR, after which it right shifts the sum in the AC and the multiplier in the MQ. But for a low order MQ bit of 0, the computer does not add but instead only shifts right. Actually, the computer being considered does not shift right directly but instead first shifts down and then up and right from the lower registers into the upper registers. We will call the latter operation a shift right for simplification, although it is really a shift up and right.

Now considering the dual register AC and MQ multiply operation in more detail, if the low order MQ bit is a 1, the MCU pulses the ADD line of the AC to enable the outputs of the adders to trigger the lower AC flip-flops. Then the MCU pulses the SHIFT RIGHT line to cause the sum to pass to the upper registers while also being shifted. The operation is different if the low order MQ bit is 0. In this case the MCU pulses the SHIFT DOWN line instead of the ADD line. Next, the MCU pulses the SHIFT RIGHT line. During the add or shift down

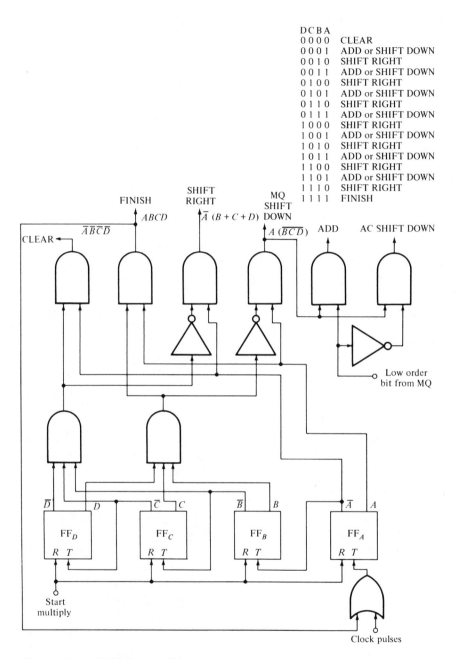

Figure 11.3 Multiply control unit.

of the AC, the contents of the upper MQ also shift down to the lower MQ. And during the shift right of the AC, the MQ also shifts right.

The MCU tests the low order MQ bit once for each bit in the multiplier or, in other words, a total of seven times. Thus, during multiplication there are fourteen steps, seven of which are add or shift down and the other seven of which are shift right. Two other steps are needed: The MCU must initially clear the AC and, as a final step, must generate a signal to indicate the finish of the multiply operation. These two steps plus the fourteen other steps are a total of sixteen steps required for multiplication.

In the MCU the control signals for the sixteen steps of multiplication are provided by a four flip-flop counter that in response to triggering clock pulses produces a count from 0000 to 1111. Except during the execution of a multiply instruction, the counter produces an output of 1111 that causes an OR gate to block clock pulses from triggering the first flip-flop of the counter. For the start of a multiply operation, a signal must clear the counter flip-flops to 0000 to enable this OR gate so that clock pulses can pass and trigger the counter.

The correspondences between the contents of the counter and the multiply steps are shown in Figure 11.3. As can be seen, the MCU clears the AC or, in other words, pulses the CLEAR line of the AC when the counter is at 0000. When the counter increases the count to 0001, the MCU generates the first ADD or SHIFT DOWN signal. Then, at a count of 0010, it generates the first SHIFT RIGHT signal. And so on, until the counter reaches 1111, at which time the MCU generates a FINISH signal.

For obtaining switching algebra expressions for the various signals, we assign a different variable to each flip-flop: variable A to the low-order flip-flop, B to the second one, C to the next, and D to the last. These variables head corresponding columns in the table shown in Figure 11.3.

The expressions are fairly apparent. For example, the CLEAR AC signal is obviously $\overline{A}\overline{B}\overline{C}\overline{D}$, and the FINISH signal is $ABCD$. The other expressions are only slightly less evident. An ADD OR SHIFT DOWN signal is needed whenever the A flip-flop is 1, except when B, C, and D are also 1. This signal, which is $A(\overline{BCD})$, pulses either the AC SHIFT DOWN line or the ADD line, depending upon the operation of AND gates having inputs from the low order MQ flip-flop. The AC and MQ SHIFT RIGHT signals are generated whenever the A flip-flop is in the 0 state except when B, C, and D are also in the 0 state. Consequently, the SHIFT RIGHT signals are generated from $\overline{A}(B + C + D)$.

When the counter reaches 1111, the $ABCD$ FINISH signal, which is then a 1, is conducted to the OR gate that controls the passage of the triggering clock pulses. With a 1 input, this OR gate produces an output that remains at 1 until the counter is cleared for the start of another multiply operation. Of course, this 1 output does not produce triggering, and so the counter flip-flops remain at 1111 until a clear pulse is received for initiating another multiply operation.

11.3 BLOCK DIAGRAM OF THE ARITHMETIC AND CONTROL SECTIONS

The arithmetic and control sections for our little computer are shown in Figure 11.4 in block diagram form. The number of flip-flops in each register should be apparent. As has been mentioned, there are eleven flip-flops in the SR, eight in the AC, and seven in the MQ. Further, the IC and MAR must each have seven flip-flops to permit access to any location in memory. The IR has four flip-flops for holding the four-bit operation codes.

Only nine lines, each corresponding to a different instruction, are shown as outputs for the operation decoding matrix. However, with a four-bit operation code there can be as many as sixteen output lines. These lines extend to all correspondingly marked inputs, even though, for the purpose of simplification, the lines are not completed in Figure 11.4. For example, the LDQ line is actually connected to the input of the AND gate beside the MQ although the line is not completed in Figure 11.4. Similarly, the CLA line from the operation decoding matrix is connected to the input line marked CLA for the AND gate beneath the AC.

The lower half of Figure 11.4 contains a ring counter timing unit of five flip-flops that are triggered by clock pulses (clock-pulse inputs are not shown). Each of these flip-flops has an output marked with a circled number that is connected, although for simplification is not shown connected, to all points on the diagram marked with the same number. For example, the output ① from FF_1 is connected to an AND gate input to the MAR and also to the input of the AND gate adjacent the IC.

Cycle control is produced by an instruction-execution cycle flip-flop having two output terminals marked ① and ⓔ that connect to all similarly marked terminals. At the time the ring counter is first energized, this flip-flop is in the 0 state and produces a 1 on the ① line. After five clock pulses the 1 in the ring counter circulates back to this flip-flop, triggering it to the 1 state. Then the ① output goes to 0 and the ⓔ line output to 1. Since this flip-flop is triggered once for each circulation of the 1 around the ring counter, it controls whether the computer is in the instruction or execution cycle of the execution of an instruction.

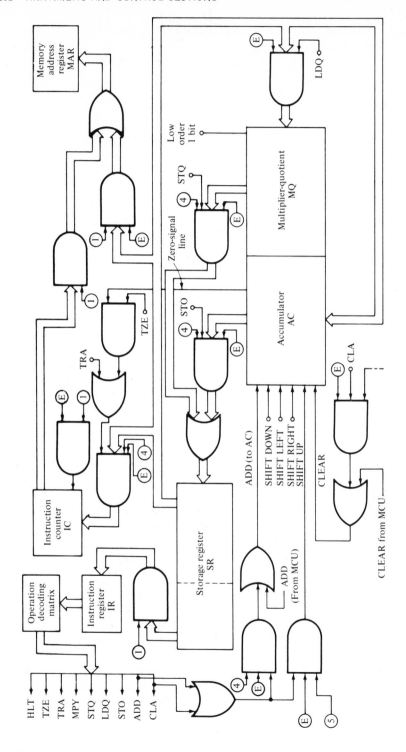

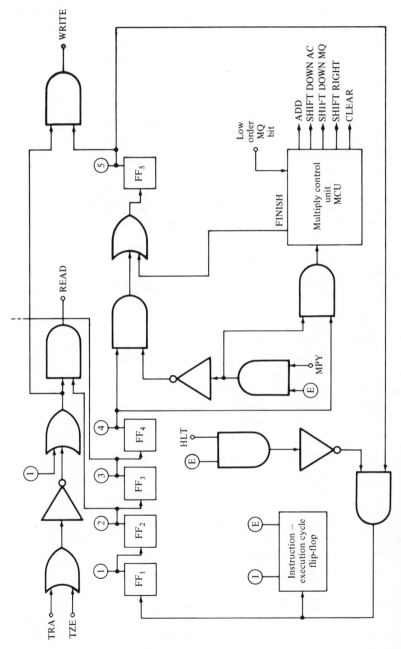

Figure 11.4 Arithmetic and control sections.

Some of the connection lines between registers and other components are shown in hollow form to indicate the presence of many lines. For example, the hollow line from the rightmost SR flip-flop is actually seven lines for single-line transfer and fourteen lines for double-line transfer. Also, the gates associated with these lines are not single gates but many, one for each line. For example, each AND gate input to the MAR represents either seven or fourteen AND gates, depending on the type of transfer.

As has been mentioned, the instruction and execution times are each divided into five timing periods: Time 1, Time 2, and so on, which times correspond to 1's on the respective outputs of the ring counter. Also, the instruction and execution times alternate, as shown below:

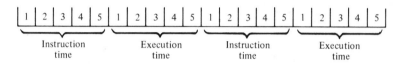

Instruction   Execution   Instruction   Execution
time   time   time   time

Instruction Cycle

During each instruction cycle, which is the same for all instructions, there is a 0 in the instruction-execution cycle flip-flop and thus a 1 on all lines designated ①. The following events occur during the various times of this cycle.

Time 1: The IC contents, which specify the memory location of the instruction that will be executed, pass through AND gates activated by ① inputs, through OR gates, to the MAR. This connection between the IC and MAR exists for the complete instruction cycle even though it serves no purpose after Time 1. This connection does no harm and to break it would necessitate additional circuits.

Time 2: A clock pulse causes the 1 in the ring counter to go from FF_1 to FF_2. Then all lines marked ② are energized. One function of the 1 on ② is to produce a pulse at the output of an AND gate that controls the pulsing of the READ line to the memory. This AND gate, which is just above the ring counter, will be called the *READ AND gate* for future reference. The other input to this AND gate is also a 1 at this time because it is the output from an OR gate having a 1 input from the ① line. Thus during Time 2 the word in the memory location specified by the MAR is read into the SR. When this word, which is presumably an instruction, arrives in the SR, its first four bits, the operation code, pass through AND gates activated by an ① signal and trigger four flip-flops in the IR which then stores the operation code.

Times 3 and 4: Two clock pulses cause the 1 in the ring to pass from FF_2 to FF_3 to FF_4 but nothing else happens.

Time 5:   The next clock pulse passes the 1 in the ring to FF_5 which then energizes all lines marked ⑤. One of these lines is an input to an AND gate, which we will call the *WRITE AND gate,* that controls the pulsing of the WRITE line to the memory. This AND gate, which is just above the ring counter, has one other input, and this input is also a 1 at this time for reasons mentioned in the discussion of Time 2. With 1's on both inputs the WRITE AND gate produces a write pulse that causes the contents of the SR to be written back into the memory location specified by the contents of the MAR. This writing, which restores the instruction to the memory, is necessary because of the destructive read-out during Time 2.

From the above, we see that the complete result of the instruction cycle can be stated quite briefly; the instruction in the location specified by the contents of the IC is read into the SR and the operation code is placed in the IR. That is all there is to it.

Since the instruction cycles for all instructions are the same, we will not again discuss the instruction cycle in detail.

Execution Cycles

After each instruction cycle the pulse in the ring counter triggers the instruction-execution cycle flip-flop to the 1 state, thereby causing all lines marked Ⓔ to be energized and an execution cycle to begin. Because the execution cycles differ for the various instructions, they need to be explained individually.

In the following discussion of execution cycles, we will assume that each execution cycle has been preceded by an instruction cycle or, in other words, at the beginning of each execution cycle the instruction is in the SR and the corresponding output line from the operation decoding matrix is energized.

CLA execution cycle

Time 1:   The address of the instruction in the SR passes to the MAR through AND gates activated by 1's on ① and Ⓔ. At the same time, the output of another AND gate steps up the IC by one in preparation for the following instruction cycle.

Time 2:   The word at the memory location specified by the MAR contents is read into the SR. This is the word the last seven bits of which will eventually go into the AC. For an understanding of why there is a read operation during this time and during Time 2 for the execution of all instructions except TRA and TZE, the reader should consider the inputs to the READ AND gate. In one input path an OR gate has a 0 output because it is energized by TRA and TZE lines, each of which has 0 on it except for TRA and TZE instructions. A NOT gate following the OR gate produces a 1 out that passes through the following OR gate to be an input to the READ AND gate which then has 1's on both inputs during Time 2. And, for the same reasons, there are 1's on the inputs to the WRITE AND gate during Time 5 except during the execution cycles of the TRA and TZE instructions.

Time 3: The AC is cleared by a pulse on the CLEAR line from an AND gate (the 1 also passes through an OR gate) beneath the AC in Figure 11.4. This AND gate has three inputs— Ⓔ , CLA, and ③—all of which are 1's during Time 3 of the execution cycle of the CLA instruction.

Time 4: The ADD line of the AC is pulsed from an AND gate connected through an OR gate to the ADD line. This AND gate has three inputs—CLA, Ⓔ , and ④—all of which are 1's at this time. The number in the SR, which is added to the zero in the AC, is triggered into the lower AC flip-flops from the adders.

Time 5: The number in the SR is written back into memory. Also, the AC SHIFT UP line is pulsed, causing the contents of the lower AC to trigger the upper AC flip-flops. Thus the number is stored in the AC.

ADD execution cycle

The execution times are the same as those for CLA with one exception: During Time 3 there is no clearing of the AC. In fact, nothing happens during Time 3. Consequently, the number in the AC is added to the number read in from memory during this cycle.

STO execution cycle

Time 1: The address of the STO instruction in the SR goes to the MAR and the IC is stepped up by one.

Time 2: The contents of the memory location specified by the STO address are read into the SR. Although the presence of these contents in the SR is not significant, the associated destructive read-out of the memory location is important since it permits writing into this memory location at Time 5.

Time 3: Nothing happens.

Time 4: The contents of the AC pass through AND gates and OR gates above the AC in Figure 11.4 and into the SR. These AND gates are activated by 1's on the Ⓔ , STO, and ④ lines.

Time 5: The contents of the SR are written into the memory at the location specified by the address of the STO instruction.

STQ execution cycle

This execution cycle is the same as that of the STO instruction except for Time 4, during which the contents of the MQ, rather than those of the AC, pass to the SR.

LDQ execution cycle

Time 1: The address of the LDQ instruction in the SR passes to the MAR and the IC is stepped up by one.

Time 2: The contents of the memory location specified by the LDQ address are read into the SR. Also, at this time the last seven bits of these contents pass from the SR through the AND gates beside the MQ in Figure 11.4 and go to the upper MQ flip-flops.

Times 3 and 4: Nothing happens.

Time 5: The contents of the SR are written into the memory location specified by the address of the LDQ instruction.

TRA execution cycle

Time 1: The address of the TRA instruction in the SR goes to the MAR but this fact is not of significance since there will be no read or write operations. The IC is stepped up by one, but this operation is not used either because the contents of the IC will be replaced.

Time 2: Do not read. The 1 on the TRA lines produces a 0 on one input of the READ AND gate.

Time 3: Nothing happens

Time 4: The address part of the contents of the SR passes through AND gates and into the IC. These AND gates, which are immediately above the SR in Figure 11.4, have 1's on their Ⓔ , ④, and TRA inputs.

Time 5: Do not write for reasons mentioned in the discussion of Time 2.

TZE execution cycle

The execution cycle of this instruction is the same as that for the TRA instruction, except that at Time 4 the AND gates above the SR are activated only if there is a zero signal from the AC. This signal can be obtained by, for example, ANDing together the outputs from the 0 lines of all the AC flip-flops.

MPY execution cycle

Time 1:   The address of the MPY instruction in the SR passes to the MAR and the IC is stepped up by one.

Time 2:   The multiplicand is read into the SR.

Time 3:   Nothing happens

Time 4:   The MCU receives a signal to multiply the SR contents by those of the MQ. During this multiplication, which continues for sixteen clock pulses, the 1 in the ring counter does not circulate. In fact, it is destroyed when the fifth clock pulse occurs, because then the output of FF_4 cannot trigger FF_5, there being an open AND gate between these flip-flops. After the multiplication operation is completed, the generated finish signal triggers FF_5 to the 1 state, and this 1 continues to circulate.

Time 5:   The multiplicand in the SR is written into the memory location specified by the address of the MPY instruction.

HLT execution cycle

Time 1:   The address (zero) of the HLT instruction in the SR goes to the MAR, and the IC is stepped up by one.

Time 2:   The contents of location zero are read into the SR.

Times 3 and 4:   Nothing happens.

Time 5:   The contents of location zero are restored.

Time 5 to Time 1:   The 1 pulse cannot circulate from FF_5 to FF_1 because the ring counter is interrupted by an open AND gate in the return line. With the operation of the counter interrupted, the computer ceases execution of instructions.

11.4   OTHER INSTRUCTIONS

Other instructions can be implemented in the arithmetic and control sections of Figure 11.4. In the following list some of them are described.

STA Y   Store Address.   The address part of the AC (last seven bits) replaces the address part of the C(Y). The C(AC) and the remainder of the C(Y) are unchanged.

STC Y   Store Instruction Counter.   The C(IC), after being stepped up by one, replace the address part of the C(Y). The remainder of the bits of the C(Y) are unchanged.

STZ Y   Store Zero.   All bits of C(Y) are replaced by 0's.

NOP   No Operation.   The computer takes the next instruction in sequence.

HTR Y   Halt and Transfer.   This instruction halts execution of the program. Then after the start key on the operator's console is depressed, program execution continues with the execution of the instruction at location Y.

XEC Y   Execute.   The computer executes the instruction at location Y after which the next instruction executed is that following XEC. However, if the instruction in location Y was a successful transfer instruction, that instruction prevails.

TNZ Y   Transfer on No Zero.   If the C(AC) are not zero the computer executes the instruction from location Y and proceeds from there. If they are zero, the next sequential instruction is executed.

ZET Y   Storage Zero Test.   If the C(Y) are zero, the computer skips the next instruction. But, if the C(Y) are not zero the computer executes the next sequential instruction.

NZT Y   Storage Not Zero Test.   If the C(Y) are not zero, the computer skips the next instruction. But if the C(Y) are zero the computer executes the next sequential instruction.

ORA Y   OR to Accumulator.   If a corresponding bit of either location Y or of the AC, or both, is a 1, a 1 replaces the contents of that position in the AC. Otherwise, that position is made 0.

ORS Y   OR to Storage.   If a corresponding bit of either the AC or location Y or both is a 1, a 1 replaces the contents of that position in location Y. Otherwise, that position is made 0.

ANA Y   AND to Accumulator.   This instruction is similar to ORA except that the operation is AND instead of OR.

CLM   Clear Magnitude.   The C(AC) are cleared.

COM Complement Magnitude.   All 1's in the AC are replaced by 0's and all 0's by 1's.

11.5 EXAMPLES

Example 11.1   Implement CLM on the sections of Figure 11.4.

Solution   Of course we must provide a CLM output line from the decoding
matrix. Then we must consider whether we want to block reading and
writing during the execution cycle. Although these operations accomplish nothing,
they do no harm and thus will not be prevented. For clearing the AC, the AC
CLEAR line can be activated at any time during the execution cycle; arbitrarily,
we can select, say, Time 3. Thus, by including an AND gate with three inputs—
Ⓔ, CLM, and ③ with an output connected to the OR gate on the CLEAR
line as shown in Figure 11.5—we can implement the CLM instruction.   ■

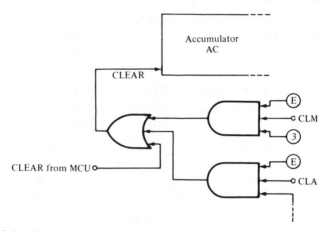

Figure 11.5   Example 11.1.

Example 11.2   Implement TNZ on the sections of Figure 11.4.

Solution   In addition to including a TNZ output line from the decoding matrix,
we must consider whether we should block reading and writing during
the execution cycle. If we read, then we will lose the address of the TNZ instruction, which address we may need to put into the IC. Thus we will *not* read or
write. These operations can be blocked by including a connection from the TNZ
terminal on the operation decoding matrix to the OR gate having TRA and TZE
inputs. This is the OR gate that provides signals for the READ and WRITE
AND gates.

The address in the SR is preferably transferred to the IC at Time 4 if there
is a no-zero signal since such transfer has already been provided for the implemented TRA and TZE instructions. This no-zero signal can be obtained from a
NOT gate connected to the AC zero signal line. If an AND gate, energized by
this no-zero signal and also a TNZ input, is connected to provide an input to the
OR gate between the SR and IC in Figure 11.4, the desired operation is obtained.
The pertinent portion of the modified diagram is shown in Figure 11.6.   ◪

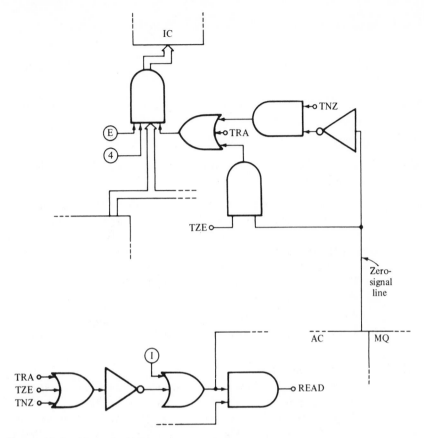

Figure 11.6   Example 11.2.

PROBLEMS

In the following problems assume that memory reading and writing are limited to Times 2 and 5, respectively, of the instruction and execution cycles.

11.1   Consider a design for an MCU similar to that of Figure 11.3 but for a system in which the data words have fifteen magnitude bits.
(a) How many flip-flops are needed?
(b) If letter variables are assigned to the flip-flops starting with A for the low order flip-flop, B for the next, and so on, what are the expressions for the CLEAR signal, the FINISH signal, the ADD or SHIFT DOWN signal, and the SHIFT RIGHT signal?

Answers (a) five; (b) $\overline{ABCDE}$, $ABCDE$, $A(\overline{BCDE})$, $\overline{A}(B + C + D + E)$

11.2 Make a diagram similar to that of Figure 11.3 for the MCU of Problem 11.1.

11.3 Repeat Problem 11.1 for a system in which the data words have eight magnitude bits.

Answers (a) five; (b) $\overline{ABCDE}$, AE, $A\overline{E}$, $\overline{A}(B + C + D + E)$

11.4 Repeat Problem 11.1 for a system in which the data words have nine magnitude bits.

11.5 For some steps of the implemented instructions, the selected times are, to some extent, arbitrary. That is, other times could have been selected and yet proper operation obtained. With this in mind, discuss the following for the CLA instruction:
   (a) What is the earliest time that the AC can be cleared?
   (b) What is the latest time that the ADD line can be pulsed?
   (c) What are the earliest and latest times for the pulsing of the AC SHIFT UP line?
   (d) What are the earliest and latest times that the IC can be stepped up?

11.6 Answer the following:
   (a) For the STO instruction, what are the earliest and latest times that the contents of the AC can pass to the SR?
   (b) Why for the LDQ instruction does the word get loaded into the MQ at Time 2? Also, why isn't a timing signal applied to the AND gates beneath the MQ?

11.7 Answer the following for the TRA execution cycle:
   (a) Why is the IC allowed to be stepped up even though this has no effect?
   (b) Why is it necessary not to read during Time 2?
   (c) What is the earliest time that the contents of the IC can be replaced?
   (d) What would happen if a write operation occurred during Time 5 even though there was not a read during Time 2?

11.8 In this chapter all the instructions are specified as being *two-cycle instructions;* that is, they have an instruction cycle and an execution cycle, each with a memory cycle. Actually, some of the instructions we considered can be interpreted and executed within the time of a single memory cycle. Identify these instructions, which we will hereafter refer to as *one-cycle instructions.*

11.9 Implement STA on the sections of Figure 11.4 as a one-cycle instruction.

11.10 Implement STA on the sections of Figure 11.4 as a two-cycle instruction.

11.11 Implement STC on the sections of Figure 11.4 as a two-cycle instruction. Can it be implemented in one cycle?

11.12 Implement STZ on the sections of Figure 11.4 using as few components as possible.

11.13 Implement NOP on the sections of Figure 11.4 as a one-cycle instruction. Can you give an instance for which this instruction might be desirable to have in a program?

11.14 Implement NOP on the sections of Figure 11.4 as a two-cycle instruction.

11.15 Implement HTR on the sections of Figure 11.4 as a one-cycle instruction. Can you give any reasons for the use of this instruction in a program instead of a TRA instruction?

11.16 Implement HTR on the sections of Figure 11.4 as a two-cycle instruction.

11.17 Implement XEC on the sections of Figure 11.4 as a two-cycle instruction. Can this be implemented as a one-cycle instruction? If so, do it.

11.18 Implement ZET on the sections of Figure 11.4 as a two-cycle instruction. Can this be implemented as a one-cycle instruction?

11.19 Implement NZT on the sections of Figure 11.4 as a two-cycle instruction.

11.20 Implement ORA on the sections of Figure 11.4. You may also have to use the diagram of Figure 11.2.

11.21 Implement ORS on the sections of Figure 11.4. You may also have to use the diagram of Figure 11.2.

11.22 Implement ANA on the sections of Figure 11.4. You may also have to use the diagram of Figure 11.2.

11.23 Implement CLM on the sections of Figure 11.4 as a one-cycle instruction.

11.24 Implement TNZ on the sections of Figure 11.4 as a one-cycle instruction.

11.25 Implement COM on the sections of Figure 11.4 as a one-cycle instruction.

11.26 Implement COM on the sections of Figure 11.4 as a two-cycle instruction.

11.27 Implement XCA on the sections of Figure 11.4 as a one-cycle instruction.

11.28 Implement XCA on the sections of Figure 11.4 as a two-cycle instruction.

12

Input-Output
Equipment

In prior chapters we have considered three of the four
principal components of digital computers: the arithmetic, control, and storage units. In this chapter we study
the remaining component—input-output equipment.

12.1 CARDS, KEY PUNCHES, CARD
READERS, AND CARD PUNCHES

Cards

Data as well as instructions are often inserted into a
digital computer with *punched cards*. And, less frequently, cards are the desired output. A card of standard
size, shown in Figure 12.1, is 7.35 in. long, 3.25 in. wide,
and several mils thick. It has 80 columns and 12 zones
or rows, although only 10 (0 through 9) are indicated.
Two undesignated rows are above the 0 row. A 1 is
stored on a card by a hole punched at the intersection
of a row and column. The absence of a hole at an intersection is a 0. The bits for coded characters can be arranged either along the rows or the columns.

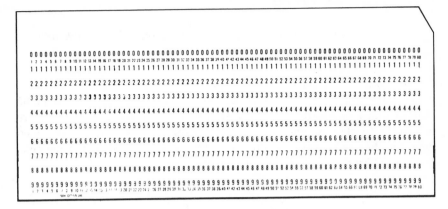

Figure 12.1   Standard programming card.

The code for the IBM System/360 has a single character per column, as shown for some characters in the card of Figure 12.2. The code for each decimal digit 0 through 9 is a single hole per column in the row corresponding to the decimal digit. That is, a one is coded with a hole in row 1, a two with a hole in row 2, and so on. The code for the letters of the alphabet has two punches per column. For each letter *A* through *I* there is a hole in the top row and one in the rows 1 through 9. For *J* through *R* the top hole is in the next-to-top row and the other hole is in rows 1 through 9. For *S* through *Z* the top hole is in the 0 row and the other hole is in rows 2 through 9. As can be seen, special characters, only some of which are shown, have codes too. Some of these are represented by a single hole per column, but others have as many as three.

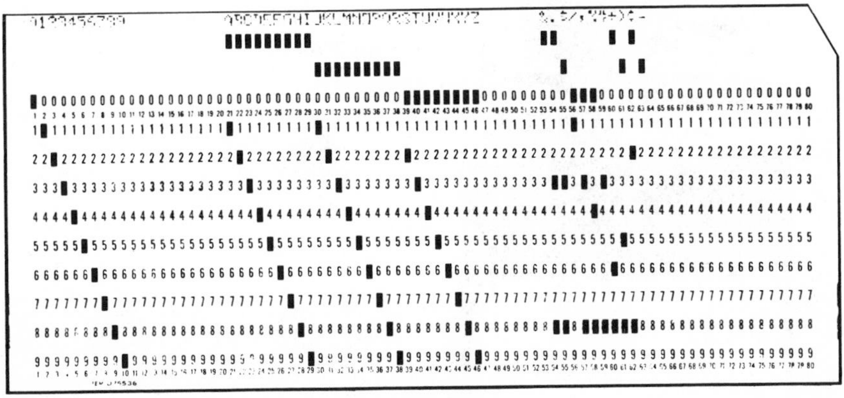

Figure 12.2   Punched card with alphanumeric code.

Key Punches

An individual can punch cards on a *key punch* like the one shown in Figure 12.3. This key punch has a feed hopper at one side for storing the unpunched cards and a card stacker on the opposite side for stacking the punched cards. During a punching operation these cards move from the feed hopper one at a time serially past a punching station under the control of an operator at a keyboard. This keyboard is similar to that of an ordinary typewriter but, of course, has added keys for the movement and alignment of cards. After a card is punched it is placed by the machine into the card stacker.

Card Readers

Card readers are electromechanical machines that sense holes in cards and produce electrical signals corresponding to the placement and number of holes. The hole sensing can be done in several ways. In one method a number of wire brushes, arranged in a row with one brush for each card row or column, wipe across the surface of cards as they move past the brushes. When holes are encountered in a card these brushes make contact through the card to a metal roller on the other side to complete an electrical connection that is sensed as a 1. The cards can be moved past the brushes with their short edges first such that the holes are sensed column by column. This is serial operation. Alternatively, for an increase in speed of reading, the cards can be moved with their long edges first or in parallel fashion. Then the holes are sensed row by row.

Figure 12.3   Key punch (courtesy of International Business Machines Corporation).

For faster reading, light is used to sense the holes, as is shown in Figure 12.4 for serial operation. There are 12 photocells, one for each row, and a single light source. Any holes in a column allow light to pass through the card to energize photocells that, in response to the light, produce electrical signals. Some card readers utilizing optical-type reading can read cards at the rate of 1000 cards per minute. One of these is shown in Figure 12.5.

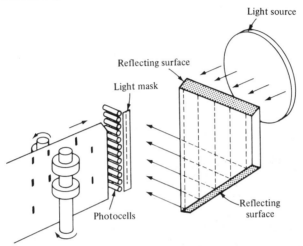

Figure 12.4   Optical read unit (courtesy of Control Data Corporation).

Figure 12.5 Card reader (courtesy of International Business Machines Corporation).

Card Punches

As has been mentioned, punched cards are sometimes the desired output from a digital computer. They are punched by an electromechanical machine called a *card punch*. The speed of punching depends, of course, on the number of columns punched per card. But, in general, the punching rate is in the range of 100 to 200 cards per minute.

Both card reading and punching can be done by a single machine called a *card-read punch,* one of which is shown in Figure 12.6. In fact, the reading and punching stations may be arranged such that the cards move past both stations in a single pass. Then data may be read from a card and the results of a calculation punched in the same card all in a single movement of the card past the stations.

Figure 12.6 Card read punch (courtesy of International Business Machines Corporation).

12.2   PAPER TAPE, PAPER TAPE READERS AND PUNCHES

Paper Tape

Paper tape, a strip of which is shown in Figure 12.7, is often used for inserting programs and data into digital computers. Commonly an inch wide, the paper tape contains longitudinally extending channels of holes arranged in rows that extend laterally across the tape with a density of approximately ten rows per linear inch of tape. The single row of small holes near the middle of the tape are sprocket holes for moving and aligning the tape. In the information channels, a hole punched at the intersection of a channel and row is a 1 and no punch is a 0.

The number of channels depends on the code used. One common code has eight channels; three are arranged on one side of the sprocket holes and five on the other. Normally, each laterally extending row of holes and blanks corresponds to a single character.

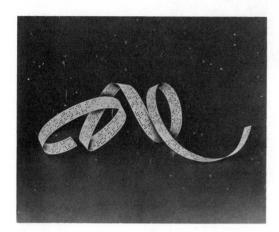

Figure 12.7 Paper tape (courtesy of International Business Machines Corporation).

Paper Tape Readers and Punches

A *paper tape punch* is shown in Figure 12.8 and a *reader* in Figure 12.9. The sensing and punching techniques in paper tape readers and punches are similar to those for card readers and punches. However, as can be seen from Figures 12.8 and 12.9, the paper tape machines are usually much smaller than the card machines. Paper tape punching may be at a rate of ten characters per second and reading done mechanically at 150 characters per second or optically at 1000 characters per second.

Often the operations of paper tape reading and punching are performed on a single unit having an electric typewriter. As the operator types out the program and makes a typewritten copy, the unit punches the program on tape. During this typing the typewriter is preferably not connected to the digital computer. Instead, after the punching, the punched paper tape is run through the reader and the program quickly read into the digital computer.

This mode of operation is especially preferred if one is purchasing computer time based on the time that the typewriter unit is connected to the computer. The typing of a program into a computer or on tape, being a slow process, is usually best done *off-line* (that is, with the

Figure 12.8 Paper tape punch (courtesy of International Business Machines Corporation).

Figure 12.9 Paper tape reader (courtesy of International Business Machines Corporation).

typewriter connected to a unit other than the computer). After being punched, the program on paper tape can be entered into the computer in a comparatively negligible time.

Paper tape has some advantages compared to cards and some disadvantages. Paper tape punching and reading equipment is usually much less expensive. But paper tape is generally more time-consuming to punch than cards because correction of errors made in punching takes more time. In both cases the tape and card can be automatically duplicated, using the punch unit, up to the error and then the punch operator can proceed from there. But a card has much less to duplicate and also requires much fewer movements and less time for the operator. Some computer users find cards easier to store. Also there is an advantage in being able to interchange cards in a deck. Others say that paper tape is as easy to store, especially if it is of the prefolded type that can be stored in a flat, rectangular package, rather than in a roll. Also, with tape there is no danger comparable to that with cards of getting them out of order in a deck as a result of, say, dropping the deck. Since cards and paper tapes each have their advantages and disadvantages, both are used extensively.

12.3   PRINTERS

Various types of *printers* are used to produce a printed output. Typewriter terminals, one of which is shown in Figure 12.10, are sometimes used for input-output purposes, and although they are often suitable for input operations they are sometimes objectionable for output since they print only a character at a time and thus are slow.

Figure   12.10 Typewriter terminal (courtesy of International Business Machines Corporation).

For higher speed printing one can use a high-speed *line printer* as shown in Figure 12.11. These line printers, which print a line at a time, can print lines of 120 characters or more at rates of over 1000 lines per minute. Some line printers print at a spacing of ten characters per inch with lines spaced six or eight to the inch.

Figure 12.11   Line printer (courtesy of International Business Machines Corporation).

One fast line printer has a chain of character type linked together in the form of a belt that is rotated past a row of electrically driven hammers. The paper to be printed moves between the hammers and the belt adjacent a ribbon positioned between the paper and belt. The belt contains 240 characters, all of which can be different, but this number of different characters is seldom needed. Greater printing speeds are obtained by using duplicate sets of characters. Five identical sets of 48 characters each are sometimes used.

In the printing operation, the information for a line of printing (that is, the types of characters and their positions in the line) is stored in the printer. Then when the character corresponding to the position of a hammer passes in front of the hammer, the hammer strikes, pressing the character type, ribbon, and paper together to print the character. Of course, after a line is printed, the paper advances a line or more and the operation repeats.

In another printer the characters are on the surface of a continually rotating drum as shown in Figure 12.12. The characters are arranged in rows along the length of the drum (that is, axial rows) with only one type of character per row. And each row has a different character. As the specified characters come beneath the hammers, the hammers are activated. In other respects the operation is similar to that of the belt-type line printer.

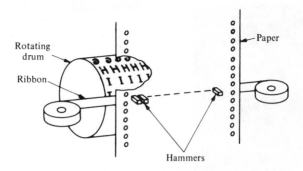

Figure 12.12   Drum printer (courtesy of Prentice-Hall, Inc.).

12.4   CATHODE-RAY TUBE

The output from a digital computer is not always de-
sired in printed or in any permanent form. For example, an airline com-
pany clerk at a desk in an airport may need updated information on airline reservations for only a short time—there is no need for a permanent
printed record. Or, an engineer may need a temporary display of
engineering drawings so that he can make changes and then have a computer incorporate these changes in the drawings in the form of a stored
program. For these and other similar uses a display on a cathode-ray
tube may be preferred. Of course, cathode-ray tubes are familiar to
everyone; these are the large tubes in television sets that produce the
pictures.

A *cathode-ray tube display station* with keyboard is shown in Figure
12.13. This station is similar to that of the typewriter terminal of Figure
12.10, with the principal difference for an operator being that the typed-
in information and the computer response are displayed on a cathode-ray
tube instead of being printed on paper.

With the cathode-ray tube display station, an operator can use the
keyboard to enter numeric or alphanumeric messages into the computer
main storage. The message is displayed on the screen as it is entered
to enable the operator to correct errors or make changes before the message is transferred from the station to main storage. Also, the operator
may request information from main storage and have it displayed. Then
he can make changes in it and have the changed material returned
to main storage. This feature is particularly valuable for an accounting
operation. A customer's account can be displayed, updated, and stored,
all while the customer is on the telephone.

A much more elaborate cathode-ray tube display unit is shown in

Figure 12.13 Cathode-ray tube display station (courtesy of International Business Machines Corporation).

Figure 12.14. This unit can display not only alphanumeric information but also almost any symbol or configuration of lines. Buildings, cars, circuit diagrams, and so on, can be displayed. The display is controlled from the keyboard or by a *light pen* shown hanging on the right side of the unit. In other words, information can be inserted into the computer by means of the light pen as well as by the keyboard.

To modify the display with the light pen, an operator places the end of the light pen against the screen and then presses a switch which may be foot-operated or may be on the light pen and actuated by pressing the pen against the screen. The light pen *receives* light that enters when the electron beam in the tube sweeps across the screen and en-

Figure 12.14 Cathode-ray tube display station with light pen (courtesy of International Business Machines Corporation).

counters the spot against which the light pen is pressed. This light energizes a photoelectric cell, which, in turn, produces an electric pulse that is transmitted to the digital computer connected to the display unit. From the time difference between the occurrence of the electric pulse and the beginning of the sweep, the computer can calculate the location of the spot on the screen against which the light pen is pressed.

The light pen can be used to draw lines on the screen to form almost any configuration. In this operation a light trail follows the light pen on the screen much the same as an ink trail follows a conventional pen on a piece of paper.

The light pen has many applications when used in this fashion. For example, the four sides of a house can be drawn. Then a program in the computer can straighten the lines and also provide a view of the house from any angle. Another use for this display unit is in circuit analysis. A circuit diagram with all the electrical components can be drawn and component values specified, all with the light pen. Then the response of the resulting circuit can be calculated by the computer and displayed next to the circuit display.

This cathode-ray tube unit with light pen is a powerful aid in the use of the digital computer and can be operated by a person having little programming knowledge. Consequently, increased use of these units can be anticipated. Unfortunately, they are quite expensive compared to other terminals and, because of communication requirements, can be used without extensive auxiliary equipment only within a few thousand feet of the central processing unit.

12.5   DATA TABLET*

We have discussed the light pen unit for inserting graphical and other data directly into a digital computer. Another unit, the *Data Tablet*, performs a similar function. A Data Tablet, shown in Figure 12.15, has a writing surface of a thin film of metal oxide covered on top and bottom by protective glass layers. This sandwich is transparent for placement over, for example, the screen of a cathode-ray tube or any viewable matter.

An electronic pen for the Data Tablet is constructed such that electrical signals applied to the thin film induce voltages into the pen when it is placed on the writing surface, the particular voltages induced depending upon the position of the pen. Associated electronic circuits operating with a digital computer detect the horizontal and vertical positions of the pen from these induced voltages.

---

* Trademark, Sylvania Electric Products Inc.

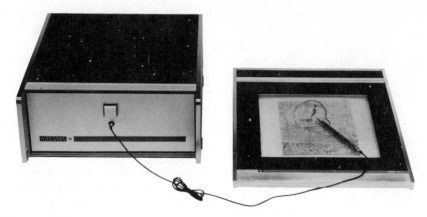

Figure 12.15   Data Tablet (courtesy of Sylvania Electric Products Inc., a subsidiary of General Telephone and Electronics Corporation).

The Data Tablet can be used with a cathode-ray tube unit in the same manner explained for the light pen. However, the Data Tablet has further applications. It can be placed over and used with maps, circuit diagrams, pages of books, and so on. But then, of course, there are no light traces as there can be with the cathode-ray tube.

12.6   TIME-SHARING

A *time-sharing system* provides digital computer service to a number of persons, all of whom use a single digital computer *apparently* simultaneously. Such a system may have 50 or more terminals of various forms, all of which can be operated at the same time. One of the most popular is the typewriter terminal of Figures 12.10. But card readers, printers, and other input-output units can also be used. Terminals can be any distance, even thousands of miles, from the processing unit, the only requirement as regards distance being a communication link between the terminals and the processing unit.

Perhaps the basic philosophy leading to the development of time-sharing systems was that a large digital computer can operate so rapidly, a single user cannot keep all components busy all of the time. In other words, humans act and respond so slowly compared to the speed of operation of a digital computer that an *information interface mismatch* occurs between user and computer which results in inefficient computer use. This mismatch can be alleviated by increasing the number of persons using the computer at the same time. The resulting increase in efficiency in computer use not only decreases the cost for computer time for each user but also permits more programs to be processed in a given time.

Many time-sharing systems are almost unbelievably complex in structure and operation and, in themselves, are a topic for extensive study, Thus, in our brief treatment we can do no more than discuss some features of the more simple systems.

In these systems, even with many terminals operating at the same time, the various programs are not processed at the same time. Instead, each user is given a slice of computer time—often a small fraction of a second—for processing his program. The programs to be processed are placed in peripheral storage (drums or disks) and are brought into core storage one at a time for processing. In other systems, more than one program may be in core storage at any one time.

If a program is not completely executed in the allotted time slice, the program and intermediate results may be moved from inner core memory to peripheral storage and then the next program brought into core for processing if it is not already there.

Complete processing of a program may take many of these time slices but the computer is so rapid in operation that the user often receives results so quickly that he is unaware that the computer is not completely dedicated to his use. However, if there are many users, any one of them may have to wait a short time for results. But usually the response time of the user is so slow in typing in a program, in correcting errors diagnosed by the computer, and in interpreting intermediate results, that the computer can give him results soon enough to make him unaware that there is another user.

With time-sharing and remote terminals a user can insert his program, have it processed, and receive results all in a few minutes at a convenient location. This use is in contrast to *batch processing* in which the user usually takes his program punched on cards to the computing center where his deck is run with others in one pass without time slicing. The time between submission of the program and reception of results is, typically, several hours.

A time-sharing system with remote terminals is illustrated in Figure 12.16. The remote terminals are connected by *data sets* to the communication lines, here shown as telephone lines. When a terminal is transmitting to the central processor, the data set at the terminal converts the digital bits to audio-frequency signals for transmission over the telephone lines. At the computing center another data set converts the received audio-frequency signals to digital signals. For transmission in the opposite direction, from the center to a remote terminal, the operation of these data sets is reversed.

Subscribing to a time-sharing service is often preferable to purchasing a small computer. A time-sharing terminal such as a typewriter terminal

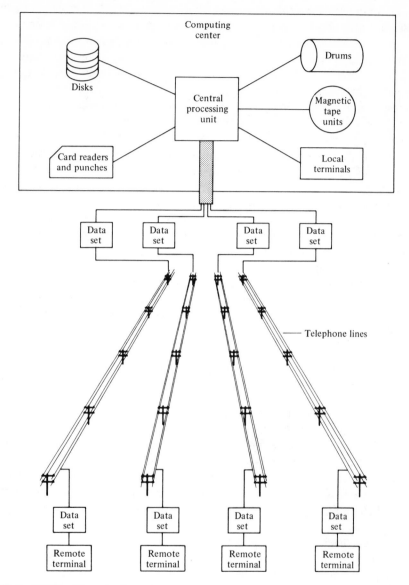

Figure 12.16   Time-sharing system.

is inexpensive; one can be rented for less than $100 per month. In addition to this rental cost there is the cost of the communication link and that for using the central processor. But, the total cost is often less per computation than with a reasonably sized small computer. Also, a user at a terminal has the power of a large computer at his disposal.

Sophisticated languages and application programs are available that
are not available with small computers. However, in many applications
a small computer is adequate and more economical. Thus we can expect
both time-sharing systems and the use of small computers to increase.

12.7   DIGITAL-TO-ANALOG CONVERTERS

Conversion of signals between analog and digital forms
is a frequent need. A basically digital system may have an output that
must be converted to analog form for controlling or moving an analog
responsive component. For example, the plurality of voltages corresponding to the various bits of a digital output may have to be converted to a single voltage for controlling the rotational position of a
shaft. In hybrid computers (computers with interconnected analog and
digital converters) the conversion of digital signals to analog and vice
versa is a normal continual operation.

By the term *digital signals* we mean, of course, signals that take
on discrete, or really ostensibly discrete, values. Actually, as a practical
matter, the signals vary somewhat around the specified levels. In contrast, an analog system has voltages that can assume any value over
a single continuous range that is often quite large, for example, from
-100 to $+100$ V.

The unit that converts a signal from digital to analog form has
the unlikely name of *digital-to-analog converter* or simply *DAC*. Another
name is *decoder*. It converts the bits of a binary number into a dc
voltage having a magnitude directly proportional to that of the number
and a polarity that corresponds to the sign of the number.

A block diagram of a general DAC is illustrated in Figure 12.17.
The digital number to be decoded is placed in a register, the flip-flops
of which have positional significance. For example, if the register has
four flip-flops, the bit in the first flip-flop may have a weight of 2^{-1}, that
in the second flip-flop a weight of 2^{-2}, the third a weight of 2^{-3}, and the
last one a weight of 2^{-4}. A resistance network, that depends on the type
of DAC, and an *operational amplifier* produce an output analog voltage,
the magnitude of which corresponds to the contents of the flip-flop
register.

The operational amplifier is a very high gain amplifier that, among
other features, draws negligible input current. Although not shown, there
are really two input lines and also two output lines. One line on the
input and one on the output are seldom shown because they are understood to be grounded. One other important fact about the operation
amplifier: The shown input line can usually be considered to be at

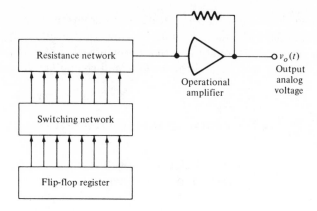

Figure 12.17 Digital-to-analog converter.

ground or zero potential because with its very great gain the operational amplifier needs only an insignificant input voltage to produce the output voltage of 100 V or less.

Because the digital signals from the register are not sufficiently precise for direct inputs to the resistance network, they are used only to operate switches that switch the resistor network inputs between two reference voltage levels that are often 0 (or ground) and 10 or 100 V. These switches may be electronic components called *level amplifiers,* but sometimes standard inverters are used. For our purposes we can consider the reference voltage system to be voltage-operated switches and a reference voltage source.

Weighted-Resistor DAC

A simplified *weighted-resistor DAC* is shown in Figure 12.18 for converting a four-bit binary number to an analog voltage representation. The four flip-flops of the register control different switches such that if a flip-flop contains a 1, it operates a switch to connect $+10$ V to an input of the resistance network. But for a 0, it switches this input to ground.

For an understanding of this circuit, the resistance network and the operational amplifier must be considered together. In our analysis, we will call the output voltage v_o and the four switched voltages v_{-1}, v_{-2}, v_{-3}, and v_{-4}, all of which are referenced with respect to the potential (usually approximately ground) on the shown input line to the operational amplifier. With this convention, the five currents into the operational amplifier are as shown in Figure 12.19. The sum of these currents

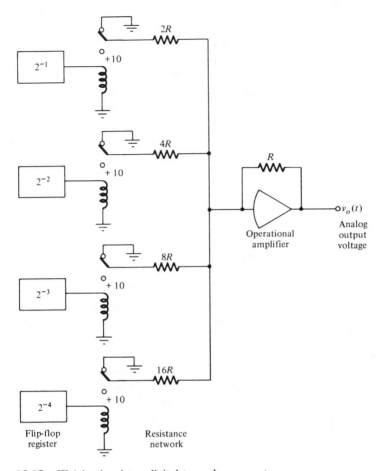

Figure 12.18   Weighted-resistor, digital-to-analog converter.

must be zero since the amplifier input does not draw current. That is

$$\frac{v_{-1}}{2R} + \frac{v_{-2}}{4R} + \frac{v_{-3}}{8R} + \frac{v_{-4}}{16R} + \frac{v_o}{R} = 0$$

or

$$v_o = -\left(\frac{v_{-1}}{2} + \frac{v_{-2}}{4} + \frac{v_{-3}}{8} + \frac{v_{-4}}{16}\right)$$

In this expression for the output voltage, the input voltages appear in weighted form with the weights corresponding to the positional values of the bits in the binary number. Consequently, the magnitude of the analog output voltage is directly proportional to the numerical value of the binary number stored in the flip-flop register.

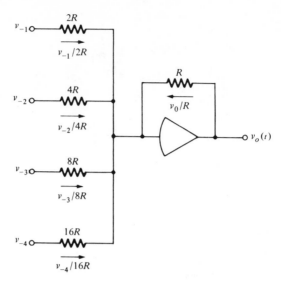

Figure 12.19   Weighted-resistor DAC with input currents.

This weighted-resistor network is impractical for a resistor network with a large number of inputs because of the resistance values. The smallest resistor in the network, the feedback resistor, R, has a practical lower limit of a few thousand ohms to avoid overloading the operational amplifier. And all the input resistances are powers of two times this resistance with the power increasing with the number of inputs. Thus, for many inputs the resistors for the most significant inputs have extremely large resistances approaching insulation values and cannot be obtained with any precision. A popular resistance network not having this disadvantage is the *ladder network*.

Ladder Network DAC

The *ladder network*, shown in Figure 12.20, has practical resistance values since the resistances are either R or $R/2$.

An analysis of the ladder network would show that it has the same output as the weighted-resistance network. But we will not make this analysis since it requires a background in network analysis that the reader may not have. However, the analysis is trivial for anyone who has studied network analysis.

The illustrated digital-to-analog converters do not have, for the sake of simplification, provision for a sign bit. Obviously, the sign bit of a decoded binary number should control the polarity of the analog signal. Although we will not discuss the matter further, it should be mentioned that a brief search into the literature will show circuits that provide polarity control with only two additional operational amplifier circuits.

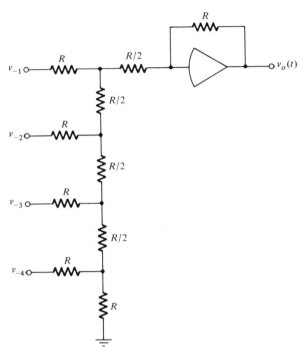

Figure 12.20   Ladder network DAC.

12.8   ANALOG-TO-DIGITAL CONVERTERS

An *analog-to-digital converter* (ADC), or *encoder*, samples analog signals, often at periodic intervals, and produces a digital signal corresponding to the analog signal. The input to the converter is a continuous signal that may vary over a wide range, as has been mentioned, and the output is a discrete representation for a binary number.

Analog-to-digital conversion is much more difficult than digital-to-analog conversion and the converters are approximately five to ten times more expensive than DAC's for approximately the same precision. And, in fact, an analog-to-digital converter usually contains at least one DAC.

In analog-to-digital conversion the analog signal is compared to a standard or generated signal by circuits called *comparators*. In one comparator, which utilizes an operational amplifier, the standard signal and the analog input signal are applied with opposite polarities to the amplifier which is connected to add the two input signals. If the positive input signal has the larger polarity, the amplifier, with its large gain, produces a large negative output signal. And if the negative input signal has the larger magnitude, the amplifier produces a large positive output signal. Comparators will be used in each electrical converter we study.

Of the several electrical analog-to-digital converters, we will consider the *simultaneous,* the *successive approximation,* and the *incremental* converters. We will also consider a *mechanical* converter.

Simultaneous Converter

A block diagram of a *simultaneous analog-to-digital converter* is shown in Figure 12.21. Its output is a two-bit digital number the value of which depends on an analog input voltage that varies from 0 to V V in magnitude. For this conversion to two bits, three comparators are required. And, in general, for a conversion to n bits, $2^n - 1$ comparators are required. A voltage-divider network of four resistors (2^n resistors, in general) energized by a source of V V provides three standard inputs to the comparators of $V/4$, $V/2$, and $3V/4$ [$V/2^n$, $2V/2^n$,

Analog voltage	C_1	C_2	C_3	FF_1	FF_2
0 to $V/4$	−	−	−	0	0
$V/4$ to $V/2$	+	−	−	0	1
$V/2$ to $3V/4$	+	+	−	1	0
$3V/4$ to V	+	+	+	1	1

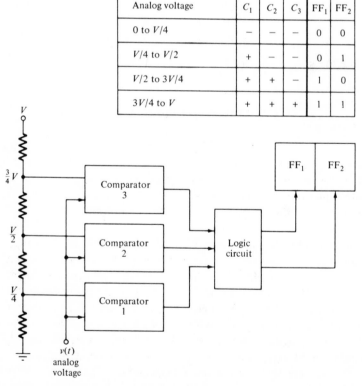

Figure 12.21 Simultaneous analog-to-digital converter (courtesy of Wiley and Sons, Inc.).

. . . , $(2^n - 1)V/2^n$, in general]. Of course, the analog signal to be converted is also conducted to these comparators.

If this signal is less than $V/4$ in magnitude ($V/2^n$, in general), the standard input signals control the polarities of the output voltages of all the comparators and all are, say, negative. If the analog input voltage is between $V/4$ and $V/2$ (in general, $V/2^n$ and $2V/2^n$), this voltage predominates in the input of only the first comparator and, consequently, its output goes positive while all the other comparator outputs remain negative. If the analog signal voltage is between $V/2$ and $3V/4$ ($2V/2^n$ and $3V/2^n$, in general) this voltage predominates for the inputs of the first two comparators. Hence the outputs of these two comparators are positive but the output of the other comparator is negative. And so on.

The comparator outputs energize a logic circuit that controls the setting of flip-flops in a register in the manner indicated in the table with Figure 12.21. If all the comparator outputs are negative, the flip-flops are set to zero. If only the output from the first comparator is positive, a 1 is stored in the register. If the first two comparator outputs are positive, 10 is stored, and so on.

The simultaneous converter is faster acting than the other converters we will discuss, but it requires an excessive number of comparators for a large resolution system. As mentioned, a conversion to a number of n bits requires $2^n - 1$ comparators.

Successive-Approximation Converter

The *successive-approximation* or *closed-loop analog-to-digital converter*, shown in simplified block diagram form in Figure 12.22, is extremely popular, especially for hybrid computer applications. In this converter, a control unit controls the activation of a digital

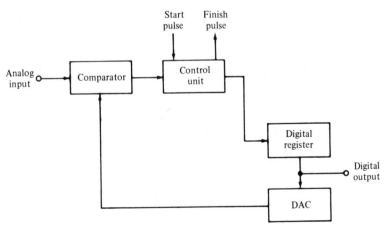

Figure 12.22 Successive-approximation analog-to-digital converter.

register, which, after the conversion process, contains the binary number corresponding to the input analog signal. In response to the register contents, a DAC produces an output analog signal that is applied along with the input analog signal to the input of a comparator. When the difference in magnitudes of the two signals is sufficiently small, the control unit stops the incrementing of the digital register and generates an output finish signal.

Considering the operation in more detail, initially the control unit clears the digital register and then gates pulses to the most significant register flip-flop, triggering it to the 1 state. Then, in response to the register contents, the DAC produces an output analog signal that the comparator compares with the input analog signal. If the input analog signal is greater in magnitude, as determined by the polarity of the comparator output voltage, the register flip-flop with the 1 is not disturbed. But if the input analog signal is smaller, the control unit resets this flip-flop. In this way the most significant bit of the corresponding binary number is determined. Next, the control unit gates pulses to the second register flip-flop, setting it to the 1 state. Again a comparison is made between the input analog signal and the output of the DAC. If the magnitude of the output from the DAC exceeds that for the analog input, the control unit resets this second flip-flop. Otherwise, the flip-flop remains in the 1 state. This process continues for each flip-flop in the digital register. After the comparison for the last flip-flop, the control unit generates a completion pulse indicating that the conversion process is complete for the sample. Then the digital register contains the digital approximation to the input analog signal.

In this converter the number of steps equals the number of bits in the resulting digital number, including leading zeros. Hence this conversion process takes longer, considerably longer, than does that of the simultaneous converter. But, on the other hand, the circuit requires only one comparator. Because the digital register is set to zero at the start of each conversion, the conversion of each sample is independent of the preceding one. And the number of steps is the same for each conversion. A typical rate of operation for this converter is in the range of 20,000 to 50,000 conversions per second.

Incremental Converter

In the *incremental converter*, also known as the *continuous converter*, the digital register is an up-down counter. which, in contrast to the register in the successive-approximation converter, is not reset to zero after each conversion.

For an understanding of this converter, consider the block diagram of Figure 12.23. When the conversion process is initiated, the comparator

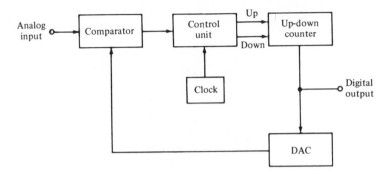

Figure 12.23 Incremental analog-to-digital converter.

makes a comparison between the analog signal and the output of a DAC excited by the contents of the up-down counter. If the magnitude of the analog voltage input is greater by a certain threshold value, the control unit applies a pulse to the counter causing its contents to increase by 1. Then another comparison is made. If the analog input is still larger, the counter is stepped up again. This process continues until the magnitude of the DAC output and that of the input analog voltage are within the threshold value of operation of the control unit. If the analog input magnitude had initially been less than the magnitude of the output of the DAC, then the control unit would have stepped the contents of the counter down instead of up.

For samples of a single input that do not change much, from one sample to the next, the counter does not change much, which means that the conversion process is much more rapid than that of the successive-approximation method. Of course, the time required for a conversion is a variable, being proportional to the change in input analog signal during the time between conversions.

Mechanical Encoders

In some applications a shaft angular displacement must be converted to a binary number representation. This can be done conveniently with a *mechanical encoder*, like the one shown in Figure 12.24, which has a disk for attachment to the shaft. This disk has concentric regions or bands containing segments of insulating material (light areas) and conducting material (dark areas). A set of conducting brushes is in physical contact with the disk with one brush per band. Each brush produces a separate output signal. For the illustrated disk, the angular displacement is converted into a three-bit number, the number of bits equaling the number of brushes and bands. Obviously, the precision of the encoder increases with an increase in the number of concentric bands.

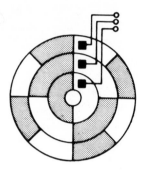

Figure 12.24   Binary-coded disk encoder.

When a brush is in contact with a conducting region on its band, an electrical connection is completed that produces a 1 for the output of that brush. But when the brush is on an insulated region, there is no electrical connection and a 0 is produced.

In the encoder of Figure 12.24, the insulation and conduction areas are arranged to provide a binary-coded output of 000 for an angular displacement between 0 and 45 degrees, of 001 for an angular displacement between 45° and 90°, and an output of 010 for an angular displacement between 90° and 135°, and so on.

This encoder has a serious operational problem resulting from the pattern of insulated and conducting areas and the significant brush widths. For an illustration of this problem, suppose that the angular displacement is approximately 0°, say, 1°. With the unavoidable significant brush widths, some of the brushes may make contact with the conducting region of 111, and it is possible, depending on which brushes are making this contact, to obtain any output from 000 to 111. Consequently, serious errors are possible and even likely. A similar condition, but to a lesser extent, occurs at some other angles.

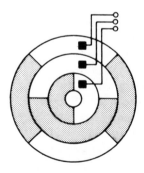

Figure 12.25   Gray coded disk encoder.

One way of alleviating this problem is to use a Gray coded disk as shown in Figure 12.25. With this coded disk the bits change value one at a time for successive binary-coded numbers. Consequently, there cannot be an error of more than one in the number being encoded.

PROBLEMS

12.1 A cathode-ray tube unit with light pen has a screen 18 in. high and 24 in. wide. The electron beam sweeps over the screen from left to right and from top to bottom in $\frac{1}{60}$ sec with 500 evenly spaced lines. A signal is obtained from the light pen 0.00312 sec after the beginning of a sweep. Approximately where on the screen is the light pen pressed, if retrace time is negligible?

Answers   3.38 in. down and 14.4 in. to the right

12.2 Repeat Problem 12.1 if the time the signal is received from the light pen is 0.01234 sec after the beginning of a sweep.

12.3 Repeat Problem 12.1 if the time the signal is received from the light pen is 0.00564 sec after the beginning of a sweep.

12.4 For the weighted-resistor DAC of Figure 12.18, what values can the output voltage $v_0(t)$ have?

12.5 The weighted-resistor DAC of Figure 12.18 is designed on the assumption that the binary number is a fraction. What changes are required in the circuit if the binary number is an integer and the positional values for the flip-flops are 2^0, 2^1, 2^2, and 2^3?

12.6 A weighted-resistor DAC has 32 inputs. If the feedback resistor R has a resistance of 1000 Ω, what is the greatest resistance in the network?

12.7 Analyze the ladder network of Figure 12.20.

12.8 Design the logic circuit of Figure 12.21 assuming that the comparator outputs are the correct magnitudes for 1's and 0's. Use positive logic, NAND gates, and as few levels as possible. Assume that the flip-flops are of the J-K type.

12.9 Repeat Problem 12.8 for a simultaneous analog-to-digital converter that makes a conversion to a three-bit number.

12.10 Repeat Problem 12.8 for a simultaneous analog-to-digital converter that makes a conversion to a four-bit number.

12.11 In a simultaneous analog-to-digital converter a voltage divider of 32 resistors is energized by a source of 100 V.
(**a**) What is the number of comparators?

(b) How many bits are in the resulting binary number?

(c) What is the range of the analog signal?

12.12   Repeat Problem 12.11 for a voltage divider of 64 resistors energized by a source of 50 V.

12.13   Could the successive-approximation analog-to-digital converter function properly if the gating of pulses to the digital register was in reverse order; that is, if the pulses were applied starting with the least significant register flip-flop? Discuss.

12.14   For the encoder of Figure 12.24, what are all the possible erroneous outputs when the angle of rotation is at

(a) 1°?   (e) 181°?
(b) 46°?   (f) 226°?
(c) 91°?   (g) 271°?
(d) 136°?   (h) 316°?

12.15   Show a mechanical encoder like the one in Figure 12.24 for converting the shaft rotation to a four-bit number.

12.16   Show a mechanical encoder like the one in Figure 12.24 for converting the shaft rotation to a five-bit number.

12.17   Show a mechanical encoder using the Gray code like the one in Figure 12.25 for converting the shaft rotation to a four-bit number.

12.18   Show a mechanical encoder using the Gray code like the one in Figure 12.25 for converting the shaft rotation to a five-bit number.

Appendix

COMPLEMENT ARITHMETIC

Some digital computers perform the four basic operations (addition, subtraction, multiplication, and division) by either addition alone or subtraction alone. Ways of obtaining multiplication from addition and division from subtraction should be apparent, but it may not be so obvious how subtraction can be obtained from addition and also addition from subtraction. This will be shown. One advantage of performing all four operations by just, say, adding is that a computer need have only adder arithmetic circuits instead of both adder and subtractor circuits.

With only adder circuits or only subtractor circuits, a computer utilizes an arithmetic that may be unfamiliar; it is called *complement arithmetic*. In this arithmetic, complements of numbers are formed, as will be explained. The complement of a number added to another number produces a sum that may be the difference of these two numbers. Or, the complement of a number subtracted from another number produces a difference that may be the sum of the two numbers.

For complement arithmetic the numbers must have a fixed number of digits, for reasons that will be apparent. This restriction is not severe since the numbers in many digital computers have a fixed number of digits regardless of magnitude, assuming, of course, that the magnitude is within a proper range. For example, the numbers may all comprise fifteen bits. In this case the integer ten (decimal) is 000000000001010 and the integer one hundred (decimal) is 000000001100100. Leading zeros complete the fifteen digits.

Two complements are used commonly: the *radix complement* and the *radix-minus-one complement*. In the decimal system they are the 10's complement and the 9's complement, respectively. In the octal system they are the 8's and 7's complement and in the binary system the 2's complement and the 1's complement.

For convenience we will limit the present discussion to the treatment of positive integers only. And we will not take special notice of mixed numbers for they pose no difficulty. In a mixed number the radix point can be ignored and the number treated as an integer. Then, after the complement is obtained the radix point can be reinserted. Alternatively, we can apply complement arithmetic directly to mixed numbers. The rules for this procedure follow rather simply from those presented for integers. Finally, in this discussion we will assume that all the numbers (addend, augend, sum, minuend, subtrahend, and difference) are in the range of the system.

Decimal Complements

The 10's complement of a decimal number in an n-digit system is 10^n minus this number. To obtain the complement we can perform this subtraction or, alternatively, we can express the number in the form of n digits (this may require inserting leading zeros) and subtract each digit from nine, and then add one.

Example A.1 Determine the 10's complement of 329 in a five-digit system.

Solution For the first procedure we subtract the number from $10^5 = 100000$.

$$\begin{array}{r} 100000 \\ -329 \\ \hline 99671 \end{array} \quad \text{10's complement}$$

In a five-digit system 99671 is the 10's complement of 329. Alternatively, we can express the number as five digits (00329) and then subtract each digit from nine, which yields 99670. Then we add one for the result 99671. ∎

The 9's complement of a decimal number in an n-digit system is one less than the 10's complement, or just the number subtracted from

$10^n - 1$. The result is the same if we express the number in n digits and subtract each digit from nine.

Example A.2   Determine the 9's complement of 4678 for a six-digit system.

Solution   By the first procedure

$$1000000 - 1 = 999999$$
$$\underline{-4678}$$
$$995321 \qquad \text{9's complement}$$

With the second procedure we subtract each digit from nine. The result is still 995321. If the 10's complement is known, which is

$$1000000$$
$$\underline{-4678}$$
$$995322 \qquad \text{10's complement}$$

and we subtract one from this, the result is the 9's complement

$$995322$$
$$\underline{-1}$$
$$995321 \qquad \text{9's complement} \qquad \blacksquare$$

With either the 10's or 9's complement it is possible to subtract by adding. For this process the 10's complement of the subtrahend is formed and then added to the minuend. If the resulting sum has $n + 1$ digits, the n least significant digits of this sum are the desired difference.

Example A.3   For a five-digit system determine $3452 - 629$, using 10's complement arithmetic.

Solution   We form the 10's complement of the subtrahend

$$100000$$
$$\underline{-629}$$
$$99371$$

and then add this complement to the minuend.

$$3452$$
$$\underline{+99371}$$
$$102823$$

The sum has six digits but the system has room for only five digits. Thus the most significant digit—the 1—is dropped and the least significant five digits— 02823 (the correct difference)—are retained. $\qquad \blacksquare$

This example illustrates obtaining a difference by adding. Of course, forming the complement requires subtraction, and indeed if this were always the case, complement arithmetic would have no advantage for subtraction. However, as will be shown, forming complements in the binary system, which is the system used in digital computers, does not require subtraction.

For a justification of this procedure assume an n-digit system, a minuend of M, and a subtrahend of S. Then the 10's complement of the subtrahend is $10^n - S$. This added to M produces the sum: $10^n + M - S$. If this sum requires $n + 1$ digits, then $10^n + M - S > 10^n$, which situation occurs if the subtrahend is less than the minuend. The 10^n part of the sum is represented by a one in the $n + 1$ digit position. Since the digital system has no room for this digit, it is dropped and only $M - S$ is retained, which is the correct difference.

If the subtrahend is greater than the minuend, the sum $10^n + M - S$ is less than 10^n and thus is contained in n digits. The sum, which is not the desired difference, is detectable by the absence of a surplus digit. In this case it is necessary to take the 10's complement of the sum and then make this result negative (recall that in all of this discussion we have assumed that the minuend and subtrahend are positive integers). The 10's complement of the sum is $10^n - (10^n + M - S) = S - M$, and the negative of this is $-(S - M)$, the correct difference.

Example A.4 Use 10's complement arithmetic to determine $3728 - 4567$ in a five-digit system.

Solution We take the 10's complement of the subtrahend

$$
\begin{array}{r}
100000 \\
+4567 \\
\hline
95433
\end{array}
$$

and add this complement to the minuend.

$$
\begin{array}{r}
95433 \\
+3728 \\
\hline
99161
\end{array}
$$

Because the result 99161 contains only five digits and thus is incorrect, we must complement again. The 10's complement of this sum is

$$
\begin{array}{r}
100000 \\
-99161 \\
\hline
839
\end{array}
$$

Then we insert a minus sign to obtain -839, the correct difference. ∎

It is possible to add by subtracting the 10's complement of the addend from the augend. In this process it is necessary to provide a borrow for the augend.

Example A.5   Using subtraction and the 10's complement, determine $463 +$ 1239 for a four-digit system.

Solution   We form the 10's complement of 1239

$$
\begin{array}{r}
10000 \\
-1239 \\
\hline
8761
\end{array}
$$

and subtract this complement from the augend, plus borrow.

$$
\begin{array}{r}
1\overset{\frown}{0}463 \quad \text{borrow} \\
-8761 \\
\hline
1702
\end{array}
$$

The result 1702 is the correct sum.   ■

This procedure can be explained by assuming an n-digit system, an augend A, and an addend B. Then the 10's complement of the addend is $10^n - B$, and the borrow plus augend is $10^n + A$. The difference is $10^n + A - (10^n - B) = A + B$, the desired sum.

Perhaps it is not apparent that a borrow is needed for the augend; that is, is it possible for $10^n - B$ to be less than A? If it is, a borrow is not needed. The answer is that a borrow is always needed, for if $A + B$ is within the range of the system, then $A + B < 10^n$ and hence $10^n - B > A$.

The rules for the 9's complement differ only slightly from the above. For subtracting by adding, we add the minuend to the 9's complement of the subtrahend. Then we add one to the sum when this sum is contained in more than n digits. This addition of one is obviously necessary since the 9's complement is one less than the 10's complement, and if adding the 10's complement produces the correct result, then adding the 9's complement produces one less than the correct result. If with the 9's complement the sum is n digits or less, then the one is not added and instead the 9's complement of the sum is formed and a minus sign inserted. A justification for the 9's complement approach will not be presented since it follows directly and obviously from that presented for the 10's complement.

Example A.6   Using the 9's complement, determine $342 - 212$ for a three-digit system.

Solution   We form the 9's complement of the subtrahend

$$
\begin{array}{r}
999 \\
-212 \\
\hline
787
\end{array}
$$

and add the minuend to the 9's complement, and then add one.

$$
\begin{array}{r}
342 \\
+787 \\
\hline
1129 \\
+1 \\
\hline
1130
\end{array}
$$

The three least significant digits of the sum, 130, form the difference. ■

Example A.7   Using the 9's complement, determine $212 - 342$ for a three-digit system.

Solution   We take the 9's complement of the subtrahend

$$
\begin{array}{r}
999 \\
-342 \\
\hline
657
\end{array}
$$

and add this complement to the minuend:

$$
\begin{array}{r}
657 \\
+212 \\
\hline
869
\end{array}
$$

Since this sum is less than 10^3, we must take the 9's complement and insert a minus sign.

$$
\begin{array}{r}
999 \\
-869 \\
\hline
130 \rightarrow -130
\end{array}
$$ ■

The process of adding by subtracting the 9's complement of the addend from the augend plus borrow, should be apparent. Since the 10's complement produces correct results and is one more than the 9's complement, then it is obviously necessary to subtract the 9's complement plus one.

Example A.8   In a four-digit system, determine $3764 + 4672$ by means of the 9's complement and subtraction.

Solution   First, we determine the 9's complement of 4672

$$
\begin{array}{r}
9999 \\
-4672 \\
\hline
5327
\end{array}
$$

and then subtract this complement from the augend plus borrow. Finally, we subtract one.

$$
\begin{array}{r}
13764 \\
-5327 \\
\hline
8437 \\
-1 \\
\hline
8436
\end{array}
$$

The sum is 8436.   ■

Binary Complements

We are mostly interested in complement arithmetic as applied to binary numbers since conventional electronic digital systems are inherently binary.

For an n-digit system we can determine the 2's complement of a binary number by subtracting this number from 2^n. Or, equivalently, we can place the number in n-digit form (by inserting leading zeros if necessary), subtract each digit from one, and finally add 1. Perhaps the easiest procedure is to put the binary number in n-digit form and then change each zero to a one and each one to a zero and then add one. This procedure, which does not require subtraction, is often used in digital computers. Thus subtractors are not necessary for forming the 2's complement.

Example A.9   Determine the 2's complement of 11011101 for an eight-digit system.

Solution   With the first procedure we use 2^8, or 100000000.

$$
\begin{array}{r}
100000000 \\
-11011101 \\
\hline
00100011
\end{array}
$$
   2's complement

In the second procedure we use $2^8 - 1 = 11111111$.

$$
\begin{array}{r}
11111111 \\
-11011101 \\
\hline
00100010 \\
+1 \\
\hline
00100011
\end{array}
$$
   2's complement

In the third procedure we change each zero to a one and each one to a zero.

$$
\begin{array}{r}
11011101 \rightarrow 00100010 \\
+1 \\
\hline
00100011
\end{array}
$$
   2's complement   ■

The equivalence of the second and third procedures is obvious since $2^n - 1$ comprises all ones and the subtraction of one from one is zero and the subtraction of zero from one is one, and so in effect each one changes to a zero and each zero to a one. Of course, in the second and third procedures we must add one since the minuend is one less than 2^n.

To subtract by adding, we add the minuend to the 2's complement of the subtrahend. If the result requires $n + 1$ digits, or is equal to or greater than 2^n, the n least significant digits form the correct difference. However, if the result is less than 2^n, then we must form the 2's complement of the sum and insert a minus sign. The justification for this procedure is similar to that presented for the 10's complement approach.

Example A.10   Determine $11011101 - 1011101$ in a ten-digit system. Use the 2's complement.

Solution   We form the 2's complement of the subtrahend

$$
\begin{array}{r}
1110100010 \\
+1 \\
\hline
1110100011
\end{array}
$$

and add this complement to the minuend.

$$
\begin{array}{r}
11011101 \\
+1110100011 \\
\hline
10010000000
\end{array}
$$

Since the sum has eleven digits, the correct difference is the ten least significant digits: 0010000000 or just 10000000.   ∎

Example A.11   Determine the difference $1011101 - 11011101$ in a ten-digit system using the 2's complement of the subtrahend.

Solution   We take the 2's complement of the subtrahend

$$
\begin{array}{r}
1100100010 \\
+1 \\
\hline
1100100011
\end{array}
$$

and add the minuend.

$$
\begin{array}{r}
1100100011 \\
+1011101 \\
\hline
1110000000
\end{array}
$$

Since the sum has just ten digits, it is incorrect and we must take the 2's complement of it and insert a minus sign

$$
\begin{array}{r}
0001111111 \\
+1 \\
\hline
10000000
\end{array} \rightarrow \ -10000000
$$

which is the desired difference. ∎

To add by subtracting, we form the 2's complement of the addend and then subtract this complement from the augend plus borrow. The justification for this procedure will not be presented since it is similar to that presented for the 10's complement.

Example A.12   In a five-digit system, determine $1011 + 110$ using the 2's complement of the addend.

Solution   We form the 2's complement of the addend. It is 11010. And then we subtract this complement from the augend plus borrow.

$$
\begin{array}{r}
101011 \quad \text{borrow} \\
-11010 \\
\hline
10001
\end{array}
$$

The sum is 10001. ∎

The 1's complement approach can be used instead of the 2's complement approach. The 1's complement, which is one less than the 2's complement, is best found by placing the number in n-digit form and then changing each one to a zero and each zero to a one.

In using the 1's complement for subtracting by adding, we add the 1's complement of the subtrahend to the minuend. If the sum requires $n + 1$ digits then we add one to the sum. The n least significant digits of this second sum are the correct difference. However, if the first sum requires less than $n + 1$ digits, then the 1's complement of this sum is taken and a minus sign inserted. Because the justification for this 1's complement approach is quite similar to that for the 9's complement, it will not be presented.

Example A.13   Determine $11011101 - 1011101$ in a ten-digit system using the 1's complement approach.

Solution   The 1's complement of 0001011101 is 1110100010. We add this to the minuend.

$$
\begin{array}{r}
1110100010 \\
+11011101 \\
\hline
10001111111
\end{array}
$$

Since the sum has eleven digits, the correct difference is

$$1111111$$
$$+1$$
$$\overline{10000000}$$ correct difference   ■

Example A.14   Determine $1011101 - 11011101$ in a ten-digit system. Use the 1's complement of the subtrahend.

Solution   The 1's complement of the subtrahend 0011011101 is 1100100010. This complement added to the minuend yields

$$1100100010$$
$$+1011101$$
$$\overline{1101111111}$$

Because this sum does not have eleven digits, it is not the correct difference, and it is necessary to take the 1's complement and insert a minus sign. Thus the correct difference is -0010000000, or just -10000000.   ■

In adding by subtracting, we subtract the 1's complement of the addend from the augend plus borrow and then subtract one to compensate for the use of the 1's complement instead of the 2's complement.

Example A.15   In a five-digit system determine $1010 + 110$ using subtraction and the 1's complement of the addend.

Solution   We form the 1's complement of the addend. It is 11001. Then we subtract it from the augend, plus borrow.

$$101010 \quad \text{borrow}$$
$$-11001$$
$$\overline{10001}$$

Then 1 is subtracted

$$10001$$
$$-1$$
$$\overline{10000}$$

The sum is 10000.   ■

The preceding discussion of binary complement arithmetic is not completely applicable to digital applications, and in particular, to digital computers. For example, in digital computers the numbers do not have plus and minus signs. Rather, bits designate the signs with a one frequently representing a minus sign and a zero a plus sign. Furthermore, in some computers, minus numbers are in complement form. That is, they are complements, including the sign bit, of the corresponding positive numbers. In this representation, negative sums or differences are not complemented, as explained above, but are retained in complement form. This matter is discussed further in Chapter 8.

Octal Complements

In the octal system the radix and the radix-minus-one complements are the 8's and 7's complements, respectively. Since from prior discussions the determination of these complements should be apparent, the procedures will not be discussed.

In using the octal shorthand, we can conveniently represent the complements of binary numbers in octal. If the number of digits in the binary number is a multiple of three digits to the right and to the left of the binary point, then the 8's complement of the corresponding octal number is equivalent to the 2's complement of the binary number. Also, the 1's complement and the 7's complement are equivalent. Even if this correspondence is not present and thus the octal and binary complement numbers are not equivalent, it can be shown that one can still employ the octal complements. However, in our use of the octal shorthand we will always have this correspondence.

Example A.16   Given the binary number 111010 for a six-digit binary system, determine the 1's and 2's complement of this number and then the decimal values of these complements. Next, convert this binary number to octal and obtain the 8's and 7's complements and the equivalent decimal values. Compare.

Solution   The 2's complement of 111010 is 000110 and the 1's complement is 000101 for which the corresponding decimal values are six and five, respectively. Converted to octal, the original number is 72. The 8's complement is six and the 7's complement is five as are the corresponding decimal values. We note that the decimal values of the 2's complement equals that of the 8's complement, and the decimal value of the 1's complement equals that of the 7's complement. ∎

From this example we see that when binary numbers can be grouped into groups of three bits each, then the octal shorthand can be used regardless of whether the arithmetic is of the conventional type or is complement arithmetic.

PROBLEMS

A.1   Determine the 10's complements of the following decimal numbers for a six-digit system (use leading zeros, if necessary, to complete the number of digits):

(a) 4729   (b) 89.2356   (c) $\frac{1}{8}$

Answers   (a) 995271;   (b) 10.7644;   (c) 999.875

A.2   Repeat Problem A.1 for

(a) 628   (b) 97.634   (c) $\frac{1}{16}$

A.3   Obtain the 9's complements of the numbers of Problem A.1.

A.4   Obtain the 9's complements of the numbers of Problem A.2.

A.5   Determine the 1's complements of the following binary numbers for a seven-digit system (use leading zeros if necessary, to complete the number of digits):

(a) 110111   (b) 0.01101   (c) 110.11

Answers   (a) 1001000;   (b) 11.10010;   (c) 11001.00

A.6   Repeat Problem A.5 for

(a) 1101   (b) 0.01111   (c) 11.1011

A.7   Determine the 2's complements of the numbers of Problem A.5.

A.8   Determine the 2's complements of the numbers of Problem A.6.

A.9   Determine the 8's complements of the following octal numbers for a six-digit system (insert leading zeros, if necessary, to complete the number of digits):

(a) 726   (b) 0.034   (c) 672.376

Answers   (a) 777052;   (b) 777.744;   (c) 105.402

A.10   Repeat Problem A.9 for

(a) 777   (b) 77.777   (c) 76.207

A.11   Determine the 7's complements of the numbers of Problem A.9.

A.12   Determine the 7's complements of the numbers of Problem A.10.

A.13   In the following decimal additions and subtractions, use 9's complements and then repeat with 10's complements:

(a) 3724 + 2826   (d) 492 − 264
(b) 472.65 + 682.4   (e) 3567.2 − 2937.645
(c) 400927.6 + 38.456   (f) 4928.64 − 7824.689

A.14   Repeat Problem A.13 for

(a) 765 + 98   (d) 569 − 28
(b) 424.5 + 372.6   (e) 4723.64 − 876.5
(c) 670329.53 + 4928.76   (f) 5392.48 − 8923.673

A.15   In the following binary additions and subtractions use 1's complements and then repeat with 2's complements:

(a) 1101 + 111   (d) 1101 − 111
(b) 111011.1 + 1001.11   (e) 1101.11 − 11.101
(c) 1100110101.0011 + 110.1   (f) 111011.101 − 11110011.1

A.16 Repeat Problem A.15 for
  (a) 11001 + 1111
  (b) 11001.1 + 11001.1
  (c) 11011001111.1101111 + 11100.1111
  (d) 11101 − 1111
  (e) 110101.101 − 11110.11
  (f) 11001111.11 − 11101111.1111

A.17 In the following octal additions and subtractions, use 7's complements and then repeat with 8's complements:
  (a) 4725 + 3214   (d) 4125 − 314
  (b) 5427.3 + 675.1   (e) 52134.62 − 7720.345
  (c) 600372.4501 + 7707.773   (f) 6432.3 − 70042.654

A.18 Repeat Problem A.17 for
  (a) 476 + 5322   (d) 6732 − 734
  (b) 673.432 + 324.5   (e) 46327.327 − 5727.77
  (c) 7200765.324 + 37027.777 (f) 7654.32 − 77777.777

A.19 Find the radix complements of the following numbers:
  (a) $A29F.615_{16}$ (b) 532.62_7 (c) $B75.4A_{13}$

  Answers (a) 5D60.9EB; (b) 134.05; (c) 157.83

A.20 Repeat Problem A.19 for
  (a) 324.51_6 (b) $MFA.5L_{24}$ (c) 1111.1101_{17}

A.21 Repeat Problem A.19 for
  (a) 120.112_3 (b) $9AF.GE8_{18}$ (c) 222.021_3

Bibliography

BOOKS

A. Switching Circuits

Dietmeyer, D. L. *Logic Design of Digital Systems*. Boston: Allyn and Bacon, 1971. An introductory but comprehensive and readable presentation.

Hill, F. J., G. R. Peterson. *Introduction to Switching Theory and Logical Design*. New York: Wiley, 1968. An intermediate-level book.

LePore, P. E., R. A. Holmlund. *Modern Logic Design*. Sylvania Electric Products, Waltham, Mass., 1970. A practically-oriented book for a company-sponsored course.

Malmstadt, H. V., C. G. Enke. *Digital Electronics for Scientists*. New York: Benjamin, 1969. A readable, introductory book for scientists and engineers wanting a practical working knowledge of digital circuits.

Marcovitz, A. B., J. H. Pugsley. *An Introduction to Switching System Design*. New York: Wiley, 1971. A readable, introductory presentation.

Marcus, M. P. *Switching Circuits for Engineers*. 2nd ed. Englewood Cliffs, N.J.: Prentice-Hall, 1967. A readable, introductory book containing considerable relay-oriented material.

McCluskey, E. J. *Introduction to the Theory of Switching Circuits*. New York: McGraw-Hill, 1965. An intermediate-level book.

Sifferlen, T. P., V. Vartanian. *Digital Electronics with Engineering Applications.* Englewood Cliffs, N.J.: Prentice-Hall, 1970. A readable, introductory presentation with much practical material.

Signetics Corporation. *Application Memos.* Signetics Corporation, Sunnyvale, Calif., 1969. A collection of application memos of practical circuits with explanatory material.

Wickes, W. E. *Logic Design with Integrated Circuits.* New York: Wiley, 1968. A small readable book that is applications oriented.

B. Computers

Bartee, T. C. *Digital Computer Fundamentals.* 3rd ed., New York: McGraw-Hill, 1972. A readable book written at an introductory level.

Chu, Y. *Digital Computer Design Fundamentals.* New York: McGraw-Hill, 1962. Considered a classic by some, this book has extensive and thorough treatments of many topics and especially of arithmetic operations. It is written at an intermediate level.

Eadie, D. *Introduction to the Basic Computer.* Englewood Cliffs, N.J.: Prentice-Hall, 1968. A readable, introductory, and practically-oriented book.

Gschwind, H. W. *Design of Digital Computers.* New York: Springer-Verlag, 1967. Somewhat introductory but comprehensive.

Heilweil, M. F., G. A. Maley. *Introduction to Digital Computers.* Englewood Cliffs, N.J: Prentice-Hall, 1968. A small basic book for computer technicians.

Ligomenides, P. A. *Information-Processing Machines.* New York: Holt, Rinehart, and Winston, 1969. A readable, introductory book containing material on both switching circuits and computers.

Nashelsky, L. *Digital Computer Theory.* New York: Wiley, 1966. A small readable book on digital computer basics.

ARTICLES

Garrett, L. S., "Integrated-Circuit Digital Logic Families," *IEEE Spectrum,* Vol. 7, No. 10, October, 1970, pp. 46–58. This is the first of three excellent and practical articles on current digital logic families. The other articles are in the November and December, 1970, issues.

Howard, H., "Why MSI?" *EDN,* Vol. 15, No. 9, May 1, 1970, pp. 49–54. A readable, introductory article on multiplexers.

Kvamme, F., "Standard Read-Only Memories Simplify Complex Logic Design," *Electronics,* Vol. 43, No. 1, Jan. 5, 1970, pp. 88–95. Like all articles in *Electronics,* this is readable. An excellent introductory article on ROM's.

Norman, R. H., "Staying Ahead of the Game," *Electronics,* Vol. 41, No. 22, October 28, 1968, pp. 106–108. This is the first in a series of 31 excellent articles on memories extending over many issues of *Electronics,* the last being that of Sept. 15, 1969.

Ruff, R. E., "J-K Properties Ease Karnaugh Map Application," *EDN*, Vol. 15, No. 21, November 1, 1970, pp. 45–47. This article describes a superior method for programming J-K flip-flops.

Sirota, J., J. Marino, "There's a Read-Only Memory That's Sure to Fill Your Needs," *Electronics*, Vol. 43, No. 6, March 16, 1970, pp. 112–116. A readable introductory article on ROM's.

Uimari, D. C., "Field-Programmable Read-Only Memories and Applications," *Computer Design*, Vol. 9, No. 12, pp. 49–54. This readable article describes some ROM applications.

The August, 1966, issue of *IEEE Transactions on Electronic Computers*, Vol. EC-15, No. 4, contains some excellent articles on memories written at intermediate and advanced levels. Some of these are

1) Brown, J. R., "First- and Second-Order Ferrite Memory Core Characteristics and Their Relationship to System Performance," pp. 485–501.

2) Gilligan, T. J., "2½D High Speed Memory Systems—Past, Present, and Future," pp. 475–485.

3) Pleshko, P., L. M. Terman, "An Investigation of the Potential of MOS Transistor Memories," pp. 423–427.

Index